TALK '90S WITH ME

23 Unpredictable Conversations with Stars of an Unforgettable Decade

MATT PAIS

ISBN 978-1-7352504-4-1 (hardcover)

ISBN 978-1-7352504-2-7 (paperback)

ISBN 978-1-7352504-3-4 (ebook)

Cover design: Trent J. Koland

For my family

Table of Contents

Preface

"In West Philadelphia, born and raised ..."

There is a very good chance you know the rest of the lyrics. You or someone you know almost certainly remembers declaring, "It's morphin time!" And it is likely that at some point, maybe having to do with hockey and maybe not, you have yelled, "Quack! Quack! Quack!"

Or not. Maybe you learned along with Cory Matthews and imagined joining the All-American Girls Professional Baseball League. Maybe you froze to make sure the T. rex couldn't see you or perfected your best impression of Roger Klotz or Zoidberg. Maybe you just miss the days of movies about rollerblading and whales. (Though never in the same story, unfortunately.) The list of movies and shows that connected in the '90s, so much of which remains important to so many whether or not it's been rebooted or remade, is endless, and the people and work included in this book are, obviously, just a snippet of the decade.

During my 11 years as the movie critic for the Chicago Tribune's RedEye, I interviewed hundreds of people, many of whom were important to the '90s: Wesley Snipes, Harrison Ford, Will and Jada Pinkett Smith, Halle Berry, Antonio Banderas, Salma Hayek, Mark Wahlberg, Ice Cube, Emilio Estevez, Jodie Foster, Edward Norton, Angela Bassett, John Malkovich, Kevin Costner, Diane Lane, William H. Macy, John Turturro, Chris Tucker, Bob Saget, Marlon Wayans, Juliette Lewis, Jason Schwartzman, and Thomas Ian Nicholas. I also interviewed 22 cast members of "Saved by the Bell" for my 2020 book "Zack Morris Lied 329 Times! Reassessing every ridiculous episode of 'Saved by the Bell' ... with stats."

For this book, I wanted to approach the era more broadly and see what new material could be gathered about long-beloved movies and shows through extended conversations with people who made them special. Each one would begin by asking, "What's something from the '90s that you're nostalgic for?" and "What movie or show from that time— something you were not in—meant or still means a lot to you?" And then dive into the person's work in particular.

When I started this project, I had no idea who would be interested. I wound up surprised at both who said yes and who didn't. More importantly, I was thrilled by the conversations, which without fail found unique angles, insights, reflections, and stories that you simply won't find in other interviews with these people. The discussions averaged about 60-75 minutes, with the shortest being 35 and the longest being 108. Time, obviously, was not unlimited; the calls lasted as long as they lasted, and questions had to be chosen carefully. Only by knowing what's been asked can you know what hasn't been asked, and that means

i

reading, watching, and listening to previous interviews, on top of watching/re-watching the actual material to be discussed. That might sound overwhelming; sometimes it is. But it's really fun, and it's what leads to discoveries.

These pieces don't claim to be profiles but rather interactions that bring you closer to the actors and feel fulfilling, entertaining, and even deep. I hope the conversations (all conducted in 2021 and edited for clarity) remind you why you love these movies and shows while also providing new ways to think about what they meant at the time and now.

Because nostalgia is everything at once: bringing the past into the present, the present into the past, and all of it as part of us into the future. Ideally accompanied by a Cap'n Geech and the Shrimp Shack Shooters sax solo.

Luke Edwards of 'Little Big League,' 'Newsies,' 'Undressed'

In 1994's "Little Big League," a seemingly absurd adolescent fantasy (a 12-year-old kid takes over as owner and manager of the Minnesota Twins) becomes a hilarious and undeniably goodhearted exploration of approaching work with joy. Sincere but not sappy and deceptively wise in its perspective on fun, the movie arrived after more-beloved kids' baseball fare like "Rookie of the Year" and "The Sandlot" but deserves a place on the same mantle.

What grounds the entire thing is Luke Edwards, who in his first starring role (following supporting parts in 1992's "Newsies" and "The Wizard," which opened two weeks before the calendar turned to 1990) combines everything Billy Heywood needed to be: knowledgeable, passionate, mature, yet also a little naïve and inevitably in over his head when needing to deal with the egos of a failing Twins team and also maintain delicate pre-teen friendships.

Edwards—who lately has coached actors and appeared in movies like "Adverse" (with "Rookie of the Year" star Thomas Ian Nicholas)—may not have gone on to the adult stardom that young viewers would have expected (and Edwards has incredibly honest thoughts about why that happened), but he deserves to be regarded as one of the '90s' most quietly great performers. And there's nothing subtle about how wonderful he was in conversation.

What's something you feel nostalgic for about the '90s?

Boy, there's probably a lot of answers to that. The '90s was like my time! [Laughs] I miss the music; I miss the fashions. Boy, I miss the video games, I miss Mario Lemieux … [Laughs] I could go on and on. I was probably having the best time of my whole life in the '90s. On and on.

I definitely didn't think you were going to say the fashions.

[Laughs] Well, it's ridiculous, but it was great in its ridiculousness. I'm working on a thing—I write a little bit—and it's in the '90s. That's pretty deliberate. I kind of want to bring some of that stuff—I don't want to bring it back; I just want to put it on the screen and remind everybody how ridiculous it was. And kind of fun. [Laughs]

1

Well, I know we're both sitting here in our jean jackets …

[Laughs] And I guess my experience is of a specific thing, which is hip-hop and techno and crazy, big, baggy jeans and all kinds of weird stuff. I was wearing lots of weird stuff.

It's funny, the things that you find yourself missing. The people who didn't experience things like that, it's like, "Wait, you miss giant pants?" I wrote down next to this question "Buying CDs at Best Buy." Simple things like that.

Oh my god. I don't know how much experience you have of L.A., but Tower Records— we're still not OK about Tower Records being gone. We're all just living in mourning. That's one of a few stores, but for us that was the one. Yeah, just to go to the music store and poke around. It doesn't even matter if you buy anything; it's the best place to be. [Laughs] And you kinda can't do that anymore. There's still record stores, but I really miss Tower Records.

In terms of that era, can you think of a movie you weren't in that means a lot to you? It could be another kids' sports movie, "The Fugitive," anything.

Oh, man, there's so many. It's so hard to drill in on one or two things. Some of my favorite stuff. Especially in terms of film and TV, it's changed so much. I really miss big, dumb comedies. Comedies are kind of dying in film. It's sort of alarming for me. One of my buddies, his dad worked in the industry, and he got us an advance copy of "American Pie." We all sat around and watched that, and it just blew our minds. It's so dumb, but we just loved it. It was hilarious. I miss big, dumb comedies a lot. Was "Deuce Bigalow" In the '90s?

I believe the first one was late-'90s. [Editor's note: Yep, it was 1999.]

Those movies are so stupid, but I love them. Anyway, you're not going to get much more of that. So that's movies. Do you know what "Mr. Show" is?

I quote "Mr. Show" more than anyone I know.

Is that right? [Laughs]

I love "Mr. Show" so much.

Oh my god! That's like seminal. It's so important for me. Quoting is one thing, and I do quote it, but mostly people are like, "What?" It's the thing that I reference the most in terms of when I'm having life experience. It's really strange, I don't quite understand why, but every time something happens I'm like, "Oh, yeah, it's just like that one episode [of 'Mr. Show']." Man, I really miss "Mr. Show." They tried to bring it back for a second. I was hopeful, but it didn't work.

2

I thought the Netflix version was funny, though. It's hard to pick a favorite sketch, but one that jumps to mind in making me laugh the loudest is "Teaching by Billiards." Do you remember that?

[Laughs] Yes! "The great train disaster of ..." [Laughs] Oh my god. Man. Bob Odenkirk, he's doing drama now and it's great, but that guy is so funny, man. That same friend that got us the advanced copy of "American Pie," he worked on "Mr. Show." He was just a PA, but his dad was kind of part of the production of it and so he's actually in an episode. When Bob Odenkirk is a rapper and has a DJ, my friend was the DJ. My friend also gave me VHS copies of episodes of "Mr. Show," which I still have.

That's about as '90s as it gets.

Right! [Laughs] I don't watch 'em. I don't have a VCR, but I still have 'em.

Between "The Wizard," which was almost the '90s, and "Newsies" and "Little Big League," something that struck me at the time and now is that you always seemed wise beyond your years. I know you talked about being cast in "The Wizard" for having a focus that other kids didn't. Can you remember the first time you were aware of that about yourself, or that someone pointed that out about you being sort of an old soul?

[Laughs] Boy, my memory is kind of spotty. I don't know if I could tell you if it happened before, but it definitely happened during and a lot. Those exact words: old soul. I never quite understood what that meant. But I got that a lot.

To frame it a different way: I saw a quote from you where you said, "I've always been the very sensitive type, which serves me in my pursuits as an actor but then of course doesn't really serve me very well in lots of other hard life experiences. It's always a trade-off, I guess." What do you see as the trade-off? Is there a story or example that articulates that?

I think it's just been my experience, but part of that old soul thing, whatever people are seeing there. I think we have a lot of different terms that probably describe the same thing, or different parts of the same thing, and in general, in this time of my life, my overall mental health isn't great, and I think they're part and parcel. I think being really sensitive, or also being somebody who has a very active mind, those things come with. That's just my experience. I'd love somebody to prove me wrong. It's like having the inclination to be a skeptic or an analyzing sort of person. [Laughs] You know, ignorance is bliss. If that's true, somebody that's trying to know a lot, or has a desire to think about things, pick 'em apart, know more about 'em, the thing that comes along with that is—I'm tempted to use the word misery; I'm sure there's a better way to frame it. Does that make sense?

3

If only we could think of an example of something that wasn't going well in the world, I might be able to understand that better.

[Laughs] Yeah, boy. Any number of things.

And you're talking to someone who wrote a book counting the number of times Zack Morris lied on "Saved by the Bell." It's hard to have that sensitivity because you pay attention to things other people don't see. I'm going to save the "Little Big League" questions until after "Newsies," but it makes me wonder if Billy Heywood was an adult, would he even take the job? Or would he say, "Baseball's not as important as my work fighting climate change"?

[Laughs] I've thought about that a lot because I have played a number of these young characters. I've thought a lot about what they would be like as adults. It's really interesting. Billy Heywood, he knows so much about baseball in sort of an obsessive way. Maybe he's a little obsessive [Laughs] or has a little Asperger's. Hyper-focused on something, it always has kind of a downside.

Do you think about what Les from "Newsies" would be like grown up?

Yes. Less because of the era; that was turn of the century, so Les would just have so many crazy things lined up for him. Give or take he's 10 years old at the turn of the century, so he's going to see the Great Depression and World War I and all this crazy stuff. [Laughs] And Les is poor, so he's going to probably enlist and go fight and stuff like that. Boy, I haven't thought about that one very much just because of the different era. [Laughs] Jeez, Les would probably see two world wars if he survived them.

That's a slightly less joyful note than the ending of the movie.

[Laughs] Yeah. Les is also, other than having an adoration for Jack Kelly, he's not terribly dynamic. So it's more interesting for me to think about the character from "The Wizard" or "Little Big League" because they are unusual people.

The extrapolation that you did from "Newsies" is fair though because it's sort of an adult story for a kids' movie in terms of the rich trying to take advantage of the poor, unionizing, fame equaling success, and salesmanship. Did any of those messages really sink in for you?

Oh, yeah. Without a doubt. It framed a lot of stuff for me. Pulitzer and Hearst, they're the villains give or take of that story, and I don't think I really knew much about either of those characters at the time, but it was my intro. So ever since I've been really interested to learn more about those guys. I just saw "Mank," and it was so great and so fascinating. I went to Hearst Castle last year or two years ago. It's fascinating stuff. Are those guys villains or not? There's certainly some villainous behavior, but any captain of any industry is sort of villainous in their own way. Every Disney movie—it's the running joke, right—is so dark if you frame it differently. And that one is no exception.

Is it weird for you to see it with that different lens right now? When I think of "Newsies" as a kid, I loved it, but I also remember performing "Seize the Day" with a friend in the elementary school talent show, and the music teacher then teaching it for years after, but it wasn't because I connected with the material so much. Maybe it made me want to be a journalist, I don't know. I know I loved the songs.

[Laughs] Well, they're great songs, however you cut it; that's great songwriting for sure. I think I was 11 maybe when we shot that, and I was pretty aware of—I just feel like I've always been aware of the dark stuff around. I couldn't ignore it or filter it out or turn off my awareness of it. So even at the time, I think we had conversations about it, some of the actors: "This is a story about street kids who have nothing." I don't know. [Laughs] That's what Disney movies do, they take a really super-heavy, dark subject and paint it a certain way.

It's hard not to wonder how many years it will be until a kid sees "Newsies" for the first time and is like, "What the hell is a newspaper?"

[Laughs] Oh man. Well, they'll have something else, right? They'll have something that stands in and serves that same function in their lives; it just looks a little different. But they'll still have news!

There will just be a new cut of the movie where they dub the word "website" over the word "newspaper."

[Laughs] So the kids can appreciate it? [Laughs]

On a happier subject, when you think of that experience, is there something vivid that comes to mind about the making of the movie, or building rapport with Christian Bale? No one admires Batman the way that Les admires Jack.

There's good stuff and bad stuff. As far as trying to build rapport or work with Christian, that was really easy because he's a really cool guy. [Laughs] Just in regular old life, he's a very nice guy, very personable. Or at least he was at that time. I have no idea; people change. So that was easy. I wasn't doing any work there really. [Laughs] One of the better, nicer, fonder memories is before we shot, we did maybe a month, I'm not sure how long it was, of rehearsals on the Warner Brothers backlot, and every day our job was to show up and work on a little dancing, a little singing. We did acrobatics kind of stuff. Fight training. It was super fun because we didn't have to shoot. Our job was just to play around and rehearse, and we just had this big empty soundstage, and it was just a bunch of young guys hanging out and having a good time. So that was super fun. They did give me singing lessons and dancing lessons, and that's the only time I've ever done that. It was fun. I didn't stick with any of it, but in the moment that was a lot of fun. That's kind of the best memories I have is that time before we started shooting. [Laughs] And there's less fun memories I can tell you about too.

I'll take you up on that.

So there's an actor who plays my brother in that movie, his name is David Moscow. I have a half-sister, and I always kind of wanted to have brothers. I always felt a longing for that, so on "Newsies" we were working really closely together, and we kind of became that. As actors we do sort of live the lives of those characters. It's obviously not full-on, but we do live it. Anyway, so we kind of were brothers for that time, and he taught me this or that, about the birds and the bees and so on, so I've always had this place in my mind for him, this nice, fun, and rosy place, and after the movie and as we both walked through life we ended up running into each other again and again because we had similar friends. And eventually we got together and decided to make a movie together, and I don't want to go too crazy into any details, but it didn't go well. He was the director, and I was just one of the producers, but it was bad. Real bad. And that was kind of the end of any kind of friendly terms. [Laughs] So that is something that does really stand out. For me that doesn't happen with a lot of people; I tend to remain friends and friendly with most people, the vast majority. So sadly when I think about "Newsies" I can't help but think about that fractured relationship. It's too bad, really.

I appreciate you sharing that. I guess it's not terribly surprising that that would happen to every actor at least once, especially when you meet someone as a kid. It's hard to keep those relationships going decades on.

Yeah. I gave him a lot of benefit of the doubt because of our initial relationship, and that now I feel was a mistake. [Laughs]

Do you find yourself belting out a "Newsies" song every so often around the house? If I say, "That's my cigar," my wife will complete the line. I don't know if you ever do that.

[Laughs] Short answer, no. Long answer, sometimes. [Laughs] I guess those are both short answers. I'm not a musical theater guy. So it's not my thing, that's for sure. Those songs are really great. They are so well-written; they are little earworms for sure. So I know all the songs by heart. I only sang, I think, on one of 'em, but I know 'em all. I know every word to every song. They're just really well done; I think you can't help but be subject to them. But just for me in general musicals are so not my thing, so it's not a thing I really celebrate. [Laughs] I'll tell you a funny anecdote: One of my friends when I was young was Chris Evans, who's Captain America. And he is a musical theater guy; he and his whole family really love all that stuff. So he knows every "Newsies" song by heart. He's a big, tough, action hero guy, but he will belt those songs out [Laughs]. I just find that really funny.

In what setting is that happening?

In private. Strictly in private.

The two of you hanging out last week, him performing for you?

[Laughs] No, sadly, no. We lived together a couple different times. We were close when we were younger actors. We're still friendly and everything, but he's off in another world. [Laughs] He's a big old movie star. But if you run across him, ask him to sing a "Newsies" song. He'll probably do it. [Laughs]

Last "Newsies" question. This is a deep cut, but I wanted to ask: Even the most down-to-earth people probably have one high-minded thing about them, or that they like. Is there anything about you that's "real hoity-toity"?

[Laughs] I kind of struggle to understand what that really means. [Laughs] Jeez, I don't know, what is hoity-toity? I really try not to be that, for sure in my life. But I'll talk about philosophy; is that hoity-toity?

People who aren't interested in engaging intellectually probably would say that it is.

[Laughs] That's what I mean. It's different things to different people. I'll talk about Kierkegaard, and definitely some people will be like, "What?"

That's fantastic. Moving on to "Little Big League" stuff: Setting aside child labor laws and anything else in terms of logic, do you think a failing team hiring a child manager could work?

Sure! Just in the realm of possibilities? Absolutely!

Yeah, if it was legal—the Tigers were bad when the movie was made, and they're bad now. If they decided to hire a 12-year-old ...

Yeah. My answer is yes. And I don't think it's that far off. We're in this world now of sports of analytics. There's people working in front offices of these big sports franchises, and all they do is crunch numbers. Why couldn't a kid do that? I'm sure they could. [Laughs] I'm sure that's happening sooner than later. Well, I don't know. That's an idea.

And especially with how many failed managers keep getting recycled. I don't know why teams don't try something new.

7

[Laughs] Well, experience does count for a lot. [Laughs] It's a hybrid thing. I feel personally you've gotta have the old guard guys around because they're so wizened. But of course new ideas and new blood is how things change. So it's like you've gotta do both. You've gotta have the old, cagey vets and the hot rookies and such.

I feel like if a team is going to insist on another round for Dusty Baker or any of these managers who have had 25 jobs—and maybe I'm just a biased Cubs fan about that era—but they should be legally obligated to also hire a child who knows what they're doing.

[Laughs] I think there's something to it. They both gotta understand their arena, where their expertise is most valuable. But there's something to it. Teams are already doing this. The guy that manages the Leafs, the biggest franchise in hockey, is a pretty young guy. It's not just that it could happen; it's happening.

Could you rank the major sports in order of how well it would go to have a 12-year-old as the manager or head coach?

[Laughs] I think it's a challenge in any sport. There's just so much money. It's a challenge no matter where you are. These big sports teams, each one is like its own corporation, and corporations don't like risk. So [it's a] huge, huge challenge no matter who you're dealing with. The NFL is the most old-school, old guard, so I don't know about that one.

What do you think about people who say that if you can't play, you shouldn't manage? They're often the ones who say if you can't act, you shouldn't be a critic. Is there logic to that? Billy was a bad hitter but a great manager.

[Laughs] There's one scene in the movie where I actually have to play baseball—or stickball. And it was so painful because I was so bad. I'm still so bad. I'm a terrible baseball player. It was such a chore making that scene for me. For everybody because everybody saw how terrible I was at it. No, I don't think that's true at all! I think you should play and you should love the game, but you don't have to be good at it … the management, it's more about personalities and delegating and all those kind of things. It's so much more about brilliantly understanding the game. Every sports reference I'm going to make is a hockey reference because I love hockey. Wayne Gretzky was a terrible coach! He had a terrible record as a coach, and that's the most cerebral hockey player who ever did it. How come?

That's a good point. After all, part of why Billy succeeds is he gets on the players' wavelength, whereas Dennis Farina's character is just a jackass the whole time.

Right. What's the point of that movie? The love of the game. And Billy himself of course forgets and gets caught up in the nonsense. But the bottom line of that whole story is your love of the game will carry you. So when he remembers that and remembers to remind others, everything kind of works. Not necessarily that they even win—which is one of the things that I really love about that script. But that they just have a good time while they're doing it. I think that's a big challenge. Whether you're successful or not, you can have a good time in what you're doing.

Absolutely. On a different note: One of the things that struck me while rewatching the movie is that, like several other kids' movies of the era, it asks kids to confront death. I'm wondering if you have an early memory of when a piece of art or entertainment first brought that to your attention.

Wow. I think part of being a real sensitive person is that almost every piece affects me. I'm the person that will cry at every movie. Even if it's a bad movie, there's a part that I'm crying. Like, why am I crying?

"Deuce Bigalow" too?

[Laughs] I will cry about it right now! He's so kind to the women who people are so mean to. And he's just kind to them. And that makes a difference. Break my heart. "Deuce Bigalow" has got some levels to that. [Laughs] I'm not going to go down that road. I don't have a real clear memory; when you first asked the question, I just went straight to "Bambi," but I think that was a thing I formulated later on in life because I'm not sure if "Bambi" really affected me all that much. [Laughs] The short answer is the first movie that had death in it. Like, "Oh, damn." That had a huge effect on me.

I don't have a better word than interesting to talk about the way that movies for kids are used to try to start conversations about that. But I also have to wonder: How many families that saw "The Wizard" or "Little Big League" had conversations about death after they saw the movie?

[Laughs] I'm going to guess not very many. Just simply because people don't really like to talk about death. [Laughs] It's not our most enjoyable topic. That being said, we did a thing last summer, two summers ago, [where] I talked with the writer of "The Wizard" at length. Because "The Wizard" has a really dark side to it too, and he told me that story about the family, it kind of came to him early in his life and he lived with that for a while. It was just in his mind, working on that. Anyway, I'm not sure where I'm going with that. There is a heavy thing to that story. That's always the stuff that I latched onto. "This is the meaty stuff; this is where it gets good because it's interesting." Most people aren't there for that. They're there for "Mario 3."

For sure. And part of why it's fascinating is because that's not what people are going for. You'd hope death isn't the first thing people discuss after "Little Big League" because there's so much else to talk about and enjoy. My first memory on this topic is going with my mom, a friend and his mom to see "All Dogs Go to Heaven." It's right there in the title, but I think they must not have processed that

this will force young viewers to confront death. We left 10 minutes in and walked into "Prancer."

You guys walked out?

We left the movie and walked into a movie about a reindeer, who I believe does not die if I remember correctly. I think they just thought, and I don't blame them, that, title notwithstanding, a G-rated kids' movie was safe. And I bet there were people who thought that about "Little Big League" too and had to have some conversations.

[Laughs] Oh for sure, for sure. Any time you set out to tell a story—there's just no avoiding it. And by it, I just mean difficult, dark stuff. That's life. I don't have kids, so I don't quite connect to this yet, but the sheltering of kids. Of course I understand it, but life is going to happen eventually. So if kids are introduced to the idea of death in a movie or in real life or in a conversation, no matter what that moment is going to occur. Each human mind has to tackle it eventually. [Laughs] And stories are about conflict. The stories that don't have any conflict, we detest. We forget about them. The greatest stories are the ones with the most conflict. If you're going to make a kids' movie, it's going to have some tension, struggle, conflict. Otherwise it's not a story.

And it would've been so underwhelming if it was just, "Grandpa decided to retire and give you the team."

[Laughs] Right! Where are the stakes? [Laughs]

This is a ridiculous question, but when you saw "Magnolia," which was five years after "Little Big League" and has Jason Robards playing a dying man and Tom Cruise sort of in the Luke Edwards role as his son, did it go through your head, "Oh, he's about to give Tom Cruise the Minnesota Twins"?

[Laughs] That is so funny! I bet I did have that thought! At some point or another. It's really bizarre to work with all these performers as a kid and not really understand who they are, what the context is, and then walk through life and understand who they are and see their other work and see this actor up on the screen in this movie that I had nothing to do with and go, "Oh, Grandpa?" I've had that experience a lot. [Laughs] I wish I could've seen all of Jason Robards' movies before working with Jason Robards. I feel like I would've appreciated what that moment was so much more. I was just kind of a dumb kid. [Laughs]

The answer to this could be very long, and we won't get into industry talk too much. But why do you feel like they don't make kids' sports movies like this anymore? Why wouldn't a movie like this be profitable and capture people's interest?

10

Man, I really don't know. There's all sorts of stuff I can say that is not going to be news to you. They don't make movies like "Little Big League" anymore. That's a medium-budget movie, and that just doesn't exist anymore. You know that, right?

I do.

It's also really strange to have come up in the industry in the time that I did. Things have changed so much. So many actors were reliant on those types of movies for their livelihood, and it's just gone. So there's that. But just in terms of why a kids' sports story isn't being greenlit right now, I don't know. That's a really good question. It seems as viable as anything really.

When looking at "Little Big League," and you could say "Newsies" and "The Wizard" too, it's not that movies don't have happy endings anymore, but these particular movies all touch on optimism and kindness winning out over crankiness. Obviously the world has changed so much. Do you feel like that is relevant in considering if you were trying to pitch this sort of thing, if the context of the world no longer fits?

Cultural innocence has definitely changed. In the way that everything is a paradox. The more things change, the more they stay the same. So everything has changed, and everything's still exactly the same. But it was a simpler time. Everybody was just a little more innocent in their approach to life. So things have certainly changed in that sense. If you take the whole spectrum of movies and TV right now vs. the '90s, things are darker. And that's just cultural. Global warming or climate change was a different problem in the '90s. It's not that it wasn't a problem; it was. But it was far less dire. So things like that have an effect on everything. And there's still of course room for optimism and those kind of stories. Maybe now more than ever, honestly. I hear that a lot from friends who are writing and pitching stuff is there's gotta be an optimism in the story or else people won't buy it. I think people are dying for a happy ending, for some kind of reason to be optimistic with the state of everything. [Laughs] Complicated questions. The more things change, the more they stay the same. [Laughs]

Looking at the '90s as a whole, I remember being so happy to see you pop up on MTV's "Undressed." Do you remember where your head was at that time? I'm sure kids would think that an actor who is a lead in a movie would get a ton of other lead parts, but did you feel like the movies we've discussed—and there's a whole other conversation to have about child stars transitioning into adulthood—provided credibility, or it was more like it was a kids' movie, so people shrugged it off?

Um, this is also kind of complicated. The answer is both. [Laughs] It did matter, and at the same time it didn't. I did "Little Big League," and I did one movie after that, a TV movie ["The Little Riders"], and then I stopped, and I kind of chose this. My mom and I moved out of L.A.; we moved to a town outside of L.A. called Ojai. And it was harder at that point

11

to go to auditions, and on top of that I was a little burned out and kind of wanted to just be a regular kid in school for a minute. So I stopped. I stopped auditioning and everything and was just in high school. And nobody warned me about that. That's a really bad idea, and especially at that age was a really bad idea. An agent can tell you better how this works; I don't know if I had momentum or something. There was something that I had. Anyway, I lost it. So I came back after high school as an adult, more or less. Eighteen, you're not really an adult. Anyway, what I found at that time was I kind of have to start from scratch. And that was really tough. I'm still sort of reeling from that moment. Nobody warned me. Nobody told me how that works. Maybe they didn't know themselves. But the experience of coming back to L.A. as an adult and going out for stuff, I definitely got opportunities because of my credits, but I wasn't reading for the lead role in this or that. It was all more supporting. I think it really was about being an unknown commodity as an adult. So yeah. [Laughs] At the time I did "Undressed," I think I was 19 or something, so I was just kind of coming back to it, and I was really hungry for some work. And "Undressed" was a TERRIBLE show. And when I say that, in terms of the production—because MTV is a horrific company to work for. They just cut corners everywhere. It wasn't a great shooting experience, nor in many ways a particularly great end product. But I was just dying for some work. I was happy to have it.

It always seemed like you had a good head on your shoulders, and I'm so happy you're the solid, down-to-earth guy that comes through in this conversation and in the research I did beforehand. We know that doesn't happen with a lot of kids who grow up in the industry. If you could do it differently, would you?

Oh, yeah. [Laughs] I try not to spend too much time thinking about that. [Laughs] Regret and all. [Laughs] But yeah, oh my god. I would have never took a break. I would have never stopped if I knew—when I was a kid and I first started, I didn't set out to be an actor. It wasn't a thing that was like, "Oh, I want to do that." I really had no investment in it either way. People were like, "You should try it." I tried it; it was fun. Like, "OK, I'll do more of that." The upshot of that is I didn't really appreciate what it was. How rare it was, how difficult it was. I just kind of did it and was going with the flow more than anything. Now, of course, however many years later and however many jobs I haven't gotten [Laughs] and years of struggling to pay my rent and stuff, now I have a different perspective, different context for it. Finding success as an actor is so tenuous. Try to put your finger on it; you just can't. It's not just being talented; it's also being sort of good-looking and having some luck and knowing that person and also being kind of charming. It's just a million things. I teach some actors, and it's really hard to see young people or just novices, if they're in different stages of their life, approach it. Because they're going "Why am I not successful? Why am I not getting this job or that job?" And I wish I could give them a simple answer, but it's unbelievably complicated. So the fact that I ever had success, now I kind of look back at it, it kind of blows my mind. That was a different life. I wish I could have kept it going and done that. It's a really difficult transition from the late teenage years into adulthood. That's where a lot of kid actors don't successfully transition. And to go back and do it again and really do that transition right would be great.

12

Whether it's your role in "True Detective" or anything else, I'm so glad to see when you're on screen. I'm reminded of Anna Chlumsky, who did it as a kid, went away and came back in the comedy world. I'd be so happy to see that for you.

There's another part to that. Which is that none of the things that I was a part of were ever actually hits. They weren't. "Little Big League" has this cult thing now, but at the time it was a failure. Same with "Newsies." "Newsies" was a colossal flop. And same for "The Wizard." "The Wizard" was a modest success, basically. So I've never been a part of a hit. Again, it's complicated. There are all these factors, and that's a big one. Really a big one. So Anna Chlumsky, she was a part of a bona fide huge hit movie. So there's a thing there that she can leverage later in life. And I don't have that.

Were there any other auditions in that era as you were transitioning into being an adult actor that would be worth mentioning as a close call?

[Laughs] Yeah, there were a lot of those. That is the life of an actor. Ask any actor, "Tell me about all your near-misses." I guess the one that stands out most in my mind is "The Fast and the Furious." In all honesty, I blew the audition. I felt like they really wanted to hire me, and I couldn't put it together. It was all this technical stuff about cars. I didn't know anything about any of it. I tried and just failed. I remember reading that script and kind of going like, "This is dumb, but whatever." And obviously it's a huge hit. And you go, "Ah, damn."

For the Vin Diesel part, I assume?

Yeah, right. [Laughs] Yeah, the lead. No, not the lead.

Which role?

I'd have to go back and see the movie to see who played it. It was one of the supporting guys. Like a real gearhead, car nerd guy.

I'm not a car guy myself. If I had to use the lingo, I'd have trouble too. I'd just be like, "I don't care about this."

[Laughs] Well, that is our job as actors, right. To fall in love with whatever it is. That is literally our job. I gotta own that at that stage of my life, my work as an actor, I wasn't doing it. I wasn't doing my job. That particular audition stands out. It's dumb; it's probably not true, but I just have this feeling that they really wanted to hire me [Laughs] and all I had to do was come in and say the words and it would've been fine, and I just couldn't. [Laughs] But we've gotta do that: "Now I'm a doctor." "Now I'm a lawyer." And sell it. That's our job.

I want to see that movie, where the job changes every 10 seconds.

[Laughs] Yeah. It's a movie about an actor.

I guess that's "Catch Me If You Can," where every few scenes it's "I'm a pilot," then "I'm a doctor."

Right! He was a great actor, Abagnale. He was a great actor, that guy. His point wasn't the acting, but he was good at it.

Gabrielle Anwar of 'Wild Hearts Can't Be Broken,' 'Scent of a Woman,' 'For Love or Money,' 'The Three Musketeers,' 'Body Snatchers'

The year is 1991. Two young actresses deliver major parts in old-fashioned, Disney live-action movies. One is Jennifer Connelly, who is good in "The Rocketeer" and goes on to have a robust movie career, including daring projects like "Dark City" and "Requiem for a Dream," an Oscar for "A Beautiful Mind," and eventually being typecast as a wife whose husband is cheating on her ("Little Children," "He's Just Not That Into You").

The other is Gabrielle Anwar, who is charming and fantastic in the lead role of "Wild Hearts Can't Be Broken" as Sonora Webster, a real-life horse diver who thrived in that work even after going blind. She soon appears with Johnny Depp in a Tom Petty music video, anchors an instant-classic scene with Al Pacino in "Scent of a Woman," stars alongside Michael J. Fox in a romantic comedy, and is named by People as one of the world's 50 most beautiful people.

Somehow a perfect storm of talent and buzz led to, if you're graphing it, one of the most V-shaped career paths you will ever see. Despite nearly playing Rose in "Titanic" and turning down "Shakespeare in Love" (!), Anwar spent the late '90s and early 2000s making so, so many movies that you almost definitely have not seen or heard of unless you like memorizing IMDb pages or watching the most obscure movies you can find on Tubi. This was driven in large part by Anwar's personal life, in which she found herself divorced and raising three kids as a single mom.

A few years later, though, she was crushing it again on "The Tudors" before being a total badass for more than 100 episodes on "Burn Notice" and a recurring, delightfully wicked villain on "Once Upon a Time." Track down her "Law and Order: Special Victims Unit" episode as well to see her character's heartbreaking desperation, a huge difference from the aforementioned roles of late, or the warmth, intelligence and sophistication she brought to even brief appearances like "Scent of a Woman" or "Beverly Hills, 90210."

Oh, also: In 2017 she directed and appeared in "Sexology," a documentary about female sexual fulfillment, which was edited by her Oscar-nominated father Tariq Anwar

("American Beauty," "The King's Speech"). Point being: Lots to discuss with this courageous actress/filmmaker, who after approving my interview request through her publicist sent the following email:

Matt,
Super curious.
Gabrielle

What are you nostalgic for from the '90s? It could be anything you miss.

My youth! [Laughs] I'm nostalgic for my youth.

When you think about that, what specifically comes along with it?

The world being my oyster. Now I feel like the crusty shell.

That's quite an image. I don't know how many people can look at the start of a decade and feel like it was, for lack of a more original metaphor, like a rocket ship taking off. Do you think of the beginning of the '90s as being when things got insane for you?

I don't know about insane. I think I was very busy, and I was very focused on work, so I wasn't really too sidetracked into too much that could get me into too much trouble. But I do remember feeling very alive and very capable and excited by life. Of course, this was before the techno-plex that has taken over all of our lives. So there was an innocence there. And almost a generational naivete, not knowing what was about to implode in our personal and public universes.

I just want to make sure I'm understanding you. Are you referring to opportunities you had then that wouldn't be available to a young actress now?

No, not really. I think there was a freedom that was very prevalent in the '90s that doesn't exist anymore because of technology, because of this sort of cancel culture, the Me Too. I think there was a freedom that is now lacking, and without that liberation, there seems to be a tremendous amount of restraint on our liberty.

It's a tough balance because things like that of course bring along a lot of important change. The conversations that are being had now and behaviors getting better. When you say that, is there something specific that you feel gets lost?

I do. I'm all for Me Too. I'm all for taking care of my own. [Laughs] Genetically speaking. And at the same time, I feel like we've lost something. We've lost an element of freedom. Of choice. Of expression. And I miss it. I miss it terribly. I think that from my experience of the '90s and being in a world dominated by powerful men, the choices I made were a deliberate attempt to protect myself. And I am very proud of those choices, and I maintain them to this day. And I think that may have been lacking in that era, and now of course the repercussions are sprung upon us, and there's a lot of canceling within the culture, and I have to say I find it disturbing.

Because it doesn't leave room for conversation and is too binary?

Both of those. But also it's not a fair judicial system. There is no trial. It's just hearsay, and a lot of implied guilt while still innocent. I think there's an innocence that we're overlooking, and it saddens me. As a very tactile, sensual human being, I feel sad that we're so restricted in our expression of self currently. And that wasn't the case in the '90s for sure. It was the absolute antithesis of that.

In terms of guilt and innocence, the other question I've asked everyone before diving into specific work is asking them to name a movie from that era that they weren't in that means a lot. But I previously heard you talking about your love of "The Shawshank Redemption." So I'll ask why you love that movie, or, if the movies we love say something about us, what loving that movie says about you.

[Laughs] That's a good question. I think it says I have damn good taste in screenplays and performances. [Laughs] I think I love a well-told story that has deep, implicated integrity and moral impact.

And it's also a movie about someone rising above a system that's done them wrong.

Yes. Yes. Yes. I can identify with that. Thank you.

It's funny to look at the things we love and ask what it says about us.

No, but I think you're right. I have to concur. I would say that that is a huge part of my passion for that film is that he rises above a system that's so corrupt that I really get a kick out of it.

It was great to dive into a lot of your work for this interview. For "Wild Hearts Can't Be Broken," I know that a few years before that you were kicked out of school after some things you said got you punched in the face. Then for your first major leading role, you punch someone in the face, say you have never been punched and, "I think my big mouth just got me in trouble." To what extent was it cathartic to have all those things happen in the movie because of what happened for real?

[Laughs] Well, I think to this day that has gotta be my favorite film experience I've ever had. There were so many elements about stepping into that role and into that film. It was so unique and magical to me. It was extremely cathartic. Like most character roles. We choose them for maybe subconscious but definitely distinct reasons. I didn't really choose that role; that role chose me. I remember the auditioning process. I remember everybody was auditioning for that role. All of my contemporaries were wanting that character because it was so damn fun. And a true story. And I got to meet the real Sonora Webster, who was an extraordinary woman. It was just a journey I will never forget.

The role's fit for you had me thinking about the notion that bands have their whole lives to make their first album and it's the one that's most authentic to them. And often the second album isn't as good and doesn't connect with them in the same way. Is there something to be said for that being true for actors as well, in that their first big part is true to them in unintended ways? Or is that not fair to say?

Well, I think that that might be very much wrapped up in that first taste of success and of accomplishment. Which is impossible to repeat. So I think that that first album or first breakout role just tastes so sweet. And who doesn't like to get attention from their work? It's not really why most people work for a living, but it's certainly nice to be recognized and seen. So the response to a first album is so precious, and you can't repeat that ever again. There will never be another first in so many areas of life. So I think there's a true, deep appreciation for that first experience coming out of the gate. Even though I had done other projects for quite a few years prior to that film, it was such a delightful role and probably the first delightful role I had been offered. And perhaps one of the last. [Laughs]

The movie is so winning in so many ways. Do you feel like people have stereotypes about horse girls? How do you feel they are perceived?

[Laughs] That's so funny. [Laughs] You know, it's funny you should say that because people who do remember that film are all equestrians. They're all women, and they're all equestrians, and they're all very much involved in horse-girl movies. Listen, I'm very proud to be a horse girl. I would rather be a horse girl than an elephant girl. Although I have to say I have a real soft spot for elephants. But I think there's something about horses that I'm actually obsessed with. In fact, my husband and I only have these exquisite photographs of horses in our bedroom. So that says something very erotic about how I feel about the equine. [Laughs]

What is it about horses that creates these horse girls or these horse women?

I think there's something extremely seductive about a horse. I think the way they move, the way they feel, the way they feel between your legs! Everything about them is just this exercise of eroticism. And I think young girls, when they start entering puberty is usually when their obsession with horses begins, and I think there's definitely a correlation. There certainly was for me. [Laughs] I confess!

And the landing for elephant diving is not quite as smooth.

No, I'm sure. I'm sure. That would be quite a plunge.

When I was a kid in the '90s, I probably looked at that stuff a certain way. But now that my 3-year-old son's favorite animal is horses, I look at them differently. It's interesting to hear you talk about them in terms of eroticism and their connection with women in particular.

Well, I think that there's definitely an element that would feel sort of similar with a male. We both have that yin and yang in us somewhere. So I'm sure that there are definitely men who have that same experience and bliss.

Something notable about 1991 is that Disney released two old-fashioned, live-action movies: "Wild Hearts Can't Be Broken" and "The Rocketeer," which are both great. They also released "Beauty and the Beast," which I would argue is not nearly as empowering but made way more money and was nominated for Best Picture. I'm wondering what you think about the empowerment that comes from the live-action versus animated properties. It's a generalization, but it's hard not to look at that batch of movies and wonder why things connect the way that they do.

Hmm. Interesting. As far as the success is concerned, I think that children can watch the same movie indefinitely. Ad nauseum. Trust me, I have three of my own, and they can watch the same piece of film over and over again. So box office-wise and video sales-wise, you don't get a better audience. Which speaks volumes about most animated films. It's just repeat viewing. I don't know if that's the same for live action. Certainly the promotion of "Beauty and the Beast" was a much bigger financial investment than that of "Wild Hearts." Because I don't believe they spent any money on advertising "Wild Hearts" at all, as far as I remember. So I don't know if people even know about the film's existence, whereas with "Beauty and the Beast" the advertising was significant. And parents love to stick their children in front of an animated film. There were elements to "Beauty and the Beast" that really spoke to me in this idea of this horrible man trying to bring down this unusual, super-, uber-unique other man who looked like a wild animal. I found that fascinating. To be perfectly honest, I'm not much of an animated movie fan unless it's "Shaun the Sheep."

Because those movies, the Aardman stuff, it's really funny and entertaining without poking away at it, but if you do want to talk and think about it that way, it holds up. Whereas in "Beauty and the Beast," Belle is seen as so unusual just because she reads, and the love story is so superficial. We don't need to go down this rabbit hole; this type of thinking and conversation doesn't earn one many friends. But Sonora's story and her as a strong female lead, it's hard not to wish movies like that were the norm rather than the exception, instead of movies that I question what makes them so beloved.

Yeah, I couldn't agree with you more. I'm certainly not going to debate that. I was very disappointed that the film wasn't better received.

I know that what people get offered can be influenced by box office. Do you remember what you were being offered after "Wild Hearts"? Was it more awesome, strong female lead characters? Or 25 more horse movies?

[Laughs] Do you know, I was not offered another horse film after that. I did appear on a horse in "The Three Musketeers," but I didn't do any other "Black Beauty"-esque type things. I was being offered strong female leads. I ended up choosing "For Love or Money" with Michael J. Fox, and before we started shooting, they rewrote the script and turned her into an embarrassment from my perspective. And I had no control over that. I remember many conversations with my agent at the time being devastated that now a really strong, independent female role with a history that was relevant had turned into a prostitute overnight. And I had no control.

How was the character drawn originally before the change? What did we not get to see about her?

It was completely rewritten. When I read the script, I think I was in Alabama shooting "Body Snatchers," and I had been offered a bunch of stuff, and I chose "For Love or Money" because I thought a romantic comedy would be a really fun and novel thing for me to do. Originally the female lead was a model-actress-singer who was trying to make her way through New York, and meets this concierge who's a great guy and has it made but is also torn between this older gentleman who she actually really loves. And she had some incredibly funny dialogue and some incredibly self-effacing humor, and she was from New Jersey, so she had this very specific dialect, which I was working on with my dialect coach who was with me on "Body Snatchers." Then we get to New York, and there was probably 10 days of prep and wardrobe and makeup and camera tests. During those 10 days, I was aware that there were rewrites, and I expressed my concern to Michael J. Fox. He said, "It's just going to get better and better. You'll see." And then when I was just so offended and affronted and furious. His role got funnier and cuter, and my role became such a stereotypical, weak cliche. There was nothing I could do. I spoke to the director, Barry Sonnenfeld, who was far from sympathetic. And I spent the rest of the film in sort of a bad mood. [Laughs]

Have you seen Michael J. Fox's comments about that period? He said, "My decision-making was ridiculous. It wasn't based on truth." So you were justifiably unhappy, and he was just acting out of terror after his Parkinson's diagnosis. Talk about a movie that could have been so much better but probably shouldn't have even been done based on what was going on with everyone involved. Hindsight, I guess.

I remember Ron Howard and Brian Grazer taking me out for dinner when I got back to Los Angeles. I was excited and impressed and flattered. We left that dinner, and I wanted to go home and bury my head in my pillow and cry for days. It was one of the most insulting experiences I've ever had. I think that the dinner originally was intended to talk about perhaps another couple of films that we could perhaps work on. Because I was, I guess, one would consider somewhat of an ingenue. But I just took immediate offense to the conversation, and it was just a really superficial and typically Hollywood experience with no depth or real perspective on life. It was like meeting with two aliens that had no—what's the word—authenticity. It was really kind of a horrifying experience, that dinner. Not as horrifying as working with Barry Sonnenfeld.

That's terrible to go through an experience like that. I'd never seen the movie until recently. Watching it now, it almost looks like an accidental indictment of what it's probably trying to celebrate. It just seems like a rich guy's fantasy that I would hope people now see as despicable. It was interesting to read reviews where some people criticized the character, and others criticized you. Maybe this is a stretch, but there's almost something impressive about being great as someone bland. When given a role of substance, you obviously are so capable. It's ridiculous that someone would see that movie and think that the issue was the performer, not the character.

Well, I appreciate you saying that, but I have to disagree. Because I think I sucked! I think I sucked! I know I sucked. There's no question in my mind. I couldn't do it. I couldn't do it.

I also find myself wondering if you were wondering about something. In "Wild Hearts Can't Be Broken," the horse gets used to your smell. In "Scent of a Woman," of course you're being smelled, and then in "For Love or Money" you were being smelled again. You had to have been like, "Why is my character getting smelled in every single movie?"

[Laughs] You know what, I had never made that connection. That is hysterical. That is so funny. Oh my god. Yes, what a bizarre turn of events. Who would have thought?

Someone who runs a trivia night needs to ask who the only performer is to be smelled in a movie in three consecutive years. Although maybe not because that just sounds weird to say out loud.

[Laughs] Yeah, it does. It is a little strange. It's a little strange.

For "Scent of a Woman," I know you didn't rehearse with Al Pacino, and your time on screen was meant to have a lot of spontaneity to it. Did you ever get a chance to talk to him then or afterwards about playing blind, which is something you had just done in "Wild Hearts"?

Um, I did not. I'm very cautious when I'm working with actors of either gender. I grew up in the industry. My father was a film editor, and I was often around actors and actresses. My mother was an actress. And I was very aware of the ego of an actor. So I'm extremely

21

cautious, particularly until I get to know somebody well. I keep a very—what is that expression—tight hand, you know, in gambling. I keep myself very much to myself. So the same applies with Pacino in that I was fully available if he was to embark on a conversation with me, but I certainly didn't begin any conversations, and I have to say that is part of my technique. [Laughs] Around particular people, and actors are definitely among those people.

No problem if you can't answer this, but was that informed by seeing what happens when that isn't done?

I don't like conflict. I don't like to not feel liked. And I have experienced, prior to doing "Scent of a Woman," egos that [were] intimidating, and I developed a protective mechanism where I am very introverted, unless of course I need to be extroverted. I think that's probably why I became an actor. But I definitely went to turn it off [versus] turning it on.

I saw an article that suggested the role followed you for a while in terms of people asking you to do the tango. Was there a best and/or worst time that happened?

It still happens. It happens all the time. Allllll the time! Everywhere I go. It's like it's the only film I ever did.

Have you ever actually done it with someone who asked?

I did, actually. I have performed the tango a few times since then because I was asked to. Inevitably it will be as a charitable act because I figure if I can help someone by doing a few steps, why the hell wouldn't I? So, yes, I have performed the tango when I didn't want to. [Laughs] And have lived to regret it.

I'm sure there are many people who have been part of memorable moments and can't run away from them. I wonder what the goofiest example is, like if someone was in a memorable scene where they smashed a chair over someone's back and people are constantly asking them to smash a chair over their back.

I think that probably happens more than we know. When people meet actors, they often ask for something really, really ridiculous. As though an actor is not a human being but they're just a function of your performance. Oftentimes you're having lunch with your kids, and someone will come over and say, "Take a picture with me!" [Laughs] As though you're part of the public domain. Of course, if you respond with anything other than, "Yes, of course, my friend," then you're going to feel their wrath.

We talked about what was happening to you in the beginning of the '90s, and I caught up with some of what you made in the late '90s. I know there were a lot of things going on for you personally that impacted what was going on professionally. When you think about the challenge of making decisions in the early '90s vs. the late

'90s, and I know you consider yourself an impatient person, how do you contrast those? Does it feel like the decade is divided in half in a wild way?

Well, in the beginning of the '90s I was a single, wild, crazy, free, narcissistic actress. By the end of the '90s I was a single mother, very much involved with my daughter, and trying to make ends meet. So it's a huge bifurcation, and I made specific choices that were very detrimental to my professional career. And I was aware of that during the process of figuring out my future. At one point my agent said to me, "Are you sure you want to have that baby now?" I was thinking, "Well, the baby's already in there." [Laughs] It's not like I'm making a decision to get pregnant or not. The baby is already alive and deep within my womb. So the question seems somewhat paradoxical.

People definitely don't realize what would happen for a performer when they're making decisions for financial reasons. They may want to believe every creative choice is made because of passion, but that probably happens less than they would hope.

No, that's not my story. Not even close. Not even close.

I mean this in the nicest way possible, then: Was there a project from the late '90s/early 2000s that you remember turning down? [Editor's note: Anwar answers this from earlier in the '90s.]

Yes! First of all, I was in the running for "Titanic," and for about 24 hours was told that that would be mine. That role would be mine. And then I think Kate Winslet did what Kate Winslet does, and the next thing you know, that's not the case. [Laughs] And then I turned down a fabulous film because I was pregnant, and I couldn't shoot it. I can't remember the name of it. I think Julia Ormond ended up playing the character. It was starring Brad Pitt. Oh, "Legends of the Fall"! Which was a fabulous movie, and she did a great job.

When something like that happens with "Titanic," does that take a few years to get over? Or because of what was going on in your life and actors expect situations like this, do you move on? Did it weigh on you?

At the time, no, because I was very much focused on my child and trying to be a good mom. And that was such a priority in my world that I really wasn't thinking much about my career at all, which is very emblematic [Laughs] of my filmography. But over the years, as I have witnessed Kate Winslet's career, of course I'm looking at it, going, "Oh, damn. Look at the opportunities this actress has had. What a blessed career, and how impressive." And I think she's extremely talented. So there's not an envy there, but definitely jealousy. Definitely jealousy.

I don't know if it makes you feel better or worse that there's a review on IMDb for "Board Heads" that calls it the best movie of 1998 and says, "The only problem

is that it is only 90 minutes long. The premise easily justifies a four-hour epic or maybe a trilogy."

Oh my god. I love that! That is hysterical. Oh my god. It's funny; I actually can't remember probably 65% of the films I've done. And there's a reason for that.

On that topic, and hopefully this segue is reasonable. I love the quote in your email signature: "Life shrinks or expands in proportion to one's courage." When you think about your career from that era or whenever, is there a time you can point to that you felt like you were courageous, and a time when maybe in retrospect you weren't?

I think it was courageous of me to have a baby. I can't compare any of my film career to that courage. There is no comparison. They're worlds apart. I think motherhood really put my entire life into perspective, including my vocation.

That's awesome. Is there anything you look back on and wish you would have done differently or had a different courage in the moment? It seems like you're great at being outspoken and speaking up for yourself, so I don't know if there is an example. Or if everyone has one.

I'm sure there are many, many, many times where I have been weak in the courage department. I have been outspoken. I learned that from my father, who's the best. And I think it's gotten me into a lot of trouble. And some of it has been to my detriment. In fact, quite a damn lot has been to my detriment. But I do feel confident that I have maintained my integrity throughout all these years.

It can be fascinating to look at a person's filmography and things that surprise you, and there's something to being able to be good in a bad movie. Now the trajectory for some actors is predictable, so it's interesting to see outliers. I hope it helps fans see performers as people and that it's not a straight line from starting to the top. And thanks to streaming devices, all those movies are out there.

I know, isn't that shameful? It's so bad. It's so, so bad. I just remembered another film that I did turn down, actually. It just popped up in my head, and that was "Shakespeare in Love."

Why did you turn that down?

Because it was an early rendition of the script. The script was fantastic, actually, but it was very early on in their pre-production, and I remember thinking to myself, "I am so small. I'm only five-foot-three. I can't play a man. I could play a boy, but I can't play a man." So even though I loved the script, I just thought, "This is not realistic." And I made that choice. And do you know, I've never seen the film?

24

And it would've been a moot point anyway because they put Gwyneth Paltrow on nine-inch stilts the entire time.

They did?!

No. I wish someone would do that one time, but no.

That is too funny.

I think it's fair to say that Americans sometimes make generalizations about people from England. In terms of the roles that came your way, whether it's "The Three Musketeers," "For Love or Money," "The Tudors," you're so good so I'm not saying this is a bad thing, but I'm wondering if you ever felt limited by any perception of being elegant or classy?

Um, I guess. I have played such an array of personality types over the years. I think that the fact that nobody's seen most of those movies is kind of irrelevant to why I chose them. [Laughs] I think I was trying to break any kind of stereotype for a long time and to feel challenged by a character or a script. I mean, I'd rather be thought of as elegant than white trash.

That makes sense. And there are actresses who are typecast in roles like that.

Yeah, and they're usually the best character actors there are because they're usually nothing like the character that they're playing, which is obviously impressive.

Between "Burn Notice" or "Once Upon a Time" or even your episode of "Law and Order: SVU," your range speaks for itself. This is a basic question, but do you feel like the last 10-15 years has felt like a different lifetime professionally?

Yeah. I think I've experienced many lifetimes. Without a doubt. Which is probably why I have such a memory dysfunction. I'm not kidding; I literally can't tell you half of the things I've done or who I was in the film with or what the experience was like. Which doesn't fare well for interviews. [Laughs]

It just speaks volumes about what was going on with you at the time.

For sure. That's the case in any profession.

I have to ask you about "Sexology." Before you moved forward with the project, were there any questions that you asked yourself?

Well, no because originally the documentary was going to feature Catherine Oxenburg and I going on this journey together as two girlfriends. So I was very comfortable with that. I was very specific about directing it because I didn't want to put myself in a situation where I didn't feel I was in control of my vulnerability. So what ended up happening was Catherine actually experienced this journey prior to my filming mine, so that was a surprise. [Laughs] And I didn't really have time to sit back and say, "Is this a wise decision or not?" Because I was very gung-ho to bring this information to other women. And I was willing to sacrifice my own private experience in order to share with other women that they're not alone in their private experience.

Which you say somewhat casually, but I think it's awesome that you were willing to do that. There are probably a lot of people who wouldn't. I imagine you heard from some who were thankful that you did.

Yeah. I haven't heard anybody say anything negative about it. Although perhaps they just didn't say it to my face. I feel very proud of the project, actually. It's a pity that it wasn't promoted in any shape or form. But I do still direct a lot of women to the documentary, and they're very happy to see that they're not alone in this epidemic of sexual dysfunction on our planet. Particularly in this space.

There's a discussion in the movie of how sex is presented in a contrived, fantasy way in most movies and shows. How much does that inform people's perceptions of sex, love and relationships? At one point you say you want the ape man but are horrified whenever he does ape-like things. There are many romantic comedies that hinge on taming someone or at the end one big, romantic gesture cures everything that came before it.

I think that there's no truth in most depictions of relationships and sex in TV and film. I think it's part of the problem, actually. We all have such high expectations of what a relationship is supposed to look like because we've all seen Jennifer Aniston, and why don't I look like Jennifer Aniston? Why don't I have her breasts? [Laughs] Why don't I have her legs? Why don't I have her humor? Why don't I have her hair? It's very confusing. There's no real discussion or really authentic perspective of what we all look like. I often say to my husband, "Their marriage sucks!" And he says, "What do you mean? They've got it all together." And I say, "Look, if you were a fly on the wall of their kitchen when they get home from dinner tonight when we say goodbye, you will see the truth." Even reality shows aren't real. So there's no real depiction out there of what life really looks like, and what it can look like. More importantly, what can it look like? What is available to us?

Is the issue the type of characters featured or the reality of what we learn about them? You are so right, obviously, but I'm sure some people would say, "Yes, but this is coming from someone who was named one of the 50 most beautiful people in the world, so what does she know about what people go through?" Part of the

issue maybe is just that no matter who the story is about, it's presented in such a shallow way. Or is it both?

Well, I think television and film is such a specific medium that there's only so much time you have to create a character, so cliches tend to be the nature of the beast. Because it just tells a better story, but every now and then you'll get a piece of art that's not stuck in the genre of cliche. And those are the gems. I was just reading about Elliot Page, who's just come out as transgender. I actually messaged him on his Instagram to say, "Is it OK to have a mourning period for Ellen Page?" Because I loved her. And I loved the characters she played, and I loved everything about her. And now she's gone! I did not hear back from him. [Laughs] His career when he was a her was a wonderful example of playing characters that are nuanced and they do have a level of authenticity and a level of depth to them.

On that note, in "Sexology" you talk about spending so many years being who people think you are versus your authentic self. Can you elaborate on the difference?

For me personally, I was a very uncomfortable child. Very, very internal and kind of terrified. So in order to function as I grew, particularly in my teens, I had to project something more viable. [Laughs] So that I didn't get beaten up. Again. So I sort of very subconsciously invented personalities that would work in a situation. Which is quite damaging because it's very hard to remember who you once pretended to be. It's kind of like liars. It's easy to tell the truth because you don't have to remember anything, but if you catch yourself in a lie you have to regurgitate the beginning, the middle and how the end is going to materialize. So I was playing roles that would work in any given situation. And of course being the narcissist that I am, I wanted to feel appreciated. So each attempt at feeling appreciated was a different version of self that I kind of created. So I didn't even really know who my authentic self was for a really long time, and particularly in sex, in my sexual autonomy. I was very confused.

When you talk about it being hard to remember a persona you've invented, are you thinking of a specific moment when someone caught you in a lie and you forgot what you had done?

Oh, yeah. It used to happen on a daily basis. That's when I quit lying. I literally am like the Jim Carrey character who doesn't tell a lie, who only tells the truth, and puts his foot in his mouth every five minutes. That's who I am now.

Can you give an example of what was happening every day before that?

I would get very, very anxious when two groups of friends would come together that had been divided in my life. Because I would be one way with one group of friends and another way with another group of friends, and then at my birthday party when they all came together, I was schizophrenic. I literally would turn to one person with one personality and have a conversation, then turn to the next person with another personality and have a conversation. And the entire evening was a sham. Which doesn't bode well for a happy birthday.

I'm not sure if that sounds more like a Jim Carrey movie or Hannah Montana.

Love Hannah Montana.

If you had to pinpoint what year you changed that mentality and it was all truth all the time, when did that happen?

Well, I'm still waiting for that to happen. [Laughs] It's a process. It's an evolution of self. I'll get there. On my deathbed.

"Sexology" certainly gets to a vulnerable, honest place about who you are on a number of levels. You touch on things that seem to have informed you in a lot of conscious and unconscious ways. If everyone you ever worked with had to have seen "Sexology" before collaborating, what changes?

Well, I think I'm immediately more vulnerable. I think I'm less mysterious as a woman. I was thinking about working with a man, actually. I wasn't thinking about working with another woman when you said that. I was thinking about what it would be like to work with a man who's experienced "Sexology." I think I would be less of a potential lay. And that dynamic always shows up between the masculine and feminine in my experience, unless of course the man in question is homosexual.

Casual viewers probably do a lot of speculation about those dynamics on set, whether it's a movie or a Tom Petty music video.

[Laughs] Cute.

I know you've been doing a ton of writing between screenplays, novels, a memoir, a miniseries, and writing 12-14 hours a day. Can you illuminate what comes out during that process? What material are you writing?

I have probably four, five screenplays. I have 10 pilots. I have a memoir, two novels and a 12-volume phenomenology in which I collaborated with two doctors on—actually, one of the fellows that I'm working with I met on "Sexology." He was one of my interviewees. He was my favorite interview. So we just finished a 12-volume phenomenology, four of which I think will be published in the fall. But what comes out of me is I feel like I'm in bliss. I feel like I'm connecting to source, whatever source is. So what comes out is bliss. I'll come into my office in the morning, and the next thing I know it's seven o'clock at night, and everybody's waiting for dinner.

That's a cool feeling to get lost that way.

It's heaven. I wish I'd had the opportunity to do this earlier, but I was feeding three mouths and trying to pay for school.

Which is a more accurate title for your memoir: "Wild Hearts Can't Be Broken" or "For Love or Money"?

Oh, definitely "Wild Hearts." But at the moment it's called [Laughs] "Burned, Pickled and Plated."

Is there anything about you that would surprise people who have a perception of you as being as classy as some of your characters?

Well, I'm very low maintenance. I'm very low maintenance, which I'm very proud of. And I go to great lengths [Laughs] to maintain my low maintenance. [Laughs] I would say that with the advent of COVID, my lifestyle changed very little. And I'm very grateful that my mainstay wardrobe is sweats. Because most people had to invest in a sweats wardrobe for COVID. Not I.

Has anyone ever called you Gabby?

My parents and my childhood friends called me Gabby, and I have since grown out of Gabby. If anyone says Gabby now, I feel like I have done something wrong and I'm about to be reprimanded. So most of my dear friends call me G, and my grandson calls me GG for grandma Gabrielle, and I'm very happy with GG.

Obviously your dad is an acclaimed editor. But some people would make a movie like "Sexology" and say, "I know who my dad is, but I don't want him to edit this." Is you having him edit the movie a sign of you being fearless or a sign of a really evolved relationship between daughter and dad?

Maybe a little of both. My father and I are very close, and I can't think of another editor that I'd like to work with. In the future also.

That's good that you didn't have to shy away from that for unnecessary reasons.

Right! Yeah, I wanted to reinvent intimacy. There's many forms of intimacy, not just that between partners. And my father and I have an intimacy that is incredibly valuable. Obviously it's not sexual, but it's extremely close and full of love and respect. There are many levels, many different versions of intimacy, so I was glad that we could go on that journey and really honor that.

Which movie have you thought about in any way as being more relevant or on your mind lately: "For Love or Money" in terms of misogyny and wealth inequality, or "Body Snatchers" and the cult mentalities that have been evident in recent years?

Hmm. To be perfectly honest with you, Matt, none of my films are ever on my mind.

I can't believe I'm saying this out loud. But because I read interviews you did about "Sexology" and the ways people perceive female sexuality and the vagina, and we did already talk about "Shakespeare in Love," I feel like I would be remiss, or maybe I will regret asking, what you think about Gwyneth Paltrow's vagina candle.

[Laughs] OK, so in another incarnation I may have gone the GOOP way. I think that her products are fabulous. I think that there's a slightly bourgeois element that isn't very well-received in the general population [Laughs], but I have to say that there are days that I go onto their website, and I will look at some of the products that they're selling. Just out of curiosity! Not that I've purchased any. But I am curious. I'm curious. Because who doesn't want to have a happy vagina?

So your thoughts on that particular product?

The vagina candle I'm not too familiar with. Does it look like a vagina, or does it smell like a vagina?

I'm not sure if the former is true. I believe the latter was the point.

Ahh, OK. Hey, listen. The scent of a woman, what can I say?

You've talked about the different sections of your career and the ups and downs of life. Is there anything you would go back and change on a micro or macro level?

There are things I would go back and change in my personal life, but not in my professional life. It is what it is. People take themselves way too seriously in this industry. We're just making movies.

I like that. The entertainment world is certainly a focal point of so many things. The last thing I wanted to ask was to circle back on something you said earlier about cancel culture. As you said, you've been in a position where you felt like you were in a position that we know young actresses are in, in many different ways. There are things you've spoken about, and there are things that are difficult to talk about. What do you think is the right way to know how to handle these situations? Like you said, we have the Me Too movement, which is obviously an important conversation to have. What I think you were referring to is the idea that someone goes from well-respected to despised overnight. It seems to me that the list of people who have been justifiably indicted for these things is far longer than the list of people

who have had a wave of negativity come their way that they haven't disturbed. So I'm wondering how you think we should change the way we handle ourselves in these situations when something comes out, whether it's all the things about Kevin Spacey or the domestic abuse stuff about Johnny Depp. What is the appropriate way for people to handle these situations?

Well, let me start by saying that in my personal opinion, and of course I'm only speaking for myself because that's the only experience I can relate to: I was invited into a hotel room or two in the '90s, and I declined. And I was also offered heroin in the '90s, and I declined. So I think we need to start there. I have a 20-year-old son, and he's terrified of saying the wrong thing or doing the wrong thing, so he's kind of shut himself off from even dating at this point. Because he feels so ostracized by the culture right now just for being a male that he's not interested in investing in something that may go south without his even knowing. And I think that we're in a pretty traumatic state of affairs when our sons are either raping college students who are drunk or not even capable of going on a date. So I feel like we're approaching things from such a strange perspective suddenly. I feel like we're not actually dealing with the root of issues on the planet right now. We're just on this topical, social-media realm that has no depth, and I think that in order to really change the culture, we have to start looking at much deeper structures of the subject matter. I think that obviously no woman should be abused in any shape or form. It's absolutely wrong. Neither should a man be abused in any shape or form. That's absolutely wrong. So how do we make this balance without destroying people's lives? It's just shocking to me. I have dear friends, both male and female, who have been on both sides of this argument. I signed Me Too too back when it happened. On that first day I hashtagged Me Too on my Instagram account because I am a survivor of a rape and childhood sexual abuse. So I'm right there with these women. And I don't want to take someone down. I don't! I just don't. I don't think an eye for an eye is the right way to do this in any system of justice. So I struggle. I struggle with this whole redesign of how we interact with each other. Mostly from my children's perspective. I'm in a marriage. I'm very settled. I'm very comfortable in my world. But my children are exploring. They're beginning to explore, they're beginning to date, and they're in relationships, and it is an incredibly unpleasant era to experience love. And I just don't think it's right.

Not that a very big challenge can be solved in one answer, but do you have an idea of something that can be done about this?

Yeah. In fact, the phenomenology that I just completed addresses these issues in great detail and great length. So, yes, there is a solution, I believe.

Part of it is almost like what I've felt sometimes when it comes to protecting oneself during this recent period. Because going into a certain place, I might know that I'm being safe and my family is being safe, but there's so much that you can't control about what the world does that that winds up informing so much about how you perceive other people and your place in the world, and maybe that is likely to

31

result in people retreating a little bit because of feeling like things are so contentious and not really of a community. That analogy seems to track.

Yeah. Yeah. I think we've given a lot of governance to the wizards behind the web. Which is kind of an incredibly terrifying thought. That our entire world is being controlled by a few private entities. I'm scared. [Laughs] I'm scared. I'm scared for my children!

Tom Everett Scott of 'That Thing You Do!'

Just because an actor broke out while playing a fantastically nice person and constantly has come off that way in interviews for more than two decades doesn't mean that when connecting for an interview they'll be doing something kind and generous like, say, helping a brother-in-law move.

But, in fact, that's exactly what Tom Everett Scott, aka objectively nice, likable drummer Guy Patterson in universally beloved nice guy Tom Hanks' 1996 directorial debut "That Thing You Do!" is doing just before he calls. Not only that, but when I ask his preference among a batch of other movies from that year, he wants to give attention to and comment on each one, rather than just pick a favorite. A warm, present thing not everyone would do, which also goes for a remarkably endearing detail he shares about something he did on the set of Hanks' film. Via email after our interview, he doesn't just confirm the spelling of important educators in his life but includes additional praise and a link to an article about his middle-school music director retiring.

Of course, despite "That Thing You Do!" being an extraordinary movie about a young band's fast rise and abrupt disintegration that is just as lovable now as when it came out, Scott shouldn't be defined by just the one role. Though his time as a leading man ("American Werewolf in Paris," "Dead Man on Campus") was short-lived, he has worked steadily in the years since, with significant co-starring and supporting roles in everything from "ER" to "La La Land" to "13 Reasons Why" to "Boiler Room" to "Law and Order" to "One True Thing" to "I'm Sorry."

When you think back to the '90s, what's something you're nostalgic for? It could be absolutely anything.

Starbucks still had kind of a mystique about it. You could still go to a video store. You could still browse the aisles of a video store. I miss that. My wife and I would spend more time looking for a movie to watch than actually watching the movie. And argue about which we were going to rent that night, and it never mattered what we got because she'd always fall asleep 15 minutes in. I guess I miss—there was a simplicity to it. I miss that simplicity of not being reachable at all times. That you could just rely on people leaving you a message on your voice machine. You know what I mean? It's hard to even imagine that now, right?

Absolutely. It's such an instinctual thing to check email or texts. People have to actively not do it as opposed to actively do it.

Yeah, that's a great way of putting it. You're right. We just spend way too much time on our smartphones. We're so inundated with this constant communication that it's hard to even imagine that the only way you would really hear from anybody was over the phone, on a voicemail, if you weren't home to pick up the phone when it rang or calling your machine from a pay phone and listening to your messages. That's how you would meet friends out if you were out. If plans changed, you'd have to check your voice messages! It's really crazy. How old are you? I don't know; am I talking to somebody that remembers this?

Yeah, I'm 38. So I definitely remember. Even after college, which was now a long time ago, I think of how many texts or calls went back about the plan and settling things by conversation. And now that people have families and kids, the type of communication—one thing I wrote down to myself of an example that comes to mind for me about the '90s is having good conversations over the phone with friends. That just is not common anymore.

Exactly. You could just be on the phone forever. When I moved to New York City in '92; I was there from '92-2001, but right after college—you were texting after college. We weren't even texting. I would, like, sit on my fire escape. I lived in Manhattan; I was in Midtown. I was in this—not crappy because they were redone. They were called floor-through apartments or railroad apartments, where you had to walk through one room to get to the next room. I shared it with a couple guys, and we had the phone connected [near] the fire escape. You'd just open the window, sit on the fire escape, and we were all smoking cigarettes back then. We were stupid kids, not really caring about our health. So we were smoking cigarettes out on the fire escape and having long-ass conversations, and actually it was on that phone that Tom Hanks called me personally to ask me to be in "That Thing You Do!" And that whole process of him getting in touch with me was I had auditioned and I was waiting to hear back, and it had been an audition, a callback, a reading with Liv Tyler, a meeting with Jonathan Demme and then just waiting and feeling like it was close, it was going to happen maybe, and my agent was like, "Well, I'm going out for dinner tonight, and I'll have my pager on me." [Laughs] Or whatever device. And Tom Hanks called me at home in that apartment on that little phone by the fire escape. And I remember him asking me if I wanted to be in his movie, and I had to think about it for one millisecond. Yeah. That's how I got my first film. That's how I got my big break from Mr. Hanks, who is like a god to me.

That's such a memorable location and image. When you're going to get good news, being in a place where jumping for joy could lead to you plummeting several stories might not be the best place.

[Laughs] My then-girlfriend, now-wife, Jenni, we were there together. We were living there for a month before we were going to move in together for the first time. And she was there, and we were holding the phone between us listening to Tom Hanks talk on the phone. We were giddy.

I'm sure! Before we move on, I have to ask if you remember anything about the video store debates between you two that you mentioned before.

Yeah. So our local place was called Channel Video. Channel Video was on Columbus Avenue between 83rd and 84th or 82nd and 83rd. It was right in that neighborhood. We would walk up there. There was a basement. On the street-level floor there was VHS, and then downstairs was the new DVD collection. And the really good stuff was the Criterion collection. I remember looking for foreign films and documentaries. We considered ourselves fairly hip and intelligent, so we wanted to find cool stuff like that. We were usually on the same page, but sometimes you're not in the mood for that. Sometimes you just want to watch a mindless comedy. So the debates were usually when one of us wanted to watch a foreign film and you'd be like, "Ah, subtitles." But the other one would be like, "Yeah, but I want to be smarter."

I wonder if anyone ever rented a subtitled foreign version of "Tommy Boy" just to feel like they were splitting the difference.

Oh, man, what a smart thing to do! Like, "Here's what we'll do. [Laughs] This is 'Tommy Boy' dubbed in Chinese, but with the English subtitles." That's not bad; that's a good compromise. Doesn't matter; my wife would be asleep in 15 minutes. She'd just put her feet in my lap, tell me to rub them, and be like a hypnotist. Boom; right out.

"That Thing You Do!" came out in 1996. From the following list of other movies from that year, what struck the biggest chord with you and why: "Swingers," "A Time to Kill," "Space Jam," "Primal Fear," "Multiplicity," "Sling Blade," "Jerry Maguire."

OK, so a couple of those I haven't even ever seen. I've never seen "Space Jam." I know that's going to freak you out because you're 38, but I'm 50, and it didn't hit me. I didn't get hit by "Space Jam." I missed it. And my kids aren't really sporty, so they didn't watch it either. And they're older now, so I apologize for not seeing "Space Jam." I know people love it. "Multiplicity," I know that's Michael Keaton, and I know that Julie Bowen, who was in "American Werewolf in Paris" with me, was in "Multiplicity," but I didn't see that either. "A Time to Kill," that was a John Grisham novel, maybe?

It was.

Who starred in that? I can't remember.

That was Matthew McConaughey, Ashley Judd and Samuel L. Jackson.

Yeah. I know it, and I probably saw it, but I don't really remember it. The obvious choice is "Swingers" because I went to the premiere. I've seen the movie multiple times since. It resonated with me because I was an actor and went through all the stuff that those guys went through. We were all coming out at the same time. "Swingers," I love that movie. So that's the obvious answer for me. But what were the other ones?

I said "Primal Fear," "Sling Blade," "Jerry Maguire."

I loved "Sling Blade." I was talking like that guy for weeks after that. Billy Bob. "Sling Blade" is a good movie. That was the first time I'd seen Dwight Yoakam ever do any acting; he's a good actor. And the late, great John Ritter is fantastic in that movie. I love "Sling Blade." So that's a close second. What were the other ones?

I appreciate it. I don't want you to feel like you have to comment on each one. I was just asking your preferences.

I do. That's how I am. I'm very thorough.

That's excellent. "Primal Fear" and "Jerry Maguire" were the others.

I don't remember what "Primal Fear" was about. Was that Harrison Ford?

That was Edward Norton's breakout in the dual role.

Oh yeah, yeah yeah yeah. That's right. He switches to that other guy. The courtroom drama. It was OK; to me it's not a memorable movie outside of it being Ed Norton's breakout. And "Jerry Maguire," I really like that. I may have maybe only seen it once or twice, but I really enjoyed it. I got to work with Renee Zellweger after that, and we stayed friends and we have the same manager. I love Renee very much. I think she's amazing in that movie. I like that movie; I think that movie has some very memorable moments. For me it's "Swingers," and then "Sling Blade" probably second.

I appreciate how thorough you are. That speaks volumes.

[Laughs] Yeah. I don't know. Ask my wife how wonderful that is. [Laughs]

Well, I'm so excited to dive into "That Thing You Do!" a movie that has meant so much to so many for so long. And I used to be a drummer, so it's great to talk to you about that aspect too. I know your parents wouldn't let you play drums when you were a kid because they were too loud—

Wellllll, sort of. I mean, they probably would have let me play the drums. I think what they were was grateful that I chose the trumpet. Let's put it that way.

Was that a debate at home? What do you remember about the time when you weren't sure which way you were going to go?

OK. I have three sisters. Two of them are older. We're all about two years apart. This is the way it worked in my family when I was growing up in East Bridgewater, Massachusetts, public school system. It had a very good music department. There were three people in charge of the music department there: [high school music director] Dan Lasdow, [co-leader of spring musicals] Mary Wilcox, and [middle school music director] John Fantucchio. All three of them were wonderful influences on me. Dan's relationship with me was wonderful because he was a trumpet player; I'll get to the story here. So my older sisters, they both picked the flute. So in fourth grade, Dan and John and maybe some other students would come to your classroom and demonstrate the different musical instruments that you could play in the fourth and fifth grade band. And if you liked music and being in band in fourth and fifth grade then you stuck with the program through junior high and high school. And because these guys were so good, there were competitions, statewide stuff. There was like a whole program. Cut to the short: So my sisters both picked the flute; I know that when I hit fourth grade they're going to come to my classroom because I've already been exposed to this in my family. I know that I'm going to choose an instrument. In my mind it's like, "It's going to be drums. I'm going to pick drums probably." Because I really like drums. I like drumsticks, I like banging on things. I just kinda had a feeling that was going to happen. And they come to the room and they're demonstrating the instruments, and Dan Lasdow who demonstrated the trumpet, what does he play? He plays the "Star Wars" theme. I saw "Star Wars" when I was 7, 8 years old. That was the most impressionable thing in my life that could have ever happened to me. The only thing he could have played on the trumpet that could have persuaded me to play anything other than drums was the "Star Wars" theme. It was this really sneaky move by Dan Lasdow. So I chose the trumpet. That's how that happened. And I played the trumpet all the way through to twelfth grade. Sometimes I was first chair. I would get into all these music festivals and competitions. Because I'm very competitive, I really enjoyed it. Some of my best friends through school were other trumpet players. We were this little gang of trumpet players. It really shaped my life. I knew that I wasn't going to go into music because acting was a bit more of a force in my life. I was a bit more drawn to that, but it could've been music. I probably wasn't good enough. At this point if I was still trying to make it in music I'd be failing. Luckily, I found something that I'm pretty good at.

Was there a musician you really looked up to at that time? Or to put it another way: Who was your Del Paxton, and how would you have reacted to playing with them?

It wasn't any trumpet player. I liked playing trumpet, but I didn't really respond to any trumpet players. There was Doc Severinsen. Herb Alpert, my dad had his albums. But I was more attracted to rock 'n roll and MTV, and I like Van Halen and the Police. This '80s version of music for me. Huey Lewis and the News. I wouldn't say I had horrible music taste, but it's better now. The older I got, the more exposed to more than just my small town and my small environment, the more I got exposed to better and better music.

I can say with confidence that if you release an album of trumpet covers of Van Halen songs, people will buy it.

OK, all right. I see what you're saying. I might have to do that. You're right. Can you imagine if I could play the trumpet as good as Eddie Van Halen played the guitar? Where would I be right now? I wouldn't be helping my brother move into his Woodland Hills home. I'd be hiring somebody to do that. [Laughs]

You talked about how excited you of course were when Tom Hanks called you about the role in "That Thing You Do!" Obviously Guy's nervousness leads to him speeding up the tempo and creating the band's success. Did you have any nerves or need to do anything to calm yourself in order to be able to actually execute this life-changing role?

Early on, after I got cast and before I headed out to L.A. to shoot it, there was this month where I was taking drum lessons and preparing, and they were sending us all this stuff to watch from 1964 to get in the mood. And I was feeling this mounting pressure, anxiety. And I hadn't done much in my life at that point. Nothing of this scale. Nothing. This is it. This is the biggest thing that had ever happened to me. It's probably the biggest thing I've ever done since. But something clicked in my brain, some other part of me told myself that I was going to make mistakes. It's inevitable. It's human. To allow myself to make mistakes. To tell myself, "You have permission to make mistakes. Take the pressure off yourself, and enjoy this." It was one of those moments, the moment of clarity, where you actually give yourself some good advice. So moving forward, yeah, there were moments where I was nervous around Tom. He was amazing. He would recognize it. He had said some really important things to me during the course of filming, especially early on where he was like—with a lot going on on a movie set, I was easily distracted. I also grew up in a place where if you see somebody carrying something, you offer to help. So I would see grips and electricians and stuff doing stuff, and I would try to help them. I was trying to help everybody make the film! [Laughs] And Tom Hanks said, "Come here, come here. Listen. This is one big machine, and you're just a cog in this machine. You have your job. Everybody has their job. You've just gotta do your job." [Laughs] It was such sage advice. It's such good advice, and it's something I've taken with me since then. It's enough to just do your job and do it well. There was also a real moment of recognition during the filming where—I actually realized this when I read the script, that I was Guy, and Guy was me. There was this parallel thing. I'm going to go on this journey that Guy's going on. He's going on for music; I'm going on it for acting. So whenever Tom would give us a direction like, "OK, you're coming in here, and you're at the Pittsburgh show, and it's a big deal and there are going to be 1,000 people in the audience and you're just like, 'Wow, I can't believe this is happening to me.'" [Laughs] And I looked at him and I was like, "Yeah, I think I can probably replicate that." [Laughs] So there were moments. And there were moments of like, "Pinch me, I can't believe this is happening." Does that work? Are you really supposed to pinch yourself when you think you're dreaming?

Good question. I've never done that.

But there were definitely moments where we would look at each other, me and Steve and Jonathan and Ethan would look at each other and be like, "Wow. I can't believe this."

That's funny that he had to tell you "That ain't your job," which is also a line in the movie.

[Laughs] Yeah. That's right. I loved working with Obba Babatunde. He was just so great. He had so many great stories. He is so great in that movie.

And there are people way older than their mid-20s who would love to have that enlightened perspective, allowing yourself to make mistakes in a life-changing moment. I think that's hard for a lot of people. So that's great that it helped you take that step.

Yeah, it was really lucky. I think it was a combination of the pressure and the desire to do a good job. And there was a part of my logistical side of my brain that was just like, "All right, there's one way we're going to be able to do this, and it's if we allow there to be mistakes." I don't know where that came from. My mom and my dad were really good at raising their kids to think about things. My mom especially just really prepared me for a lot of the decisions I had to make. She's a very kind person who believes in kindness. She also was really good at analyzing a situation and thinking about good options. I came from a good background, and I'm really glad that I did.

Clearly the trajectory of the band is influenced by a lot of things. When you think of the busy touring schedule, the life of a band on the rise, what aspect of that lifestyle seems most difficult to you?

I think a band on the rise probably isn't that difficult at all. Because everything is new, everything is positive. Those are the things you remember the most. Like me, same with playing the role of Guy Patterson. All the memories are great from that time, and everything that was happening was great. It's when you've done it a few times and some of the newness and freshness wears off, and then you realize, "Oh, every time we do a movie we've gotta do press, and every time I do something I gotta get up at 5 a.m. and do radio interviews for hours with disc jockeys who all want to know what it was like to kiss Liv Tyler. OK." So it's later. It's not the first time, it's not on the rise that you have a bad time. It's later where you kind of realize a little bit of cynicism. You get a little jaded, you get a little of this, that or the other thing. Your own expectations are changing. I think that's where the difficulties come in. Otherwise, you're just young and having a great time.

I think that's a smart insight. In my previous job part of my role was being the music editor, and over time I've grown fascinated with bands who just released one great album and that was it.

Mmm hmm, yeah. That's true. One of my favorite albums growing up, and like I said my music taste has changed, but the Outfield was this band that had this great first album, and then their second album was such shit. I think that guy just died recently during the pandemic. But I used to love that. It was also I realized that that first album is years of developing that music, and if it's a hit you have a much shorter time to come up with all this great new music. And it's just so much harder to come up with something in less time, and once the expectations have been set up.

The song "My Paradise" by the Outfield is a song I love that when I listen to it, it feels like no one is listening to it except for me.

Was that off the first album?

It was one of the highlights they had after the first one.

I am going to look that up. I can't wait to hear that: "My Paradise" by the Outfield.

Yeah, I always loved that song, and that's awesome you're a fan of them too. I also wanted to ask: Which do you think changed more, the music industry between the mid-'60s and mid-'90s, or the movie industry since 1996?

That's a good question. The more significant change in the music industry I want to say has been since the mid-'90s. Since it's not about making albums that you sell in record stores. The music industry has probably had its most impactful change since then. Movies from mid-'90s to now, it's probably similar to the music industry, which really changed. In the mid-'90s, you were still able to make "That Thing You Do!" You were still able to make $20-$30 million movies that weren't blockbusters. And then the spectrum of indie films. In the '90s there was indie fare that was still kind of popular, Sundance movies and stuff, that was really popular, there were tentpole movies, and then movies like "That Thing You Do!" That doesn't really exist anymore. They don't make those movies anymore. Those movies are miniseries streaming on demand. It's completely changed. Most stuff didn't change as much from the '60s to the '90s as from the '90s to now because of technology. I was having a conversation with my friend John Hyams about this: "The Godfather" probably would not be a movie released in the theaters now. If no one had made it yet, that would be developed into a limited series on HBO or Netflix or Amazon or whatever.

Wow. That's so true. And part of what I think is so resonant about "That Thing You Do!" is that it's so pure of heart, it has no villains, and it's nice in a way that can and should be taken as a compliment. All that is to say, and this is a bigger question without a binary answer, but were the '90s nicer than now?

Without getting too political, we gotta look at how things were this past year. What happened. And it wasn't just this past year; it came to light this past year. There are significant changes in how we see whether people are nice or not, to put it generally. "Nice" can be you're caring, but it's politicized now. Whether you care about somebody or you don't, that's been politicized. [Laughs] That's crazy, but that's kind of it. There has been much more emphasis placed on being inclusive and being caring of others, for others, than there was back in the '90s. The '90s is still kind of—some people have been living in this blissful ignorance state. But I will say, because I'm sick of hearing myself talk about stuff like that, on an interview like this I don't even want to pretend that I could get into this in a short interview; this is such a huge discussion. But to answer that question, and how it applies to the movie I made in the '90s, that was Tom Hanks' story about a time of innocence. The last moment of innocence for our country. Because it was 1964. It was before Vietnam; it was before major events that changed everything.

It's a big question, and I appreciate how you brought that all together.

And as a dad though, I think I'm forced to teach being nice. Not forced to; I choose to. Raising other humans, you're talking about being nice and fair all the time. So I think it's regardless of when it happens, you're always trying to instill that in your kids.

At least, we would hope that's what people are doing. Yesterday my 3-year-old son wasn't putting away some toys we were playing with outside, and my wife told him that if he can't be responsible for putting his own toys away, we'll have to give them to the neighbors. He was like, "OK. We should do that." We said, "I think you'd be upset." He said, "No, I have other toys. Let's do that." And he was upset we didn't jump to do that. It was like, "We have raised you really kind, and you're calling this bluff."

Ohhhh. Well, there you go. You got a good one.

Thank you! Part of the impact of "That Thing You Do!" is the trajectory of Guy and Faye's relationship. And of course the impact of "La La Land" speaks for itself. You had a great quote about that: "It's about how you can't sometimes be who you want to be as an artist and then also have the love of your life. It's just this tortured decision that they had to make, and it just makes your heart break." Obviously "That Thing You Do!" also deals with being an artist and the impulses and pressures in that world. I was wondering how you'd compare the relationship messages of "That Thing You Do!" and "La La Land." Are they saying the same thing?

That's interesting. I never really saw that parallel, but it is there in both movies. Jimmy is not able to have the relationship with Faye and have the artistic goals. He's unable to do that. I've been with Jenni—we met in college, and we've been together since before "That Thing You Do!" I don't think I've given anything up to be with her, and I don't think that relationship has done anything negative to my artistic endeavors. If anything, she's provided me with opportunities to be artistic. So it's not a blanket thing. But I do see that parallel now between characters in "La La Land" and Jimmy and Faye in "That Thing You Do!" It sometimes doesn't work. Sometimes you need to go after your dream, and if it seems like a relationship is going to squash that, or be too controlling or distracting, you do have to make that choice. Sometimes that is more important. Sometimes you're not in the right relationship, and that's more what it is. In "La La Land," they're really in love. They really are. They are in love. And it's very passionate. But it proves that it doesn't work. You see where they have conflicting feelings. And I think Damien Chazelle really spells that out. It's not symbiotic; there is too much conflict. And that is the heartbreaker that it didn't work because of those things. And then in "That Thing You Do" Guy ends up with Faye, so everything works out great.

And if you look at what happens to the members of the band, Jimmy being the one who was arguably the most focused on professional success, he's the one who has the long-term career in the industry, but I don't recall anything about his relationship future.

No. Right. We always talk about what would the sequel be. I would be hesitant to do a sequel just because sometimes when a movie is so good—and I can say that confidently. "That Thing You Do!" is this really wonderful movie, that it would be hard to put a sequel and mess with that. But if there was a sequel, I would love to see it in the '80s. I would love to see what Tom Hanks does to the '80s like he did with the '60s. And make it more of one of those pathetic one-hit-wonders having to get back together. But when I start seeing it I start seeing all the bad versions of that movie. [Laughs] That's why I hesitate to go any further.

It just becomes "Hot Tub Time Machine."

You know it does. [Laughs]

Well, in terms of pushing the story forward, have you given any thought to what the conversation would be like between David and Mia on the way home from the jazz club in "La La Land"?

Oh. Like would he even have registered a little something? I don't know; I think she would have kept that from him. Why open that up with your—I mean, who knows? Maybe she decides to let it out so she can—maybe that's the kind of relationship that David and Mia have is where she can say, "This is what happened." Who knows?

I have a few lightning round questions to ask you. Which is a better/worse band name: the Heardsmen or the Chordvettes?

Oh, the Heardsmen is better. Chordvettes is just too punny.

Who is a one-hit wonder that you like?

42

Level 42.

I don't think I know them.

They had one hit. [sings doo-doo-doo-doo] It's an '80s song. "Is There Something About You?" Is that it? Let me look. I've got "My Paradise" in my queue. Level 42, "Something About You." That was their one hit.

I'll have to check that out. What's a ballad you'd love to hear a version at a faster tempo?

"The Love Boat" theme.

Would you rather star in a biopic of Keith Moon or John Bonham?

Ooh! Oh, wow. I think I'm Bonham. I think I'm John Bonham. But I love Keith Moon. I love the craziness. I just don't think I look like I could play him. I could probably get away with playing Bonham.

Are you better at poker or drums?

[Laughs] I'm equally mediocre at both.

Who will win another World Series first: Your Red Sox or my Cubs?

Oh, well well well. There's some connection between those two teams and their success. The Red Sox are really rebuilding right now; I think it's going to be a few years. What about you guys? Where are the Cubs at?

Same position of being much farther away than you would think.

Who are the core players?

They still have Javy Baez, Anthony Rizzo, Kris Bryant, Willson Contreras. [Editor's note: That was true at the time of this conversation.] But they've gotten rid of a bunch of people and have no pitching left.

Jon Lester's not there anymore?

He went to the Nationals along with Kyle Schwarber.

Is Theo still GM?

No, he left.

I don't know then. I don't know, man. That's a good question. It might be 10 years before either one of them wins.

Seeing as you were in "That Thing You Do!" and "One True Thing," settle it once and for all. Who is the better, more talented person: Meryl Streep or Tom Hanks?

[Laughs] Who is the better, more talented person? That's not fair! I can't answer that. They both were so wonderful to be around. Literally the nicest big stars there could be. Yeah, I can't pick one or the other. They're both awesome. *[mock California voice]* They're both wonderful!

And not in the lightning round format, I listened to a podcast where you talked about the late '90s, being that age at that point in your career and having to guide yourself after "That Thing You Do!" When you think of the offers that came in at that time, do you look back at that time and laugh? Of course everyone is grateful for the opportunities they have but also sometimes look back with different perspective. What do you remember of the hubbub that must have followed after "That Thing You Do!"

Well, yeah, I certainly have 20/20 hindsight. There were decisions that I made that I would like a redo. But it's hard to know, and I didn't have any real experience—I tried to make the best, well-informed decisions that I could. I definitely thought a werewolf movie would be this fun thing to do. I didn't realize how sticky the fake blood would be, how cold it would be to work at night all the time. [Laughs] It was fun, but it was also a little miserable. I had never been to Europe before, so in many ways it was one of the greatest things that I've ever done in terms of I was in my mid-20s on a studio feature film in Europe, in Paris, at night, running around, and it was such a cool, singularly unique experience of any of the other things I've done. But as a movie and what it did for my career, maybe I could've waited a little longer and made a better choice. Same with "Dead Man on Campus"; I had a great time, but I probably could have been a little more patient, a little pickier. I think that's something I didn't have. As I've grown older, I've been better at making decisions. And that happens. Older actors who have been around for a while before they get their big break tend to make better decisions [Laughs] than the younger ones. But I'm happy. I'm happy with my career. There was like a stack of scripts, and there were tons of meetings that I took, but there are so many other variables in play that you don't have any control over. Like whether a movie's going to be a success at the box office or not. Unfortunately.

I just saw "American Werewolf in Paris" for the first time, and you're incredibly charming in it regardless. You're so likable in everything.

Oh, thank you, man, I really appreciate that. There was a long stretch where I just didn't want to even look at those, and I have recently looked at them with my kids because they were like, "Come on, let's watch your movies." I was like, "Oh, yeah, yeah. It isn't bad. It isn't bad." But it is tricky to have no box office success. If you have it, it certainly helps with the next job. If you don't, Hollywood's just going to move on to somebody else. It's sad, but it's true. But I've also been able to have this really wonderful, long career, so I'm not really complaining. Just taking notice.

I also saw you comment about how much testosterone was on the set of "Boiler Room," which came out just a few weeks after the '90s ended. Of course "That Thing You Do!" was also about a group of guys in close quarters. How would you compare those experiences in terms of that testosterone and what you remember about "Boiler Room"?

"That Thing You Do!" [was] obviously a wonderful experience, my character is in every scene, and I think it's more about being there every day and being a bigger part of it. Whereas with "Boiler Room," Ben Younger specifically wanted me to play the boss. He wanted me to play against type, and it was fun. It was a great group of guys to work with. It was nice to just bop in, do my thing, and bop out. We were expecting our first kid at that time, so it was kind of a perfect job for me. But the experience was so good. We went to Sundance. The thing about "Boiler Room" that I always think about is how I've been to the Sundance Film Festival twice. First with a movie that I produced with a friend who wrote and directed it called "River Red." We were there as a selection; we weren't in competition. We weren't in competition, and we had to pay our way, and we had to beg, borrow and steal just to get a shack to sleep in while we were there. And it was fighting for every invite to any party, and it was just totally difficult. Whereas when I went with "Boiler Room," it was on New Line's dime, we were there in our premiere, it was red carpet everywhere, all access passes. I was like, "Oh my god. In three or four years, I just experienced the two ends of the spectrum at Sundance." And "Boiler Room," even though it wasn't a big-budget movie, it was still a high-profile film. And I got to work with my buddy Giovanni [Ribisi]. It was like we switched roles. He was more the supporting to my lead in "That Thing You Do!" and vice-versa in "Boiler Room." It was good to work with Giovanni again. He's a good dude. We had fun on that.

And lastly I'm a huge "Law and Order" fan. If my eyebrows are getting a little long, my wife accuses me of looking like Jack McCoy.

[Laughs] Yeah.

I mention this because, not that they are necessarily similar, but if I made a list of my favorite characters with a strong sense of goodness and morality, Guy Patterson and Jack McCoy would both be on that list. You talked about working with Sam Waterston. Why do you feel like that experience with him or that character is so resonant as an extension of that line of thinking, that driving goodness?

He was fun to work with, and he's a wonderful guy. That's another production where I got to play against type, which I always really love and value. He's just such a great person to bounce things off of because he's just been there. He's been there and done it, and he's done it well. "We're married to the same woman," he said. Our stories about our wives are just so similar. They like to mix idioms; they like to leave cabinet doors open. We always had fun working together. I love Sam.

That's awesome. I think the longevity of both "Law and Order" and his character and "That Thing You Do!" both—they're so different, but when I think about the stuff I like returning to, you could argue there's a certain pursuit of idealistic justice, success, happiness. Maybe this is an absurd connection to make.

It's not a terrible one. No. You're right; they're very similar characters. They're both trying to do the right thing.

Karyn Parsons of 'The Fresh Prince of Bel-Air,' 'Major Payne,' 'Class Act'

Contrary to popular belief, it is not easy to be obnoxious and likable, unintelligent and vulnerable, self-absorbed and welcome. As Hilary Banks, the spoiled oldest cousin for Will Smith on "The Fresh Prince of Bel-Air," Karyn Parsons played this potentially disposable role so well for six years that, not surprisingly, people didn't realize how much else she could do.

She wound up appearing as intelligent, kind counterpoints to over-the-top characters in movies like "Major Payne" and "The Ladies Man," on top of being a love interest in "Class Act," one of the four (!) movies starring Kid 'n Play.

The real Parsons is capable of a whole lot, though, including writing novels ("How High the Moon") and starting her own nonprofit called Sweet Blackberry, which strives to bring stories of achievement by real-life Black heroes to a wider audience through books and movies. There's a lot of material here, complex and inspiring and funny (anyone who watched the "Fresh Prince" reunion on HBO Max saw an honest combination of laughs and tears that proved surprisingly resonant), and Parsons makes great company to break it all down.

What are you nostalgic for from the '90s? What's something that you miss?

I miss the decade for me because that was when I was a lot younger and running around and [Laughs] working on a job where I was getting a really good paycheck. [Laughs] So obviously that. But in the '90s in general, I really long for a time before cell phones and the internet. With all of the good stuff about it, I feel like people were so much more in the moment. Obviously they weren't trying to document things every second, and they weren't trying to document it and then share it with everyone. Things are so curated now for an audience, for how people are going to see it as opposed to just being ourselves and raw in the situation. And also I think if that had been around at the time, I probably would have been much more measured in my behavior and more careful because I was afraid someone would catch me saying something wrong or doing something that could be mistaken or judged a certain way. I think that affects people now. People aren't as organic probably in some way, in some respects. I like that kind of raw innocence that people had. At the same time I never thought that I would be nostalgic for the sitcoms. I was on a sitcom, so I wasn't like, "Oh, I just love sitcoms." I was on a sitcom, so I was allowed more cynicism probably about them. But I remember when reality TV took hold, we all thought, or a lot of us, myself included, thought, "Oh, it won't last. Where can they go with it after 'The Real World' and 'Survivor'? What can they really do?" And it just kept growing and growing and growing and kicking the sitcoms away. And I didn't realize how much that tradition came from vaudeville, from a stage play in front of an audience. It had a certain design to it, it had a family thing to it. It had all these elements that got lost as well when it got pushed out. And I talk to people all the time about it who say how much they miss it. And I think there was really something beautiful and special about it that joined people that we don't have now. That's a surprising thing for me. And I used to watch music videos back then and really enjoyed it. I guess I'm older now. [Laughs]

When it comes to sitcoms, do you think the laughs or the lessons that those provided are more needed and missed at this point?

One thing that they did really well—and like I said I was a little cynical at the time about some of it and have come to be much more appreciative of it—which is something that people do in comedy often, and they do in sitcoms and in "Fresh Prince" they did really well, is they open an audience up with so much laughter and silliness that when they hit them in the gut when they least expect it, hit the audience with something more serious to think about that's a little heavier, it really would land and people would feel it and be like, "Whoa," and it stays with them. I see how well the "Fresh Prince" writers did that, and Will and the cast were able to nail a lot of that, and it really resonated for people. People talk about so many of the shows to this day. While they love the show and it was funny, there were a lot of really meaningful moments that hit them hard and stayed with them. And I think that was a really beautiful thing that the sitcom was able to do. It was stuff we all relate to, situation comedy, we relate to these kinds of characters, somebody knows somebody like that and like that, and you know these situations that you get in that are also silly and funny, but then you're also able to in the middle of those laughs and other things, to a trusting audience, [address things] that are a little bit heavier and need to be said or need to be looked at, and I think without being preachy about it. And I think the sitcom was a way of doing that.

When you think of that era, is there a movie or show that you weren't in that meant a lot to you, or that you still go back to?

That's hard because I was so busy working. There were things I discovered later because I worked all day, I came home, I had to eat and get my changes to the script and go over them and get up early the next day. When I wasn't doing that, I was out running the streets acting crazy. [Laughs] Yeah, I don't know. I might think of something, but not yet.

You've spoken a lot about the cast of "Fresh Prince" being a family so quickly. When you say that, what do you think of in terms of specific moments? Was there a first thing that happened that set you at ease to turn it from colleagues to family?

I think about the first week, for one. We shot the pilot; we didn't get a full week, I think we were short a day of a five-day week. I think we had four days to pull it together. I just remember we kind of fell in with each other immediately. Immediately we were welcoming, excited, like, "We're all here, we're putting on a show." Nobody was fronting, nobody was posing, nobody was trying to be better than anybody. Everyone was rabidly excited about this thing we were doing, and it was such a great energy, and everyone was so appreciative of everyone else. Everyone thought, "Oh, god, you're great, you're great," and it just lifted and buoyed all of us. And Will, who was already a star, didn't feel like a star in that way. He was so accessible, and there was no separation, no detachment, no "It's great to work with you guys." It was all of us together. And we very quickly pulled that episode together and had a blast, and that felt great and bonding right away. We bonded so quickly. And then we were all back and thrilled that we got picked up, right away we'd all go to lunch together every day, we all had our dressing rooms open, our doors open all day long, so everyone was free-flowing in and out of everyone else's room. We just felt so quickly comfortable with each other, and always if you came on the set at any time, somebody was hugged up on somebody else. We were always hugging and laughing and having really deep, heavy, heavy conversations because we had a lot of time to kill while the writers worked on stuff upstairs. Everyone trusted each other, and I always felt that. I always felt a sense that I could be myself. I was seen, I was accepted. I was different from everybody else as Karyn, but I always felt seen. And I think we were all like that with each other. There was never a [cliquey] thing or you have to think this way. Everyone was very much accepted for who they were as individuals, and I don't feel like that everywhere I go. And I'm able to recognize that because of how much I felt myself and loved and seen there. I'm able to recognize, "Hey, I don't feel that everywhere." [Laughs] That was part of, too, what made it a really unique, familial relationship.

I know I certainly don't remember all my great, deep conversations as much as I wish I did. But when you talk about those heavy conversations you had with the cast, do you remember anything in particular?

We talked about current events. We talked about race. We talked about our own personal experience. We talked about all sorts of things. The climate wasn't always the way it is now about race—things are very intense now. But we did have lots of … it's like anything. Current events sparked conversations, things that other people were going through sparked it. I can't remember specifics; we just talked about things. It would get really heavy, and we'd pick things up later. People didn't get mad at each other. They wanted to hear each other. But the thing is, we were challenged. We didn't just say, "Just because you said this, that's right." It wasn't just a lot of nodding and saying, "Yeah, yeah." People would speak up and say, "But I don't know; what about this?" People like James Avery were really great for that, him being part of that. Because he was older and wise and had so much experience and wisdom to bring to conversations and think a little bit more. Because the bulk of us were younger people—I guess half. It was good. For me they were really good, stirring conversations that I looked forward to. In the six years that we were on the show, I don't think—I might have a friend that would tell me that I'm lying here—but I don't think I ever didn't want to go to work. Aside from being sick, which rarely happened, I always looked forward to going in and hanging out with those people. And the crew as well.

That's great to have a family that can sit around and debate thought-provoking ideas. I don't know if every real family out there can say that they do that.

Yeah. And I don't know how everyone was about it, but for the most part most of us I would say were really good about it and really got a lot out of it and enjoyed it. That's true; a lot of families don't do that. [Laughs]

As you mentioned, there were so many family sitcoms at the time. Do you have any sense of if this felt like the norm of the era, where people cast as families bonded this way?

People used to come by our set, all sorts of people, whether they were actors or musicians or entertainers or not, and they would always say, I would hear this all the time, "You don't know what you have here. You guys don't know what you have here. You don't understand. You don't know what you have here." You'd hear that all the time and go, "Oh, yeah, isn't it great? It's so great." Because we were all so happy, and it was fun, and it was just lively. People would come to Friday nights just to hang out. People would always say, "You don't know what you have." And it's true; after that, every one of us went on to other jobs and felt like, "Wow, we had something really, really unique." You go on and meet other great people in your life and have these relationships with the cast and crew of things, but this was really special. I don't know that other people were having similar experiences. They may have been.

You've talked about at first worrying about people hating Hilary. When that was going on, how did that impact you? Was that keeping you up at night? How did you handle that worry?

[Laughs] No, it didn't keep me up at night. I enjoyed playing her, and I certainly wasn't making my castmates mad. Directors, producers were laughing. People were laughing, so I knew there were people that thought it was funny. I just stated that people were thinking that stuff was funny but that I was a little bit of a villain in a way. And it was confirmed here and there that there were people that really didn't like me. I think a lot of people grew to like her in a strange way, and certainly decades later Hilary gets more love now than I ever got when I was on the show. [Laughs] People are always now saying, "I'm just like her. I love Hilary." And I didn't use to hear that all the time then. It didn't keep me up at night. I wasn't worried about it like that. The only time I remember being worried about it was when Will was taking a few of us to Philly to something, and the show was going to be brand-new, and I thought, "Oh, shoot, people there love Will so much, and the characters had this antagonistic relationship, that people are going to be like, 'I don't like her.'" I thought there was going to be like that "Ugh" attitude toward her. I was wrong. They were actually cool; they knew that was an actor. But it didn't bother me. It's like I said; I really enjoyed playing her. It was fun. I would much rather play that character than not play her just to get people to like me.

It's a cognitive whirlwind to one moment worry that people aren't liking her enough and then decades later worry that people are loving her too much and enjoying the self-centeredness more than they should.

Yeah, that was interesting too, how that started to become people whispering, "I'm just like you." I'm like, "Don't tell anybody that! That's not a great thing." But people have fun with it. There are a lot of people that like her ambition. She's so confident and she's so cutting, and so people really enjoy that. I just hope they don't take it too far in some areas.

You were fantastic in the role, and Hilary has many shades, so just to call her selfish and spoiled and a daddy's girl would be an over-simplification. But you've talked about the role Uncle Phil, her father, had in enabling her. How do you think James would have parented her differently than his character did?

Oh, yeah, he wouldn't have taken anything. [Laughs] James would not have taken her mess. I think he would be the kind of dad that was like, "I don't need to be your best friend. I'm just going to do what's right by you." And that means maybe a little tougher than Phil. Uncle Phil, or Dad in her case, he was smitten by his daughter when she was young probably, and enjoyed being a dad and having this first child, this little girl, and then became this monster that he had created. [Laughs] That's how I saw it! But not James. I think James wouldn't have taken any mess. He was much tougher than that.

Do you have a sense of that being any type of escape for him? You're describing a conscientious mentality as a person that is great but can also be tiring. I can see how his role would have been freeing in the way he parented Hilary. Not dissimilar to the way you are an accomplished, intelligent, engaged person, I imagine there's a freedom to be able to put that aside from an "Ignorance is bliss" perspective.

Well, it's fun playing characters that aren't like you. For me it's definitely fun to step into somebody different from you. I'm sure for James—sometimes there's sides of you. Sometimes there's not. But you get to feel those things, and it's fun. And I'm sure James got a kick out of being a sucker for his daughter sometimes. Which he was. He was a big mushball sometimes. He was so sweet, and he was a sweet man, so he'd bring that part of him. I know for myself playing a character that I believe was not like myself was really freeing and fun. Really fun.

What kind of parent do you think Hilary would have been?

Oh gosh. That's interesting because I would have answered that differently when I played her than now because now I've got kids. [Laughs] So there are areas where—I think Hilary would have wanted friends. She wouldn't want to be a parent—she wouldn't want to be a nag. She wouldn't want to have to say things over and over again to someone. She'd want somebody to be her friend. She'd probably be lousy, boy, [Laughs]. She's really self-serving, like, "What do I need right now?" And unfortunately when you're parenting you don't get that luxury. And you see yourself become something that you didn't want to be often. It's not always the most attractive, to be like nagging. I feel like a nag, like I say the same thing every single day. I don't know. Hilary would probably be a pretty lousy parent. She'd just want to have a buddy, so she'd do what she did with friends.

The cliche is you either perpetuate the things that were taught to you or go out of your way to reverse them. So the question is if she would raise her children the way that she felt her parents gave her a long leash, or if she would do the opposite and parent the way that Phil looked after Will.

I think it would be the long leash. I think it would just be the easy route, and the easy route often would be, "OK, you go ahead and do that. Maybe you know what you're doing." [Laughs] It's easier that way! Than saying, "You don't know what you're doing." She might have fun trying the other thing on, but ultimately I don't think she would stick with it. In the beginning it would be fun to put on an outfit for her, to put on the whole dress-up of mom, "I'm a mom. I'm going to be a mom." But after a few years, I think she'd be over it. She didn't have that marathon thing in her.

I was thinking of the time years ago when I interviewed Chadwick Boseman about "42." I'd asked him about kids' sports movies that meant a lot to him, and when I mentioned "The Sandlot" and "Rookie of the Year" those didn't connect. He mentioned "Remember the Titans" instead, and at the time I feel like I was oblivious to that. I mention that in terms of if you have a sense of the fandom for "The Fresh Prince" and what people connected to. The show was a hit, but in the reunion you talked about it maybe not being as much of a smash as it seemed. Do you have a sense of the demographics that connected to it? Did you feel like it crossed boundaries in terms of who the viewers and fans were?

Yeah, it did. It's definitely more a popular show I believe today than it was—it feels like it anyway. That's what I receive. I didn't get the response then that I get now. I've talked to so many people, and I've had so many people decade after decade say, "It was my favorite show, and now it's my kid's favorite show." You hear this, and then ten years ago by and you hear it again, and you hear it again, so you know it's reaching a lot of people. I'm talking all different types of people. It's not just a Black audience. However, I will say that when I was on the show and I would look in TV Guide and see if we could crack the Top 20 shows, the Top 10, we didn't. I don't think we cracked the Top 10 in TV Guide ever. But now when I talk to Black people that grew up then, people were like diligent about it. And they were serious. That was a big, iconic show. I think for a lot of people, but especially for Black people. I talk to people that it's entertaining and all of this, but I think there were a lot of things about it that made it really pull them in and some of those things were that we were a diverse—we were a Black family, but you've got Ashley, who's this really bright, woke kid who you can see is so smart, and smarter than everyone else. Except maybe Geoffrey. But smarter than everybody else and witness to all of it, and at the same time we see her going so far. And Carlton, who is a Black Republican. And Hilary, who is a fashionista, superficial—who people wanted to call a Valley Girl, but we lived in Bel-Air, so it wasn't the Valley. You've got Will from Philly, and you've got Uncle Phil who's got this multi-layered life, and he came from the south and he was an activist, he was a lawyer, he was a judge. And you see the pool shark side of him, and you know that there's all this history and layers in him. And the mother, Aunt Viv, who was a dancer, and she has that history and a lawyer and a professor. So you've got all of this—and Geoffrey, of course. So you've got these really rich characters, and they're all very different from each other. And I think it made a lot of people feel like, especially Black people, that there isn't one way to be. There wasn't this one code that everybody understood. Because Hilary wouldn't understand that one code, and Carlton wouldn't understand that one code. They were all different, and that was really nice I think for people to see. Not this monolithic Black family being one thing. They were all so different from each other.

That makes a lot of sense. On that note, you said, "At some point the writers wanted to make Hilary a strong Black woman, but some people are flawed and you can learn from them too." How do you think the lessons would have changed if they had taken a different path in what they were describing there?

You mean if she had become a strong Black woman?

It seemed like you were suggesting they created an arc for her that may or may not have been necessary in your mind.

Well, they were trying to make her go there. It didn't really happen. Not the way that I think people were trying to make it happen. She became a little more mature in some ways. Not really to me. We had so much say, that if I had gone to the producers and Will and said, "I think it's time that she becomes enlightened," I think they would have enjoyed writing to that. And they were so talented that they could have made it work, I'm sure. But I enjoyed her being like she was. I enjoyed Archie Bunker on "All in the Family" being Archie Bunker, even after Edith had passed away. I didn't want to see him all of a sudden change and he's a different man. I like to see that man, that flawed character, affected by things. It's more interesting to me to see Hilary, to see her, that woman, be affected, like when her fiancé died. To watch her have to go through it and be affected and try and mourn him and move on. Watching her go through it, it's able to be bittersweet. It's funny and it's sad. Instead of everyone being stoic and together. I don't find that always so interesting.

It leads to my next question, and I feel like I should acknowledge that I am white and Jewish. I would be an example of what I am about to describe here. In the reunion, Alfonso said that it was a Black show that was not necessarily represented in the writers' room. The show is wonderful and so beloved, of course. But since he brought that up, I'm wondering if you have a sense of how that impacted the show,

or if there was an issue in the writers' room that was difficult to address because of where the stories were originating?

Well, I can only imagine that it limited things. It limited viewpoints. I will say two things. One, Andy and Susan Borowitz, who created the show, they didn't stay with the show past the first year. But they set the tone for a lot of things, and one of the things was after we would run through the show, everybody would sit down with the writers and everybody and the first thing they would say was, "How did it feel to you?" That was the first thing, was us. So they completely deferred their respect to this Black cast. We had some Black writers, not many. But they'd say, "How did it feel?" And we were able to say, "This part felt really strange to me. This felt unnatural." And James Avery would often speak up as the patriarch and say, "I don't believe that a Black father in this situation would say this or would go to this person and do this or I think there needs to be more of this." And people would speak up. Tatyana, I remember her speaking up for Ashley, saying on some things, "I don't know; I think my parents would not let me get away with talking like this." So there were some areas, even though it was this wealthy family, there were definitely elements that people chimed in about their own experience and their own Black experience. Where they said, "This felt wrong. This note felt wrong as a Black person." So there were some of those things that were still brought in. In that regard I guess you would say it wasn't a whitewash. And just because they were wealthy didn't mean that these things, these ways that Vivian and Phil were brought up, wouldn't come into the rest of the family upbringing. So Andy and Susan started that, and that went on for the whole six years. We spoke up about what felt wrong to us, what felt right to us, or what could be better, and they always had respect for that. So that was really a beautiful thing, and every producer that came along honored and respected that and listened to us. And that's another way where we were really spoiled by this show. 'Cause you don't get that much where people are coming to you, the actors, and saying, "Before we go any further, I want to know how you felt." And they're all taking notes and taking changes and if you said, "I don't feel right about this," they changed it. But also Will Smith, he early on stopped going to lunches with us and spent a lot of time upstairs with producers and writers talking things through with them. He was a young man, but he was very involved in the direction the show was going and doing what he could to make it better and keep things on track, and I think to have the true voices heard and represented on the show.

Are you able to think of a specific example of something that changed because of any of that communication?

I wish I could think better, but I know there was something with Ashley. I think it was a boy thing where they wanted her to go to Will and talk to Will about kissing a boy, and she was like, "This doesn't feel right. I would talk to my sister or my mom." And I think it was also something where she spoke up to her parents and talked back really harshly and she was like, "Uh uh. This would not happen in my house." And James was laughing. He would say the same thing, like, "There is no way that little girl could say that to me and get away with it." I think those were things that they were both from separate places, James and

Tatyana, they were bringing it from their experience as Black people and saying, "In our Black household, that doesn't fly, and it doesn't feel right." And they took note of things like that. And things like that would continue, because then that helped develop more layers to the character so going forward writers would recognize, "Hey, that character wouldn't do that." They would hop onto other areas of the character. And like I said, we did have some Black writers in the writers' room, Rob Edwards, John Ridley. We had people in and out of there. Winifred Hervey Stallworth was our exec producer at one point, and that's a Black woman. We had guest Black directors as well. Debbie Allen was the director of the first two episodes. So there were people in there who were really strong personalities who were, I'm sure, speaking up on behalf of Black families everywhere to say, "Yes, this rings true, and maybe that doesn't."

That's great. In terms of the world beyond "Fresh Prince," then, I listened to the interview where you were talking about self-doubt, audition sabotage, stage fright, that type of thing. Hilary is so much the opposite of that, of confidence-plus. Did you ever feel like inhabiting that role created a contrast? Was there a relationship between the confidence of the character and the challenges you experienced when you weren't playing her?

That's interesting to bring up. Because I mostly ran into those challenges after I was no longer inhabiting Hilary. Which is interesting. When I played the role, I rarely had problems. In auditions I don't think I experienced difficulty. I think it came after the show was off the air and I wasn't playing her anymore [Laughs] that it became—she was so confident, and it was so great to just put her on like a catsuit, zip her up and have all of this. And it was so great to have all of that confidence. Yeah, that was something Karyn suffered separately. I don't know if it had any part of it, if I had still been playing her if I would have more confidence. Maybe because my confidence muscles were actively engaged [Laughs], I don't know.

So anyone imagining you in the room before an audition looking in the mirror and saying, "What would Hilary do?" would just be making that up?

Yeah. I didn't think of her like, "Hilary! There she is over there." I can think of her that way decades later, especially when I've changed so much from her. I don't resemble her anymore because I've aged, and I've changed. But when we still had the same shoe size and we still could be mistaken for each other, then I think my relationship to her was different. I could look at her as separate now, and I can appreciate the confidence that playing her probably gave me. I can appreciate it now, and I can appreciate things in her life—and you're right. I can probably look at her now and go, "What would Hilary do?" [Laughs] And summon her. Which maybe I should try sometime.

The movies of the '90s had some notable messages about teaching kids with positive or negative reinforcement whether in "Kindergarten Cop," "Billy Madison"

or "Major Payne." You're a mom and do a lot of work with and for children. When leading kids, is it better to go too soft or too hard?

Oh, well no "too." It shouldn't be "too." Definitely not too hard. I understand, I get tough love and all that, but you can coax kids into the right place often. There's definitely a medium. Because if you're too soft for too long, the bird will never get out of the tree. You can't get it out of the nest; it's just not going to happen. You're going to probably have to give a little nudge to make it happen, which might seem cruel. But at some point, mama bird knows it's ready. And baby bird doesn't. [Laughs] I think "Major Payne" would be a terrible dad. [Laughs]

It's very much a '90s movie, but it reminds me of some of the conversations that have or haven't been had in recent years about masculinity and speaking vs. listening. If it came out now, there would be elements that are relevant. Have you thought at all over the years about the movie and change that has or hasn't happened in the years since?

[Laughs] I haven't thought about it, but I do understand what you mean. That is what that is a little bit because he did come around to seeing it her way. But I haven't given it much thought. [Laughs]

That's fair, and we could talk all day about the roles written for men and women and what the movies focus on. But there's a subgenre of movies that feature a woman who is a wonderful woman who is shaping and supporting an obnoxious dude. And that can play out in a lot of ways, whether it's "Major Payne" or "The Ladies Man" or almost every Adam Sandler movie. You've talked about how few roles were out there at the time, and when there's a Halle Berry in the world, that's that. As you made the transitions in your life that you did in terms of what roles you did and didn't take, and getting into writing and other professional pursuits that connected with you more, to what extent would you have felt different if the roles had been different? Or were you ready for those changes regardless of the opportunities?

It wasn't as conscious, but it was definitely a part of it. I had a lot of fun playing the characters that I played in "The Ladies Man" and "Major Payne." I had great experiences. However, you know, basically characters like that, and there's so many of them, especially in comedy, like you said Adam Sandler stuff, where the woman is really there—it felt to me like, "I'm here so you know he's a straight male. I feel like that's my purpose. [Laughs] That's it." In both "The Ladies Man" and "Major Payne," the guy's kind of alien. Who on earth, in the real world, would be attracted to and would have a relationship with this strange character of a person? But I put my hand on my hip and wag my finger and teach him a lesson and bring him around, and then at the end want to make him my husband. [Laughs] It was a different time. We see that still, but we see fewer parts like that, where [now] women are allowed to be a little more well-rounded and have a life of their own and not just be there to send a message about his character, which is all those were there for. Almost an appendage to let you know this is a straight male character here, and I basically am letting you know that that's what he is. If I had had interesting parts, if I had had things that were challenging or exciting or interesting—I had some things along the way, but not a lot, of interesting projects that I landed. I auditioned for things that I got really excited about and remember that feeling of, "Oh my god, this would be amazing to work on." I remember that feeling many times, but I didn't end up getting the part. It's hard. It's not like it beat me up. I happen to be really grateful for my experience, and I feel really fortunate. And things in life just happen as they happen, but I will be honest when you look at it as an actor, if I had gotten some of these other roles, my attitude would've been different, I'm sure. You want that experience. You go in for that excitement and that thrill of being creative and being part of something that's exciting and fulfilling, and those weren't those kinds of parts. So I'm sure it changed my relationship to my acting career. It changed my relationship to acting, certainly. Even being on a sitcom changes—if that's all you do, and you're not ever stretching other ways, it'll change your muscle. It changes what you're used to doing. You can create habits if you don't do other things to balance yourself out. All of that probably happened a little bit. I was affected by the work that I was getting, by the parts. And then when I was off the show, a friend of mine really wanted me to go to a writing class, and I went and all of a sudden that excitement, that thrill, that challenge was there for me. And that fulfillment, that feeling of wanting to get in there and do something creatively was there. So I found something else that I was excited about. I didn't lose my interest in acting; for the first time I found something else that I really wanted to do.

Are you able to mention one of the projects you referenced that you got close on that excited you?

Um, I guess so. [Laughs] When I got "The Fresh Prince of Bel-Air," I was down to the wire on a project. It was called "Hurricane" at the time. It ended up being called "One False Move." And it was down to Cynda Williams and I, and Cynda got it. And I got "Fresh Prince." Just going back and forth, and it was a very different kind of character than Hilary Banks that's for sure. A drugged-out girl, very different, dramatic project. I think it would have changed my trajectory as I approached work. I imagine it would've; I could be wrong. Who knows? Maybe my experience would've been horrible. What ended up happening was I had six years of bliss doing a sitcom. And then after that I'm sure there were lots of projects that I went in on. Some things that I don't want to mention. We can always imagine, "Oh, things would have been so different if that happened." Yeah, it may've been different, but not in the way you like to think. You never know.

On the topic of changes, when you were talking about movies like "Major Payne" and "The Ladies Man," it's nice that they have a happy ending, but I always want to see how those relationships play out. After a year, how are these couples that we've been told will be together forever actually doing?

Yeah, you're not supposed to think that far ahead. [Laughs] Or if they bring you a sequel it's all fun and games again. Unless you couldn't get the actor. If they were like, "Oh, Karyn's asking for too much money for the sequel, so I guess they got a divorce!" [Laughs]

There's no good segue from that to Sweet Blackberry, so I'll just move on to that. What you're doing is awesome with that, and I wanted to give you a chance to talk about it in a different way than in some other interviews. I moderate discussions for a couple movie clubs, and when we talk about the issues a movie addresses, including but not limited to race, we talk about what the goal of the filmmaker was, and what audience is being targeted. I mention that to ask you, in terms of the stories of Sweet Blackberry, do you have a sense of who you want to find this material? Does change come from creating advocates or reversing prejudice? Targeting the middle or the edge?

I want everybody to read these stories. There are families who are teaching their kids these stories already. But the children don't know them yet, and when they discover the story of Bessie Coleman how inspired they're going to all of a sudden become by her and how empowered they're going to feel when they recognize that, "She did that and I can do that. I look like her." I hate the idea that these stories are relegated to just being Black stories, like an elective at school, like it's a side thing. This is everyone! This is important. And these stories in particular that we're telling are American stories, and they're stories that shaped America. Some people want to roll their eyes and they can do that all day long, but that's just because a lot of the history that we've been told deliberately omits a lot of things. People have to decide what to put in the textbook, and they also have to decide what not to put in. I think it's important that we bring these stories to everybody because they're for everybody. Ultimately, yes, it's going to empower Black and brown children, but it's also going to empower other children too that don't look like these heroes just finding out these accomplishments. Because what did a lot of them have in common, besides for the color of their skin? They had to overcome incredible obstacles, and I think for any child, that's what most stories that they read, adventures and stories of heroes, are people that had to overcome things and found greatness in themselves because they had to get over these huge hurdles. And that's what I want to bring to kids. I want them to recognize what they're capable of in the face of challenge. And that's for all children. And also of course I want them to learn about these people, these real people. I don't want their stories to be lost. But bottom line is I want all kids to be inspired and excited and feel emboldened. There will be people whose families already know a lot of this stuff, but it's just as important to push the stories there as it is to push the stories out a little bit to the people on the sides who are thinking, "Oh, this isn't for me. This is Black history, and I'm not Black." No, no, no. This is American history. This is all of our history. It's this unfortunate switch of first it was a prideful thing, "This is Black history." And then became, "It's Black history. It's cute." And it was relegated to the shortest month of the year. We need to get past that and recognize this is all of our history. It's relevant, it's important, and it joins us too. I want it for everybody. I want everyone to recognize it belongs to all of us.

That's fantastic. On the one hand I can see that getting easier with some awareness in the last few years, but with the value spectrum that's been identified I can see that getting harder too. Do you find yourself going back and forth between hopeful and frustrated?

Yeah, I think more I'm seeing in the last couple years—we had to change our little reel that plays in the front. We haven't put it up yet, but it goes on the front of the website. Because before it was kind of imploring people to, "Hey, this is important stuff we're talking about!" That's what we've been doing for so many years, is trying to get people on the same page as me to understand this history is American history. It's important, and why it's important. To get people listening and on board. In the last few years, everyone gets that. And I've been trying to tell people, do you understand how this impacts a child and how it changes the landscape of race for them as they enter the world if they're introduced to these stories about people of color at a young age? Regardless of what color you are, you recognize your value and your neighbor's value and everything from a young age when you come into the world, that changes how you look at race. So we can do that. But I've been trying to push this on people for years, and finally with things that have happened over the last few years, there's less imploring people to listen and understand and more of saying, "Hey, we're here. We've been here, we are here, we have this stuff that will help all of us. It can help our kids and help us bring these stories to them." People I think are ready for it finally. The world has come around to where this is on their minds and not having to explain to people why this is important anymore. They get it. And it seems so silly now to go, "Wow, I can't believe I had to have part of my discussion always be why it's important." Now everyone gets it. Of course it's valid and important.

I wish I could remember a time after watching an episode of "Fresh Prince" my friends and I sitting around and talking about something topical. But I would be lying if I said I thought that happened, and it's interesting to think about the reasons why that didn't.

Yeah. It was a different time. Different priorities and things on the table. Different times.

I have a couple goofy, quicker ones to go out on. Better song: "Gettin' Jiggy Wit It" or "Miami"?

"Gettin' Jiggy Wit It."

How come?

Because I know it better. [Laughs] And I never liked Miami that much. I know Will just loves Miami so much, and I went to Miami expecting to love it so much. I guess I'm just not the same party animal that he is. [Laughs] I don't know, maybe that's it. "Gettin' Jiggy Wit It" is very Will to me.

What's something that parents just don't understand?

[Laughs] Oh gosh, that's so funny. That girls just want to have fun. I don't know.

In "Class Act" your character has to cite a very specific name of a science article that I bet took a lot of time to memorize, so I'm wondering if you remember what that was.

God, I don't! Tell me!

It was lipopolysaccharide-induced modulation of human monocyte urokinase production and activity.

That sounds familiar. [Laughs] But I didn't remember.

You picked Regis Philbin as your favorite "Fresh Prince" guest star and mentioned you would've loved to do a spinoff with him. Can you imagine what the premise for that would have been?

I would've loved when the show ended for Ashley and Hilary to both take off for New York, and she'd be my assistant and work on the show with me, on my talk show with Regis Philbin being my co-host together. And Hilary and Ashley as roommates and co-workers with that kind of relationship in New York City. Hilary in New York would be scary, and I think Ashley would just take to it like a fish to water. I think that would've been fun.

Do you have a Will Smith movie you can identify as your favorite and not favorite?

Uh, I know as soon as I say something I'm going to think of something else. I loved "Pursuit of Happyness." Everybody was crazy about "Independence Day." It's just a lot of action. And Will was really funny. It was overhyped for me. It was a lot of effects. It may not have helped that Will showed me how some of the effects were done on a model. [Laughs] So I'm watching going, "I know how that happened." And I told him this too, whenever my kids would watch "Shark Tale" I felt like I was in the room with Will. And he said the reason why is, "Aside from 'Fresh Prince,' that's the only job I've done where they let me do whatever I wanted." So he was himself as a fish in "Shark Tale," and that's why it felt like I was hanging out with Will whenever we watch that movie.

Have you seen "Seven Pounds"?

I think that was my favorite performance of his.

Oh.

Yeah, I know people hate the movie, and it definitely has a little bit of—I can't remember the term. But I love his performance in that. And I love Rosario [Dawson] in that. But I know people [didn't like] that film.

And I wanted to get your opinion on something less fluffy: Obviously Hilary was a TV meteorologist. I've always been baffled by the history of that role being so often occupied by attractive women who are then objectified. Do you have any thoughts on that strange tradition?

I would actually love to look into that, where that started and why it hasn't stopped. Very strange, right?

Yeah. Most importantly there should be nothing that is a given that is harmful to anyone but also the idea of where there would be a subconscious motivation for any type of person to go into that type of work because they think that's where the opportunity would be. It's strange on a number of levels.

Yeah, but there are definitely women or girls who watch other young, attractive women who are being thought of as attractive in that field and they think, "I want to do that." Because they're thinking of themselves that way too. It just keeps going. And they're the ones that show up for the jobs, and that's who the station wants to hire. It's like people have gotten used to that being what's delivered is the pretty girl delivers the weather. It's weird. You've got men like Storm Daniels—not Storm Daniels. Ha. [Laughs] But guys that are reflective of weather all the time. And you've got the really attractive female who has a different look from the anchor person. It is interesting.

Something tells me nationally televised meteorologist Stormy Daniels would not accomplish what we're going for here.

[Laughs] No no no no no. No need to go there.

And lastly, I wish I didn't have to ask this question but feel like I need to: With Karen becoming synonymous with ignorant white lady, does that grate on you to hear that as someone whose name is Karyn? Do you have a suggestion of a different way we can refer to these people who are terrible and need to learn?

Well, my kids say Jennifer instead of Karyn. They just switched it because they don't want to offend me. And then my daughter has told me on a number of occasions, "It's not you, though, because yours is with a 'y.'" [Laughs] I just think it's funny. I just wish it wasn't my name. [Laughs]

Charlie Korsmo of 'Dick Tracy,' 'Hook,' 'What About Bob?' 'Can't Hardly Wait'

There are many reasons to admire the accomplishments of Charlie Korsmo, who happens to have a physics degree from the Massachusetts Institute of Technology and a law degree from Yale.

But he should also be celebrated for the astonishingly professional presence he brought to his high-profile roles when he was a kid, appearing alongside legend after legend in "Dick Tracy," "Hook," and "What About Bob?" He also delivered exactly the likable touch that the role demanded in his one and only starring role as an adult in "Can't Hardly Wait."

In conversation, Korsmo, also known as Case Western University professor Charles Korsmo, is joyful, thoughtful and intelligent, mixing a ton of laughs with a clear view of the material and his role in it.

What's something you feel nostalgic for from the '90s? It could be absolutely anything.

Oh my god. [Laughs] I don't know. It was a weird decade for me obviously. I went to college in the '90s, so I feel nostalgic for college. In terms of pop culture, I guess the video games and such. "Mario Kart" and "Goldeneye."

Why do you think that's where your mind goes?

It might be just because my kids are now at an age where my son in particular is very much into video games. So I'm playing them again for the first time since the '90s and seeing how much they've changed.

And you're also nostalgic for being a student in college as opposed to an educator?

Yeah, absolutely. [Laughs] As you get into middle age you start to miss the carefree days of yore.

What aspect do you miss? Is it staying out until 4 a.m. or just waking up with less to do? Or both?

I'd say a little bit of staying up 'til 4 a.m. but more generally just not having as many responsibilities to others. [Laughs] Where your future is still very plastic and you can do any number of things whereas as you accumulate more responsibilities your ability to take risks goes down.

In terms of pop culture, if you had to think of a '90s movie that you weren't in that you find yourself returning to a lot or that means a lot to you, what comes to mind and why?

Oh, jeez. [Laughs] I don't know. In terms of movies I wish I had been in, the one I look back on, there's two that I look on with regret. One that I was actually cast in but didn't end up getting to do because I got pulled to do another movie that I was on contract with. Was "Terminator 2," where I was supposed to play John Connor in that. I love the "Terminator" movies, and that would've been a different direction for my career had that happened instead of "What About Bob?" And then when I was doing "Can't Hardly Wait," in that era I started auditioning for other movies again and I got close on a couple that I didn't get. I'd say the two that I look back on that I think "Boy, I would've been good in those, and that would have been a good [help toward] an adult career" was "The Ice Storm" and "Wonder Boys." Both of which Tobey Maguire got. [Laughs] I got to the last stage on both of those and didn't end up getting them. But I love both of those movies and would have been a nice way to at least keep open the option of doing acting as an adult.

Sure. I didn't know about any of that. Regarding John Connor, in a world where you do that movie, do you have a sense of how you see things playing out differently? Which I only ask because obviously Edward Furlong wasn't quite able to make himself a household name.

[Laughs] Didn't hit it! It's not over, I suppose, but it didn't end well for him, I suppose, right. I don't know. I never moved to Los Angeles and lived in Hollywood, and I never saw myself committing to a film career, but I really enjoyed doing it. If I had gotten to a level where I could've done it part-time and done other things outside, that would have been great. And that might've given me that [chance]. I didn't want to be Leonardo DiCaprio, but if being in a James Cameron movie and [being] his Bill Paxton where I could just show up every couple of years and do a movie [Laughs] and go back to my regular life would have been nice.

I love that comparison. And am now thinking of you in the Bill Paxton role in "True Lies" too.

[Laughs] I was a little young maybe, but nowadays I'd be great for it. [Laughs] Especially since I haven't had a haircut since summer with the pandemic. I look like a 1970s used car salesman.

So then starting off with "Hook," Charlie, if you think of the sequence that stands out the most in your mind, what do you remember best?

Ah, gee. The one I probably remember filming most vividly is the sequence in the clock shop where I'm smashing watches, smashing clocks with Captain Hook. That or the flying sequence at the end of the movie where we're flying back from Neverland.

The smashing seems self-explanatory, I guess. When you think of the flying, what do you think of?

The whole experience. It's always weird when they find out you've been in a movie, they ask, "Did you meet Robin Williams?" [Laughs] "Well, yeah, of course I did! It's not all done with green screen!" But it's a very weird job and you work extremely closely and you're with these people for 18 hours a day for six months, and then might not see them again for years. I just remember doing these flying scenes, we're in these harnesses and hanging up there above the stage for 12 hours together, him, me, and Amber Scott who played my sister in it. It's like being in a high school play where you're just thrown together for months at a time, and there's this very intense relationship and then never see each other again.

When suspended in the air, do people talk the whole time to pass the time or do you just hang there, waiting?

[Laughs] We talked most of the time. Robin took it upon himself to make sure everyone stayed entertained when faced with that kind of tedium.

It's not hard to imagine him playing emcee in that situation.

Exactly. And anytime Steven Spielberg needed one of the kids to smile or laugh or anything like that, you could just put Robin behind the camera and let him go for a few minutes. It was very easy.

When someone asks if you've met Robin Williams, is that a sign they haven't actually seen "Hook" or just taking his character's parental absence to the extreme?

[Laughs] You know, I don't know. The questions people ask sometimes don't make any sense. I don't think it's that they haven't seen the movie; I guess they think "There's no way someone I'm meeting could have possibly been around someone famous." [Laughs] They think of them as these otherworldly personages.

That's a funny way to put it. In terms of Steven Spielberg, what comes to mind about the way he directs child actors?

Well, it's interesting. I feel like I'm a little skewed by the fact that it was "Hook," which is like the one movie he always says he's not happy with the way it turned out. [Laughs] So

I'm not sure it was the typical experience on a Steven Spielberg set. In that usually he shoots very quickly and comes in under budget, and "Hook" went way over-schedule and way over-budget and took twice as long as it was supposed to take. That and "Jaws" I believe are the only movies he's ever made that ran over schedule and over-budget, and I think he felt a lot of pressure by the end of it. But as far as kids, he was very respectful. He didn't treat you like a prop. Some people talk about these child actors in the same terms as animal performers in movies. [Laughs] You just see them moving them around the set and having them do tricks. And he was not like that at all. He really treated you as a part of the creative process, and some directors—not really anyone I've worked with—will give kids line readings. "Read it like this." Which for an adult actor is the most insulting thing you can do. [Laughs] And he never did that with kids either. He'd talk to you about what the scene was supposed to be, what you're supposed to be feeling and what [to do] with it. He also was an unusual combination of running this massive shoot with a huge budget and thousands of people working on it and everything, but he's also extremely spontaneous. He's got a lot of things that he's planned out how he's going to shoot it, but he's also very willing and in fact insists on the ability to call an audible and if something looks cool shoot it in a new way. So he's constantly trying new things on the set, which is very hard to do when you're dealing with such a massive production and so many different parts.

Do you remember an example of that?

I remember during the big sword fight between Captain Hook and Peter Pan. I was there, obviously, but that wasn't really me [fighting]. While they were doing it, he had the idea that someone would swish their sword over some candles and the candles would light up. There are a million movies where someone swipes their sword and the candles go out, but now they light up! And we spent the whole morning trying to figure out how to make that work. [Laughs] And shot it. But he'll get behind the camera himself and figure out the camera moves on every shot rather than have it all storyboarded beforehand. It's just very unusual in such a big, special effects-heavy production.

So in terms of his work with kids, then, the rumor isn't true that when you did well he gave you a treat and for mistakes he smacked you in the nose with a newspaper?

[Laughs] Yeah, he threw me a sardine if I did a good job. A trained seal. [Laughs] No, not how he did it.

Well, the scene where Hook is looming over you threateningly with a hook, even though it's not real I'm sure there are some young actors that would want some guidance from the director in a scary moment like that.

I suppose, although in reality when you're filming anything like that the circumstances aren't anything like they end up looking on screen. [Laughs] In your closeup shot the other actor's not even there. [Laughs] You're just pretending that the hundred grips and cameramen aren't standing all around. So none of it feels real while you're doing it.

Absolutely. Then the last question about "Hook": "Peter Pan" is a story that has been retold and retold and retold. What do you think about that? Obviously within nostalgia is, fittingly, an effort not to grow up, or at least remember the past. Are you on board with returning to stories repeatedly, or at some point do we need to move on?

You know, it doesn't bother me, frankly. There's a reason some stories stand the test of time. I often think people try too hard to reinvent the wheel on movies when they're adapting an old story and work very hard to change it, which—not always; sometimes it's really amazing and you discover something new—but often I wonder why you're doing it. The old story works for a reason and has a built-in audience for a reason. There's a reason people respond to the "Peter Pan" story, and that's not going to change in the near future. So I don't mind remakes and fact-faithful adaptations. Actually the "Peter Pan" story [Laughs] is one that never really appealed to me. As a kid I never felt like, "Boy, I wish I could remain a kid my whole life." I wish I could have remained 25 my whole life, but not 10 my whole life. My kids are now getting to the age I was when I did that, and they don't like Peter Pan either. They can't wait to grow up.

Well, my next question was going to be about you negotiating your own salary on "Dick Tracy." Many adults aren't good at negotiation, so to do it at that age is pretty remarkable.

Well, I am now a lawyer. [Laughs] So it's built in, right? I guess it was a bit of an unusual case as a kid in that it was my choice to go into the career in the first place. I was the one that wanted to start going on auditions; it wasn't my parents pushing me into it or anything like that. Maybe this is hindsight, but I don't feel like I was a completely oblivious kid that just had things happening to me outside of my understanding. I was an active participant in it all at once.

Sure. My son is 3, and he can negotiate his way into an extra Daniel Tiger song or whatever it is pretty effectively.

[Laughs] Kids can be pretty convincing. They're willing to walk away. They can outlast you.

So in terms of the filming of "Dick Tracy," what do you remember most vividly? Is it just how much food you had to eat or something else?

Well, that was my second movie, but it was my first big-budget Hollywood movie. The first one had been a fairly small production in comparison to "Dick Tracy" and "Hook." So just the scale of it and how long it took and filming at Universal Studios, and we had a dozen soundstages with all these massive sets and everything like that. And seeing the first cut of the movie after we'd made it, it looked nothing like what I had pictured it looking like when we were doing it. So seeing how little of a movie is actually in the filming of it, and how much is in the assemblage of it and everything else was amazing. In hindsight I just remember how long everything took, that you'd spend a full day getting 10 seconds of footage. The amount of craft that went into it was amazing.

It seems like child actors understandably don't always have a sense of context of who their costars are. When you think of yourself as being in the center of all these people in that movie, does that make you laugh, that you were natural in that environment? I don't know if you think about how different it would feel now if Al Pacino, Madonna and Warren Beatty came to your house now.

Yeah, it certainly would. I did not feel out of place at the time. I was only 10 when we were making it, which seems really young to me now. That's how old my daughter is. Most of the people in that movie, the big stars in that movie, were people who weren't exactly in kid movies. Warren Beatty had been around for a long time, but he wasn't someone I was acutely aware of as a 10-year-old as a big Hollywood star. Al Pacino, I'd seen "The Godfather" I'm sure at that point, but I don't think it connected to me who he was. Obviously I knew who Madonna was, but being a 10-year-old gives you a different relationship with Madonna than if I'd been 20 or something like that at the time. Frankly the thing I appreciate the most about having done the stuff as a kid was to me they were just people. Which of course is true. That's what they are. I was saying a few minutes ago, a lot of people seem to think movie stars are these celestial objects and they're certainly different from other people. My first interaction with people like this was as people, and people are people in some respects. And getting to experience that at age 10, by the time I was able to be where I would have been over-awed by rich and famous people, I had already had the experience that rich-and-famous people aren't that different from everybody else. Which was a valuable lesson. But yeah, I remember it being weird for my family. I was invited over to a dinner at Warren Beatty's house where we were all sitting around the kitchen island. It was me, Madonna, Al Pacino, a couple of other people. And my mother had not been there. I was staying with some other relatives at the time in Los Angeles. And I was on the phone with her afterwards. "What did you do?" "We just sat around, and I was talking to Al." [Laughs] "You mean Al Pacino?" "Yeah, that's right." It didn't seem weird to me at the time.

It almost puts you in a position where you don't want to be a name-dropper, but to tell the story of your day you have to be specific.

Yeah, it doesn't feel like name-dropping to a 10-year-old, though. [Laughs] It wasn't intentional. My mother found a book that I kept. I used to have people—kind of like a yearbook, at the end of a shoot I'd go around and have people from the cast and crew sign my book. The entry from Madonna was, "Someday you'll appreciate me." [Laughs] I thought that was a funny thing for her to write.

What do you think she meant by that?

Well, I think just that I wasn't thinking of her as someone big, fantastic star. She was just a person I was working with. I think she probably wasn't used to not having a big effect on people.

And then she went on to make the classic children's film "Body of Evidence."

That's right. Classic. "Truth or Dare."

You've been justly praised for your performances from that time, and I came across an article raving about you that shared the Nora Ephron quote that I'm sure you've come across too: ""When you do find the right kid and he or she gives a wonderful performance, it really has nothing to do with you, because with kids what you see is what you get." Do you think that's true, that kids aren't acting, just cast to be who they are?

I don't know. And I'm not sure how accurate my memory of it is. I certainly have heard that Nora Ephron quote, and it's not how I felt at the time. I didn't feel like "what you see is what you get." I did feel like I was acting in these movies. I remember when I was being considered for "Dick Tracy" and the casting director from my first movie, which was called "Men Don't Leave," was called about the experience of working with me, and he apparently said I wouldn't be right for the part in "Dick Tracy" because "Charlie's a sweet kid. He's not a streetwise orphan kid" like the character in "Dick Tracy." I remember being a little indignant about that. [Laughs] "I'd be acting in either one of these movies. I'm not the character I played in 'Men Don't Leave,' and I'm not the character I played in 'Dick Tracy' either." So I always kind of [Laughs] resented that kind of thinking that a kid actor is again just sort of a prop where what you see is what you get. But I know that that's the experience some adults get from working with them from time to time. I hope I was kind of an exception to that. Looking back, I acknowledge I wasn't as much in my head as I would be if I were on a movie set now. I'm sure it was easier to be a natural performer as a 10-year-old than it would be now.

Sure. That's an unusual disclaimer to have to make: "One of the stars of my movie, just so you know, is not a streetwise orphan."

[Laughs] That's right. "You better cast someone else." But I remember the same concern with "Terminator 2." Edward Furlong obviously had a more authentic rough background than I did, than a middle-class kid from Fargo. [Laughs] Again, it's acting. I think back to the story about Dustin Hoffman and Laurence Olivier working together on "Marathon Man." Where Dustin Hoffman was in his method acting days and torturing himself to feel like he was in pain in these scenes, and Laurence Olivier said, "Good God, Dustin. Try acting." [Laughs] I was always more on the Laurence Olivier side. Not that I'm like Laurence Olivier [Laughs], but in terms of the philosophy of acting. You don't need to be the character to play the character.

I think we have the headline for this story: "Charlie Korsmo calls himself the Laurence Olivier of the '90s."

[Laughs] "The second coming of Laurence Olivier."

On the topic of any degree of tension on a set, and certainly I don't expect you to pull back the curtain on anything, but in terms of Frank Oz saying "What About Bob?" was a tough movie to shoot, do you feel like as a kid that was news to you based on your experience?

No, not news to me. I certainly was less acutely aware of it than I would have been as the director. But I think everybody knew that there was an awkward tension between Bill Murray and Richard Dreyfuss that worked really well for the movie but I think made for an uncomfortable set at times. Although I think it's probably overstated. They were both professional on the set, although I hear they had some interactions off the set that were less congenial. The producer of the movie, who had also drafted the first draft of the screenplay, Laura Ziskin, who went on to a very prominent career as an executive. I believe she was one of the first female heads of one of the large studios. She and Frank Oz and I guess Bill Murray were at odds the entire film as well. I was aware of that in that there were confrontations that everybody heard about between her and Bill Murray at one point that led to her leaving town. So I was aware of it at the time also. I didn't view it as my problem or responsibility, so it wasn't weighing on me as much as the fact that we ran over schedule and if we had finished on time I would have gotten to do "Terminator 2."

I think that's a fair perception for an 11-year-old to have.

[Laughs] "I knew about it, but not my problem." I can get along with everyone.

It's interesting, the notion of if when you create a character that's supposed to irritate a lot of characters, I'm sure Bill Murray isn't the only performer who would be tempted to mess with people.

Yeah. He's an interesting guy, obviously. And I guess has gotten more and more interesting over the years. Probably the questions people have asked me the most in the last 30 years about my time as a child actor are 1. "Was Robin Williams really like that in person, wild and crazy like that?" And 2. "Was Bill Murray really like that in person?" What's interesting is the answers are the opposite. Robin Williams definitely was not like that. He would turn it on and off. He had the ability to be a wild comedic force. But in his real life he was always a very quiet, almost shy, contemplative, introspective guy. Whereas Bill Murray was always on, which I think as an 11-year-old I found it hilarious, but as an adult trying to work with him I can see how that would be really tough to deal with at times.

Well said. What you said about "The Ice Storm" and "Wonder Boys" is interesting for a number of reasons, one of which is that some pieces about you returning to acting for "Can't Hardly Wait" make it seem like you only did that for that movie in particular, as opposed to you auditioning for a lot and that just happening to be the movie that you made.

Yeah. An embarrassing amount of my career decisions were driven by the desire to avoid school. [Laughs] I viewed acting when I was just starting as a great way to get out of having to go to middle school, which I found absolutely awful. Then once I started high school I actually enjoyed high school and had a good time, so I stopped auditioning for things and I didn't do anything. Then I got to college and was studying physics and was finding it fairly soul-sucking and decided to start sending in audition tapes that I would make in my dorm room. And I got close on a couple of things, and I hit on "Can't Hardly Wait" and filmed it while I was going to school and flying back and forth from Boston to Los Angeles every week while we were filming it. I was still looking for other experiences like that, but I never dropped out of school to pursue it full-time, and nothing else really hit.

In all of your work, you have a unique ability to be great and memorable no matter what the role or movie. I must admit when I saw "Can't Hardly Wait" in high school I hated it. It seemed like such a fantasy that at the time I called bullshit on it. It wasn't trying to be real, but at the time I just said, "Yeah, right. I wish." Rewatching it now it's fun, and never more fun than in your drunken karaoke performance of "Paradise City." And not even because of anything absurd; it's that there's such uninhibited joy in that moment. Is that something that takes any different preparation than you'd put in for any other scene?

No, not really. In fact, originally they were planning on choreographing it, and I went in to have a session with this dance choreographer, and after playing around with it everyone was like, "You know what? It's going to be better if we don't do that and let [you] go nuts and see how we should film it." And not have it be some pre-planned set piece. So no. I kind of found that movie almost effortless to film. It's not the best movie I was ever in I don't think [Laughs], but it was certainly the most fun to do.

Did you ever find yourself in karaoke situations in real life and perform that song again?

No. Although every time—it happens less often now—but I have certainly been at karaoke places or somewhere with a jukebox, and someone thinks it's going to be very funny to put on "Paradise City." And what they forget is it's like a nine-minute-long song. [Laughs] So the first two minutes are funny, and then after nine minutes of "Paradise City" the joke wears off. [Laughs]

But "Welcome to the Jungle" would work better.

Much better. That I could do. Though trying to sing Axl Rose, the Ethel Merman of hard rock, is impossible to imitate. In fact, that was the first thing we did; it was a weird situation in that they originally cast somebody else in that part and started filming and decided they were going to go a different direction and they hired me without even meeting me just off of the ridiculous audition tapes I had sent in from my dorm room that my friends and I had filmed. And when they flew me out to Los Angeles the first thing we did was took me to a recording studio and recorded me singing "Paradise City." [Laughs] So I was a little worried they were going to have second thoughts after they saw what I was doing to it.

Because that wasn't the first thing they did on other sets you were on?

No. [Laughs] You usually sort of ease into the shoot.

In terms of what your perception of what high school is like now vs. when "Can't Hardly Wait" came out, do you have a sense of how that movie plays at the moment based on how geek culture has evolved or the personality types as defined in the cliques of the '80s and '90s are less defined?

I have no idea. I feel so disconnected from what teen culture is at this point. For the first time in my life I feel like I have no idea. I know it's not an original insight, but with social media and everything else, everyone having smartphones, I get the impression it's so different than it was 25 years ago. It's a black box to me. I have no insight into it, and I'm terrified of my kids getting there. So far they don't have phones, and they're not on social media, and I'm terrified of the day they do. I'm a law professor, and when I first started I was 30 and the students had been teenagers when "Can't Hardly Wait" was around [Laughs], so I'd feel like there was some kind of connection. Whereas now most of them weren't even born when that movie came out. I'll know more in five years. I have a pretty good idea what third grade is like in 2021, but I don't know much about senior year other than everyone's on lockdown. I feel sorry for anyone whose senior year was in the last year.

Then in terms of the way things change over time, when you think of the quantity and quality of what was coming your way after "Hook" and after "Can't Hardly Wait," was there anything you turned down that would be worth mentioning? The concept of "momentum" can be so arbitrary, but it seems to apply to child actors.

I think it's true that once you step out, you lose that momentum. Although I was going to lose it anyway. If I'd stayed with it, I probably would have done more before I'd hit puberty anyway and my voice would have started to change, so who knows. So my timing was [wise] in it was a voluntary decision to walk away rather than being kicked out, but I probably would've been kicked out anyway. Most people are. [Laughs] There were movies I turned down: "My Girl," I remember. I feel like the first two or three movies that Elijah

Wood was in were all stuff I turned down at the time. [Laughs] But nothing that I look back on like, "Boy, that would have been great to be in!" It's more stuff that I came close on when I was 19, the "Can't Hardly Wait" time, that I look back on and think, "Boy, that would have been nice."

I saw that you're still exchanging Christmas cards with Steven Spielberg. Let's say he calls and says, "As you know 'Hook' is one movie I felt we didn't get right."

"We need a redo!"

"Yeah, we're going to do a sequel, and I want you to play the dad role. What do you say?"

Well, I need to get a trainer. [Laughs] Look, it's fun. I don't know. Last year, or I guess it was two years ago now, a friend from childhood who's a filmmaker now asked me to be in a small independent movie of his ["Chained for Life"], just took a couple weeks to shoot. I said, "Sure, not a problem." It's a lot of fun. I would be happy to do it, but it's not something that I would uproot the life and career I have now to pursue outside of a having-fun-with-it situation.

Did you say you would need a trainer to take on the part with Spielberg?

[Laughs] I'm 42 years old now. I'm no spring chicken.

On that topic then, the irony is impossible to miss in terms of Robin Williams' character's lifestyle in "Hook" and your eventual profession. To what degree do you feel like Jack Banning keeps you in check as a lawyer/dad?

[Laughs] I don't know. I don't really identify with the character. I've gone out of my way to make career choices that give me time and flexibility and time with my family and everything else. I was briefly an actual corporate lawyer in New York billing the 3,000 hours a year. But as soon as we decided we were going to have kids, my wife and I, I bailed out for academia where I could have a much more civilized and reflective lifestyle. [Laughs] So even though I still do corporate law, I do it from the comfort of my home for the most part.

I think that shows great, strategic choices. There are people in a lot of industries that don't have that balanced life.

Anything that makes having anything else going on in your life, that never really appealed to me. I had a small part in a movie "The Doctor" with William Hurt, and he at the time I think was really miserable and felt he was working all the time, was never at home, didn't feel like he had a normal life and schedule and everything else. It's not like it's working in the coal mines, doing movies, but you have very long, unusual hours away from home and away from your loved ones, and it can be very alienating from everyday life. I remember having the discussion, like, "You're a famous actor at this point, right? You could do one movie a year, one movie every two years and then the rest of your life have a normal life." And that's been the kind of balance I've been looking for in my career where it doesn't crowd out everything else that I care about.

That's great. Whatever anyone's doing, you'd hope they'd be able to share that.

Yeah. Sharing my 12-year-old wisdom with William Hurt.

Certainly. You mentioned that as you've been teaching longer, the students get younger—

The Matthew McConaughey line, right? I don't mean it that way. [Laughs]

For sure. Has anything changed about the way you address your movies with students?

Absolutely. I think people still know about it, but it's not something that is that big a deal to anyone at this point. When I was starting there was so little difference in age that I wanted to do anything to build a separation between myself and the students, and I was petrified that people would be focused on the movie stuff. I remember my first year teaching, I got my first teaching reviews, student evaluations, and one of them wrote that, "Professor Korsmo never addressed the elephant in the room." [Laughs] By which was apparently referring to my acting career. [Laughs] So for a few years I would make sarcastic references to my prior career, but now I think A. everyone knows about it and B. nobody really cares anymore. [Laughs]

And I feel like it would only seem to be bubbling at the surface if you were bad at what you were doing now. I saw at least one video of you giving a presentation, and it goes without saying but obviously you are knowledgeable and the type of authority anyone would expect for that type of person.

[Laughs] I would hope so. That must have been a fascinating video; I apologize.

Of course people's perceptions of everything change in adulthood as opposed to when you're 10. But as someone who was so outspoken about what a waste of time school is as a child, what strikes you about how much you wound up getting an unbelievable education and then became an educator yourself?

My views haven't changed [Laughs], at least with respect to fifth grade. [Laughs] I learned way more outside of school than I ever did in school. That was one of the huge advantages of the movie career was you got a one-on-one tutor. You had to do three hours of tutoring, but you could do a lot more in three hours with a tutor than you did in eight hours of screwing around in school. And seeing my own kids, the extent to which school is just daycare rather than any real education is depressing.

Why is fifth grade such a hot button for you? Should people just skip from fourth to sixth?

It's just people are in very different places in their life in fifth grade. Physically and emotionally and educationally. I don't believe in the schools and the teachers, frankly, but trying to be everything to everybody doesn't really work at any time, but especially in those years where some kids are ready for a lot more than they're going to get in fifth grade and some kids are really struggling with what they have to deal with, and they're all sort of clumped in together. I don't know that it ends up working all that well for anybody.

After fourth grade everyone should get a form where you can either check "Go to fifth grade," "Go to sixth grade," or "Become an actor."

[Laughs] That's right. Go to Hollywood. Try to save up some tuition money.

And finally I have to ask: Your character in "Can't Hardly Wait" was William, and your son is named William. I assume the answer is no, but was that on purpose?

[Laughs] No, it was not on purpose. He's named after an old relative on my wife's side. [Laughs]

Dave Holmes of 'Wanna Be a VJ'

Many people likely consider themselves experts on '90s pop culture. Not as many have done it professionally.

Yet when someone makes a documentary about, say, Woodstock '99 or the late, disgraced Backstreet Boys and NSYNC founder Lou Pearlman, it's not surprising that one of the interview subjects is Dave Holmes. Despite having no prior broadcasting experience whatsoever, Holmes placed second in MTV's inaugural "Wanna Be a VJ" contest in 1998 and went on to host numerous MTV shows ("120 Minutes," "Say What? Karaoke"), as well as hosting FX's "DVD on TV." His path from knowing he was terrible at his marketing job to being unexpectedly comfortable on live TV to publicly coming out as gay to his role as an editor-at-large for Esquire is chronicled in Holmes' entertaining, conversational memoir "Party of One."

If there is a non-actor expert—who also happens to have almost won a reality show before that was semi-common—to talk to about the '90s, it's Holmes.

In "Party of One" you have a section that directly states, "Man, I miss the 1990s." So I know you will have no shortage of answers for a question about something you're nostalgic for from that era. It could be anything you miss.

Wow, where do I begin? I think more than anything I miss being unreachable. The idea that at the end of the day, the day would be over. And you'd go home. If you had an office job, you'd go home, and that would be that. You could not be reached. You could sort of unplug in a way that is not possible now. You are glued to your devices at all times. It was significantly harder back then to be a person with ADD. Because there were fewer things to distract yourself with. So you had nothing to do but get lost in your own thoughts. I miss the world before the internet. It's been good; it's brought us some things. But it's also destroyed our minds.

The notion of being unreachable is certainly something many can relate to. Are there aspects of that that make it particularly a challenge for you, just because of having a Midwestern mindset of being generous and saying yes to things and also the notion from your book of missing having an internal life? Part of being reachable is once someone can connect with you, a person like you then has to put something out into the world as well.

All of this stuff is good. It's all positive. You can get a little drained. But as much as I miss unreachability, universal connection has been really good. Before Twitter was the trash can that it is now, you could meet people from all over the world with similar sensibilities. I've made good friends and collaborators through it. So that's good. But it's also just such an energy suck. I also kind of miss having thoughts that I didn't feel compelled to share with the world. What used to be a journal or a private thought is now a Twitter feed. Which is not as much fun.

Right. When you could have a funny thing that made yourself laugh as opposed to having to validate it because it made 20 other people laugh.

Yes. Say it to the person next to you, and then forget it. Those were the days.

And I know there are many things you can say to this next question as well. But if you had to narrow it down to one or two movies or shows, when you think of something from the '90s that still means a lot to you, what comes to mind?

It's not a movie or a TV show, it's the whole Boston independent music scene of the early '90s. I was in school kind of near it, but I didn't really go into town to take advantage of it too much. But there was Lemonheads and Juliana Hatfield and Buffalo Tom and all of these incredible bands making music that was the soundtrack of my tortured inner emotional life. Even when I listen to it I'm still absolutely back there. They're not from Boston, but I'm wearing an Ocean Blue T-shirt as we speak, and that was just the soundtrack of my soul. I would have to say just the world of Boston music in 1993. I listen to it, and I'm right back there.

I of course am familiar with those artists, but if someone weren't and asked you why these sound like the '90s to you, how would you answer them?

Huh, that's a good question. It was sort of sweeping and emotional in a way that music had not been. It was mostly boys screaming their hearts out. It had kind of a jangly guitar thing that built on what R.E.M. built in the '80s. It was sort of emo before emo.

Did you also, as I did, spend the morning listening to the new Toad the Wet Sprocket album that came out today?

No, I didn't even know about it!

I was surprised to see it when I did my usual Friday-morning Spotify search.

Wow. I had no idea. That is great news, though.

It felt like a wink from the universe since I was talking to you today.

Yeah! Yeah. Wow. I'm excited. But I had no idea.

I know I'm part of a large group of people that was rooting for you on "Wanna Be a VJ." How much did your experience on that show inform your own reality TV viewing in terms of how you perceive who wins and whether that person "deserves" it?

Um, well, a thing like that had not yet happened on TV. So showing up I didn't really have any expectations. There was no template that I thought the whole thing was going to follow, so I didn't really know much. But I did know that as soon as I showed up for the Top 10 and Jesse Camp was there, I was like, "Well, that's who is going to win this thing." If it's up to an audience vote, what MTV viewer wouldn't look at him and listen to him and be like, "We have to get him this job because it'll just be total chaos." I was pretty sure that was how that was going to go down. Honestly, it was kind of freeing to know that. Because it was like, "Well, now my objective is not necessarily to get this job this way. It's to make some connections, talk to some people, and find my backdoor in." The objective became to lose well. Also, it's funny, talking about it now with people who watched it, uniformly the one misconception is that it was a show with a season. People are like, "You were on the first season of 'Wanna Be a VJ.'" Actually, it was like one day. [Laughs] It was a couple of little events on a Wednesday and a Thursday, and then there was a four-hour thing on a Saturday. And that was it. It all happened so quickly that there wasn't time for story development or character development or for me to wonder what my edit was going to be. It was three or four quick live events, and then it was over.

That's a really good point. When I talk about the perception of a reality TV contest, I was curious if your own experience makes you perceive other winners differently, almost thinking more about who's voting for them than the contestant themselves. I remember in 2001, a few years after "Wanna Be a VJ," VH1 did a show called "Bands on the Run," and there was a band called Flickerstick in the final two. I was sure they were the better group and of course everyone else would think so, but they lost. So between that and "Wanna Be a VJ," I was just like, "There is no justice in reality TV."

Well, I mean, I don't know. Maybe there is, maybe … I don't know. A thing like this that is down to an audience vote you really can never quite predict. "American Idol" took us around some twists and turns around the early 2000s. You can never be quite sure what people are going to vote for when you're giving them the power to vote. I kinda didn't see it that way; I didn't really see the thing as a reality show at the time. Just because we didn't have those yet.

And there's something more subtle about what you bring to the table.

Thanks. I came in thinking if this is going to be a live event and the audience is going to be voting, I'm not exciting in that way. I felt like, "Oh, this is a job that I could probably do, but I'm not a big character." So I thought if I have a chance, I need to A. get in early, and B. my way in is not going to be through the audience necessarily. It's going to be through the producers and the people behind the scenes who were my age and sort of music nerds like I was. And that proved to be true.

I know you get a lot of questions about Jesse, and I'm not going to ask you any. I just want to know if you think Jesse gets questions about you.

Oh, I'm sure he does not. I'm absolutely certain he does not. Yeah, no, there's no way. Yeah. I'm sure he does not.

When you think about that competition between the two of you, in some ways I was reminded of the "Saved by the Bell" episode in which Jessie is the knowledgeable, informed, passionate person, and she loses a school election because Zack cheats his way into it, and he just wants a free trip. Obviously you can make a parallel to a certain presidential election as well. The cliche is that reality TV is not like reality in any way, but it's interesting to see that when it comes down to a final two either in reality TV or reality, is this an inevitable dichotomy between the informed, integrity side and the loose cannon?

I think there are people who look at things like these in terms of disruption. Especially something that is as frivolous as "Wanna Be a VJ." I can see 14-year-olds watching this and being like, "Well, let's fuck them." [Laughs] "Let's take this person who is charismatic and a character but also way out there, and make this network have to put him on live TV." I totally get that. That's fun. And I'm sure there are people who are just like, "No!" Taking it seriously, which is equally crazy. It's all very silly. That I understand in terms of a reality show or something that is kind of silly and meaningless and on TV. The bummer is when it is an election, an actual election for real office, and it's like, "Eh, fuck it, I don't know. He makes up good nicknames for people, and he's going to be the president." That to me is, like, no. There are some things that you have to take seriously. A goofy contest on TV, have fun. But when there are real stakes involved, let's approach it with some sobriety, folks.

And it seems like you wouldn't have to point something like that out, but it's maybe not unreasonable to connect these things and wonder if it planted the seeds of these extremes in people's heads.

In 2016 and 2020, my mentions were crazy. There was a lot of that kind of chatter on Twitter. Hillary vs. Donald Trump thing, harkening back to "Wanna Be a VJ." It was like, "Eh, I don't think I'm going to engage with that." Because I am not as smart and prepared as Hillary Clinton, but there was a lot of that in my inbox and my mentions around both elections. It's a thing that comes up.

It's been awesome to see how much success you've had after that show, and it seems like part of it is because you have credibility and authority as a voice that's informed but opinions too. Like the difference between the play-by-play announcer and color commentator. It's not just play by play from you, but I imagine people

think a VJ or host isn't allowed to have their own viewpoint. You've talked in your book and other interviews about things that didn't come up because of the way things were in the '90s, but were there ever times where you felt you had to hold your tongue and be forced out of your natural critic position and just do the play by play instead?

Well, I look back at it now, as somebody who at that time in my life, I was 27 when I got that job, I had been out of the closet since college. And I never was out on the air. There are a lot of reasons for that. We didn't have blogs and social media and stuff. What you were on TV was kind of what you were to the public. There was no other way, except through the press, that you could [identify] yourself. But I certainly did have a lot of time on live television where I could have said something and I never did, and I look back and I'm disappointed in myself for that. We're promoting the shit out of Eminem, and Eminem's lyrics are crazy homophobic, and it's very weird to me that I didn't feel that I could say something about that. But I didn't. I wish I had been a bit bolder in that respect, but you just didn't do it, I guess, at the time. I don't know. And I wasn't the only one. It's very strange how different our culture is now, and it's just wild to me that I'm on live TV with somebody who says the word "f****t" 375 times on his album or whatever, and I didn't bring that up. Like, what the fuck? I'm disappointed in that, in myself for that. I don't know. I guess it was just the time. I do wish that I had been a little bit bolder and more spontaneous. But it seemed like a much bigger deal at the time, like it would have created a big distraction that I wasn't prepared to do. I remember on "Say What? Karaoke" I said something. There was a girl doing a Britney Spears song, her navel exposed, and it was very sexy, and I was like, "Ooh, the straight boys are going to go crazy." And our producer was like, "Let's take that again. You said the straight boys are going to go crazy. Just say the boys are going to go crazy." And it was like, "OK!" And just did it and didn't question it. It's like, what the fuck? I should've maybe dug in a bit more, but I didn't.

It's so hard to even put yourself in the mental position of the way things were at the time. I even meant a case of you having to introduce, say, a Kid Rock or Limp Bizkit video. You're not being asked to have an opinion about those, just introduce them. In no way am I trying to get you to talk negatively about anyone, but I'm curious if being in that position was ever uncomfortable. Because you have good taste and we've seen the impact, in the "Woodstock '99" documentary and beyond, of those artists and feelings you may have had but maybe weren't able to express.

We played a lot of music that I didn't like, that wasn't my cup of tea. But there's a thing that happens when you're on that set, especially if it's live, the audience is there and the songs are playing on these incredible speakers, and there's so much joy in the air that it's like, I'm singing along anyway. And my personal feelings about fuckin' "Bawitdaba" or whatever, which I don't like, I put them aside for a minute because in this moment everybody is in this one place and they're together and enthusiastic and it's on TV. And the energy and joy level is through the roof, and in that moment, it's like, "When this is over,

I'm not going to listen to it again," but in the moment it's like, "OK, I like it." You get swept up in it. You kind of can't help it.

If MTV came to you and said, "Dave, you won't believe this, but we asked Eminem if he wants to sit down for an interview about homophobia and all the things he's said and done. He wants to talk to you for an hour-long live special." Is that something you're interested in, or would you pass?

I would do that. They won't. So I feel very confident saying I would do that because it would never happen. But, yeah, of course. Because there's so much more to get into than just him saying the F-word a million times. Our culture has really changed, and people's hearts and souls and minds have really changed, and my heart and soul and mind have really changed. I would love to talk to him about his experience and where his head was at the time. But I also, as I said, contributed to this problem. I was an out gay person in life who wasn't out on the air. I could've pushed things forward in ways that I didn't do. I would love to talk to him about it because there is a lot that I would like to atone for and get off my own chest.

In "Party of One," you make positive mention of the music of some people like Eric Clapton, Elvis Costello, Ryan Adams. These are all people who have had personal things come out about them or made statements or done things that don't make them seem like great people. Are we at a point where people care about what type of person an artist is now in ways they didn't in the '90s? Is there an argument to be made for separating art from artist?

If you look at Eric Clapton, Eric Clapton's always been shitty. This is not like a heel-turn like a wrestler with Eric Clapton. He's been garbage for decades. Literally there would be no second-wave ska if not for Eric Clapton being shitty. He made terrible comments about immigrants at a concert in the '70s that led to the formation of Rock Against Racism that led to 2 Tone Records, and all these racially mixed dance parties and new music genres and all that. It's a problem we've been wrestling with for a long time. I think it's just artists now have more opportunities to display the fact that they're garbage if they're garbage. And I'm on air on SiriusXM, and we certainly play a ton of Eric Clapton and Van Morrison and people who I think are not people I want to have in my home, but it's also what people like. Fame is more of a 360-degree experience now, so if you're shitty it's going to come out. I personally don't need to be good friends with the artists that I listen to. I'm not as personally invested in anyone's personal life. But I don't think any of the conversations we're having are new in any way. We're learning about people in different ways, but people have been stepping in it forever.

So is it fair to say that if people look back on the '90s as being more innocent, is that just because we didn't know as much about people sometimes?

I don't know if it was more innocent. It didn't seem more innocent at the time. Yeah, your public persona could be much more polished. A publicist had a lot more power in that time because they were in charge of crafting your public image. Now, you are, and not everybody knows exactly how to do that. We know a bit more, but I don't necessarily think it's less innocent now or people are shittier now. We just get more than we used to get.

It's a cliche for every generation to look negatively at the new generation of music. You talk about in your book, even when the Strokes came along, and felt like you were out of the loop about the next wave of new stuff. I definitely have been the guy looking at Soundcloud rap, for example, and groaning, "Rap was so much better when I was younger." While it's easy for every generation to think of the entertainment industry as being better when they were younger, at some point isn't somebody going to be right about that? The feeling that things were better in the '90s than they are now, potentially?

When people say music was better when they were young, two things. First of all, you're right. You're absolutely right. Things are so much easier to make now. There's no barrier to entry. I myself could record an album and put it out into the world by 5 p.m. today. I could start when we get off the phone, and by 5 p.m. I could have a full album out in the world. I shouldn't because I'm bad at it. I don't have talent in that way. I can do it, but I shouldn't do it. And there are a lot of people who are doing it who shouldn't do it. So, yes, you're right. The second thing is, you're wrong when you say it. Because the stuff that does connect with young people connects with young people for a reason. They bring to it the experience of being young right now, and the music that connects with them speaks to them within that context. They know things that we do not know. Post Malone could not do less for me, but he's saying something. He's connecting in some way with teenagers that I cannot understand, and I should not be able to understand it because I am 50. My pop music exposure is strictly through SoulCycle classes and rides in an Uber, and that's the only time I ever hear current pop music. It all sounds very much the same to me. The beats all sound alike. When there is a rapper, that rapper is mumbling. It does not make sense to me, but it's not supposed to make sense to me. It is supposed to make sense to young people, and it does. And those young people will someday be my age, and they won't understand what the 16-year-olds of that time are listening to. It is just the way that it goes.

Hindsight can warp everything, and the present doesn't know what the future will hold, but it's definitely felt weird to look at how much aggression there was in some of the material of the '90s and how much now is so laid-back. I'd think it would have been the opposite.

Yeah. It's funny, you look back at the Woodstock '99 of it all. The very angsty tone of the music, the rock music anyway, of the '90s, and it's like, we had it good back then. The '90s were good. I know that there was an overall feeling of angst and ennui or whatever, but the economy was fucking booming. It was largely peaceful for those of us who are lucky enough to live in the United States. We could at least pretend that there was world peace.

Things were good. And our rock music was very dark and angsty. And now it's like the world's really dark and angsty, and the music is a bit sunnier. Which is good. I turn to music to feel better and to escape what we're all feeling at this particular moment. Looking back at the '90s and all of those fucking furious white boys at Woodstock '99, it's like, "Guys. You guys! You're about to graduate college and get a job. And you're the last people in America who are going to be assured of that. Be happy."

And as you said, the young people who are experiencing the new music that the more seasoned ears can't understand now, it connects to them for different reasons. But so much has changed about the movie and music industries from the '90s to now in terms of what gets made. Is there an argument to be made that modern kids are losing out by not having the type of movies and music and TV that '90s kids did? Aside from everything being rebooted, so much of that '90s stuff is not there for kids. I think of the things that meant so much to me or I related or responded to, whether it's something as easy but beloved like "The Sandlot" or the medium-budget movies that don't get made much anymore. Are modern kids' childhoods losing out in a way not having that stuff?

Um, I don't think so, no. Because that stuff is still getting made. Movies that get press are these superhero movies and reboots of old properties and things like that, so they get the attention. But it doesn't mean that it's the only thing that's getting made. I think kids today actually have it a lot better. The stuff that I grew up on, I really had to strain to see myself reflected in it. I'm still of that generation where you would get indirect representation. There was a character who was sort of like you, who you could a little bit see yourself in. But now if you're a teenager and you're questioning your gender, there are 30 characters written by gender-queer people or trans or questioning people. It's direct representation. It makes you feel a lot less alone. Certainly if you're a young, queer kid, there's all kinds of stuff for you. There's an array of different lifestyles and role models available to you. The big summer movies, I couldn't care less about, but there's so much more entertainment being made. There are fuckin' YouTube stars and TikTok stars and all kinds of different ways for kids to envision a future. And, on top of it, because we all have access to everything we want at the snap of a finger, they also have "The Sandlot," and they also have fuckin' "Annie" or whatever. They have everything we had at the push of a button and then all of this incredible new stuff. Yeah, I actually think kids today have it a whole lot better. There is no such thing as scarcity anymore. The thrill of finding a VHS of a movie that you thought you were the only person who ever saw. Or that record that they made 500 copies of, and that's all that ever existed, and you find one in a record store for $5 because they don't know how valuable it is and, like, holy shit. That kind of thing I miss. That's a thrill. But I think it's a pretty fair trade.

That's what I was about to say, to play devil's advocate: It's not as if standing in Best Buy, waffling about whether to buy an album was the heart of the meaning of the experience, but it was certainly a good chunk of it. It's a whole other discussion about physical vs. digital media. My son is 3 and hasn't had to make a decision

about this yet, but the idea that young kids will just move freely from a show to a movie to an album and not care about it in the way that I kept all the CDs that I cared about the most, and why would I get rid of those?

Oh, same. Same. When you like an artist and you really wanted their album, it was like a vote that you were making with your dollar. You had a finite amount of money; you could only buy a couple of things, so it really had to matter. So when you bought the thing and you liked it, you would come back to it because you had a personal investment in it. You had spent $18 on it. It would sit on a shelf and be a reminder: "This is who I am. This is what I like." So you had kind of a relationship with it because you had made a personal investment of your time and money. Now it's much more ephemeral. You gave a listen, and then it's gone. I am still a big music nerd, and an album comes out that I'm really into and I listen to it for a couple of days, and then I forget about it. Because it's not on my shelf. It's on a playlist somewhere, and the algorithm isn't serving it to me anymore because I've listened to it a bunch and it wants me to be constantly swimming forward. So I forget about it. And there's great music from the last 15 years. When I listen to a song that I was obsessed with a decade ago, it's like, "Holy shit! I just completely forgot about this." Because I don't have a reminder just hanging out anymore.

With you being someone who misses a lot about the '90s for a lot of reasons, we've seen so much from the '90s coming back in reboots or bands reuniting or otherwise. As of today, "He's All That" is on Netflix. Even if it always happens that the thing from 20-30 years ago comes back, is there a point at which we might be teetering into over-reliance on that? Or is there no such thing, and we'll take the good with the bad? There must be a reason we're seeing this so much now.

Well, what it is is the entities that have money to spend on productions are operating out of fear. They're not operating out of a need to innovate. They're trying to maximize value for shareholders. As somebody who has pitched a lot of shows, you go in with an original idea, and if people nod and smile and are very polite and they're like, "Can you do something with a Rubik's Cube or the Mario Brothers? Can we make a Tic-Tac-Toe Movie?" You're like, "Well, maybe. I can't." Everybody is frightened to death to lose money, so they hedge their bets by going with existing intellectual property. And that will of course burn out. And I think if we're going "He's All That," we're pretty close to the bottom of the tank. It'll come back around, for sure. It's an uncertain moment in entertainment history, so everyone is going to go back. You need to have an extra angle to bring people in because all of these things are risky investments. It'll come around, it's just we're in a moment of recycling.

In your book you talk about the trendiness of gay friends in the '90s and '00s. As with all social change, we had to push through stereotypes to get to the truth beneath it. While I think anyone who deals with pop culture is reluctant to use the word "responsible," to what extent do you think the movies and shows of that era contributed to that environment?

The way that we get out of tokenism and the sassy gay friend and the sassy Black friend and all of those kind of tropes is by centering characters and voices that are not straight and white. The straight, white, particularly male was at the steering wheel of popular culture from the beginning of time until like 45 minutes ago. So everything that wasn't that person's experience was kind of exoticized and tokenized. The gay people, the Black people, anybody that wasn't straight and white was just there to push the straight, white person's story forward. So now because there are as I said a lot fewer big productions but there are infinitely more medium-sized productions and there are so many more venues and apps and streaming services. Fuckin' IMDb has original programming now. So it's harder to get rich in entertainment, but you can keep your nose above water in entertainment because there are a lot more jobs. And those productions are now starting to center voices and experiences that are not that of the straight white guy. So now you get a thing like "Pose," which is such a deep dive into the queer experience. And you get things like "Insecure." You get much richer depictions of real life because people are telling their own stories. And it's really only happening because it was no longer economically feasible for it not to happen.

That's a good way to put it. I'm not suggesting that the two things I'm about to cite are the same at all. But in "Party of One," you talk about the way that you were able to host 90 minutes of live TV without having a panic attack despite having almost no experience was that you were in shock. I have some broadcast experience as well, and I remember my first time on live TV. It was not good, and I was very nervous. It took years of doing segments to feel comfortable and not feel like I had to memorize what I would say. It was definitely a process. I bring this up because on a much different topic, when you were talking in the book about your experience of coming out and relationships and what you described as your own "HIV panic," when talking about hookups you used the phrase "the fear drowned out the thrill." And when you said that, it made me think about the way in which you very much didn't let that happen on live TV, and I was curious if that is a reasonable interpretation of your experience previously learning not to let the fear drown out the thrill. Or is that two totally separate things that are ridiculous to bring up together?

Oh, no no no. That's a good question. I will tell you, and this is a thing I've come to understand really only within the last few years, and I think I kind of knew this all along but I didn't really fully get the diagnosis until I was in my 40s, but I have a fairly severe case of ADHD. So if you are familiar with the condition, it can make a person very anxious because your mind is spinning. When I got on live TV for the first time and was the one in charge, the one steering the ship, I felt truly calm for the first time in my life. Because the external chaos matched my internal chaos. There were a million things that I had to pay attention to, I'm reading a teleprompter and a producer's screaming in my ear because something's about to change and somebody in the audience looks like they're about to throw up and so-and-so is late and I'm supposed to do a segment with them. There are a thousand things going on, and my job is just to make it seem like everything is going exactly the way that it's supposed to. And I was like, "Oh, this is what I do. This feels good to me." And I've spoken to other people who also had that job who also have ADHD, and they say the same thing. It really was like, "Oh, this is the perfect job for me." I didn't understand it at the time. I was just kind of like, "Oh, I know how to do this and I feel good about it, and I feel calm." I didn't really know why. Now I know it's because that is a job for someone with ADHD. If you don't have it, you won't do as well. If you have the ability to focus on one thing, that's not really going to help you in a world where you have to focus on 20 things. So that's what did it for me was just having a broken brain really made me the guy for the job.

And the last question I want to ask is about when in the Woodstock '99 documentary there is a suggestion that Kurt Cobain's suicide changed the trajectory of the '90s and to some extent between the pop culture being made and there being a different sensibility before and after. Certainly not everything in society is founded in the pop cultural world, but if his suicide hadn't happened, is there a butterfly effect that you see things being massively different? Or do you think everything that happened still would've happened?

Wow, that's a good question. His suicide was at the very end of my senior year of college. I remember I was driving. I heard the news on the radio driving from Boston to Worcester, and on campus everybody had found out. It was mass mourning on a scale that I had not ever seen. Obviously it was a heavy and profound moment, but I don't know that it necessarily changed the course of the decade. What was already happening by the time he died is that the big record labels were learning all the wrong lessons from the success of Nirvana. They I think just heard the noise and the strange fashion and didn't pay attention to the kind of progressive nature of his lyrics and his public persona and all the really progressive, queer-positive and feminist stuff that he put out there got lost in the shuffle, and all the big labels were just like, "Well, we need loud guitars." And so they went out looking for loud guitars. And they found Limp Bizkit. I don't chalk it up to his death as much as I just chalk it up to big corporations doing what big corporations do, which is trying to make money and doing it in the dumbest possible way.

I agree. I guess my question is that artists like Limp Bizkit were so successful and embraced by the public. So is that on the record labels? Do you get a sense that artists like Nirvana that had something to say were losing out because artists like Limp Bizkit were rising to the top?

No, I just think it was the record labels were focusing on the noise rather than the message. And that big, loud, sludgy guitar thing was cathartic enough for angsty young boys, and so it sold really well. But the progressive message and all that got kind of washed away. Although I did just see Foo Fighters last night at the Forum. They played their first big show at the Forum since lockdown, and that pure joy with the clanging guitars and heavy drums, it was such a big, sweeping, optimistic, emotional show. So it's not gone. The post-Nirvana alternative moment was just kind of loud and dumb.

Amy Jo Johnson of 'Mighty Morphin Power Rangers,' 'Felicity'

In her role as Julie Emrick on "Felicity," in TV movies like "Killing Mr. Griffin," on the three albums she released, as director of features including 2020's "Tammy's Always Dying," Amy Jo Johnson does so much to represent authenticity, vulnerability, sincerity, generosity and kindness.

And then there's the start of her career in 1993 as Pink Ranger Kimberly Hart in "Mighty Morphin Power Rangers," where she was all of the above too but surrounded by a strange, corny, cult-following superhero world that is almost impossible to summarize concisely. Yet also shouldn't be ignored as a source of inspiration to fans worldwide.

"Can you become a new version of you?" asked the "Felicity" theme song. It's both trite and mandatory to connect that to Johnson (who asked to leave "Felicity" to grieve the loss of her mother and was raised in a born-again Christian cult), who no longer acts and has transitioned among several creative pursuits on her way to finding new purpose as a filmmaker.

When you think about the '90s, what's something you feel nostalgic for? It could be absolutely anything that you miss.

Probably, if I'm going to be honest, that time in my life had such a freedom. I was living in Los Angeles at the time. It was during my 20s, so it just gives me a feeling of—I partied very hard, Matt. [Laughs] I had a lot of fun.

When you think about that, where are you and what are you doing? What do you remember specifically?

I spent a lot of time on Sunset Boulevard in a bar called the Red Rock. It was right across the street from the Blockbuster, which is no longer there. And that was sort of the corner—my best friend lived right up the hill right there, and we spent a lot of time right in that neighborhood.

I won't ask you to share any lurid details from partying hard.

[Laughs] I never did drugs, but I did like to have a good time. [Laughs]

When you think of that era and movies and shows you were not in, is there something you saw at the time and connected with or something that when it's on now you watch and really connect with?

Yeah. You know what, it's kind of funny—this is not the answer you're looking for. I was a "Nick at Nite" girl, and I would just every night watch old sitcoms from the '70s in the '90s. So that's probably the wrong answer for you, but that's what I would binge at that time is "Mary Tyler Moore." [Laughs]

Why is that what connected with you then?

I think it just gave me a sense of comfort and familiarity of my childhood and growing up and what my mom and dad used to watch all the time.

That's excellent. That's so much of what art can represent for people is that comfort food feeling, especially when it's connected to people in your life. When it comes to "Power Rangers," you've talked a lot about the beginning of your career and your feelings about acting over time. But I wanted to start by noting that you obviously kicked a lot of ass and ask how much that empowered you in any way. Was there a correlation between that and how you felt as a person?

It's funny because I didn't really connect physically that sort of empowerment with a character until I did "Flashpoint" in my 30s. In my 20s, in the '90s when I was playing Kimberly and then went on and did "Felicity," I was very, very naive and very insecure as a human being in general. I grew up as a gymnast, so for "Power Rangers" it was just second-nature for me to do gymnastics and sort of fake the martial arts, but I don't think at that time it necessarily made me feel more confident. But I only say that because when I went and did "Flashpoint" and ran around holding that gun and storming in and being a police officer, my first day on the set I was just like, "How am I going to do this? This is not me." And then by my last day on the set, I didn't even know how to shake that feeling or that role of being Jules and being this more grounded, confident person than I was when I began the role. So that's why I say that because it was a moment in my life that I did not feel when doing "Power Rangers."

So was that then just because of where you were at in your life? Or was that influenced by the heightened reality/fantasy of "Power Rangers"?

Sure, sure. Probably both. But I definitely think it was a time of my life. When I was 35—I was pregnant the first season, had a baby, which always grounds a person and makes them more confident. And I had left Los Angeles and moved my life to Canada, so I sort of extricated from my life back in Hollywood, in L.A., and I needed to do that as well. So the "Flashpoint" time was definitely a different time of my life where it was time to get grounded in your late 30s and actually find confidence. And so in my 20s doing "Power Rangers," sure, maybe because I'm fighting putties and monsters I can't see [Laughs], maybe that wasn't so grounding. And it was my first job. I had never done any of that before. It was a bit like, "Whoa! What am I doing?" Some reality check of, "What is my life right now?"

One of the first things the group is labeled as is "Teenagers with attitude." Would you describe yourself that way at that time? In so much of your work you've showcased what a thoughtful, introspective, reflective person you are, including as a musician and filmmaker. But I guess everyone has that in their life. Maybe.

Um, no. I don't think I ever was. But I would say that we were kind of bratty, all of us. [Laughs] I think that we had bratty moments more than moments of attitude. We were all so new and naive. It was all just happening so fast that I can look back and cringe at certain moments of maybe everybody taking themselves too seriously as we're running around in Spandex. [Laughs]

Do you have an example of that in mind?

Honestly, Matt, I'm just thinking of examples from other people like David [Yost] and Jason [David Frank], and that's not really very fair. [Laughs] So I won't tell any of those stories. But I was the same as well. You know what? I'm going to give us a break because we were also working on a non-union show with not the best rules. It was a bit dangerous, and there were moments where I would refuse to do something because I felt like my life was in danger a little bit. But I'm sure that blurred the lines here and there as well.

And I didn't really know that whole dangerous backstory until doing research for this interview. I would imagine that would impact people's feelings about things.

For sure. Me and David caught on fire once, and one time I was like dangling at least 20 feet in the air. I'm like, "What am I doing?" And then me and Austin [St. John] were dangled over this gas flame, and I remember at that point refusing—like crying and saying, "Let me down!" And Austin standing up for me and saying, "We're not doing this anymore!" It was a whole thing. [Laughs]

That's a weird day at the office.

Oh, yeah. There was a lot of weird days. And I think in the second movie "Turbo" we did an underwater sequence, and I remember one of the lights fell in the water and thank god no one was in the water because they were not underwater lights. People would have died. It was a little crazy. It was non-union; it felt like guerilla shooting in a way.

Even outside of the serious injury stuff, the show and movies are so surreal. Did you ever have a moment where you were looking around and thinking, "I'm using my legitimate gymnastics experience to pretend to fight people in demon bird suits?" Did it ever just feel weird?

Sure. Like I said, I would have reality checks all the time. Like, "What am I doing?" But I was also super excited, super grateful. I literally got a job six months after I moved to Los Angeles, so I did feel pretty lucky. But in my head, I was like, "OK, this is the start. This is my first job." And I didn't expect it to become as popular, and I really didn't expect it to have the longevity of popularity that it has had. Which is crazy. And so surprising. I'm so grateful for that as well because that comes with its own gifts. At the time, I just really thought, "This is my first gig. I'm going to do this, jump off this and try to get another one."

And you've talked about being at conventions and people telling you stories that are heartbreaking or inspiring. Is there something that comes to mind that you feel comfortable sharing? Admittedly I missed the show by a couple years. It was more my younger sister's time, so I'm curious what people connected with that was heartbreaking and inspiring.

I hear a lot from people who either their parents were going through a divorce or they had lost a parent or something traumatic had happened in their childhood. They were bullied at school—whatever it was, "Power Rangers" and the TV show was almost like their best friend, and they would go home and they would watch this show and we were all sort of a part of their lives, and they felt connected, and all the shows had these positive messages. So I think kids that needed it really identified with the characters, and I think it just supported them and helped them. So that's what I get a lot of at the conventions is people thanking me and the other people who played the Rangers for all that support, and like we were their friend. It's really beautiful. This one kid, his name is Matt, he's probably in his 30s now. He's in a wheelchair, and he thanked me for helping him learn how to laugh. Which I was just like, oh my god. Because he said that he was so sad growing up because he was different and disabled, and then the "Power Rangers" came on and it made him laugh and it helped him to find the humor in things. I thought that was pretty special.

Absolutely. It's been interesting to hear you talk about discovering your changing feelings about your passion for acting. Do you feel like you were aware of that from the start? Did you expect that to go away? When "Power Rangers" exploded, did you hope those doubts would go away, or did it only become clear in hindsight?

Um—sorry, I got distracted in my brain for a second. [Laughs] I really didn't start to have doubts—I wasn't unhappy until I was in my early 30s. So through that whole first decade of me being in Los Angeles, I think I showed up there around 1992, I was very driven. I was just really focused on creating a career as an actor while also, like I was saying before, fighting my insecurities that I had. My shyness, my stage fright, but at the same time I just wanted to be famous, and I wanted to be a performer. But deep down I didn't really want that, I suppose. And then in my early 30s I just started getting more and more miserable and then I finally was like, "OK, I need a major change here," so I just packed everything up and just left and drove cross-country and went back to Cape Cod, to my hometown, to decompress a bit. And ended up getting a movie in Montreal, and that brought me to Montreal, and I was like, "OK, I'm going to try this out." And I got "Flashpoint," which brought me to Toronto. Sorry, I've left out the fact that my mom died when I was 28. So I think that was the beginning of my being unhappy and really spiraling. So when I left I just needed to kind of go and leave and figure my life out. So when I got to Toronto and was doing "Flashpoint," honestly, Matt, I don't know what to tell you. At the end of "Flashpoint," I just felt like I was done. I was hitting my 40s, and I was like, "I don't want to grow old on camera. It's hard enough for a woman to age. I don't think I love acting enough to want to be so vulnerable." But as soon as I wrote and directed my first short, I was like, "I could do this! This feels like what I've always set out to do; I just didn't know it."

I know that there were frustrations of people saying, "Oh, that's the girl from 'Power Rangers'" when you were auditioning for other things. Do you think in that era if you had been cast in, say, "Shakespeare in Love" or something else where they didn't give you a chance despite how good you are, do you think that would have changed how you felt about anything? Or it had nothing to do with that?

Huh. I've never really thought about that. Probably. Well, I don't know. Because, look, I was handed "Felicity." I auditioned, and I worked hard to get it. But I got "Felicity," and the caliber and level of people working on that show was really quite outstanding and pretty amazing and a huge gift to me that I did not appreciate in the moment. Because I think I was so sad about losing my mother that I quit the show. I left. I asked J.J. [Abrams] if I could leave. So I don't know how to answer that question. I don't think so. I don't know. If I got "Shakespeare in Love," who knows? My whole career could have been completely different, but my mother still would have died, and I still would have been sad and miserable and unhappy. So I don't know. I don't know how to answer that question. I would say probably not.

And it's such a remarkable transition from "Power Rangers," this big, loud thing, to something beautiful, quiet and private on "Felicity." You've said the former was like college and the latter was like grad school. It's not insightful to say that those two shows are different. But did that quiet, private sense have a really different impact on you?

Yeah. We did the pilot, and then my mom—actually, my mother was already sick when I got the pilot. So that sort of muddied the water of everything for me. And we started shooting in June. My mother died in August. So I never really got a chance to just enjoy the moment. And really appreciate it and learn from it and dive into it. I was just so preoccupied with grief. [Laughs] And I lasted two-and-a-half years, and I was literally falling apart. So I never honestly got a chance to appreciate that moment.

Understandably. That you gave the performance you did with all that going on is remarkable. It's common for people to play characters who are younger than them, especially with stories set in high school or college. How do you think you would have played Julie differently if you were 18 instead of 28?

It's so funny—I watched the pilot with my daughter, who's 12, and my boyfriend like three weeks ago because it was on Hulu or something. I was like, "Do you want to check it out?" and I watched it and I was like, "What am I doing?" Hopefully I stopped doing that after the pilot, but I could see me trying to act 19. [Laughs] I was 28 playing a 19-year-old, and I can see me trying to be 18. Yes, I think if I was 19 playing 19, I probably would've been a little bit more grounded in the role if that makes sense. Although I'm judging it based off of one episode. I didn't continue watching with my daughter, and I have not seen it since we shot it. [Laughs] So I'm not really sure how I did the rest of the episodes.

What was the thing that stuck out? Was it the moment Julie wears a backwards hat and says, "Hey, do you guys like Britney Spears?"

No, nothing of what I was wearing. It was my voice. I can hear me—the look in my eyes. I remember doing that. When I was in my late 20s still playing teenagers, I would do this thing with my eyes where I could make my eyes look really innocent, and my voice has this almost Britney Spears thing going on. [Laughs] I don't know, I would just talk kind of [uptalking] like this. And you can hear it in the pilot! I'm like, "Oh my lord." And I remember J.J. actually one time saying, "You know, when you can really finally someday drop into your voice, in your gut, you're going to be great." [Laughs] He said that when we were in New York at the upfronts. I hope that I finally did drop into my voice. I should skip ahead and watch a few episodes to see if I sounded [different]. [Laughs]

The show is great at exploring both friendships and relationships. Which of those do you think is harder to end?

Oh, they're both so hard to end. I think friendships, the majority of the time, last longer, so they can be harder. Right? Only sometimes do we have a really long-lasting love relationship.

There's no handbook for ending a friendship. People have the tools or expectations of what you do when a romantic relationship is over, but when a friendship is over there's a sense of not knowing what to do.

Yeah, it's true. And a lot of times I think friendships can just disappear. Just sort of dissolve. You just lose touch a bit, where a relationship you have to end it if it's going to end. I've lost both. I've gone through both, and I think both can be just as sad.

You talked about the personal connection fans made with Kimberly. How would you compare what people have said about Julie and how they were inspired by her?

I imagine those conversations could have been heavy. Or is there lightness to it sometimes?

Honestly, at these conventions is where I've really truly met fans and people who have followed my career, so the majority of the comic-con [conversation] is "Power Rangers." So I haven't had a ton of conversations besides meeting new people and them just being like "Oh, I loved your character on 'Felicity,'" and they liked the music. I haven't really gotten into a lot of conversations about my character on "Felicity" as much as Kimberly. Just because "Felicity" fans aren't really comic convention people.

That would be a fascinating idea: a comic convention for the WB shows of that era. It would have such a different feel to it, but I wonder if it would be rewarding for people in a different way.

Yeah, maybe. I've noticed a change and a shift in the comic cons for sure in the last five years, because I think I only started doing them five years ago. But I've noticed because there are so many binging shows now, it's not just superheroes at these conventions now. There's lots of different shows that are there. It just seems like it's becoming more of a thing that people go to. Not just comic book fans.

Every time I go to a convention and I dress up as Ben or Noel, no one ever recognizes me. It's so frustrating.

[Laughs] I know, right?

I know that you didn't see the end of "Felicity," and I don't want to talk to you about the ending. But I will ask: If you had the opportunity to time travel like "Felicity" or teleport like "Power Rangers," which would you rather do and why?

[Laughs] I would teleport for sure! Because right now all I want to do is go see my sister on Cape Cod, and I can't! So teleporting would be great right now.

You wouldn't struggle with that decision? The opportunity to go back and see real dinosaurs, hang out with dead heroes, anything like that?

No, that sounds really frightening. I have no urge [Laughs] to leave right now. Besides the pandemic and being stuck in my house for a year, I really like right now. [Laughs]

When you think of movies like "Killing Mr. Griffin," "Susie Q" and "Perfect Body," what stands out most in your mind, and is there a memory that rises to the top?

When I think back to the different jobs I had, it's always the actual shooting of the job and the adventure of that time. I never had a bad experience; they were all very different.

I'm going through them in my mind right now and thinking of all the different places I've gone and people I've worked with. I always liked going on location because then it's sort of like summer camp and you go and just dive into the whole experience. "Killing Mr. Griffin" was shot in Los Angeles, whereas "Perfect Body" was shot up in Vancouver. So was "Susie Q." This really horrible movie comes to mind called "Infested." Worst movie I've ever done. I think worst movie that was ever made. [Laughs] It was shot in Long Island, in Warwick. And that was probably the most fun I ever had. Terrible movie. [Laughs] But we had a blast! We were Hamptons-adjacent. They said it was the Hamptons, and then we got there and you could see the Hamptons, like across the water. [Laughs] And I brought my dog, and it was so much fun! I had so much fun. I watched that a little while ago with my boyfriend. Oh my goodness! Remember those movies in the '90s that were so campy and crazy that they were funny? Reese Witherspoon did one with Kiefer Sutherland. You have to look it up. It's really funny, and it's fantastic in a funny way. This I was hoping would be that way. It's not. Those are so bad that they're funny. This is so bad that there's nothing funny about it.

I have to say that anyone who grew up in the '90s would probably love to have been a fly on the wall for conversations you had with Michelle Williams and Mario Lopez on the set of "Killing Mr. Griffin."

Oh, yeah. Me and Michelle used to hang out a lot. She used to come and sleep over at my house. And I was, what, like 24, 25 when I did that. I think she was only 17. She got emancipated when she moved to Los Angeles on her own.

I have to ask if you remember anything about those sleepovers, conversations, anything.

I just remember her coming and staying at my house. I remember right when she got "Dawson's Creek" she was at my house, and she was super excited. Honestly, she was so young, and I was in my mid-20s, partying hard. So I probably gave her alcohol when I shouldn't have or something. Anyway, let's not talk about that. [Laughs]

Or you could have been informative for her in playing Jen Lindley!

Maybe. Who knows? I don't know; I haven't talked to her since. [Laughs]

I just watched "Tammy's Always Dying," and it certainly doesn't seem like a movie by a second-time director. I know you took inspiration from your father's own challenges with alcoholism, and I hope you don't mind me asking if you've talked to him about this movie. In having your own personal connection to the material, are you hoping there would be any reaction or impact that way?

My dad right now, so exciting, is doing so well. He's in a nursing home, so he's been sober since September because he can't drink in the nursing home. And when somebody's sober for 90 days, their brain unpickles and you can get your scruples back. And so I can actually have real conversations with him. He's making friends. Anyway: Things are looking up in that area, it's so nice to see. At the time, when I did "Tammy," it was the complete opposite. It was a very different picture. And when we went to TIFF, a journalist actually called him to verify some of the stuff that I had said. I gave her the number and said, "Call and ask." And he was so proud and really honest with her and just told her that, yeah, he had an alcohol problem, and she just verified all the information through him, and he admitted to all of it. Now, I don't think he's ever seen "Tammy's Always Dying." Or maybe my brother showed him? But I had written this one movie years ago called "Crazier Than You" that I haven't made yet, and it's really based off of his life and my mom's life, and I think he thought that he was going to be watching that. [Laughs] Because he read that script before. So I think when he was watching "Tammy," he's like, "Who am I?" [Laughs] I think he thought he was watching "Crazier Than You." Anyway, the point is I'm very proud and excited for my dad right now because I think he's had a turn of events in the past year which is a miracle really.

That's fantastic. It sounds like he's talked about the movie then, but the two of you haven't talked about it together. Would that be accurate?

Yeah. Yeah. No.

And you have a new project that's getting up and running which seems really ambitious, and ambitious concepts aren't being made a lot anymore. At this point, how do you define success as a filmmaker?

Hmm. I don't know. All I know is that I had a year last year, as we all did with this pandemic, or being isolated and alone in our own little worlds, and I just used that time to write a story that I had been ruminating in my head for a few years. And I actually flew to Newfoundland to write it and isolated there on top of a little mountain, looking at the ocean. And I'm really proud of this epic love story that I've written called "Ends of the Earth," and right now we're casting it. I can't mention who has the script because who knows, but I'm really, really aiming and hoping to shoot this in summer 2022. Hopefully the world will have healed a bit from all of this by then. I know people are shooting stuff now, but I want to shoot it in Newfoundland, and I would love to not have all the restrictions of COVID shooting. I'll do it, but who knows where we'll be by next summer. Anyway, I'm super excited because things are moving and happening with this story that I dreamed up, and it just makes me super excited. That feels successful. It took me a year to make "Tammy's Always Dying," which is so fast, but it was such a fun, hardcore mountain to climb, and now the movie's out. So I'm really reminding myself, and it sounds so cliche and stupid, but it really is the journey of getting a film off the ground and getting it made because once it's out there, that's it. That's great, but that's not the fun part. Yeah, I finished writing that one in September [2020] and that one has some momentum, and now I've spent the last three months, and I almost have my first draft, of another movie—right now I'm calling it "Vivi La Vita," or "The Italian Villa." That will probably change, but I'm living in my head in

Italy because I miss Italy and I really want to go, so I'm writing this "Big Chill" meets "Love Actually" that takes place in a villa in Italy. And it's going to be just fun, and I want a fun, big cast, and I just want to shoot this really beautiful, big, epic movie in Italy that is healing. And I would like to spend about four months in Italy shooting it. So that's what I'm manifesting right now, Matt.

I would say that after making a story set against 9/11, spending four months in Italy to have a different emotional register sounds nice.

No, I have to say with "Ends of the Earth," it is not a 9/11 movie by any means. It just happens to be a woman on one of the planes that is grounded in Newfoundland during 9/11 is the backdrop of the premise, but I would not call it a 9/11 movie. It's a love story.

I'm really curious about that and excited to check it out. I want to go back to the "Power Rangers" stuff and the stunning details about what people were paid and the danger involved. I'm glad to hear it sounds like you spoke up about that sometimes. When you think back on all that, do you ever wish you could do or say anything differently? It sounds like it was fun and rewarding but also weird and dangerous. Do you think about that at all?

I really don't because I'm not a woulda-coulda-shoulda kind of person. I think maybe the only regret in my career that I have honestly is not appreciating what I had when I got "Felicity" because I was dealing with losing my mom. But my one regret might be I wish I hadn't left. I wish I had stuck that out and just gotten through it, my grief, and just focused on the work there. I don't think I was appreciating what I had. I don't think I realized what it was at the time. And with "Power Rangers," I have no regrets because that was my first job. I learned so much. And even though we got paid nothing, I just feel like the benefits of the power that that show had with young kids who are now adults is just worth all the pain and worth all the ridiculousness of that time. Because I really feel blessed and lucky to have that support now from all these people who are now adults.

And there's a difference between being electrocuted and almost electrocuted. As long as people are only almost electrocuted, then they're fine.

[Laughs] I didn't die. [Laughs] I came out in one piece. It was a little dangerous, but I'm scrappy. I can handle it.

See, that's an extremely badass perspective. Look at how far you've come.

[Laughs] Right? Totally! And none of what went on on that set would ever happen now. It could never happen now. Union or non-union, there's so much safety in place on sets now just because of stupid accidents and horrific accidents that have happened in the past that I think it's such a safer environment.

And the last question I wanted to ask was this. I listened to an interview in which the interviewer said you were his first crush. I know people are flattered to know someone is watching them and happy they made an impact, but when people look at you as that type of thing—and I imagine if people made a list of stars of shows of that time who were people's crushes, you would be on there—is it just like, "Cool, thanks for watching"? Or when you hear that, is it, "I wish you would've paid attention to the character, and that feels weird to me"?

I think that it just kind of is what it is. And there's a part of me that, at this point in my life, having just turned 50—[Laughs] I was about to say something I probably shouldn't even say—there's a part of me that kind of likes it, Matt. [Laughs] As an aging woman— no, I'm kidding. It doesn't bother me. It used to creep me out. It doesn't creep me out anymore because I've met enough of the people who have said that to me that I don't necessarily get a creepy vibe from them. No, there has been some creepy vibes, but I think I appreciate it. I think I'm flattered. That's the word. I'm very flattered at this point in my life. I think, "Huh! That's kinda neat."

That's good! And it probably depends if someone looks back on it fondly and says it innocently. But if they detail having 3,000 posters on their wall and say it in a really low tone of voice, it might not sound sweet anymore.

No, but when they were just little kids who had the first crush—a lot of times I get gay men who are like, "Oh, you helped me figure out that I'm gay!" I'm like, "Oh, that's so cool!" [Laughs]

Devin Ratray of 'Home Alone,' 'Home Alone 2: Lost in New York'

On the one hand, Buzz McCallister (Devin Ratray) was the source of maximum older-brother intimidation for young viewers, what with his smarmy, pizza-based bullying, peddling of lies about allegedly murderous neighbors, and HAVING A PET TARANTULA.

On the other, both of the first two "Home Alone" movies—the only two that deserve acknowledgement—end with a surprising moment of kindness from Buzz that leads to entirely unexpected emotional relief. Whether it's the respect offered in telling Kevin (Macaulay Culkin) it's cool that he didn't burn the house down (in the first) or giving his younger brother credit for misadventures that led to the family being together in a swanky hotel room with tons of gifts (in the sequel), Buzz provides resolution that we didn't even know we needed. It's the sense that Kevin is welcome among the many young family members who so easily dismiss him, and particularly the older brother who seems to be targeting him more and more as they get older.

Three decades later, Ratray has accumulated a substantial resume of supporting work in notable projects, including big movies like "Hustlers" and "R.I.P.D.," beloved indies like Jeremy Saulnier's "Blue Ruin" and Alexander Payne's "Nebraska," and acclaimed shows like Steven Soderbergh's "Mosaic," "The Tick" and "Agent Carter."

He also starred in an unusual mockumentary about being in love with Condoleezza Rice (and learning about the racism she encountered as a kid in Alabama, suggesting hypocrisy about benefiting from and opposing Affirmative Action, and then getting a deeper understanding of her role in the use of torture as Secretary of State) called "Courting Condi." In an exceptional 80-minute conversation, Ratray is hilarious and smart in explaining so much about so much, including why he doesn't want to talk about "Courting Condi" and a surprising parallel between "Home Alone" and "Hustlers."

What's something that you're nostalgic for from the '90s?

Our country's economy.

Why is that what comes to mind first?

I turned 18 in the '90s, and Clinton was the first president that I voted for. I guess I'm nostalgic for the feelings of optimism and hope that I had for the country and for becoming a man officially in the '90s and coming of age. It's the largest economic growth in peacetime history of our country.

It reminds me of how many conversations my friends and I had after college about the generational difference of what our parents experienced and how that changed as what you're describing faded away.

Yeah, it's also the last decade that our country hasn't been involved in two wars. Peacetime economic growth. And the biggest problem that we could possibly fathom was getting a blowjob.

So it seems like you look back on that decade pretty fondly.

Yes. I started high school in 1990, and I finished college in 1998, and I started my first rock band in 1997. I do look back on it fondly. It was my most important decade in terms of growth. Started it when I was 13 and ended when I was 23. So that's a huge period of growth from a boy to a man.

If you had to think of a movie from that period that you were not in that connected with you at the time and still means a lot to you, what comes to mind?

"That Darn Cat" with Christina Ricci. [Laughs] It's the go-to movie that would come out of my mouth when I would get up to the front of the line to buy tickets. Back in the day we used to have to buy tickets for movies standing in line. Bizarre, I know. It was a Fandango-less world. They'd say, "How many?" And I'd try to think of the most obscure movie that was out at the time. I remember being at Times Square next to my brother and saying, "One adult for 'That Darn Cat'" And my brother just kind of losing his shit and laughing. And the lady behind the booth just looked at me so quizzically and then started laughing out loud, saying, "It's not playing here!" I said, "What?! Then I'll just have two for 'Ladybugs' with Rodney Dangerfield." So this went on for about two or three minutes, just thinking of the most obscure films I could possibly think of. The rule is I never see any of the movies that I said I wanted to go see when standing in line.

So none of these actually mean anything to you personally.

No, I have not seen any of them. There were a few films that spoke to me, that really woke me up. I mean, David Fincher came out in the '90s, and I skipped school one day and accidentally might have taken some hallucinogenics and went to see "Alien 3." And even acid couldn't make that movie good, it still sucked kind of. Then "Seven" came out, and that just blew me away. I saw it in the theaters and couldn't believe what was actually happening. And then "Fight Club" in '99 knocked me out. And that was after "The Game," which I also—saw all of them in the theaters, all four of them. Yeah, Fincher was kind of

98

like, "Oh, that's the guy. That's the go-to guy that I want to be when I grow up." And never did.

Do you have a sense of how you would have reacted if you accidentally had hallucinogenics on the day you saw "Seven"?

I probably wouldn't have finished watching it. I think "Alien 3" was the last movie that I saw on hallucinogenics. I remember "Terminator 2" and "The Little Mermaid" and "Alien 3" and "Jurassic Park," and after that I was like, "These movies are really affecting my soul, and I should really try and actually pay attention and watch them in real time." So I only watched movies sober, straight after that. I was a pretty boring date in high school because girls were like holding my hand in the movie theater and trying to make out with me and stuff, but I really just wanted to see the movie. [Laughs] It kind of disappointed a lot of dates. Didn't have second dates because of that.

I think most people who went to "That Darn Cat" were just seeing it because they knew they didn't have to pay attention.

Oh, no, you have to pay attention to the subtlety of Christina Ricci's work. And that is some of the best cat acting since Bill Murray in "Garfield."

I'll never forget the time the local paper misprinted the movie listings when "That Darn Cat" and "The Saint" were both out, and they printed it as "That Darn Saint."

[Laughs] Well, that would have been probably a more interesting movie. If Val Kilmer was just this wacky cat who kept hacking up fur balls, and Christina Ricci is just like, "Oh, Val! Come on, you. Get down off of that refrigerator."

I think a lot of people would've wanted to see that.

I would've. "That Darn Saint."

If you were talking to someone who had never seen "Home Alone," how would you describe Buzz to someone in the most generous terms possible, and how would you describe him in the most critical way you could?

He's a deeply misunderstood philanthropist who knows that his family will only grow through tough love and puts added pressure on the youngest of the family knowing that the baby of large families usually gets coddled and spoiled and has a failure to launch later on in life and doesn't really achieve the goals and potential that he could. So he's a little rougher on his younger brother because he knows he can take it. He's a young athlete, a man of discipline, and good taste in adult men's magazines. He knows that the little troutsniffer has had it too easy, and this time he caught it in the butt. He just wants to have a peaceful, gregarious and generous Christmas for his family, and feels that Kevin's irresponsibility can really derail them and throw it off course and ruin Christmas if he's not careful. So Buzz really has to step in and straighten him out.

That was very generous. So then how would you do the flipside if you were looking at him more critically?

He's a really intelligent, handsome, talented, good-looking athlete who really just wants to look out for his family's best interests, and that's the end of the story. He's a really good guy.

That seems pretty objective and unbiased.

That's pretty much what Buzz would think. [Laughs]

Well, just speaking for myself Buzz certainly presents a level of intimidation, for good reason. We know that Buzz's parents are somewhat absent-minded and stressed-out. How much do you think that the way that Buzz acts is a result of the parenting we see in these movies?

All children are results of parenting if they grew up with their parents. So we see the pitfalls of white suburban privilege of the '80s, where alpha-males grow up thinking that they have the rights to rule the world, and Buzz exercised them with confidence and a pensive wisdom. He didn't rush to judgment, but Kevin really messed up. [Laughs] Kevin really messed up. Poor mom and dad are trying to give them this huge trip to Paris, and we have to spend our time in a hotel waiting for a phone call.

I can't help but wonder what he was like when he was the only one around. Was he always the way he is, even when he was younger? Or he became Buzz later to an extent?

I think pretty much the moment—he came out of the womb with a buzz hairdo. He's pretty much worn a varsity jacket since he was zero. And it's the same one; it's grown with him, it's odd. As soon as Mr. and Mrs. McCallister agreed to write "Buzz McCallister" on the birth certificate—he never has a name. It's just Buzz. [Laughs] Catherine O'Hara and I once said that. We decided that Buzz was what was written on the birth certificate. That pretty much started to mold Buzz as a young man and somebody who looks out to make sure that his little siblings wouldn't become such a troubled young man.

Many performers have talked about being recognized when they're not working and treated as if they are the same as their characters. How much did kids see you and feel intimidated?

Yes. Kids I didn't have too many problems with; kids were always more fascinated by me, and it was kind of like a giddy awe that they had for me. Usually young mothers or babysitters of kids would come up to me and tell me how awful I was and how terrible I was to Kevin. And I would always say, "Thank you, I appreciate that." And they would try and tell me, "No, you was really terrible. Why was you so mean to Kevin?" Sometimes I would take the time to explain the difference between cinema and reality, but as those lines blurred in our society [Laughs] and all celebrities were reality stars and reality stars were celebrities and characters, and people blended more and more and you can't tell which New Jersey housewife is planning on smashing a wine glass this time or which one really did, as those lines blur more and more then people would assume more and more that I was my character, Buzz. Which is sad.

It would be one thing if you wrote the movie and starred in it and you were determined to play the bullying brother. When filmmakers star in their own projects, then I think you can take issue with the person they're playing—

No! No, I don't think so. Martin Scorsese has put himself in several of his own movies, namely "Taxi Driver." And I don't think he likes to sit in the back of a taxicab stalking his wife with a .357 magnum. Have you seen what a .357 can do to a woman's face? That's where he starts off. No, I don't think if you're making a movie and you put yourself in it you are at all connected to that character. Unless you're Francis Ford Coppola in "Apocalypse Now," playing a documentary filmmaker instructing soldiers not to look at the camera, trying to make a realistic picture. For example.

Interesting. I guess I was thinking more along the lines of Woody Allen. And obviously we can have a separate conversation about him.

Ah, well, yeah, OK. I mean, Woody Allen played the same part in every movie he ever played. Yes, he was essentially playing a version of himself. Rodney Dangerfield in every movie he ever played, you didn't see a whole lot of range with him. He would pretty much be Rodney Dangerfield and go on and do his thing, and he didn't really read scripts. There are definitely people who will have a persona in film. John Wayne, you would see John Wayne making a movie. He was never going to be the sensitive scientist who was against all war. [Laughs] John Wayne was going to be John Wayne, whether he had a six-shooter or an M1 bolt action rifle, he was going to have a gun. I don't think I can think of a John Wayne movie where he didn't have a gun or shoot it. Except "The Rifleman." Charlie Chaplin made "The Dictator." That mustache was fake from the Tramp. He put on something last minute trying to come up with something for the Tramp, and that became his trademark. Which he hated. And it just happened to be a stroke of luck that Adolf Hitler also had shitty taste in facial hair, as well as most other things. Adolf Hitler had shitty taste in just about everything, and Charlie Chaplin said, "Oh, at least I can use my cinematic power and weight to mock somebody politically." And he did. And other filmmakers— Stan Lee was in every one of the "Avengers" movies just as a kitschy wink to the camera, to the audience. Same with Alfred Hitchcock. I think that filmmakers can be separated from their art and should be. Unless they really try and attach themselves to it. As in your case of Woody Allen or other people.

I appreciate that breakdown.

Bruce Lee. You're not going to see him as the wacky surgeon who accidentally took his own laughing gas. That would be more like Jerry Lewis, who tried very hard to go against the own stereotype that he propagated himself, "The Nutty Professor," "The Bellboy," or something like that, and tried to do more stuff where he was a leading man. We all saw how that went.

I did enjoy "That Darn Dragon," though, the comedic martial arts combo.

Yeah, the unsung sequel to "That Darn Cat." Can't wait. I hear they're doing a reboot.

So just to circle back to the relationship between Buzz and Kevin, how do you imagine that their dynamic evolved as they got older? Both movies have that emotional coda between the two of you that suggests the bond underneath. As adults would they have the same salty/sweet dynamic, or as they got older was it more sweet, less poking?

I definitely think that they grew closer after the second "Home Alone." I think that once Buzz realized that the little trout could actually handle himself and truly was, I would assume, the youngest person in Winnetka, Illinois, to ever get house burglars, breaking and entering, armed robbery burglars, arrested twice, I think it probably launched Buzz into thinking about his own career and maybe sent him into a lifelong dedication to law enforcement, and I would hope that [Kevin] would think about a lifelong career in home security. Have his own home security system. I think he'd be pretty good at it.

On that topic, which is more inspired/twisted: Putting a nail on the stairs, or setting a blowtorch to blow on someone who walks in a door?

I think if you're going to try and set a human being's skull on fire, that might indicate that you should seek therapy. I think electrocuting somebody and hurling bricks off of a rooftop, it's the sociopathic nature that my little brother has that he's always gotten away with. Golly, they just kept on coming, those two guys. I wonder what the movie would be like if there were just like 30 Marvs and 30 Harrys and all clones, and there were all these clones attacking the house at once and you dealt realistically with the violence that this 9-year-old would unleash upon these unsuspecting, poor, armed intruders. Each time a brick was hurled off a building it would just lodge in one of Harry's, or I guess Marv's foreheads, and you'd see brains squirt out of his ears. Or at least one of 'em would die from some sort of dysentery from a rusty nail going through the foot.

Though I don't think interesting is the word for it, it's interesting that as a kid it just seemed like home defense, and watching it now I realize how Kevin's defense is much more violent than anything I imagine Harry and Marv ever doing to anyone.

If the movie took place in Texas, it'd be a much shorter movie. Because Kevin would just have a bunch of guns, his dad's guns, and he would be legally in his right to just blow the guys away when they come through the door. [Laughs] And everybody would actually kind of like that movie more, I think. [Laughs]

A short film about home defense for children.

Yes! It could even be an educational film that they show in class: "This is what you do if somebody tries to come into your home."

The movie obviously plays these violent encounters lightly. Would you say "Home Alone" is more like "Looney Tunes" or "The Good Son," the film Macaulay made soon after?

[Laughs] Very much "Looney Tunes." [Laughs] That's an easy one. He did "The Good Son" to try and change his image. The father really fought for him to do that movie. They actually had to hold up production while they finished "Home Alone 2" for him to go do "The Good Son." Because he didn't want him being pigeonholed as a sociopathic "Looney Tunes" character. Instead he wanted to be pegged as a sociopathic real-live little boy.

I could see how that would be an important career navigation. In terms of your own experience as a kid as this was happening, you've talked in other interviews about how surreal it was for the first movie to be a huge hit for your whole freshman year of high school. For someone at that age the psychology would have to be difficult. Many people in that situation would have a roller coaster of their ego going up, then down, then getting full of yourself again. Did you have to check that at all?

Uh, no. I was truly unaware of the status level of fake celebrity that I could've had. I did not cash in on riding that wave at all. And my parents certainly—partially they didn't know how to exploit a huge movie franchise, but they also didn't want to. They kept me grounded. Literally grounded, but also I was broke. I was a broke teenager asking my parents for $20 to take someone to go on a date to a movie. I was very unaware of the influence that being in that movie might have had on other kids around me who may not have been my friend if I wasn't in it. I never talked about it. I never bragged about it or boasted about it. It was out of my radar. I was still trying to work on being a teenager in New York City in high school in the '90s.

It's surreal either way, right? Either you're a kid who skyrockets to fame quickly and has to figure that out, or you're trying to keep your head on your shoulders while

everyone else says, **"Holy crap, this has been number one for 15 weeks in a row,"** and you're just like, **"I'm studying for an algebra test."**

Yeah, it was. I had to be reminded of it a lot. And truly was naive. There were teachers in high school who would bring it up every day in class. Every week in biology class Mr. Gelbaum would bring up, "'Home Alone' is number one again." Or other teachers would try and make comparisons to the movie. "The single solo neutron inside an atom is all alone. Poor guy is *home alone* while the electrons fly around him, and protons even farther away. The protons are the parents. They're far away! They're flying outside in the outer shell of the atom by Paris." I'm sitting there just being like, "Really? This is a poor comparison to chemistry, the production of the atom." I guess Kevin would be the neutron in the center. And the negative electrons circling around the neutron would be Harry and Marv, and the parent protons were circling far outside trying to get back home! Little things like that. And the class would of course all just groan and look at me and I'd be like, "It's not my fault, man."

I can only imagine how using bricks in gym class for dodgeball went over, then.

[Laughs] Luckily in high school I was a drama student at LaGuardia, and they felt that taking dance once a week was enough physical activity, so I didn't have to take gym. Luckily.

You've talked about the confidence that you felt in the sequel because of the first one being such a hit, as well as not liking your performance in the original. That if you could do it again, you'd be funnier and meaner and better all around. Can you think of something specifically that you'd change?

Barfing up the pizza, I always thought I overdid that too much. That whole scene got a little comical. Sitting in the French embassy—it was shot in the French embassy. When we're supposed to be at our aunt and uncle's place watching "It's a Wonderful Life" in French, I just would've handled things ... I took it seriously, and I took it sincerely, and I learned all my lines and I rehearsed and I practiced in my hotel room, I just generally think that I would've been better. I'm a method actor, so I really would have regurgitated vomited pizza on Macaulay's face and adorable little head.

Was there ever a discussion of using more authentic Chicago pizza in that scene? Giordano's or Lou Malnati's or something?

No, no, man. Little Nero's. That's the pizza for the McCallister family. That's it. Little Nero's, they'll get that shit to you no matter what. They will break any driving law that exists to get that pizza to you as quick as possible. They will knock over any garden gnome that you have. They will knock people down on the street just to race up to get that pizza to you. They really want you to eat that pizza. So the McCallister family, yeah, we're Little Nero's, faithful, loyal fans through and through.

As a Chicagoan, I now found it surprising. But I guess it's good they're loyal to local, despite how affluent they are.

I mean, sure. Sure. They're probably local. The delivery guy, he seemed to know his way around the neighborhood pretty good. But it's like, Chicago's not really a town known for pizza anyway. So it's all going to be shit if it's not New York-style pizza, right?

We could possibly debate that.

[Laughs] Come on! Does Chicago really have any good pizza anywhere? Sure, if there's like a New York-style pizza place that opens up there. I can go on the record saying that, right?

Yeah. If you like something folded and takes half as long to eat and is a minimization of its ingredients, you could go for that.

Sure. And if you want a pound of lasagna with some more bread around the lasagna and call it a pizza, sure. You can have a two-and-a-half-thousand-calorie, one slice of pizza that'll take a half-hour to eat, no problem. I love lasagna! [Laughs]

Part of what's fascinating and mind-boggling about the way that our perspectives change over time is that it's almost unimaginable that people didn't think about something then the way they do now, and you can apply that to anything about which the understanding has evolved. If the original movie came out now, if you speculate about how it would be taken and then think about how it was taken at the time, that's a thought-provoking contrast. Has that been strange for you to see the culture change but the movie still exist in the way things were in 1990?

In '90, the biggest problem that the film had was people saying, "It's too violent for children. And what are we going to do about all this violence? And should we be taking kids to it?" Any film or any massive experience that takes over a society's psyche, a film that the whole nation is thinking about, people will criticize or try and look negatively upon it. When "Gremlins" came out, they said that "Gremlins" was too scary for children. Now TikTok is giving children unrestricted access to adult-themed songs to recreate. There is always a lashback [sic] from the conservative side of our country to make sure that nobody has pure fun or positive experiences with something. If "Home Alone" were to come out today, it would be, I think, well-received, but it would be kind of swept under the rug. It's a film that technology has really taken care of a lot with cell phones and GPS and trackers and even home security systems. The film will have to go through a very creative and thoughtful revision if it's redone, and I'm very excited about seeing what would happen if the film were to come out today. I think it could definitely work. Even without the automatic nostalgia tag that's latched onto the film, I do think that it would be a very interesting concept: One kid defending his home against bad guys. It's a great concept.

I feel like home invasion horror movies and thrillers have been some of the scariest to come out in the last decade or two.

Absolutely. Anything from "The Strangers" to "A Quiet Place." It's defending your home and your family against outside forces, and sometimes they're bungling burglars, and sometimes they're large men with burlap sacks tied over their heads. It's a concept that everyone can identify with and say, "What would I do if my home were being defended?"

To whom do you attribute the things that Kevin does? Did Buzz teach him, or did he learn from someone else?

Buzz definitely did not teach him that. Buzz tried very hard to school him in hand-to-hand combat. I do think that Buzz was responsible for Kevin honing his talents for booby traps and wanting to burn people alive because he had to defend himself against bigger, larger forces like older brothers and older sisters always going through his stuff and assuming that whatever was Kevin's was the rest of the kids and he was the runt of the litter, the last of the pecking order, and he had to find ways to out-navigate them. So I do think Buzz had more of an on-hands approach to training him, so to speak, but he learned how to become so wily and nimble to survive in the harsh, bleak, dystopian world of the McCallister family Christmases.

It's almost surprising that he's still messing with him in the sequel. After I learned that my kid brother was so sadistic and the things he's capable of, I'm not sure I'd put candles behind his ears for fear of retribution.

Oh, Buzz would destroy Kevin. Buzz has no fear of Kevin whatsoever.

If aliens came and wanted one movie to represent the U.S. and you could only pick "Home Alone" or "Hustlers," which would you pick and why?

Can I blend the two together and just give them "Hustlers Alone"? Constance Wu has to defend her strip club from Wall Street guys with no money, and they keep finding a way to get into the club, but luckily J. Lo is a sweet, angelic pigeon lady who shows Constance Wu how to defend herself. [Laughs] There would be a lot of high kicks on poles, there would be a lot of action. And a whole lot of shenanigans in the back room. In the changing rooms of the club there would be hilarious hijinks. I guess it would be these Wall Street guys trying to break in and try to get into the back room. To answer your question, I think both films would give a rather distorted version [Laughs] of American society. One where it's completely OK to beat up [Laughs] and terrorize white men. And the other one's "Home Alone."

Until talking about this I'm not sure I realized how similar the plots of those two movies are.

[Laughs] Yeah, I stumbled upon that too as you posed the question. I was like, "Wow, they're nearly the same kind of movie."

Something that's very different that I just watched for the first time is "Courting Condi." What can you say about the genesis of that movie, and was the response to that or controversy or anything like that in line with what you expected would come from that?

I would actually really prefer not to talk about "Courting Condi" too much. [Laughs] I really would prefer not to. I don't quite want to acknowledge it. It was something that started off as a political mockudocumentary and ended up being another farcical—I really don't want to talk about it. I really would not want to include that in this. I'm not proud or pleased with how the project ended up. It went for the easy laughs rather than examining one of the most corrupt Secretaries of State that we had, at least in our lifetime. It was really supposed to be more of a fact-finding mission to let people know about this whole administration and ended up being just silly and vapid and the director trying to get me naked on film. He went for a different route than what was presented when we were trying to come up with the concept, and editing just went completely for cheap laughs. It was also too late. It came out the year that the administration just moved out. It was at the end of their second term; if it had come out sometime earlier then it would've had more of the impact that I was hoping it had. It could've been farce taken seriously, or at least mirroring some really serious, serious issues that changed the face of our country. We still have to take our shoes off because of the shoe bomber. I think his first name was Michael, I forget. One guy set his shoes on fire Christmas Day 20 years ago, 19 years ago, and we still have to take our shoes off because of that. Also the entire way that we travel has been forever altered from 9/11, and the Bush Administration was just wildly, incredibly incompetent, or almost, it seemed, deliberately knowing to look the other way in many, many aspects. There were a whole lot of things we were really trying to accomplish that we never did, that never got finished. It's been a real sore spot in my career, and it was the last project of that type that I will ever do where I'm not more hands-on with the editing process of it.

I certainly didn't mean to bring up a sore spot. You did a great job of explaining your feelings about that. Are you comfortable with including that for anyone who comes across the movie and wonders?

Yeah, I'm really torn. At least I want my say out there, but I don't want to bring any more attention to it than it is. The director just wanted to make me look foolish, and I wanted to make something important. Yeah, yes, OK. We can.

And I ask about it only because it's my job to ask about something I think people might wonder about. But don't want to do anything that makes you uncomfortable either.

[Laughs] Well, I should've thought of that before I signed up for the film.

I appreciate you explaining that and have no more questions about "Courting Condi." On a much better note, you were fantastic in "Mosaic." Steven Soderbergh is so known for being incredibly efficient, and there aren't that many filmmakers that get the type of name recognition and respect that he does. Could you explain his secret sauce after working with him in terms of efficiency or viewpoint, or is that like the cliche or trying to talk about dancing or something?

Well, first of all may I say that he is a fantastic ballroom dancer. Many nights in the editing suites after shooting he would don a tuxedo and just glide through the room. No, I'm kidding. He has the approach of, "I know exactly what I'm doing, and I know how to do my job, and I think that if I task people who know how to do their job, then they can do their job and I will do mine." I think he's a huge believer in casting is the most important process in making films with actors. He goes for a cinema verité, a realness, that a lot of directors say, "Well, I want this to look real and gritty so I'm going to spend three hours setting up a shot on a movie set so it can look real. Then I'm going to step out of my camper, my trailer, and walk in and the actors are going to feel real as they walk onto a set." Soderbergh will bring people onto a set utilizing the light that is available. I very rarely ever saw him set up a light. But his films have such a unique look because there is an inherent reality in it. Unforced reality. And he doesn't pressure people to do rehearsals. He will sort of sit and let the organic, reverse entropy of the scene—we walk in and the scene hasn't been constructed yet, or at least that's what I think. He probably already has the whole thing set up. And there were a couple times where I would initiate saying, "Can I rehearse this?" And he'd go, "Sure!" And we would feel it out organically. He would very much see how we felt the space of the room, the environment we were in. Then he would look at it and say, "OK, we'll do twin 88s. One over the shoulder of Dev, one over the shoulder here." And we would do it. Now of course there were more complicated scenes where there's lots of extras and an excavation crew and bodies being exhumed and I had to hit this mark and this mark and this mark, and it would be a three-page take. Those were the ones where he absolutely had everything marked. When we had the time to have a scene grow organically, then he would graciously give us the time for that with no pressure. And when there was a good deal of pressure, it didn't feel like it because he already had a very comfortable plan for you to hit mark A, B and C. I think he feels if he gets the right actor for the part, which is pretty much anyone he wants because everybody's dying to work with him, then he knows that they're not going to be bad. I can do my job, and he can do his job. It's a very strange dynamic of making a film. And there was a 572-page script, which would take anybody a year, years. A script is 120 pages. And we did 572 pages, and it was in a matter of weeks. Also his unending energy. It's this calm nucleus that will not run out of power. We say the sun goes down when it's nighttime. The sun's not down; the sun is just hidden, and it's still doing exactly what it was doing when the sun was up. So to speak. He's like that. He's editing films while I'm sleeping. Would you please hold on for one moment? The assistant director of [a film I'm doing next] is calling on the other line.

Sure.

Thank you.

(Three minutes later)

Hello?

Hey, Devin.

Hi, I'm so sorry about that.

No worries. I so appreciate your time, and I hope everything is good with that other call.

Yes, it is. Things are changing rapidly. It's ironic that that happened. I happen to be getting ready to shoot—well, I'm in quarantine in L.A. right now getting cleared to shoot Steven Soderbergh's new movie. So that was his first assistant director on the line.

That's so exciting. I loved what you were saying before, and I think it's amazing the degree to which he's so effortless in what he does well that he can do a movie like "Logan Lucky" or "High Flying Bird," and people almost take it for granted. Is that something that's more common with filmmakers or actors? I could see how some of your work has an effortlessness that people sometimes probably don't appreciate the precision that to them seems effortless.

Absolutely. Everything on camera has been rehearsed. Not necessarily for that project, but in my life. I am constantly absorbing other people's behavior and watching other actors and trying to observe the pacing and the atmosphere that other directors create for films. Everything is rehearsed on film. That is not to say that there isn't improv. That's not to say that there aren't spontaneous ideas that come up on the set that are worked out with the other collaborators. The producers, the writer, people on the set. Sure, we came up with things there. When my wife is blocking my exit in my office, trying to put an idea in my head, and I'm so baffled and confused and befuddled, sure, a lot of it was having to remember what order to take off my supply belt, my utility belt, so to speak, and remember to take the battery out of the walkie-talkie and put it in the charger, take my gun out, keep the safety on, all that is going on. I was a little confused and befuddled by that. But when I turn to her where she's like, "Nate, Nate." And I turn and just, "Whaaat? Baby, whaaat?" That came directly from a conversation and argument that I'd had with my girlfriend at the time from just a couple weeks ago. And she saw it with me and kind of gasped and turned and said, "That was you! That's what you said; that's how you said it." First she kind of understood my exasperation a little bit more at the time and how distracted I was, and how it wasn't meant to be dismissive. [Laughs] It actually helped our relationship, seeing it. But she was also like, "Wow, that was you on screen." And I said, "No, that was Detective Nate Henry in a situation that I could relate to." It's all rehearsal, and when you call action that's when you can bring things out that seem effortless. And I watch other actors do this, things that we never notice. I remember 20 years ago, when DVDs used to have the actors, they would have narration where actors would talk over the movie and talk about, "Oh, well, this scene we did this." Do you recall what I'm talking about?

Sure. Commentary.

Commentary is the word that I didn't know to say until this very moment of my life. Commentary! Brad Pitt's commentary on "Fight Club," the scene where he puts chemical burner on Ed Norton's hand and holds it there and makes him hold it. You know the scene I'm talking about, in the kitchen.

Of course.

He takes out a jug of vinegar and says, "Now, listen, you can rush over the sink and make it worse and pour water on it, or you can hold it and realize that this is your moment and neutralize it with vinegar." He pulls up the jug of vinegar and flicks off the cap with his thumb, and it's a very small, seemingly effortless thing. And it looks cool. And it's so what Tyler Durden would do. Tyler Durden is just always cool and always one step ahead. Of course he flicks it off. Brad Pitt mentioned that. He was like, "Finally got that cap off with my thumb there." Ed Norton was like, "Aww, that was brilliant. That was so good." The scene suddenly became—between the two of them, the scene was about Brad Pitt flipping the fucking cap of the vinegar off the bottle, when none of us in the audience were ever thinking about that. They're like, "Oh my god, oh my god. Get that vinegar on his hand. Jesus, this guy, is he a psychopath, and why is Ed doing this, and god could I possibly go through burning myself and what is happening?" This incredibly intense, dramatic scene, and the two of them are just sort of giggling about how physically apt Brad Pitt is. And he is a very physically suave, smooth actor, but even little things like flipping the cap off the vinegar bottle was rehearsed again and again that made it seem so effortless and he's so suave and cool and has the whole situation under control. It's all rehearsed. It's all part of characters. And Soderbergh will first create an environment where people can feel relaxed and be able to bring ideas to the character. And if it works, it works. Nobody gets to the NFL by luck alone, and nobody doesn't know the severity of that type of pressure and that type of absolute physical demanding. I'm not at all saying that we're anywhere like NFL athletes who put themselves through the most abusive, aggressive, violent physical achievements in almost any sport. But you don't get to be at the top of the line, which I consider Steven Soderbergh the top of the line in terms of living, working filmmakers. And you have to bring all of your observations that you have accumulated over your life. I mean, I watch commercials and I think, "Jesus, why did he get that part in that dog commercial and I didn't?" Everything is practicing for what's going to go on film. Boy, that's a long answer of me saying the same thing over and over again.

Those were perfect examples, though. That was great.

[Laughs] Thanks.

My last question for you is about Harry and Marv being known as the Wet Bandits. I always take note when that type of lighthearted label is used for real criminals. Like if a bunch of people in Mets hats are stealing purses and they're called the Mets Marauders. When thieves are labeled with cute nicknames like that, is that something you are for or against?

[Laughs] An odd question. To put it in the ancient terms, [in old-timey voice], "It's a way to sell papers, kid!" It's a headline. It's a way to get the audience—that's the thing. When news shows refer to their ratings or audience members, they're not audience; they're citizens trying to be informed. But they need them to remember. You've heard of the Night Stalker, but you might not know that his name was Richard Ramirez. They all will remember a quick, catchy piece of information. Something that the neurons in people's brains can latch onto quickly. The Central Park Five. My brother knew those kids, and they were totally innocent. They were set up and forced to confess to something. You remember the Central Park Five in New York. You don't know their names, but you remember that situation. It's just name recognition. And not sure if it's a good or bad thing. I'm not sure if the Unabomber is a very good name for a guy who would send packages to people and blow up their faces with nails. I'm not sure why he was a "uni." [Editor's note: It appears Ratray was thinking of that name as being spelled "Unibomber."] Like a unicorn bomber? Or he just liked sea urchin and Japanese sashimi? And, yes, I just came up with that example right now as I'm trying to open a bottle of Pedialyte. It kind of trivializes it. But that's why sometimes criminals have to take matters into their own hands and control their own social persona in these days of social media. And they weren't happy with being called the Wet Bandits either. I'd appreciate if you'd refer to them as the Sticky Bandits now.

If you're going to rob a bank on a pogo stick, you deserve to be called the Pogo Stick Bandit. But if you hurt people really badly while doing that, "Pogo Stick Bandit" might be too cute.

Right, right. In their case, though, you actually have to look at the fact that they never hurt anyone. As much as they tried, they never landed a single blow [Laughs] on anybody. You can't really add assault onto their charges. They never hurt poor Kevin. They threatened to. Menacing him, threatening him, sure, those are crimes. But the Wet Bandits, they got a bad rap. In fact, what happened to Old Man Marley? Shouldn't he get at least attempted murder or something? He took a snow shovel to the back of a guy's head! Why didn't he get arrested?

You don't think that's a self-defense case?

What the hell is he doing in that house?! That's breaking and entering! Maybe he was part of the whole robbery! Maybe it was a three-man job, and things just went sour between the burglars. Kid comes along, they get spotted, he eyes all of them, Old Man Marley thinks,

"Oh, well, maybe I can talk my way out of this." He turns on the other two, wham! Slam! Knocks them out. And then is like, "Look at this, kid, I saved you! Haha, mum's the word."

I never thought of it that way, and now that's the only way I will think of it.

Good! I never thought of it that way either until this very moment.

Hill Harper of 'Get on the Bus,' 'He Got Game,' 'Steel,' 'In Too Deep,' 'Married with Children'

It doesn't get much more versatile than Hill Harper's run of notable roles in the '90s.

Following a five-episode arc on the broad comedy of "Married with Children" (a part won over Dave Chappelle), he appeared as aspiring filmmaker Xavier in Spike Lee's "Get on the Bus"; an eyepatch-sporting, Shaq-shooting villain in "Steel"; Coleman "Booger" Sykes, the supportive and less height-gifted cousin of Jesus Shuttlesworth (Ray Allen) in Lee's "He Got Game"; and Breezy T., a drug dealer serving under Dwayne "God" Gittens (LL Cool J) in "In Too Deep." The unifying attribute is Harper's immense likability, even when playing characters who do bad things.

Offscreen, there are almost too many good things to speak of, including but not limited to: The actor is a friend and Harvard law school classmate of President Obama and has two other Ivy League degrees to go along with Harvard Law. He adopted a baby as a single dad and named him after his former co-star Pierce Brosnan. He is also the author of multiple books and a cancer survivor and a creator of the Black Wall Street app. If you hear him on a podcast, it is less likely to be about his onscreen work (which includes major roles on "CSI: NY," "Covert Affairs" and "The Good Doctor") than about his expertise in cryptocurrency.

When you think about the '90s, what's something you feel nostalgic for? It could be anything you miss from that era.

I would say the sense that anything was possible and there was a lot of joy. I think there was a lot of hope, a lot of creativity, and the sense that anything was possible that definitely permeated that time.

Why did people have that feeling in a way that they didn't at a different time?

I just think that it had to do with a time and a place coming out of a real stretch of creativity. Music really tells the tale and moves the meter for most all culture. If you really think about what moves the meter, I think coming out of the '80s you had a lot of color and feel-good and dance, and the '90s it was more a cool vibe, but at the same time people were ambitious and wanted to do interesting and cool things. So to me, it just had a real vibe of possibility. Which was really good. So I think that always going back to the music, music tells the tale. All the time.

Even the quantity of one-hit wonders makes it seem like there were a lot of new people to know in the '90s. Montell Jordan, Crystal Waters. There are some classic songs from that era that other decades may not have as many one-hit wonders, or that were as good.

Like you say, there were a lot of people creating a lot. I was in L.A. and New York during that time, so just saw a lot of creativity.

When you think of the '90s, what's a movie or show you weren't involved in personally that you're a big fan of? Either you loved it at the time or return to it a lot now?

Man, that's hard. I don't think in terms of times like that, so that's really hard for me to do. I think of older projects, but I don't think they were in the '90s. Hmm. When did "Jerry Maguire" come out? Didn't "Jerry Maguire" come out in the 2000s, or was it in the '90s?

That was '96, actually.

OK, there you go. "Jerry Maguire," that's a good one.

Why is that what comes to mind first?

I saw it several times; I really was motivated by that film. I thought the storytelling, the acting, what it was trying to say; it just really resonated with me about goals and dreams and life and overcoming obstacles, but also having a light energy. I love that film.

On the subject of goals and dreams, you have such a unique, fantastic background in terms of what you did before getting into acting. I certainly don't intend to make you the representative for this question, but we of course are a long way from being anywhere close to having enough representation and enough diverse roles. When you think back to when you were getting into acting and looking for opportunities in the '90s, what stories were being told and what was out there for you, what do you think about from that era?

I really think about the independent film movement and all of the young independent filmmakers because I felt like that's where I could find roles and do work. So I really leaned into the independent film space and really enjoyed it. That's really where I focused a lot of my energy and a lot of my time, and loved that. Super creative, super indie. Everyone's doing it because they want to make a project, and it wasn't about the money or anything like that. Independent film, particularly African-American filmmakers, in the '90s, telling stories in the independent film area was just spectacular.

Absolutely. And having "Get on the Bus" being the type of movie that it was, and the type of opportunity for you. What was the first thing that struck you about what makes Spike Lee distinctive as a filmmaker when you were working with him?

Yeah, I remember when I was doing my audition for "Get on the Bus" he was looking at his watch. And I was like, "Oh, I clearly didn't get this role." I could see him doing it during, and I was insulted because it's like, "Dude, I'm doing my best work here. And you're looking at your watch." The other thing I remember is him really encouraging his actors to act and create characters and not wanting to over-direct. I think he saw a lot of successful directing as successful casting. And that's one thing I've learned: Probably 80-90% of directing is casting. That's in part why I think we see the quality of film projects and the quality of acting decrease over time because we don't spend the time in the room auditioning actors anymore, working with directors. People just make a tape and send it in, and you end up with not the best results. He just is somebody who really wants his actors to act. He's not intimidated by actors, and he really wants to get out of their way and offer a few little gems when necessary. He's a phenomenal director.

Did you feel like that audition moment when he wasn't paying attention was a directorial strategy?

I think he'd already made his decision. I think that he makes decisions pretty definitively, and I think he was like, "This is the guy." I think he makes the decision if you're not the person and if you are the person, and he clearly made the decision that I was getting the role. So he was like, "OK, I made that choice. Boom. On to the next."

For a movie like that, where the material is so rich and on-topic, does that result in the cast having meaty discussions on set? Like because the material is so heavy you have to stay on point on set? Or is it the opposite and you don't want to be message-message-message day in and day out?

I was really lucky for that film that my character on the bus sat next to Ossie Davis' character most of the film. So I got to sit next to Ossie, and he was telling me stories about Godfrey Cambridge, telling me stories about the Negro Ensemble Company in New York, telling me stories about Malcolm X coming over for breakfast or dinner and being at the house. And so I got a chance to just talk to Ossie Davis for three weeks, sitting next to him, which has truly informed my career, I think, to a great degree. Because he told me actors shouldn't just act. We're here for a bigger purpose, and we're here to represent something to make the world better and make the conditions of life better. So those discussions definitely were had. But in the movie, you sat next to certain characters. I don't know what Roger Guenveur Smith was talking about in the front of the bus, but I know what I was talking about back with Ossie Davis.

Does that inform the performance, the mental space those conversations put you in? As opposed to if you and Ossie were talking about sports or something?

Absolutely. Everything informs performance. Everything. And the atmosphere that's created on the set informs so much of all performance. So no doubt about that.

Using that to pivot to "He Got Game" and the concept of achievement, when you think about that story, is Jake Shuttlesworth an overbearing father, asking too much and fouling Jesus too hard on the court? Or are Jake's choices necessary for Jesus to be great?

Oh, I think they're necessary. My dad was like Jake Shuttlesworth, and unfortunately now me as a father I'm not like Jake Shuttlesworth. I have to be more like Jake Shuttlesworth.

I know your son is younger than Jesus is in the movie, but why do you think if you embrace Jake's approach that you haven't been following that path?

Because I think that that type of parenting creates success, but it also drives a wedge between the parent and the child. Because the child starts to associate the parent's love with hardness and also with their success. I think that can drive a wedge.

To what degree did becoming a father impact your view of your past work, particularly a movie like "He Got Game," which is so much about fathers and sons? Do you see the movie differently now?

I'll watch that movie with him sometime. I can't answer that question because I don't know; I haven't seen it in so long. And I have a very personal relationship to that movie because there was a huge storyline that was cut out, so when I see that film it brings a little bit of twinge of pain, unfortunately. I don't watch it very often.

I'd seen you mention previously about that, what got cut. In the movie Booger comes off as supportive and that he hasn't suffered because of Jesus' success. Cutting a scene of him talking about Jesus' success being detrimental to him changes the character dynamic completely.

Yeah. But it wasn't just that scene. It was a whole storyline about how Jesus would defend Booger because he couldn't read. So you see him getting teased in school, and he couldn't read. So Jesus would defend him, so that kind of relationship where he felt like he was living in Jesus' shadow and he would also support Jesus but Jesus was also defending him. It was a whole storyline at school, and they would tease me because I couldn't read. It was really good.

You being on the court with real NBA players in the movie really makes me miss Spud Webb and Muggsy Bogues. Kids growing up now are missing out on the shorter NBA stars of the '90s.

Yeah! Those guys. The super-short guys, and then also the semi-short guys like Allen Iverson. Allen was so great. And also a lot of people don't know Kobe Bryant was supposed to star in "He Got Game." It wasn't supposed to be Ray Allen. Kobe had basically signed a deal, and somehow the deal fell apart at the last minute. I don't know exactly what happened, but it fell apart at the very last [step].

You have the very unique credit to say you worked with Ray Allen and Shaq, both athletes adapting to acting roles. It was Ray's first; Shaq had had a bit of experience when you worked with him. When you think of them learning and what it took for you to be involved in that, how would you contrast those experiences?

I mean, they're very different. A superhero movie that's kind of tongue-in-cheek is very different than "He Got Game." "He Got Game" was attempting to achieve something very different, and so what was required of Ray Allen in that role was significantly more than what was required of Shaq in the role of Steel. But they both brought truth and fun and hard work to their roles. And I think that's ultimately what made them both so successful is they worked very hard, and they want to be good at everything they do. Including acting in the role. It was great working with both of them.

Was Ray able to see you as a source of guidance? When Denzel Washington is there, it might be hard for anyone to feel like they can add some pointers. Were you able to help or leave that more to Denzel?

Yeah yeah yeah. I could definitely help, but he had an acting coach on the set as well. She's worked with Angelina Jolie, and she's amazing. She was on every day, and I would talk to her as well. So he didn't have too many voices in his ear, I would say things to her. "Hey, he can do this. Maybe we'll ad-lib here." That way he was always hearing things through one person.

When looking at "Steel" and "In Too Deep," two movies where you play criminals and very different people than the other roles we've been talking about, there's such a sense of glee you bring to these characters and likability in spite of what the people do. It seems so obvious, the notion of effortless likability. You'd think many actors would have that, but I don't think you can say that about everyone. Is that something you think people are casting you for on purpose? Is it something you've had naturally your whole life?

To me it's more I think all characters take actions for reasons they think are positive, even though they may not be positive. So if you find that, then that comes through. And I love playing bad guys; I just don't get cast enough as a bad guy. I wish I got cast more as the bad guy, but I just don't. And it bums me out.

If anything, there's a pattern of journalism in your career. You're an aspiring filmmaker in "Get on the Bus," a reporter in "The Skulls," "Live Shot," and "All Eyez On Me," and then hosting the news program "How It Really Happened." What do you make of that through line? Are those parts finding you? Is there an inherent connection uniting all of those?

You know, maybe? I think people associate journalists with writers, and because I am a writer as well maybe there's some type of subconscious [element] of that. There's never been a conscious side to that. It just happened to fall out that way.

And of course playing doctors a few times, and other authority figures. There are plenty of people who have convincingly played doctors, lawyers, journalists, officers, who don't have multiple Ivy League degrees, but the notion of someone radiating intelligence or authority is interesting. I don't know if that's something you've ever felt aware of personally or professionally.

Both of my parents were doctors, so the doctor piece feels very organic to me and familiar. Now I went to law school; what's ironic is I don't think I've ever played a lawyer. I've played cops and FBI agents and CSI agents, so law enforcement. But I've never played a lawyer.

Has there ever been a surprising experience on set with someone in terms of a reaction to your background and education? Of course you'd hope everyone would be curious or admire it, but sometimes people don't respond the way you might expect.

Not really. Because I don't talk about it much. Sometimes people bring it up, but I think that most people I work with don't necessarily know my background. They're not familiar with it. You'd have to look me up and do research to know that. The vast majority of the time it doesn't ever come up.

You have many credits, including but not limited to some of what we've discussed, that tackle race. Obviously this is a big question. How do you feel about the ways in which material like this helps advance the conversation about race? "Get on the Bus" is 25 years old. There have been strides in some ways since then, but there are countless things that should be way better than they are. If you look at a movie like Spike Lee's "Chi-Raq," I thought that was really thought-provoking and different and impactful, but sometimes movies like that only get seen by a small audience. Representation is good, and it's better to have material than not have it. But how do you feel when you look at the work of the '90s and today and the way that this stuff advances the conversation or doesn't?

118

It's tough because when I look back at the work of the '90s and all the different filmmakers, the different voices, I feel like in certain ways we were further along then than now. There was an ability to look at nuance, an ability to show characters that are multi-faceted, diverse in different ways. I look at the independent films I did in the '90s. To me, a film like "The Nephew," films like "The Visit," a film like "Loving Jezebel," a film like "Love, Sex and Eating the Bones," those are all films that to me present these really interesting, multi-faceted characters that the story and the characterization is not specifically about race but about the character that is this Black person or person of color or multi-racial person or what have you and living life. And to me that is so much more rich and interesting than doing projects that are specifically just race-driven so to speak as far as the story. Obviously race is a part of it, but only one part that informs the character's reality and how people react and respond to the character. So to me I don't feel or see the progression that I would have expected to see and would have liked to have seen. Spike's work, and we'll use Spike as an example, Spike's work back then, when it comes to race and issues around race, was so much richer and deeper and better than, for instance, what's the movie with John David Washington?

"BlackKklansman."

Yeah. To me, "Do the Right Thing" [1989] and "BlackKklansman," they're not even close. "Do the Right Thing" is probably one of the greatest films ever made. I would put it in the Top 3, minimum Top 5, of greatest films of all time. And then you have another film like "BlackKklansman" by the same filmmaker taking on race, violence, and other things, and to me that's one of the best comparisons of how the depth of the work in this area has not improved. It's actually gotten worse.

Why has that happened? Is that a reflection or industry changes or society as a whole? What's the explanation for why you feel like things used to be better?

And if I could answer that question, you'd call me a genius. I have no idea why we're regressing. I think part of it has to do with a whole systemic movement toward dumbing people down. Just fundamentally speaking, the last 40 years we've taken so much money out of the public school system, and there's been so much emphasis on just how can you squeeze as much money out of people as possible? So therefore you come up with the idea you make people more stupid, and you take their money. And therefore if you make something that's nuanced and rich, you'll never make money off of it. So people realize, "Oh, if I make dumb material that speaks to the least among us, or the least thought-provoking, then I'll make more money." And unfortunately that's the world we're in right now with the proliferation of misinformation, the proliferation of really poor entertainment products, the proliferation of stupidity.

And if we believe this art can have a positive social impact, it stands to reason that to not have that strong material, then society is potentially not growing in tandem.

Without question! It's atrophying. And people are being taken advantage of. More is not better. Just because there's more ways to look at videos and more ways to consume content doesn't mean the content is better. [Laughs] Unfortunately.

On the concept of where our heads are at about things, it must have been something to go from a show like "Married with Children," which I know was a great opportunity for you and involved some difficult circumstances about leaving—

And the fact that I beat out Dave Chappelle for that role! I mean, that's pretty awesome.

Absolutely. What I wanted to ask you was about the portrait of masculinity within that show compared to the work you did in just the few years after it. Looking at it now, which of course is 25-30 years later, it seems like a remarkable whiplash. Of course hindsight is 20/20 and it's easy to say, "You could never get away with that now, and you shouldn't." But at the time did you feel aware of this jarring difference between the voice of a show like "Married with Children" compared to some of the other work you did that was exploring masculinity in a really different and non-misogynist way?

To be honest, not really. Because I think comedy, and necessarily so, has to hold its own space. If you're worried about who you're insulting in comedy, then you're ultimately not going to be funny. And part of doing comedy is that folks are going to get insulted and are going to be made fun of. And that's comedy, and that's where some of it comes out of. People used to say Richard Pryor insulted people and enraged people and angered people. And I'm not in any way comparing "Married with Children" to Richard Pryor. But at the end of the day it's still comedy. I love the fact that the head writer on "Married with Children" was Black, and nobody knew it. That's impressive. And the fact that the original pilot of "Married with Children" was called "Not the Cosbys." It was going to be a Black family, but they changed it to a white family. Which is sad, right? One of the most successful, long-running sitcoms could've been another Black sitcom that could've been making fun of Black families. "Married with Children" was a huge opportunity for me, and I lost it because I was attempting to do other things. There's a whole story behind that. But I look back with fondness because I fought to get that role. I fought so hard. I brought cookies, I brought gumbo. It was crazy.

And this is all hindsight. It was an extremely popular show, and people laughed at it at the time. To play devil's advocate when you talk about comedy, to me so much of it derives from asking what is the target, and if someone is making fun of someone are they being taken to task? Or is the laugh track just going along with that? That show is known for doing a lot of fat-shaming of women, and the audience

laughing along. It's notable the ways that people justify to themselves about laughing at certain things. I feel like the questions should be who is the target, and why am I laughing? Those weren't being asked in the '90s, so it can be useful to think about how to perceive that now.

Yeah, I agree with you. And obviously there's always a way to be smarter. And I think that asking those questions pushes a person to be even smarter with their comedy. Because there's not only one way to make people laugh, and that's to insult people or a group of people. You can figure out new and different ways to do it, and the more that those questions are asked, the more I think comedic minds are pushed to come up with better and better and more nuanced comedy. But at the same time, that has to be tempered with a thought process of, "Hey, can I still make people laugh and not be too precious?" I never want to be precious with my acting, as an example. I want to play characters truthfully. So the point that you're making now is similar to a point that was made in a speech I gave. Someone stood up and said, "Hill, you said that you never do characters and projects that are denigrating to Black people, but you played a drug dealer in 'In Too Deep,' and that's insulting and a glorification of the drug community." I was like, "No." I said, "If you listen to what I say, I said I don't play characters that participate in films that the overarching message is denigrating. I don't judge the character. I want to play bad guys. I want to play the character that does the wrong thing at the wrong time. I want to play the character that says horrible things because that's truthful to that character. Now if the film at the end glorifies that horrific behavior, and that's to your point about a laugh track, if it glorifies that without checking it, then that's not good. And I totally agree with you. If "In Too Deep" would have ended up with LL Cool J and myself in a hot tub drinking champagne saying, "Dealing drugs is good," as opposed to what happens is we actually have a comeuppance for our activity and the person who was doing the right thing actually gets the benefit in the movie, then I wouldn't have done that film. And so it's really about, to me, the overarching message more so than the individual character or act. So we have to be careful with that. And the reverse is true too. There are movies that I think are some of the most denigrating films in history to Black men, to the Black male, people celebrate as great films and folks have won awards for participating in. I sit back and say, "How could this even be? This film is treacherous in the message it sends." But we have to look at it and say, "The performances are good; the actors were good. But the actual message of the film"— and I'm talking about right now a movie like "Monster's Ball"—"is one of the most insulting and denigrating messages to Black men in the history of filmmaking." And it's horrific. Yet awards were given out for that film. So I get it. I completely agree with you that being able to look at things historically and take them to task is important. But at the same time not being too precious is important as well.

Megan Cavanagh of 'A League of Their Own,' 'Robin Hood: Men in Tights,' 'Friends'

If you haven't seen 1992's "A League of Their Own" in a while, your memories of Marla Hooch might just go to the moment in which the news reel adoringly/leeringly covers many of the other players on the Rockford Peaches only to show Marla at a distance and declare awkwardly, "Marla Hooch … what a hitter!"

But 1. Watching the movie through adult eyes of course adds better understanding about how the movie comments on sexism rather than perpetuating it to get a laugh and 2. In fact, Marla, the talented, switch-hitting second basewoman played by Megan Cavanagh, gets a major introduction early in the film, scouted and ultimately recruited after Dottie (Geena Davis) and her sister Kit (Lori Petty) ensure that the scout (Jon Lovitz) doesn't pass on Marla just because he prioritizes the players' appearance over their abilities. The moment in which Marla tells her dad, "I'm not going to know anybody," before leaving for an opportunity that changes her life (becoming a star player and meeting her husband) is beautiful and heartbreaking, and an important scene that elevates the moving film's emotional stakes.

In addition to appearing in a short-lived "League" TV series, two Mel Brooks spoofs ("Robin Hood: Men in Tights," "Dracula: Dead and Loving It"), underrated ("I Love Trouble") and, um, never-adored ("Junior," "For Richer or Poorer") comedies, and many popular '90s-era sitcoms ("Friends," "Home Improvement," "Will and Grace"), she also spent years as the voice of Jimmy Neutron's mom, more than a decade touring with "Menopause the Musical," and, proudly, is a Chicago-area native like I am. We spoke for an hour and 40 minutes and could have gone twice as long.

What's something you feel nostalgic for from the '90s? It could be anything.

Let's see, my son was a baby. I'm very nostalgic for that. [Laughs] That era didn't have a lot of cell phones. I was grateful for more face-to-face time with people. And meeting people in their office. And I know there are some perks to not having that now, but I miss that. We're all tied to our telephones now, and I miss having that freedom. I miss the pool that I had in my backyard. [Laughs] Gosh, what do I miss about the '90s? Let's see, I miss Bill Clinton. [Laughs] I'm joking. Although it doesn't seem like it's all that long ago, it's so long ago. I miss my son being little, and he was little in the '90s. We had such good times.

We used to take him to this little place to play in the big ball pit. I miss those times of playing with him. But the actual '90s themselves, I don't know that I miss a whole lot. Oh, I know what I miss: I miss sitcoms! I miss the audience laugh track. I love that. Now it's all one-camera, which is great in its own way, but I miss the old-fashioned sitcoms.

Why are you pro-laugh track?

Well, it's not so much the laugh track—it was sort of like theater. You started in front of an audience. You could stop, which you can't do in theater, but it was more theatrical in that you went through the scenes to the end. And I like having a through line and not doing things out of order, although I'm happy to do things out of order. I just liked them. They were fun to do, it was fun for the audience. It was more of a connection. Really, what I'm talking about with all of this, is connection. I miss the connection between the audience and the actor, and between just friends and not being on our cell phones all the time. It's been a godsend during COVID, but I just feel like people are buried in them in a way. And I miss the connection of having a little kid and playing with him. Those days are over.

And you touched on that this type of connection speaks to people's professional lives, personal lives, and their relationship with entertainment too. On that note, when you think of the movies from that era, can you think of something that you weren't in that means a lot to you? Either you keep turning to it, or you always watch it when it's on?

I always watch whenever it's on and I catch it … it starred Tim Robbins and it was about prison: "The Shawshank Redemption." I always watch that. It doesn't matter what part of it's on. If it's on, I catch it, I watch it. I loved "Ferris Bueller's Day Off." [1986] That's a good one too. Oh, "Thelma and Louise," oh my god. That one really had an impact on me.

How come?

There are so few movies with female leads that they're strong. Of course they do end up dying in the end. But there just weren't that many movies with two female stars. That was something as a young woman that I guess I was yearning for in a way that I didn't even know I was yearning for until I watched it and I was like, "Oh my god, why aren't there more movies with women?" Granted, they were on the lam and they were running, but they were strong characters, and they had a lot at stake. And it was acted really well. I love Geena Davis, I love Susan Sarandon, and they were both amazing in that movie. And then "Fried Green Tomatoes," it was sort of a similar thing. It was strong female characters, and you don't realize that you want that until you're watching it. I'd always known there were more men in movies than there were women and all that, but you don't realize you miss it until you're seeing it. And then there's an inner response that just kind of lights you up and goes, "Wow, that was amazing, and it was women!" [Laughs] It sounds so dumb, but it's true. I guess it's what Geena Davis is doing now, with the work that she's doing with helping

123

cartoons include more diversity, more girls. She went to the cartoon makers and said, "Hey, in this scene there's only three females in this crowd scene." Subliminally, the message that's getting across is there isn't very much representation of girls. And they went, "Oh, wow, we didn't even realize that." And they started to include more girls and people of color, so everybody's included. I guess that was when I started to be more aware of my—I'm going to call it feminism back in the '90s. I kind of woke up a little bit about that.

Sure, that recognition of bias. It would be so nice if after "Thelma and Louise" and "Fried Green Tomatoes" we could say, "Then everything changed." But it's 30 years later, and we're like, "Well, maybe people are noticing some things now."

[Laughs] Right! We thought when we did "A League of Their Own," this is the beginning of—"Thelma and Louise" had just come out, and we did "A League of Their Own," which is a hugely female cast, and we thought, "This is it. This is the beginning." And now here we are, almost 30 years later, and not so much. It's unfortunate. But there's been other good things that have happened I feel like. Don't make me name 'em! [Laughs]

No, we will not try to capture the history of feminism in 30 seconds. And hopefully it would take longer than that anyway. So regarding "A League of Their Own," I want to start with you doing your own hitting and defense for the movie, and learning to be a switch hitter. It seems you went through some things the other cast chose not to do or didn't have to do. What do you remember about that process that you feel like you haven't talked about a lot?

Well, we all had to go to baseball training for about two months. And it was Monday through Friday, every day, and we all worked really hard. It called for my character to switch-hit. So while I was working on switch hitting, Tracy Reiner was working on pitching, and so was Lori Petty. It depended on what your character needed to do. And all of us, when they cast everybody, they needed to be "trainable." I'm putting that in air quotes right now. You had to have some baseball skill, and they had to be able to feel like they could train you to do more. And everybody, in whatever category they were in, worked really hard in that category. Because we were representing these women from the '40s, we just really wanted to make sure that it looked as authentic as possible, and we wanted to do them proud. I know I've said that a million times, but that is the truth. When I auditioned for the movie, I had been working with my roommate, who was a friend and was a trainer, on switch hitting. So when I got to the training for the movie, I already had some switch-hitting ability, but I never would have done that if it wasn't for the audition. I wanted to be able to do it because they're making me play baseball first before having me read, and I wanted to have my skills honed so that I could get a reading, so I could get an audition. I have told the story of when I went to go bat in the gym as Marla and they had made me come from another set and sent me in a police escort at 100 miles an hour, and when I got there [director] Penny [Marshall] says, "OK, we're going to have Megan's double do it." And I was like, "Whoa! You guys just raced me here. Please let me do that. Please give me a chance." And Penny, her knowledge of baseball and what went into it, was not her forte. She said to me,

"OK, hit every ball." And I was hitting off of a live pitcher. To ask that of a major league baseball player, you can't really ask that. So I was like, "Oh, god, here we go." If I didn't do well, they were going to bring my double in and let her do it, or try to do it. So I said a little prayer, and I went in. I did whatever I could to make contact with the ball. It didn't matter if it was the worst pitch in the world. And I did; I made contact with the pitches. It was such a surreal experience. And my arms were aching because I had taken so many swings. I don't know how many I did. It was hours' worth. The canister would run out, and they'd put in a new one. That was the only break I got between the loading and unloading of the canisters. The next day when I came to the set, they gave me a trophy that said "Batting champion." And we did a couple of other things, and Penny made an announcement, "Megan, we're not going to use any of the doubles footage. It's going to be only you." I said thank you. I worked really hard. I was doing 80 miles an hour on both sides by the time I did that scene, in the gym. And I was really proud of my accomplishment with that because it's really hard. We had really good coaches at USC. And some of them came with us and they continued on at Illinois Institute of Technology because we were shooting in Illinois first. Rod Dedeaux, god rest his soul, was the head of the USC baseball department, and he was our guy. He was the head of the whole thing. And we had some really great training. We had a lot of fun and a lot of injuries. Just talking about it just seems like a surreal, different time in my life. It was a literal dream come true. I got to play at Wrigley. I'm a Chicago Cubs fan; I'm going to cry talking about it! It was so moving. I was able to bring my dad to a closed set at Wrigley. All of that. It was the closest thing to a religious experience that people talk about, but in a real-life situation. [Laughs]

That whole process must have been so extraordinary for you. As part of that training, you obviously had some experience and potentially more comfort level than some of the others, as well as different demands for the character. Do you remember anything any of the cast talked about while that training process was going on and any successes or difficulties anyone had?

Sure. Debra Winger was our captain before Geena Davis came in. Debra Winger was originally cast, and she was amazing. She was a UCLA Bruins fan, so when we were playing at USC, she felt like it was [enemy] territory. [Laughs] So she rented out UCLA one day, and we all played there for a day. Some gals came in with more experience. Rosie O'Donnell is a great ballplayer. Freddie Simpson was a great ballplayer. Some of the gals, what we called the back five, who made up the rest of the team but didn't have lines, I guess they were considered extras, but they were with us the entire time. We were a team. So Robin Knight and Patti Pelton, all those extra five gals, they were all great ballplayers. Bitty Schram, who plays Evelyn, she was a tennis junior pro. And Madonna and Geena came in at the very tail end of the training because they were cast last. Because Debra ended up leaving, and Geena took her place. And Madonna got cast, and Madonna and Geena didn't have any real baseball training. Obviously Madonna's an athlete. Geena went on to become an Olympic archer. [Laughs] And everybody worked really hard. So during the training, we would get there in the morning and stretch and they would have different things for us to do. Some people would be doing weights, some people would be doing drills, and it was baseball training. Sliding, playing pepper, shagging balls, taking grounders. And they would work on our technique. And I had only played 16-inch softball in Chicago; that was my only training. I had never played baseball with a glove. Ever. Or softball. And I had been in track and volleyball, and I rode my bike incessantly. So I was an athlete. And I believed I could do it. That might sound crazy, but I had this whole visualization thing going on during this whole time of, "I'm the greatest baseball player in the whole world." I was really doing a lot of mantra-ing for baseball. I just wanted to be the best baseball player I could be. And I'm not a great fielder. My hitting is way better than my fielding. I'm OK, but I'm not as good as some of the other girls were. The throw from first to third, I couldn't do it at the beginning. Rosie could, Freddie could, Lori Petty could. Just a couple of gals could do that throw. And by the time we were done, I could. But it was work. And it was a lot of fun. And a lot of work.

Madonna is great in the role, but I sort of wish for your sake that the late arrivals would have been Geena Davis and Susan Sarandon to blow your mind that Thelma and Louise just showed up for the movie you're doing.

Oh my god. Listen, it was so surreal. Geena had just won an Academy Award, and Madonna was at the height of her career at that point. So it became a media circus. We would go to a baseball game as the whole team, and the whole stadium you could watch heads snap looking. Because I'm with Tom Hanks and Madonna and we're all walking in, and the whole stadium was like the wave but with heads. Of smiling heads turning and looking. We could only stay for a few minutes, and we had to leave early because the fandom was intense. So Madonna, her double had her exact body. It was crazy. I'm so sorry I can't remember people's names. I have it written down; I should've gotten that out before I talked to you. But her double did the run, when she runs the bases. And did the slide. And then they show Madonna sliding. Madonna slid, but not as full-blast running the way the double did.

Speaking of Tom Hanks, he is widely regarded as one of the nicest people in the galaxy, and this movie is a rare example of him at his angriest and meanest at times, in the "There's no crying in baseball" scene and him being furious on and off the bus. Since I don't believe he stays in character the whole time, what do you remember of seeing him switch from being extremely nice to being so cruel?

I think that he might stay in character for some of his more dramatic stuff possibly, but this was a total fun project for him. He was with all women, and he gets to eat as much as he wants. He was pretty happy. [Laughs] And he would make any kind of tense set situation, he could make it, just by joking around, he knew the exact appropriate amount to do it. So that scene in the dugout where he spits onto David Strathairn's shoe, and it's so gross, he transitioned pretty easily from nice guy to doing his job. He was really well prepared. Everybody was. Everybody was on their game, for real. Pun intended. He transitioned easily. We had a day where it was pretty tense, toward the end of the shoot, and we were doing some bus footage. It was Penny's birthday. It was in October, and there was a joke about they were going to rent a helicopter and fly in because they were keeping us on set and we could never go to our trailers because our trailers were so far away. There was a joke about how we were prisoners. And Geena had T-shirts made for all of us in graffiti spray paint that said "Free the Peaches." It was just a joke among all of us. And it was Penny's birthday, and we were doing the bus scene where he kisses Pauline Brailsford, the chaperone, and all of that stuff, and somebody had hired a bagpipist to come over the hills to do "Happy birthday" for Penny. And it was a tense day. It wasn't a good day for something like that to be happening. [Laughs] So a bagpipist is playing, and Tom grabbed me and we started dancing to it. He just made everything better all the time. He just did. He knew how to do it. He was close enough to Penny to be able to move her out of her seriousness that she was in. He's great. I cannot say enough nice things about this guy. He taught me set etiquette. He taught me how to be an actor on a film set by watching him and the way that he conducted himself. I just love him. I don't know anybody who doesn't.

I've never thought of a way to evaluate a day or a moment as, "Would it be fun or weird if someone showed up with a bagpipe right now?" But I like that.

We had been together for so long. We had been together for four and a half months at that time. Madonna couldn't get MTV, which was a problem because that was a huge thing for her. Everybody had been together too long, and only with each other. It wasn't contentious, but it wasn't all rosy. And it was hard because you wanted to go back to your trailer and relax, and you couldn't. So there was that element. So Geena, she's frickin' awesome and Mensa and funny, and making those T-shirts for us was also a way to lighten the mood. But she didn't have the relationship with Penny the way that Tom did. Tom had done "Big" with her. She asked him to do this part. It was originally cast with Daryl Hannah and Jim Belushi when Fox was doing it and David Anspaugh was directing. That had been a cast that had been cast a year before, but then it got shelved because Penny really wanted to direct it and produce it. So those guys didn't end up being in the movie. In fact very few of the people that were cast that first year were in it. I think Freddie was one of them. Maybe Tracy Reiner, who played Betty Spaghetti, I think they were originally cast, but I don't know that anybody else was. So Penny had asked Tom to do this, and he was on the rise. "Philadelphia" came after then, and that was when he won his first Academy Award. He was definitely a well-known celebrity, just wasn't as A-list as he is now. Now he's the king! [Laughs] Back then he was only the prince. And, listen, I don't want to make it sound like Penny was always in a bad mood. She wasn't. She just had a lot on her plate. She was directing a period piece outdoors. The amount of variables that go with that [Laughs] is a lot. If it was a cloudy day, we were going to do some of the dirty scenes. If it was a clear day, we were going to do some of the clean scenes. But then clouds came in, "Get 'em dirty." And we'd go get dirty and we'd have to put on our dirty outfits and get all our Polaroids. That's how they did it back then, for continuity. And get the little dirt bag, you got dirt on your knee, dirt on your cheek. And we come out and the clouds will have parted and now it's sunny. "Get 'em clean." Go back in, take all that off, wash it all off, fix up, come back out, the clouds have come back, "Get 'em dirty." "Get 'em clean." This happened all day. And Penny was out of her mind. Just seeing the dollar signs [Laughs] due to the amount of time wasted that we didn't even get a shot, she was literally rolling on the ground. Like beating her chest jokingly, "Why did I do this picture, oh god why did I do this picture?" Because it was just so much of that. And people got hurt. Somebody broke their nose, and people were going to the hospital for dehydration. [Laughs] It was a shitshow. [Laughs] Don't quote me on that; I'm just joking with you on that. It was a difficult shoot at times. [Laughs]

Certainly. That's what goes into anything, and with that much to do, people forget how stressful it is to execute. Of course, one of Marla's most memorable moments is the "It Had to Be You" performance. Was that done and directed with the same chaos and anxiety, or was there more stillness to it?

Generally anything indoors was controlled. So there was less craziness. It was the outdoor baseball in the heat, 90 degrees, 98 percent humidity in Kentucky and Indiana, that was the harder part. Middle of summer, all day long. People were getting sunburned; you could never sunburn because continuity-wise, you can't have sunburn. So there was a lot of applying sunscreen. There was always fussing over people, hair, makeup. That's more of what the stress was, the outdoor stuff. When we were inside, it ran beautifully. And that scene was shot at FitzGerald's in Berwyn, and I grew up in Oak Park/River Forest area, and Berwyn is a neighboring suburb. And the people that own FitzGerald's, I had played volleyball with one of the owners in high school. It was hometown girl does good. I came to Chicago, and people came to see Madonna, and they saw me. They were like, "Megan!" These were kids I went to high school with. So there was a lot of good feeling for me at that time because we had shot a bunch of stuff. I was getting good buzz from the people on the set saying, "Penny really likes you, and she's going to help you get a good agent." That kind of stuff. So that was all feeling really good. And when we actually did it, my parents were able to come. It was a closed set, but they were able to be there. The scene in the bar—first of all, there was so much more on the page that we shot that didn't end up in the movie. I mean, a lot more. We of course filmed it all. It was just amazing. And Penny's direction—when I did the crying in the train station, Penny was super helpful because she's an actor's director. She knows what it's like to have to cry in a scene. She shoots a lot of footage, and we shot a ton and I couldn't cry anymore. I was all cried out. So she gave me ammonia tablets. She was like *[in Penny Marshall voice]*, "When I say action, you pop it." I was like, "OK." I must have done—I don't know how many tablets. Dozens. I smelled like ammonia. And I had to eat in a scene later and all I could do was smell ammonia and I was drinking huge glasses of milk.

Oh my god!

Yeah, it was crazy. But it was my first movie. I would have done anything. I was so grateful to be there and part of a historical telling of—it was fiction, but a lot of it was based on truth—these women who had absolutely no recognition of them until this movie happened. I couldn't even find anything written about them in the library. And my mom was a librarian helping me trying to find stuff. Because you couldn't Google back then.

[Laughs] And we were telling this very important story about women in baseball. So there was a lot riding on all of it. And I just felt so grateful to be there I would have done anything. And I did. [Laughs] I did do just about anything. And I hear the song "This Used to Be My Playground," that Madonna does, talking about it gets me choked up. Some of the AAGPBL gals were with us while we were shooting, and they were reminiscing and showing us scrapbooks, and now I'm the age that they were. And I got to talk to some of the people from Amazon who are creating "A League of Their Own," the new series that's going to be coming out, and realizing I'm now in the position of Pepper. It's so beautiful and sad and wonderful and odd. That I'm in my sixth decade of life and I'm reminiscing about this amazing time that I got to play baseball and get paid a lot of money and do a movie.

This sort of seems obvious, but I definitely feel like watching the movie again recently made me appreciate how much it's about rising above sexism. Watching the "Marla Hooch, what a hitter" moment now, I saw the sexism of the news story done about the team that's sexist toward all of them. But I bet when people think about the movie they think about that line as going for a laugh at her expense.

Oh, they absolutely do. And they'll say things like, "Oh, you're so pretty. You're so much prettier." I was acting. I was trying to be a homely girl. [Laughs] When I get to the bar, I thought I looked pretty snazzy. I thought I looked pretty good in that scene. [Laughs] But absolutely, "Marla, what a hitter!" People yell that, and they mean well. And here's the other thing: I was talking to somebody recently, and they were saying, "How do you deal with any negative comments on social media?" I said, "First of all, I'm not on it very much. But when I do appearances, it's a love fest. This character is so beloved. That overrides anything personal in my life that somebody might not like." I feel so lucky that I haven't really had to deal with that. And because she was considered a homely or ugly girl or whatever, there are young women who are Marlas or feel they are Marlas even if they aren't, which most young women do. Nobody feels confident and beautiful about themselves generally. So there's a love fest in that regard of, "You portrayed us, all of us, women who are insecure about ourselves, and you overcame it through teamwork and the love of the team and then having a partner that loves me." When it first came out, I used to say, "I like to play ugly girls, and I'm laughing all the way to the bank." But that took a toll. It absolutely took a toll of playing the—and I'm saying air quotes—"ugly girl." The way that writers would write definitions of characters back then. "She's a two-bagger." They would say horrible things about parts that I was reading for. And I had to overlook that, or not audition for it, depending on what it was. And rise above it. Because I was trying to really play the reality of what growing up and being insecure about yourself, which I knew how to do. I have a confident exterior, but I know that vulnerability, and even men do too. I don't want to speak for men, but I know tons of women who all felt that, and I think that's what makes it loved, that there's a real sharing, an understanding of that within ourselves. I used to say I don't care about that, but I do know the toll—there were just little things that got in. I gained weight and thought, "It doesn't matter because the parts I play are chubby, average gals." But it wasn't good for me and my health. There were a lot of little, insidious ways [about] playing characters who are considered the "less than," if you will, in a movie. Do you get what I'm saying?

Definitely. And similarly to what I was saying about the change in perspective about what the joke is in the news item about Marla Hooch, if you go in for an audition and someone describes the character, they're not having much empathy or seeing the person as a person by just describing them as "a two-bagger." Is that what you mean by taking a toll?

Yeah. The insensitivity, which now has been rectified, that's the toll. It's the feeling, first of all, that they're calling me to play this part because that's how they see me. When I knew that I was more than that. But slowly you do enough of those and it tends to chip away: Do I really know that about myself? It started to chip away my confidence and my self-esteem. Listen, I'm grateful for all the stuff I've gotten to do and the characters I've been lucky enough to play, and that has been my signature in a way, my media signature, is to play these kind of characters. Now, as a woman in her sixth decade, I am totally beyond happy. I feel the opportunities that were given to me, I feel I embraced them and ran with it, and I am grateful for every single second. I don't regret any of it. Even though I've done some parts that I'm not all that proud of, I'm still grateful for even the ones that were [Laughs] not the best. Not my best work. Or not the best movie. I'm grateful for all of 'em because even the failures make up your backbone. It's all part of it. It's all good. It's all part of the weave of the fabric. Lots of metaphors here; let's just do 'em all.

So if you don't mind me asking, when you talk about the psychological impact of those roles or the way people were talking to you, what was the solution for you to overcome that? Was it to not take the role, to speak up in a different way, or just treating yourself differently?

Booking a job is an accomplishment in itself. So if I went out for one of those kinds of roles and I booked it, I felt good. I looked beyond the description that they were donning me and hoped that I was bringing a little bit more heart to the character than the one-dimensional person they wrote on the paper. And I think that's partly why I booked it too. I think in their description perhaps they were just doing it as a joke or not seeing her with any depth, but then I brought depth to whatever it was. I'm not saying that all my roles were deep, I'm just saying that I tried to make her a more three-dimensional character than a one-dimensional character. And I think that's probably why I would book. Yes, I had the look they wanted, but I brought more to the party. Not to toot my own horn here, but I am a person, and I am bringing a person to you. I'm not bringing you a joke. Do you know what I mean?

For sure.

OK. So even though subliminally your definition of who you wanted may not be kind, I also [rose above it] mostly. Mostly I got over it because I booked a job and I was working, and I wanted to be an actor my entire life. That's all I wanted to be. So this was a challenge, and this is what you were presenting me, this is what I'm going to do. And there were things that I did turn down because the character was not well developed. If they had a bad description and she wasn't well developed, I wasn't going to go down that road. I didn't want to play the joke. And I think that depending on the editing and all that, you could end up being a joke if that's what the director saw. But that's not what I wanted to do. I was classically trained; I'm a trained actor, and I want to do good roles. Who doesn't? And I wish that I could've done some drama in my life. I've only done comedic stuff, and I'm grateful that I got to, but I never got to really cross over and do any drama.

Dare I ask, was there a description of a character that you turned down that was so terrible it was unforgettable?

I don't remember the name of the project. It was the one with the two-bagger. I don't think it ever got made, or maybe it went straight to video. I don't know. It was horrible. She gets raped. And the way she gets treated in the script was like she's a piece of property. And I was like, "Absolutely not. Not doing this! It's not going to do anything for me, it's not going to do anything for the audience. Not doin' it." [Laughs] I use that as an example because that was the worst example, but there were other slights of description of actresses that were ugly or whatever. It was just an insensitivity in the way of describing the character and making her one-dimensional, or a one-dimensional description, let me put it that way. As an actor it's your job to be able to breathe life into a character that's a person that you care about, even if it is written like Marla was kinda. I think that Penny, who also had played characters who were not the pretty girl, understood this. She had a real understanding of who Marla was. And the scene where the bus driver throws dirt in the face of the chaperone, every time I've ever seen it I've gasped at that moment. It's just the worst moment; I can't believe it made it into the movie. I just feel like it belongs in a different movie. I feel like Pauline's character kind of got the brunt of that. She played her not one-dimensionally, but there were a lot of jokes at her expense. "I loved you in 'The Wizard of Oz,'" and she gets dirt in her face from the bus driver, and she's throwing up when Madonna poisons her so we can all go to the Suds Bucket. That character took a lot of hits, if you will. We don't get to see her go off and have some fulfillment in her life. Like Marla does. By the way, I just have to tell you this so that you know: Marla would have never left the league to get married. And in the original script she did not. It was in the editing that they made that happen. So just know that. She was traded to be near her husband Nelson, who makes cheese. She gets traded to Racine, which is the team that Lori Petty's character, Kit, gets traded to. I get traded first, and then Lori's character gets traded, and we're on the same team for the big game at the end, the world championship. And my character gets hurt, Geena Davis' character, Dottie, runs into Marla, flips her and sends her to the hospital and she's pregnant and she's going to lose the baby. It was this huge, big story that went on! Because my character was the fourth lead in this movie. My name was between Tom and Madonna on the call sheet. This character had way more stuff in it. And when they first put it together, it was like a two-and-a-half-hour-long movie, and they had to cut a bunch of stuff. So that all ended up getting cut, which was fine for the story. Quite frankly, being my first movie, I would have been happy if I was one of the players on the team that didn't have any lines. I was just so happy to be in that movie! [Laughs] Just wanted you to know that.

I'm happy you mentioned that. I also wanted to talk a little about "Robin Hood: Men in Tights." Maybe genres and subgenres are something people make too big of a deal out of, but since you worked on two Mel Brooks movies, can you pinpoint anything that feels different about making a spoof versus a comedy that's not a spoof, or is there no difference in how that gets done?

Um, that's a really good question. I played Broomhilde—if I was in "Game of Thrones" and that character played the maid to somebody, I played her, I mean it was a comedy, but I think I would have played her similarly. Maid Marian was her entire job, and she devoted her entire life to her to make sure she stayed safe and all of that. I think playing a spoof is funner; there's a lot of fun stuff that happens on the set of a spoof that happens compared to a non-spoof movie. And it was the only movie where I got to watch dailies because Mel encourages that. He likes to hear people react to different things, and it was the one and only movie that I ever saw myself during. That was fun. I don't know; it's hard to say because it's all based on the script, what it calls for and what you need to do. Working on "Robin Hood: Men in Tights" and "Dracula: Dead and Loving It," now, looking back, I worked with one of the greatest comedic directors of all time. Who really started the genre of breaking the fourth wall and all that. I don't know if there were directors, maybe in Europe, who did that. But he's the one who started that. So "Airplane!" couldn't have happened [without him]. He created that whole genre. And I got to work with him, and he's an amazing person as well as a director. I've seen some of the movies that I hadn't seen when I did "Robin Hood." I had never seen some of his previous movies. Obviously I had seen "Blazing Saddles" and "Young Frankenstein," but I don't think I had seen any of the other ones. Maybe I saw "Spaceballs." I don't know if that answered your question, Matt.

Sure. I figured it could be the same but just wanted to put that out there. And I wanted to briefly pick up the thread we had going before: Part of what makes Mel Brooks movies so successful is the menschiness he brings to it, the good-hearted innocence. So I ask this not to call anyone out, but to the point you made before about bringing humanity to the character, Broomhilde has a lot of moments in the movie and you're impactful in anything you do, but were there any conversations about either the moment the horse doesn't want her to jump on him or that Little John can throw a heavy beam but can't hold Broomhilde? Those moments don't feel as emotionally generous as other material. Is that ever talked about? Or do you just think about it, note it and move on?

[Laughs] I think about it, note it and move on. When I shot that movie, I wasn't that heavy. I was wearing a suit. A Santa suit, actually, under my outfit. I was in a theater company; it was probably two or three years before I did "Robin Hood: Men in Tights." And the artistic director of this company wanted me to wear a fat suit, and I was totally insulted. I was like, "I'm not wearing a fat suit! This character, it's not about her weight!"

132

We got into this whole thing. And for Mel Brooks, "Oh, yeah, I'll put on a fat suit and do my little dance and do whatever you need me to do." "I'm prostituting myself for Mel Brooks, but I'm not going to do it for you." [Laughs] Where is the line, right? Where do you draw the line? To not have been a heavy person when I did that, I was being insensitive in a way because I was not cognizant of—let me put it this way: Right now, I don't think that people that are wearing suits that make them look heavy—I'm not going to call it the other [term]—they are not looked upon very well right now. Or playing outside of your range and that kind of stuff. They want everything authentic now. Which I think there's reasons for that. So playing Broomhilde and not being heavy, I was sort of in on the joke. I feel like I was sort of making, "Well, I'm not fat …" So I could laugh along with what was being done in a way, even though it wasn't conscious. I'm probably going to get a lot of hate mail for this. [Laughs] There was no discussion around it, no. Absolutely not. The discussion was more about the German accent and making sure that that was good. I had to take German accent lessons, dialect lessons with a really great coach. Because when the audition happened for this, my agent called me and said, "They are looking for a big woman. They want her to be really imposing and to be heavy, and I know you're not. So can you just go and stuff some clothing in your shirt and make your arms look big?" I'm like, "I'm not doing that. But I will buy a Santa suit from Western costumes," which I did. So I went to the audition—this is what they tell you never to do—but they were asking for it, and I had the complete blessing of my agent, so I went dressed as the character. I had on a big Santa suit, I had on this big toga, burlappy kind of dress, I put my braids up on top of my head in the way that they are in the movie, and I went in with a German accent to meet Mel Brooks. And he was so taken aback. And I got the job on the spot. So that totally paid off for me, but it's so not recommended to do that, and I haven't done it since. And it was only because they were specifically looking for that. He wanted that suit that I rented. He bought that suit from Western costumes, the Santa suit. So I brought that to the movie because they wanted somebody big and I needed to be as big as possible, and I thought, "I'm not going to do this half-assed; I'm going to go and get a suit." And it paid off. But, no, there was no discussion of—there's discussion about it now, which is great. The pendulum has swung completely in the other direction, and everybody's really being looked at and taken care of now. But at that time it wasn't even an issue

Times change as they should, and it can be a surreal experience to see something with new eyes. It's almost hard to imagine something being the way that it was. Whether the moments in "Robin Hood: Men in Tights," or in "Friends," which you did an episode of, which like many sitcoms has a backstory about Monica previously being heavier, with countless jokes as if that's a punchline. I would hope no one was trying to be actively cruel, but when something is an institutionalized object of humor, I had to ask you about it. It must be so strange to be on the inside of this; it's not Broomhilde's only moment in the movie, but why did she have to be mocked this way?

As time has moved forward from that time to now and we've become more sensitive to other people, I still feel like being overweight is the last bastion of jokes. People don't tell racist jokes anymore, and thank god. But being overweight is still—it's the last category to make fun of. It's interesting. I was watching Turner Classic Movies with my dad the other day, and they were showing "Gone with the Wind," and beforehand they did this little blurb and saying—they're trying to be really appropriate, and they're trying to explain some of the inappropriateness of the script from 1930. Bill Maher talks about "People have to be so careful, and there's so much political correctness." And they're trying to censor anyone watching "Gone with the Wind." We need to have these, I feel, older movies as part of our history, and we need to look at it through the filter of our eyes now so that we see the wrong. I don't know if we cancel it out as a movie that you can watch anymore because of it. There's this big discussion going on about this right now. And I was thinking about some of the roles I played, like we're talking about now. It's really an interesting discussion. In the first movie, something of a nation, where they show the Ku Klux Klan …

"Birth of a Nation."

"Birth of a Nation," thank you, yes. The first time I saw that movie, I was horrified. But you've gotta remember the time that it was made. I know that it's taught in film history classes, and I know that there's a lot of discussion about it. Do we show this movie? This is all part of that conversation, I feel like. Playing an overweight person and having the jokes be about her weight. That was part of what was happening then. Think about in the Coen brothers movie, "Raising Arizona." There's the guy who tells all the Polish jokes, and then they show his badge and it says Kaczinski or something. "He told one Polish joke too many." The fact that everybody knew what a Polish joke was. People that are young now probably don't know maybe that that was a thing. Polish jokes were totally acceptable, and you could laugh about people being Polish and make fun of them. It's a totally different culture [now], and I think we need to know that that happened so that we can move on to treating people better. Because that's what happened back then.

That's an interesting point about characters who are heavier being last on the list to be evaluated as jokes that are cruel. It makes me think of the old Disney cartoons that now have disclaimers about the presentation of certain people. It's being done about race, but it makes you wonder if there would ever be a disclaimer about a heavier character. Should there be?

I don't know. Look, I'm not the spokesperson [Laughs] for this community.

Absolutely. And I don't want to make you out to be.

Right. But I do feel like when we do a general description of, "This was the time," like on those Disney movies, if you're watching it with a five-year-old, and the five-year-old says, "Hey, they're making fun of that guy because he's chubby" or whatever, there's a conversation that can happen then. "People back then weren't as aware that they were hurting somebody's feelings. They didn't realize that they were doing that, and it took people to tell them, 'Hey, you know what, showing these kinds of people hurts the feelings of those people, so now we don't do that anymore.'" So I think that saying something beforehand, that says, "There are some culturally sensitive things," or however they word it, it opens the door for a conversation to talk about all the things that are going on there that are not necessarily mentioned at the beginning of the movie. So I don't know that it needs its own—I guess it would depend on the movie. If it was a movie of all overweight people and they were making fun of a whole race of overweight people, there might be something said at the beginning. I don't know if there is a movie like that. [Laughs] I think we've come a long way.

I just have one more question on that topic then. If an actress who was early in her career contacted you and said, "I'm working on a project and I'm excited about the opportunity. It's someone I really want to work with. But there's a moment that is similar to jokes in "Robin Hood: Men in Tights" that is making fun of this woman because of her size and making her seem less-than because of that." What advice would you give to her?

I think of Rebel Wilson, or Melissa McCarthy—they both lost weight, interestingly enough—but they both are actresses who have probably had this issue. I think anybody overweight who is in the industry questions this. Here's the deal: Both of those women are brilliantly funny, and they know they're in on the joke. I think that if you're bringing your whole self to a character, they're going to see, much like those two women, they're going to see more than that. So the first time I ever saw Rebel Wilson was in "Bridesmaids," and she was playing the roommate of Kristen Wiig, with her odd brother. And she was heavy, and they weren't making fun of her weight. Her characters are so well-rounded and developed. And also there's a lot of body-positive, "This is my body; deal with it, you can kiss my ass. I'm all that, and you just don't see it." And I love that. I think it would depend on the character. It would depend on the comfort. If the young woman is a girl of size, or is she padded. That's two different things right there. But if you are a person of size, and you're playing a person of size who's being showcased, what's the joke? Is there a reason for the joke? Is there a comeuppance that happens because of the joke? There's a lot of things you gotta take into consideration in looking at that. Is this person a positive or negative character? Do they start out one way and end up another? It's a very nuanced thing, and I think that if you play this character as a person—even if the director views some of the stuff that you may do to make this person a more well-rounded person, because so much of this stuff is up to the director, you know you've done your job. What you've delivered to the film and the performance you did. And if you are OK with that, then I say do it. If you feel like you're making a joke at somebody else's expense and there's no redemptive quality about this person, that's an entirely different thing. So it really just depends on where the story is going and what the character is being asked to do and who she is in the story.

I appreciate that. A couple lighter, quicker ones: Tom Hanks' manager character, Jimmy, in "A League of Their Own" is very angry and gets tossed out of the game at one point. That doesn't happen as much as it used to, with managers

throwing tantrums or throwing bases or whatever. Did that behavior make the game better or worse?

[Laughs] That's a great question. I don't know. It's like watching a hockey game: Do you like to watch the guys fight, or do you not like to watch the guys fight? I personally feel like just play the game. But if something like that happens and it seems like it's valid and there was a reason for doing that, I think it's part of the game then. I think that most of the time it's justified when the managers do that. Not Jimmy Dugan; that wasn't justified. But somebody gets hit by a pitch and both of the teams start fighting and the manager comes out and he's screaming because his guy got thrown out and the other guy didn't, some of that's really valid. And I think it's just part of the game. I don't know that it's better or worse.

Did you get approval on the older version of yourself? I've never seen a movie with better casting for the older version of people.

Isn't it great? And you'll notice that the older version of me is not wearing—the Peaches are all in white, and Racine is in blue, and she's in blue. That's a little-known fact. Because they show them in the end, they have them [dressed] by team, and Marla's wearing Racine because she got traded. I did not have any say in the casting. They had all of us record our voices with their lines in case they wanted to dub our voices into the older ladies, and the only person they ended up doing that was with Geena. It's Geena's voice, but the actress is acting. And everybody else they ended up using their own voices. I very much liked her. Her name is Patricia [Wilson]. They came and we got to meet them, and I thought it was great. Madonna was very upset [Laughs] that that was what she was going to look like old. She didn't like it. But she was opinionated then. She's pretty opinionated. I loved the older Marla, and I feel like they did a great job casting the actress. That's Penny. And the casting director is Ellen Lewis. Yeah, I'm with you on that.

The ending of the movie on the field is controversial. Was it the right thing to do for Dottie to drop the ball?

OK. I get this question all the time. And here's what I have to say about this: Dottie is a great competitor. She did not drop the ball on purpose. She did not. She would never throw a game like that. That's throwing the game! It happened, and because it happened Kit gets the accolades and gets her big moment, and Dottie is happy for her. But I don't think she dropped the ball so her little sister could win the World Series. No way. No way! And the way that it's filmed, because it's in slow-motion, [that could be why people think] she just let the ball come out of her hand, but I just absolutely think she is way too much of a competitor to have thrown the game. And that's what I say about that! [Laughs]

I want to believe that. I think there's another moment in the movie where there's a big collision at the plate and she holds on, though, so that contrast could be a reason why people maybe think she dropped it on purpose.

People question it: They're like, do you think she did or she didn't? There's a big debate about it. I just feel like this time she couldn't hold onto the ball. But because they're showing it in slow motion, it looks like she's releasing the ball after. When actually I think it just happened. I just don't think that she would give up the game for her sister to win. That's just dumb. [Laughs]

I hope you're right.

I hope I am too! I'm kind of close to the whole thing, so I might not be the person to really ask. Because I have a strong opinion about that.

Billy West of 'Doug,' 'Ren & Stimpy,' 'Space Jam,' 'Futurama'

There's no way to summarize Billy West's contributions to the world of animation without sounding like hyperbole.

Because he really is that big of a deal—not just part of major projects but the centerpiece of them. That means voicing both shy Doug Funnie and his bully Roger Klotz on Nickelodeon's "Doug"; tackling both Peter Lorre-inspired chihuahua Ren and Larry Fine-inspired cat Stimpy on the same network's "Ren & Stimpy," which was the exact opposite of "Doug"; starring as Bugs Bunny and also handling Elmer Fudd duties for "Space Jam"; and being absolutely extraordinary at—hold your breath—Fry, Dr. Zoidberg, Professor Farnsworth and Zap Brannigan in "Futurama." In other words, the show that began on Fox in 1999 and got new life on Comedy Central and wound up lasting more than 100 episodes wouldn't have happened without his voice talents (and being really funny and smart and packed with a lot of other great voice actors too).

West has been a fixture on "The Howard Stern Show," voiced Woody Woodpecker and the Red M&M, served as a consultant on a "Three Stooges" movie and we could be here all day if we just make note of his credits, and none of that is new anyway. The point is that he's one of the most accomplished voice actors of our lifetimes and brought some excellent reflections to some of his most impactful work.

What's something you're nostalgic for from the '90s? It could be absolutely anything that you miss.

Let's see. I miss cartoons coming out that were groundbreakers that had nothing to do with each other. In other words, "The Simpsons" was in no way like "Beavis and Butthead," and "Beavis and Butthead" was in no way like "Ren & Stimpy." They were like three separate entities, but they all hit big, like cult status. I like when that happens because when something becomes successful you begin to see little junior versions of it, copies of it, clones of it.

And you feel like that arrival is a rarity at this point?

I'm not sure if it is or not. It's just a matter of taste. I'll audition for new cartoons, and the artwork—I don't know, I'm old-school. A lot of it looks like children's refrigerator art.

No line, no form, no shadow, no substance, no nothing. Yeah, I'm for flying by the seat of my pants like that, but people can do a lot better.

So when you think of the material from the '90s in terms of shows or movies that you were not part of, is there something that really connected with you or that you find yourself going back to?

I know it'll sound weird, but I liked "Aeon Flux." It was this MTV cartoon. And I of course was a "Simpsons" fan. I was always a big fan of Matt Groening.

Why do you think that sounds weird to mention "Aeon Flux"?

Because it was really experimental, and nobody was really sure what was going on with it. Much like "Rick and Morty." Everything happens so fast that I'm not sure what's happening, but I enjoy it for what it is. And "Aeon Flux" reminded me of that. This girl just dodging assaults here and there and overcoming stuff. Plus she was super cool.

For "Doug," where I thought it would be fun to start is that he is obviously a painfully average 11-and-a-half-year-old kid. He may have had his fantasies about Quailman or Smash Adams, but unlike modern storytelling he was just average and is average, and that's who he is. To what extent is there a certain nobility in that as we think back to the '90s and what gets made now?

I like it because in the Nickelodeon version it kept him kind of unassuming. There's always something sympathetic about a character like a Candide who just keeps walking into worlds that are unfamiliar. Discovery. But one's own fantasies lead to invention. Doug would get ideas from fantasizing, and he would solve a problem from fantasizing once he returned back to real life.

I found myself wondering about the difference that kids have watching stories where the experiences are low-key, everyday stuff versus the more contemporary stories where it seems that everyone discovers that they are the key to saving the universe.

Well, I think the latter that you mentioned is better because—I was always of a school where you don't want to mirror children's realities. If a kid is sitting there going, "Ga ga goo goo, Tata Mama Dada," you don't have a cartoon that goes, "Ga ga goo goo, Mama Tata Dada." Do you know what I mean? You don't want to mirror their own realities. You gotta take 'em on a ride. You gotta take 'em for an adventure.

That makes sense. So you feel like the notion now of people seeing that everyone has a hero inside of them is aspirational rather than intimidating?

Well, in this day and age that's why superhero movies are so important. Because I believe that's how little hope there seems to be in the real world of anything happening good. And everybody's eyes always turn to some sort of savior or hero. Whether it's a sports hero or something in real life. But that's why all the superhero stuff—we have this yearning to fix things and make them right, and I think all the movies that have been coming out feed into that.

I know that you brought some of your own experience to Doug and Roger in different ways. At the time, as you were starting out with the project and adapting to the characters and voices, how important did you feel like it was that you had your own experience to bring to those voices? Is that necessary in order to empathize with them properly?

Yes. Oh, yes. What I did was I did nothing but fantasize about stuff. I was born with ADHD, chronic low-level depression. All that stuff. OCD. And I wanted the world to be a certain way, and I didn't spend a lot of time in my body. I was always out of body. Plus, I was on the autism spectrum. So everything in real life seemed upside-down backwards to me. So I had to process it so I could make sense of things. It was very hard for me to learn things. Because everything just seemed upside-down backwards. I still can't tie my shoes right. I still can't tie a necktie. And I'm 69 years old. But in my fantasies, I can do it. I can do it better than anybody. I brought a lot of that vulnerability. And Doug, in his heart of hearts, he had a strong love. If someone just said, "Oh, that's just a crush; that's just infatuation," at the time it doesn't feel like that. It feels damn real. And you get no empathy from adults: "Don't worry, it's just puppy love." What do you mean? [Laughs] It's real feelings that are going on.

Yeah, I've been thinking about that in terms of Doug and Patti and stories of that time of life. Through adult eyes, you question about yourself, "What did I even see in this person? What did I feel for them?" But at the time it seems so clear.

Yeah. I loved the innocence of it. The newness of it. Where it isn't a full-on sex or aggression. You gotta remember, we're talking about tweeners. And my wondering what a girl was all about was just—I spent hours, as most guys do, wondering, "What is a girl about? How do I approach this? How do I say hello?" Anything that's real easy to do, you hit a brick wall when it comes to that stuff. It's like, "How do I say hi? How do I take you to the movies?" You're like an alien growing up, so you just watch everything around you.

How would you then compare the emotional experience of becoming both Doug and Roger? Doug with relating to the things you talked about, with awkwardness and fear of failure, but also basing Roger on a real bully in your own life? Did one feel more cathartic for you in any way?

Well, villains or bad guys are always more fun to play. The straight characters are not as juicy, let's say, as the antagonists. But they need each other. Yin and yang, you wouldn't know good unless there was bad, and you wouldn't know bad unless there was good. So there's always that combination of the two, and Patti makes it, what do they call it, The Eternal Triangle. Except Roger wasn't after Patti; that's what makes it a little different. Roger was just, he was a sociopath, narcissist. Everything that everybody is discovering about authority figures is true. Who knows? But I used to have this fantasy of 20 years later and Doug has to go to court and the judge is Roger: *[in Roger Klotz voice]* "The honorable Roger Klotz! Oh, look who I got in front of me today! What a record! You criminal, Funnie." *[in Doug Funnie voice]* "Uh, I just, you know, um." *[in Roger Klotz voice]* "Shut up! You got trouble written all over your face, and it's spelled wrong! You're going to jail for 50 years." *[in Doug Funnie voice]* "Oh, noooooooo!"

So did you feel like—and I don't know if this is just what viewers imagine and doesn't really happen for the people involved—either of those impacted how you reconciled those experiences that you were drawing from? Or does it not really go there?

It goes there because that particular model or flavor of bully actually existed in my childhood, and you look at Roger and everything comes to a point. He's pointing into your chest and trying to hurt you and niggling and his shoes are pointy, his hair is pointy, his nose is pointy. Everything about him is like a knife. And so I wanted him to have a voice that kind of cut and leers at you and threatens you.

Then does it feel like exorcising those demons through that?

Yes. It's a funny thing. When you're creating art, you wonder if the characters you're playing are teaching anybody a lesson because most plays or shows or movies are morality plays, and you wonder, "Does the Thanos in the audience know that he's Thanos?" It's like Greek mythology: "Am I this or am I that? Am I Hercules or am I a Medusa?" All these characters were created to show people who they are, and you always wonder, "I wonder if a Medusa recognizes a Medusa in a movie?" Probably not.

It's a great question. For Roger, he's the Doug of his life, I guess.

Um, yeah. I remember years ago in the late '80s, mid-'80s, people started rooting for the bad guy at the movies. I'd be astonished. I went to see Robin Williams in "Popeye," and when Bluto started beating him up, I noticed this stir in the audience, like, "Yeah!" They were literally rooting for the bad guy, and I said, "Is this what's going to happen to society? Is everyone going to want to be like the bad guy?" I shouldn't worry about society. I'm not an anthropologist.

It reminds me of when I interviewed Robert Rodriguez and he told me that he once walked into a room full of the guys who played the meanest villains in the '80s movies, and they're all great guys in real life.

Well, yeah. I'm glad you said that. That's a good thing to hear is that for a lot of people role-playing, like you said earlier, is cathartic. But I was gonna say if you couldn't see and you were blind and you were sitting in a theater and you weren't quite sure what was going on and all of a sudden you hear every guy in the audience go, "Ooooooh!" You'd think it was a girl showing her cleavage or something. And you open your eyes and it's the biggest gun! [Laughs] It's this obscenely big gun, a weapon. I don't know, there's a lot of fantasies with that crap too. I don't know. I've been in children's entertainment! [Laughs]

At one point I heard you say that you didn't feel like anyone would be interested in seeing "Doug" when he was 21. It's kind of surprising how many shows for kids tried to bring people into the college years, whether "Saved by the Bell," "Boy Meets World" or otherwise. Do you feel like that ever works? Or inherently a character like Doug needs to be left in the moment and it's hard to make the viewers grow up with them? Why is that so difficult?

Because you can't replicate alchemy. There was a certain resonance in the world when "Doug" was being put together. There was a certain emotional resonance in the world when "Ren and Stimpy" hit. It depends on the way people feel at a certain time why something becomes a hit or cult status. It's hard to replicate those same things. It's like alchemy; you start out with a bar of lead, and it's your job as an artist in conjunction, in concert with other artists, to turn it into gold. And years go by, and you try it again with the same elements, and it may not work. That's why alchemy was a pseudo-science. There has to be the right circumstances in the entire world, I believe, for you to strike gold again. Or you have to come back with some of the elements and change it into something completely different. Because something has to change. That's where the success of alchemy is. Something's gotta turn into something else, especially in art.

That's what I was just thinking, that part of what went wrong with the college episodes of "Saved by the Bell" and "Boy Meets World" is they tried for the same tone, and it didn't feel authentic anymore. It's almost like if they were going to continue "Doug" until he was 21, it couldn't feel like he was 11. It would have to be the R-rated "Doug."

Or Doug getting busted for something and having to go to court to find out that Roger was not only a cop after he got out of high school but he became a judge, a magistrate. To me that feels like real life. And it would be hysterically funny. *[in Doug Funnie voice]* "All I did was make some meth?" *[in Roger Klotz voice]* "Yeah, well, you oughta know better, Funnie! You're old enough to know better, Funnie!"

You of course spent more years as Fry than Doug. You've talked about how voice performances develop over time in a show. How would you compare how those vocal performances evolved for you?

Every show starts off with a certain sound. Like the way Homer Simpson sounded in episodes 1, 2, 3 and 4, he doesn't sound anything like he sounds in episode 50 or episode 80. It evolves on its own. It starts out a certain way, the characters are how you came in, and then the more you get to know the characters—and you can't know them unless you become familiar with the writing—and then you perform them the way the writers are evolving the characters. Because, yeah, at the beginning the characters sounded pretty different to me, and then they found what they were supposed to be.

If you were going on a trip and had to find someone to be in charge of your group, how would you rank these possibilities: Fry, Zoidberg, Professor Farnsworth or Zap Brannigan?

I would leave it to Fry because I'm probably only as smart as he is. And his sense of direction and all that. He gets into trouble, but he also gets out of trouble. Zap always gets into trouble. The Professor makes mistakes. And Zoidberg, he'll go wherever there's a chance for a meal. So his compass doesn't run like ours does. His due north is a meatloaf.

Part of the sung and unsung greatness of "Futurama" is how emotionally impactful it can be. When you're making those episodes that hit that way, does the preparation change at all? Does it take you any longer to access what you need to do compared to the lighter material?

No, they always ask you of things. The writers ask the performers to rise to the occasion to what they're doing. And you should be able to wring some tears out of a character or a situation. You should be able to do those things. Any good actor is called upon to do a million shades of emotion, and you should be able to do it and have it work for the audience.

Certainly. In the documentary "I Know That Voice," there's the discussion about voice acting being acting, but I think a lot of people take that for granted. They might assume it's easier, but in some ways it's harder.

Well, I don't know. If you get hired to do who and exactly what you are for a character, if you weren't famous you'd never work. You have to be famous to get away with that shit. Because people like me and all the people that I work with, your whole life depends on expanding your bag of tricks. You've gotta be able to do everything. It's like, "Can you do a worm?" "Yeah, sure." "What about a worm with a funny hat?" "Yeah, OK." A celebrity, Matthew McConaughey would just do his voice for that. I shouldn't say that—he's probably got a lot of ammunition. Who knows. But most people, they hire them for their name, and the audience doesn't want to not recognize them. It's a weird thing. It's very weird. I was never a fan of that. It's like taking a bunch of highly skilled plumbers and sending them to go win the World Series for you.

I totally agree. If you're going to hire big celebrities just because of who they are, you may as well have a split-screen where we just watch them record. It would be more fun anyway.

Yes, it would, but the thing is that there's no alchemy. When you look at the finished product, if you're A/B'ing, there's no alchemy. Nothing changes. To me that's the antithesis of art. Something has to change into something else for it to be magic.

And the way you inhabit these characters is extraordinary. Do you ever dream as them or think in their voices or have them with you when it's not intentional?

Not really. If I'm in a supermarket or some place and somebody hears some little twinge or something in my voice, they'll sort of sheepishly ask, "Are you Billy West?" And I'll say, "Yeah, I am," and they'll go, "Oh my god, can I have your autograph?" And I'm happy to do it. And I'll do a couple of voices. Because how dare I not do those things. The fans, they were good to that show. The fans were the ones responsible for bringing the show back. I have them to thank.

So in terms of dreaming or thinking in their voices, that doesn't happen involuntarily?

No. You don't want to know my dreams. [Laughs] What goes on there, you don't want to know.

Then on the topic of people asking you to do voices, I wanted to ask if you saw the Coen brothers movie "Inside Llewyn Davis"?

No, I didn't.

I mention it because he plays a folk singer, and there's a scene in which he's at a dinner party and someone asks him to play a song and he gets really upset about it. He feels like he's being treated like a trained monkey and that he doesn't ask a professor to give a lecture about astrophysics during a party. To you does that seem like someone is being humorless about the impact their art makes on people?

I don't know. I would just say "Way to be cordial. Way to be gracious. Wow, that's the way to be gracious is to get all pissy about it." If you're going to be among people, you're going to have admirers. And maybe they don't want to hear what you have to say about politics. Maybe they have an entire image of you. I forget who said it, but it's like "Never meet your idol. Never meet your hero because it could go totally bad. It could go totally wrong." Here you think about this person every day and you're wondering what they're doing and what they had for breakfast and where they're going to play next and everything, and that person doesn't know you exist. And when you meet them, it could go either way. It could be like, "Yeah, what do you want?" or "Hey, thanks a lot, man." [Laughs]

I guess I was curious—it would be totally understandable if someone of your talents and recognition felt sensitive, if people are constantly asking you to do this voice and that voice—

I don't mind. I don't mind. I'll do a dog and pony show. Did you ever see Robbie Paulsen ["Animaniacs," "Pinky and the Brain"]? If someone asks him to do the countries of the world, he'll do the entire thing. He's gracious to his fans. He's good to them. I'll do the same thing if asked. But there was one time that I was pissed off that somebody asked. I had to go into the hospital for prostate surgery. And I was recovering, and I was sick as I was recovering, so I was in trouble. I burned up four bags of blood, I had such a high fever. And then I began to wake up, I'm packed in ice, and there's four doctors looking at me and they go, "How many fingers do I have up? Are you good? How do you feel?" And then one guy goes, "Do a voice." And I wanted to tell him to drop dead!

People need to realize there's a time and a place.

I know. But doctors aren't like the doctors when I grew up. They're like kid doctors. Everybody is a kid garbageman or a kid clerk. There's no adults anymore.

There was one more thing I wanted to ask in terms of the Nickelodeon stuff. "Doug" and "Ren & Stimpy" are very different shows. I loved "Doug" growing up and never connected with "Ren & Stimpy" at the time. Do you have a sense of how the fanbase varied between the two? I have no sense of if there were people who loved both or if it was binary or what.

I think kids loved that three-cartoon block, the Nicktoons. I think it hit at the right perfect time, and I think kids loved all three of those shows [including "Rugrats"]. Maybe one more than another, or vice-versa. But it's funny. I have to remember that there was kids that were four years old and five years old and now they're 30 or whatever, and I meet them at the shows, and the way it impacted them ... I had no idea. You have no idea when it's going on whether something like that is happening or not. You can't know if you're in the middle of a cultural phenomenon when you're in the middle of it. It's later, after, on the outside looking in, you go, "Oh my god. Look at how people just went crazy." I'm always humbled. I don't expect adulation. All I ever really wanted was a chance to work. And I did; I got my wish. I worked nonstop. I was very, very lucky. Very fortunate. And then everything else sort of just happens. If you get fanbases, if people are into what you do, that's very lucky. That's asking people to be into what you do. Do you know what a high, booming request that is for people to be into what you do considering there are so many people and there's so much stuff? But I was lucky; it's happened a few times in my life.

Absolutely. You've been so open about your upbringing and how art became an escape and falling into those worlds, as many do. And we don't need to get into all of that, but I mention it because I'm curious, the degree to which you found these

remarkable abilities through that experience, I'm wondering if you've ever thought about if you still would've found these talents even if you had a different upbringing? Or if they would just be there unknown had you not had that drive for that escape?

Yeah, it's hard to know. I know that a lot of artists come from a place of being treated horribly. Or living in fear. Or whatever. Some kind of misery. And it makes you want to go in the opposite direction and create beauty. That's what it was for me. I lived in a hell house. I'm writing chapters; I've written like 26 chapters of a book that I hopefully will put out there. It's autobiographical. And discovering things, like being able to do voices or sing like a little kid or scream like a monster, I was able to do that stuff when I was 8, 9, 10 years old, and I had a teacher that said, "That shit is impossible for the human voice to do!" It was like he was calling me out, like I was the occult or a demon or something. And he just didn't understand that there's gifts. On the autism spectrum, there's storage houses in your head and they're locked, and autism is like a key to open the storage room that most people don't know exists. And in it is gifts, and you discover them. When I discovered stuff, it was like my superpower. Being able to do what I did was like being able to be invisible or fly. Like the Billyverse or something.

It's a remarkable thing to be able to do. To create that yourself, it's a cappella to the nth degree.

Yeah. [Laughs]

Sort of on a similar note, I guess, is when I was rewatching "Space Jam," there's a moment when Bugs is afraid of the dog and I was wondering if there's ever been a time for you, or anyone in voice acting, when you use something live to get you going? I know you can do anything on your own, but would it be helpful to have a dog there to prompt you?

No, no, I never heard of that. You have to be able to visualize what's going on. You have to be able to be frightened out of your skin or overconfident or giddy or jealous. A million emotions that go into voice acting, and you can only imagine a dog with teeth that have the kind of tartar that'll leave a mean infection if they bite you. There are a million things you can think of that would put you on edge, but that comes out through the character. And it gets exhausting. Your body doesn't know the difference. If you're going to war as a character and you're screaming at the top of your lungs, your body doesn't know that you're pretending. The body treats it as if you're going through those things, but in your mind you're not. It's not you; it's a character.

I feel like there is a semi-regular debate online about "Space Jam" vs. "Looney Tunes: Back in Action," which you also worked on. Have you seen that at all of being something people argue about?

I don't understand what there is to argue about. Nothing will change. No matter what you have to say, no matter what you do, you affect nothing and no one. It's just for the sake of fighting about something. I live in the present; I don't live in the past. I'm a progressive. That's why I don't live in the past as far as all the shows and everything I do. I have a life. I had a year off. What am I going to do? I'm going to write, and there is no present to speak of unless you want to go out and get COVID. And we don't even know if there's a future, but at least I was aware of the past in my own life. But as far as if I got together with a bunch of people and we were arguing about which episode of "Gunsmoke" was the best, I don't know. I find it kind of puerile. It's like everybody has their preferences. Some people loved Joe Alesky as Bugs Bunny, some people like Greg Bursen, some people like Jeff Bergman, some people love Eric Bauza as Bugs Bunny, some people liked what I did as Bugs Bunny. But everybody has their own perception of the experience. I don't know. Today people treat stuff as if it only exists to be argued over, go to war over. It makes people mean when they start warring over stuff, differences of opinion. And you get blamed; all I have to do is write a half-decent joke and put it on my Twitter and everybody's like, "Dad joke." Everybody's the arbiter of comedy. Everybody's everything because of the internet. Fighting and warring over things and having these heated opinions is just a way to keep the game going. It's the home game. It's the home version. It's a way to be part of it, and a way to play the game. I don't have any problem with it, really. I just hate to see people fighting. That's what I hate. I never go there. I don't want to go there.

You've also talked about your perspective of "Looney Tunes" characters and wanting to put teeth in them in terms of what feels right for the characters and what doesn't. As we said, voice actors are actors, and actors sometimes speak up about ways characters are being used or plotlines. Was there anything in "Space Jam" or anything where you found yourself speaking up about something the character was doing that didn't feel right, or about the plot that you didn't know why something was happening?

No. I never bring my aesthetic. Only to the vocalization and my own acting. But I don't question; my job is to make the director happy. Whatever the director asks for, you better give it to 'em or you won't have that job. That's the bottom line. And maybe if you say, "Hey, I got an idea," sometimes they'll say, "Yeah, what is it?" And you'll try something. But you want to be helpful. You don't want to undo the mechanics of it. You don't want to retrofit stuff after everything's been worked out. Your job is to just come in there and act.

That's an interesting contrast, then, between on-camera and off-camera performers.

Yeah. The thing about Bugs Bunny is I never could base my life around doing Bugs Bunny. It wasn't my gig. I didn't create that voice. I was lucky enough to be able to do it for about 10 years. But when that gig ends, it ends for me. People say, "Hey, you did Bugs Bunny," and I'll be happy to do it. I worked hard to be an originator instead of an imitator.

But I was really good at imitating and holding up franchises where the original person died or didn't want to do it. But I think being an originator is more rewarding for me personally.

There are a few silly ones I wanted to ask before a couple last questions of substance. I know you're a musician. I interviewed Andrew Bird a long time ago about the way he uses whistling in music. As such a talented voice performer yourself, how do you feel about whistling used in music?

Whistling? I liked it when Bing Crosby did it in "White Christmas." It just seems like a no-brainer. Whatever mode of expression you choose, hopefully it'll work. Hopefully people will like it. To me, I loved all kinds of music. I loved everything. I was invented before rock 'n roll was.

Do you have a favorite Beets song?

What, like "Killer Tofu"?

I was always partial to "I Need More Allowance."

Yeah, they're all fun. "Shout Your Lungs Out." It was so great. It was almost like Spinal Tap. That was Fred Newman and Dan Sawyer that made those up and sang them and played them. They were just beautiful. So clever.

Have you ever been bored and used your own voice skills to amuse yourself to pass the time?

Um, I don't know. I'm weird like that. I can jones on something. Because I have the OCD thing. If a character in "The Three Stooges" couldn't talk and he just made a noise, I'll make that noise, but I'll keep doing it and doing it. [Laughs] And I gotta pull out of it.

So it's not like if you're waiting in a doctor's office it's not like you say to yourself, "What if Fry and Zoidberg were out to lunch and the restaurant set on fire?" That wouldn't be a way you would pass the time.

No, I can't imagine myself doing it. When I was a drunk and a crazy and a druggie, I'd be dancing on tabletops, but I keep my hoopla underneath the percentium. That's where you go crazy.

When you were on "Howard Stern," were you ever contacted by someone you impersonated?

Well, "The Three Stooges," I just grew up loving them and that's where I learned to act, and that's where I learned comedy from. And I liked doing Larry from "The Three Stooges." And his sister lived in Philadelphia, and she was rattled by the impression because she said, "It sounded exactly like my brother." So I invited them to come to New York and have dinner with me. But nobody else really.

Is there something from "Futurama" that you wish was real?

Yeah! A holophoner. I really wish that there was one and I could play it. It really opened up my imagination. The idea that something like that could exist, and that Fry would be so good at it.

What would you want to conjure with it? If that appeared at your house today, what would you want to play?

Gee whiz, I don't know. Whatever tunes or melodies I had in my head, but it also extracts your thoughts apparently too. Of course I want to see the north pole and the south pole freeze over again. I don't want it melting. So my conjurings would be that everything would go in reverse. That we didn't have to kill animals that were headed for extinction. Wanting to be a do-gooder and wanting the world to be in a place where there isn't constant conflict and people don't act feral toward each other and infantile. That kind of stuff. I like harmony; that's why I became a musician in the first place.

Watching "I Know That Voice," in that movie, which came out in 2013, your "Futurama" costar John DiMaggio says he couldn't play a Black person on screen but can do one in voiceover. In the years since that movie came out, that's no longer true. I feel like I have to ask your take on the way things have changed in who is hired for voiceover roles?

I don't have much of a take on it because I just always played what I was assigned to do. Something I auditioned for. But I don't sit and go, "Uh, they had to hire an Asian guy because the guy's Asian." My mind doesn't even work like that. I'm a specialist. I get called on to do specialized things. And otherworldly type things or things that are totally out of my realm, but I'll make the stretches as an actor. As far as that stuff goes, I don't know. If it happens to me, we'll see what happens.

Is there anyone you wouldn't want to voice if you were asked?

Jeez, I don't know. That's so hypothetical. You're talking to someone that can do 50 shades of any character. Or emotion within a Swedish pubic hair of a difference between one I just did. But everybody's gotta be able to do that. Everybody's gotta be able to change in zillions of degrees, and all the people I know, all the people I work with, are certainly masters of all of that stuff.

Aaron Schwartz of 'Heavyweights,' 'The Mighty Ducks'

It's not possible to properly set up an interview that includes a discussion of what slime tastes like, a thoughtful exploration of how involved parents should be in the lives of children who are overweight, and a difficult, complex debate about some of the most serious social fractures of recent years.

So perhaps it's best to just dive into this rewarding, challenging conversation with Aaron Schwartz, whose turn as Karp in 1992's "The Mighty Ducks" led to writer Steven Brill casting Schwartz in the lead role of Gerry in Brill's 1995 directorial effort "Heavyweights" (which he wrote with Judd Apatow). Schwartz is warm and appealing and just right in the role, but the movie's eventual cult following didn't exactly turn him into a household name at the time. He took time away from acting in his teens and 20s, eventually returning to a recurring role on "Gossip Girl" and appearances on "The Kaminsky Method" and "S.W.A.T." He's also helming a documentary about child actors and, like everything we discussed, thankfully has a great deal to say on the topic.

What's something you're nostalgic for from the '90s? It could be absolutely anything that you miss.

What do I miss from the '90s? A lot of things. I miss the feeling of everything's new. The internet and all these things, it was the beginning. Even though it was dial-up and you had that sound of the phone dialing and the electronic sound when you were doing dial-up, it was just the beginning of interconnectivity is something I'm nostalgic for. Because now we take it for granted on how easy we just pick up our phone and Google something and ask a computer, basically like "Star Trek," we just ask a computer, "Hey, what about this?" And it has all the information. I'm nostalgic for the difficulty that came through—that our mental capacity to have patience with things was much greater back then, and I find myself not having patience that I used to, and I kind of miss talking to people and being connected with people in a different way with that idea floating over our heads that we are all going to be even more interconnected as time goes on. That and Nickelodeon. Nickelodeon was my childhood, not only being in it ["The Adventures of Pete & Pete"] but also watching it. The whole television, Nickelodeon, "You Can't Do That on Television," the newness of everything. It felt so new. And now it just feels like, "When is the new thing coming out?" And we have the impatience of "When is the new thing coming out?" as opposed to being in awe of the new thing.

At the time were you more interested in sliding down the pie slide in "Double Dare" or going up the Aggro Crag in "Guts"?

Oh, pie slide. Or the slime. I was so interested in slime. I was so into the slime that I started trying to create the slime. And I forget how I looked it up; I don't know if I looked it up through the internet. I don't think I did at the time 'cause I don't know if there was the internet, or if there was, it was like brand-new. But I remember finding out how to make slime. And using different recipes, and one of them was using wheat and green food coloring. And my house, my kitchen was covered in green food coloring at one point because I was trying to make the slime. [Laughs] I was so into slime for some reason. Since "You Can't Do That on Television," I was obsessed with being slimed. Never got a chance to be slimed, actually. I was in Nickelodeon a couple times, and I never got a chance to be slimed.

I have to ask: Did you ever try to eat it?

Yes, of course! I would watch on that show, it would pour all over their faces, and at the time I was already kind of acting a little bit and doing stuff, so I knew how things worked. And I thought to myself, "They can't make this stuff to be not edible for the actors to be able to have it poured on their faces," so maybe it didn't taste great, but it had to be edible. So I would definitely try to taste each one and see which was more palatable. None of them were. None of them were very palatable. They were all pretty disgusting. [Laughs]

Were you as fond of the dial-up at the time or it only seems nice in retrospect?

Ooh, I have to think back on the dial-up sound. I think I was in awe of it. I don't know if I was a fan of it. I remember at the time being like, "They need to make this quicker. This is ridiculous. How come it's taking so long?" I didn't know the science behind it, that it was dialing into a server and the server had to connect to another server. It was all just stuff that I completely took for granted at the time. But I also remember having this other side where I was just like, "Whoa! We are in the future. 'Back to the Future II' is happening now!" I think my personality, the way I am, even if I'm impatient now there's a constant sense of wonder. I always believe in magic a little bit, and I'm always filled with wonder at the new things that come out. I think I still had that then too.

Speaking of which, when you think of other movies from that era that you were not in, is there one that jumps to mind that you go back to the most or that still means the most to you?

"Home Alone." Definitely "Home Alone." "Hook." I remember auditioning for "Hook." When you're a child actor and you're in the mix a lot, two worlds collide, all the worlds collide, and things come full circle in a way. I remember "Home Alone," I was obsessed with Macaulay Culkin's career. I remember people used to ask me whose career I wanted to emulate. It was either Tom Cruise because I wanted to be an action star, and

Macaulay Culkin. Now I look back on it and I definitely did not want to have that type of fame; I'm happy I didn't. But I wanted to have that type of fame and that type of recognition. Maybe it was a sense of [that] I needed that attention. Who knows what it was at the time, but I aspired to be like Macaulay Culkin in "Home Alone." I was like, "That would be the perfect movie. It was fun, it was a cult classic," and at the time I loved Christmas. I'm a hardcore Jew, but I loved Christmas and the feeling of Christmas and the orchestra in the background. It was just that sense of magic and wonder, even with that. And then I ended up going to school with Macaulay Culkin. I don't know if my choice was because he was there. Or if I just picked the school. I think I went to the school because it was close and it was a school that I could go and do—it was after I booked "The Mighty Ducks," and I could go and do movies and they would allow the time off and they had a system that allowed time off and you were surrounded by other artists, actors, dancers, singers, performers. And Macaulay Culkin ended up being a classmate of mine, which was interesting. And also Amber Scott, who was the little girl in "Hook," she's a year or two younger than me but we were also classmates. So that's the way they came full circle. And on top of that, at the screen test of "Heavyweights" I also met two of the "Lost Boys" from "Hook." And I auditioned for it right before I auditioned for "The Mighty Ducks." So it was this weird world of what I wanted to be in and what I was in were kind of parallel. They were almost intermixing. I thought I was a wizard at the time because I would think of things, and they would happen. I was like, "Whoa, I'm making this thing happen. I wanted to be friends with Macaulay Culkin; I'm friends with Macaulay Culkin. I wanted to be in 'Hook,' but I'm friends with all the people from 'Hook.'" The magic I believed in seemed to come to fruition when I was a little kid.

Which aspect of "Home Alone" did you want? Was it that you wanted time alone to eat pizza, or to enact violent revenge on intruders?

Neither! Well, the revenge on the intruders was really awesome. I was like, "Ooh, the feathers and the tar, it's so genius." I didn't do what I did with the slime with what happened in "Home Alone." I didn't buy a heating source to put on the door handle. I didn't go that far. But I think it was the magic of "Home Alone." At the time I understood how movies were made; I wasn't some little kid who just saw movies and was like, "This is real." I understood the aspect that these were actors and they had take after take and had to change directions. I understood the magic of it. I was obsessed with magic when I was a little kid too, before I did movies. And I remember when I was six years old is when I told my mom I wanted to act, and she was not your typical stage mom. She was like, "Are you sure you want to do that?" She was very welcoming to the idea and helped me out. But I remember I chose that partially because it was a big magic trick. I lived on the upper west side of New York, and I would see movies being made all the time, and I remember watching, and I saw them stop, and I asked somebody why they stopped. Someone explained to me how they did it, and I was like, "This is a huge magic trick." I became obsessed with the idea of filming something. So I think when I saw "Home Alone," I saw the magic that was made out of these long hours of changing directions, waiting, getting in a trailer, going back up. I was hooked in a weird way to the logistics of it.

152

When it comes to "The Mighty Ducks," what role would you say Karp plays on the team? Is he a valuable contributor to the Ducks?

Huh. So you have Josh Jackson, Charlie, and he is the co-protagonist with Emilio. You have Banks, which is the conflict which has to be resolved. You have Fulton the powerhouse. The damsel-in-distress so to speak, with Marguerite. And the love interest with Guy. I think Karp, narrative-wise, is there to give the idea of the rug rat. He was like a tough little bully, but he wasn't a bully. He wasn't going to bully people, but he was this tough kid who showed the roughness of the team. He wears a football helmet, and he wears a Russian hat, and we first see him in the movie coming out and feeding his dog Petey to put poop in a purse to prank somebody. I think Karp is a grounding mechanism, maybe, to ground everybody in the story of the kids. The idea of these kids from district five becoming the Mighty Ducks. It's this rags-to-riches so to speak idea, and I think Karp has this anchoring role as being the rags part of the rags-to-riches. Gets hit in the head with the puck, he's kind of klutzy, he's kind of mean but he's part of the Ducks. He's the roughneck of the group. Fulton's definitely the roughneck, but he's the roughneck of the group that grounds us in, "We're just some street kids that became the Ducks."

He's a subliminal enforcer. You might not know you're afraid of him, but his presence is subconsciously making you feel intimidated.

Right. Jesse Hall, who's Brandon Adams, is another aspect of the same kind of feeling that we both have this roughness to us that shows that almost like we're Boston kids as opposed to Connecticut kids. We won't hold our punches. We'll tell you how it is, and we're not like the other teams where they just fall in line. We don't fall in line; we fall in our own line, and that's what makes us unique as a team.

Is there a professional role player you'd compare Karp to? Obviously professional athletes tend to actually contribute on the field or ice or wherever, but does he remind you of anyone?

I am not a sports person, honestly. Maybe Andre Agassi, you know. Except Karp was not that good at hockey as Agassi was at ... was it Andre Agassi? Who was the other one, the one that cursed all the time?

John McEnroe.

McEnroe! I'd say McEnroe, sorry. He's comparable to McEnroe, where everybody rooted for him but at the same time he'd start screaming and yelling, and then you kind of felt for him afterwards. You were like, "Oh, that poor guy just got angry over this." You have tennis, which is this sport that seems so elite. You go to the U.S. Open and everybody's drinking martinis. It seems very golf-like almost. It seems clean-cut. But then you got

McEnroe in there dropping F-bombs left and right. I think he grounded people in the reality that it's a human sport. I would say Karp is pretty comparable to that.

I love that comparison. That's perfect.

[Laughs] I was searching for some sports figures that I could even call out. Yeah, I think that's the closest I can come up with.

When you said Agassi, I was imagining you/Karp growing up and dating Brooke Shields.

Nah, nah. Maybe. I don't know what Steve [Brill] would write Karp as now. I think Karp became an MMA fighter or something. Ended up joining MMA and all of a sudden injured himself and had to go back into hockey because in hockey you can play injured all the time.

A scene that impacted me a long time ago and again recently was rollerblading through the Mall of America, which looks like the coolest thing ever. What do you remember from that experience?

So they redid it in part two through Mall of America when it was built. Part one, Mall of America wasn't there yet. It was another mall, or maybe it was the same mall that was not fully the Mall of America. It was the first time I ever saw rollerblades. Rollerblades, I don't think they were a thing when that happened. I think there might have been a movie prior to that with rollerblades in it. Rollerblades were probably in some way, shape or form out years before, but for them to become a household thing, I think that was the year when that happened. And when we got rollerblades, none of us knew what these things were. We never saw them before; it was like a new thing. People were playing street hockey with them. I think '91 was when they were a big street hockey thing. And we had no idea what they were, so it was kind of like this new thing. And we were already trained to ice skate. We got like a month and a half of training prior to shooting, so we knew how to ice skate pretty well. We were solid on ice. I could do whatever you asked me to do. I could control my skating just like I was walking basically. So when we got on rollerblades, it was so easy. I was like, "Wow, I'm good at this, and I've never even worn these things before." So it was exhilarating. It was freeing to do that. They cleared the whole place, and they said, "Just go have fun." They had a guy on a dolly and a Steadicam moving really fast, and we were just skating toward them. It felt as close to an action film—the last thing I did was "S.W.A.T." that was action like that. It was the closest to that feeling of filming an action film. As I told you, I wanted to be an action star since I was a little kid. So it was enthralling. It was amazing.

I'm not sure the origin of that adolescent goal to do something you can't normally do in a mall, whether it's sleep there overnight, rollerblade or otherwise. Something about that is so freeing.

It is. It's this place that has a lot of rules and regulations, and it's this place made for one specific thing. You go there, you shop, but you have to fall in line with everybody else and how they're doing things. And it kind of breaks that whole pattern. Like in "The Walking Dead" or a zombie movie where people are sleeping over or sleeping in the mall, there's a sense of a free-for-all. It was definitely freeing, and it was so much fun. I remember we filmed it for almost a whole day with all the shots that they had to get. And it was exhilarating. It was great. There was a stunt lady that got to get pushed into a fountain. I remember she was a woman who was a stunt lady for "Wonder Woman," the TV show. I remember everybody was talking about, like, "Whoa, that's the stunt lady from 'Wonder Woman,' and she's here doing the stunts." At one point when she had to fall in, I went over and was like, "Oh my god, are you OK?" She goes, "Just a day in the life of my job! This is what I do." I was in awe of the whole thing. And I had a blast.

I'm now wishing that in "Dawn of the Dead," as everyone is hiding out in the mall, worried about zombies, the Ducks are just rollerblading their way through.

Right? Oh, man, we gotta do a remix. The remix edition of "Dawn of the Dead" meets the Ducks. Everybody's scared, they got shotguns with them, and then all of a sudden you just see the Ducks rolling through being like, "Buncha wusses!"

I would see that movie, and I think a lot of people would too. "Dawn of the Ducks," it writes itself. In one interview that I listened to you said that when you were in close proximity to Emilio Estevez you remembered hitting him and wanting attention. Can you expand on that? Were the kids competing for him to pay attention to them?

I think that had to do with it for sure. I was younger than a lot of the kids, and there were little groups of kids. If they were a little older, they would hang out with each other. The younger—so me, Danny Tamberelli, Jussie Smollett, we were like a little group. And then the older kids like Josh and Elden, who played Fulton, and Marguerite, they were maybe a year or two older, but at that time when I was 10, 11 years old and they were 13, 14, big difference. That age difference, even if it's two or three years, is huge at that time. So I think there were little cliques going on. We were all friendly. Nobody bullied anybody or was mean to anybody. But there were moments where I think, it was just my kind of personality that was like, "Hey, you're not looking at me when I'm talking to you." Me talking, I didn't feel like I would get through unless I was tapping. And Emilio was so cool. He made you feel comfortable. He took us out to see "Wayne's World," we went bowling, he rented out a movie theater. He was just so chill and so easygoing. But I think I annoyed the crap out of him because anytime I was around him talking, I was always tapping him and tapping him while I was talking. I didn't realize that it annoyed him until we were all signing scripts before we wrapped, and he signed my script, "Stop hitting me—Emilio." [Laughs] I still have that script, it's hilarious. My good friend now, who I invited to the Ducks—I've known this kid since I was in kindergarten before I even decided I wanted to act, we both are now in the entertainment industry. He works at SiriusXM, he's been working on "Sway in the Morning," and he also has his own couple radio shows here and there on SiriusXM, and any time … he has somebody there that is connected to anything, he always has me call up or has me come down. And with Emilio he had me send a video because I was out in L.A. to say hello to him. He goes, "Yo, Emilio is on the show, and I got to tell him that I was there during the filming of the Ducks, and I need you to say hello to him." So we did this whole thing and he came with a jersey and said, "Hey, man, this is a jersey that I got back in the day. Do you mind signing this jersey?" And Emilio was like, "What? This is crazy." "Yeah, man, I was there. I have a picture of us." He showed a picture of Emilio and my friend Devin when he was like 10 years old. And then he asked me to send in a tape and I tell him I'm so sorry for constantly hitting him. It's a cool moment. It should be on "Sway in the Morning," it's a really cool moment where Emilio gets my tape of me saying that like, "Oh, man, that's crazy."

That's awesome. It's not hard to imagine with a big cast and a lot of kids of different ages, and because the movie is about leadership and surrogate dads too, a sense of competition or kids who aren't the lead role wanting to make sure they're being taken seriously.

Oh, yeah. There was definitely a lot of I guess you would call it competition within the other kids of attention-wise. And there were some talented kids there. Shaun Weiss is one of the funniest human beings I know. He was always cracking jokes. Full of talent. All these kids that if you look at all them, a lot of them turned out to be amazing. Some of them are A-listers. Some of them are doing other things and became very good at other lines of work. A group of workhorses and smart kids, so when you're around that, you definitely need to find your place, gotta get a little competition in there. And if me tapping somebody a billion times got him to listen to me, that was my goal. [Laughs] I guess I achieved it. Even though I annoyed the hell out of him, I achieved it.

We certainly see how Gordon changes throughout the movie. In terms of coaching kids vs. adults and earning respect, is there a difference in how kids need to be coached, or do the same principles apply no matter how old?

So this is interesting. A friend of mine sent me the "Where Are They Now?" and they showed the Ducks, and it was a recent thing because of the Ducks TV show. I had this suggested YouTube video, you know how the algorithm just keeps on going, and it shows what is wrong with the Mighty Ducks. And this guy just rips apart the narrative, the writing of the Ducks. Which I disagree with a lot of it; it's formulaic, and that's why it works. And that's why it's a cult classic because it has this extreme formula of heroes going against some sort of grain, being able to accomplish something and then coming out on top. That's what everybody wants to see, and that's why it was so popular. But in this they talk about teaching kids, and how when a coach teaches kids it seems to be that in all these feel-good movies, the narrative states that teaching kids means you have to tell them that winning is not important; it's all about having fun. It's funny that you just said that because I was thinking about that yesterday, actually, right when I saw that. Teaching kids to have fun is the key to allowing them to succeed, but there's a piece of me that disagrees with that. In the movie, Hans tells Emilio, "What happened to you?" "It's not worth winning if you can't win big." They break that line apart too. Hans goes, "You used to have so much fun. Now all it is is about winning as a lawyer and all this." It's a cool little metaphor that Steve Brill writes, where the lawyer is on top, he's undefeated, and he has that Hawks mentality when he goes into the courtroom, but yet when he's teaching these kids he has the same mentality that the Hawks are doing, and he's watching those Hawks that are just evil and the antithesis of what we want from our hero, and Hans shows him where the love is and how to turn that around. In theory, that sounds great, but if you want your kids to win games, there's a little taste of victory. I think winning feels good. Being able to be on top feels good. So I think when you're teaching kids, you have to have both. When you're teaching an NHL team, if you're saying, "Hey, guys, just don't worry about winning. Just have fun." You might as well not be there. They're getting paid a lot of money, there's people there to see them win. It's all about winning. It's not all about having fun. You should have fun; otherwise you shouldn't do the sport. But it's all about winning. So I think when you're teaching kids you have to have that perfect balance making them know that winning is very important, but at the same time it's not the end of the world because you're just a kid and you probably won't do this for a living so have fun trying to win.

So the "I hope you win; I'll love you the same no matter what" line.

Yeah. "I'll be very disappointed, but I'll still love you." There needs to be some reprimanding. I have a puppy now, and the way you have to teach a puppy, there's different rules of thumb on how to teach a puppy. A lot of people say positive reinforcement is key. You can't say "No" to a dog all the time. You have to just ignore and say "Yes" when they're doing good things. In theory, that sounds like a great idea, but once in a while the dog has to have a little bit of not fear but anticipation of you not being happy about something in order to not do that thing more often. Maybe I'm wrong; maybe saying no to my dog is a bad thing. But I think the same goes with kids being taught sports. They have to know that losing is not the desired outcome. Of course they know it; they want to win. But they have to know in a stronger sense that winning is the desired outcome, and losing is going to be a disappointing thing. But it also has to not be the end of the world. It has to be like, "OK, whoops. Let's go get some ice cream. Not a big deal. Next time we'll do it again." If that makes sense. I went really deep into it.

That's good because I also wanted to ask you, and this could be a conversation people have all day, but on some level the movie is about a man haunted by childhood failure and the movie rejecting a "Win at all costs, earn love through success" version of masculinity through domination.

Yeah, but we live in that world. So I feel like denying the truth of the world that we live in in order to stay positive is a fairy tale. We have to acknowledge that everybody is trying to get that dollar. Everybody's trying to be successful. People uplift successful people. If you're not successful, there is a detriment to it. But at the same time, we can't be the Hawks about that. In nature, we all want to win, but we have to have a sense of fun along the road of trying to acquire that success.

Would I be right then to say that you're advocating for lighting the fire under people but not suggesting that if it doesn't work, then they're worthless?

Yes. One hundred percent. Nowadays kids—I'm going to sound so old when I say, "Nowadays, these kids"—but a lot of kids with the immediate gratification, the immediate connectivity, don't appreciate … I think there's a little less of a work ethic. There's a little less of a fire under their ass. They don't see the road where Will Smith started out and how long it took him or what he went through—even when he was successful when he was young, what he went through to get there. Any successful person, you hear of overnight success, but you don't realize what their brain was doing to get them to that overnight success. There was a desire, a fire, a sense of "I can't lose" behind that. People get lucky on occasion, but if that wasn't there it would not have happened. If I wasn't dedicated—I was crazy. I was not a normal kid. I breathed, ate, slept, everything I did was about becoming a movie star. That was my mindset. As hokey as that sounds, that was my mindset. I woke up in the morning and I thought, "OK, gotta get the Backstage. Gotta submit to these things. Where's the auditions? Let's go. Let me learn these lines." I was obsessed. You have to be obsessed, and behind the obsession there is a fire that is only lit with the knowledge that you could lose.

I don't disagree with you, but what it makes me think about is that it's no secret that money doesn't buy happiness, and the world is full of people who worked their ass off to get to the top, got to the top and then said, "Oh, this doesn't feel like anything." When we're talking about this drive and making sure people don't shrug off the value of success and winning, how do you reconcile within this notion of coaching or ambition the idea of people asking themselves, "Why am I even trying to achieve this in the first place?"

Right. That's a good point. That's a great point. When I look back as a little kid, why was I trying to achieve this goal of being in movies? I'll just say this from a place that I understand. There was a sense that there might have been some trauma in my life. There might have been something that made me go, "I need more acceptance. I need something to fulfill me." And ultimately it probably, if I reached the pinnacle of success, and I was an A-lister and reached Macaulay Culkin's status that I was trying to get, I'm pretty positive that it would not do what my subconscious wanted it to do. So, yeah, that's a great point. What is the meaning behind your desire to get this success? I think it's all about the journey. I left the business when I was 16. I made a lot of money when I was young. Did not make a lot of money for a good 10 years. And I can tell you right now I wasn't rich at one point. I didn't have the ideal movie star or TV star life. And I was happy. And now as I'm a 40-year-old talking to you, I can say money does buy happiness. But it's not going to buy the thing that's missing. Money can buy happiness, but if that's what you're going for and you're trying to get the happiness just through that and you're not enjoying your road along—

we're all chasing the dollar, so at the end of the day, getting that dollar is great. It feels good. You're able to have freedom. Money buys complete freedom. But once you have that freedom, you're still stuck with your demons. So if you haven't worked on those and you haven't pursued a life of happiness and joy and it's only been to gain that freedom, you're just going to be a miserable person who has a lot of freedom.

That's really well said. Moving to "Heavyweights," there's a moment early in the movie when Jeffrey Tambor's character says, "We have to nip this thing in the bud." And you tell him, "You're fatter than I am; why don't you go to the camp?" What involvement do you think parents should have for a kid who is overweight? It's the crux of the movie, and I think there are some people who would say "Let kids be kids." And others would say that for social and health reasons they should be involved.

Extremely involved. I think it's equivalent to not letting your kids run across the middle of the road. Being obese as a child is—some of my costars have already passed away, and I just turned 40. It's a health problem. And this is at risk of being frowned upon by cancel culture, but I don't give a shit, to tell you the truth. I think this whole cancel culture aspect of things has really not allowed people to speak their minds and what's important. And of course it's needed for certain aspects of what's happening, but I also think it's pushing people into a cult-like mentality and not allowing them to have their own ideas and beliefs. And my personal belief is that if you have a child who you see, whether it's because of genetics or whatever the case may be, that is overweight … and I'm not talking about a little chubby. Little chubby, hey, don't let your kid eat too much sugar. Don't feed your kid crap. That's one aspect. But then you have obese kids. That movie had a lot of obese kids. At the time I was considered obese as well. I was over 35 pounds overweight. I was more than 35 pounds overweight at the time. I was a 12-year-old, and I weighed 150-something pounds. I'm 10 pounds heavier than I was when I was 12 years old, and I'm 40. And I'm two feet taller. And I'm not here to say, "Hey, I worked out, and I'm a man." I don't mean to sound critical or mean in any way. I just think that a lot of us fall to food as a source of feeling good, as a way to pacify some sort of issue that we have in our lives. And when you do that you're hurting your body. I think it's a parent's job when their child is not at the point where they're making their own decisions or they don't know enough in their life to make their own decisions, you're not going to let your kid run across the street. You're not going to let your kid do whatever they want to do, go out and party with their friends all night when they're 10 years old, go have some drinks. You wouldn't let your 10-year-old do that. Why would you let your kid eat Snack Pack after Snack Pack of sugar and crap that they're putting in their body that would ultimately harm them in future years? So that's my point of view. I'm not a health nut, but maybe because I've become a little healthier and I've seen the detriment, and I've seen friends die because of their weight, I think it's a huge issue, and I think the idea of fat shaming has blanketed our belief system when we need to pull back a little bit. It's not fat shaming if you're unhealthy. I think everybody's beautiful in every shape that they have. But it doesn't mean that everybody's healthy in every shape that they have. And we have to differentiate between the health of a person and the idea of disregarding the person because of the way they look. There's two separate things, and as a species, America especially, we have to slow down and look at what we're allowing to happen because of the idea of fat shaming or being part of a group. It's just as bad as smoking a cigarette when your child is overweight and you're not doing anything about it. Was that a little too dark and deep? I'm very passionate about that because I am into help, and I think it's really horrible that little kids are shoving sugar in their mouths every day and becoming diabetic and dying young.

Totally. It would be hard to take issue with the statement, "I want kids to be healthy and follow science and know that their body is doing what it needs to do." Where it becomes difficult is you want kids to have self-esteem and not feel like, "If I become this or I'm different, then I'll have value." The end of "Heavyweights" has a sense of moderation. I don't think those guys are going to stop eating Oreos completely. But they're just not going to only eat Oreos.

Right. That's how I live my life. I love Oreos! I think I had an Oreo last week. I love eating crappy sometimes. It tastes good; it feels good. Do I live my life that way? No, because I know it's detrimental to my health. It's a great way of putting it. It's about moderation. I also think, to hit on the point that you stated about little kids shouldn't feel that their sense of value is attached to their body weight, 100%. And I think that's another point that the movie makes. Yeah, we got made fun of, but at the end of the day we're proud of ourselves. But it should be isolated to, "OK, you're this person. That's OK that you're overweight. That's OK. You're not any worse for wear being this way. But continuing to stay on that path is a problem. It's not that you're a bad person or that who you are is connected to it. But the health of the machine that you've been given to use in this world, you're putting undue pressure and problems on this machine." It's touchy. It's just like teaching kids in sports. It's a touchy subject. You have to balance it out. You have to instill in the child that they are good, and they are worth everything no matter what they look like. But that their health—I think taking away vanity from the idea of health is the key. Don't connect the vanity—even though this world is just surrounded with vanity—to the reason you're losing weight. Even though I lost weight when I was 15, 14, and I think it was because of girls. I wanted to get more attention from girls. That's not probably the best way to do it, but that helped me understand health after getting into that mode of being healthy. I was like, "Oh, it feels better. I feel better, I can walk upstairs without losing my breath. My mental state is better." And I think it's important to separate those two. It's not about vanity. It's about health. It's about wellbeing. And no matter what, you are important. And you are loved. But at the same time, you want to continue being important and being loved for a long period of time, and not just let all the food in the world, eat all the food, and don't have any type of moderation. Moderation is key for anything. You indulge in anything in life, it hits a lazy point in somebody, and I think there's a moment where we all have to work. We all have to work on anything that we want. And that's part of working. Your body is what's allowing you to stay and continue working.

Ben Stiller's character is obviously a major catalyst for what happens in the movie. But I'm just now thinking about this: If the characters see food as a crutch for what they experience outside of camp, it would be interesting to watch an alternate version of the movie where their bonds together make them change their reliance on the food naturally because it's not the solace they previously needed. Or maybe that's not profound and that's just the principle of the camp.

I think that's what happened in a way. I think Nurse Julie in the movie—it's so funny, we're having this philosophical question, conversation about "Heavyweights"; it's such a silly movie, but at the same time, all these Adam Sandler movies, all these Judd Apatow movies, they all have this huge message, and I think that's why they're so popular. They hide a lot of this goofy, toilet humor behind this massive message, which is like, and each one's different of course, but with "Heavyweights" it was the camaraderie. It was a very "Mighty Ducks"-esque, "We're a team" kind of thing. "We're all in this together. We're all overweight; so the F what? Let's work on it together, and our camaraderie is the crutch that we need. Not the burger, not the Oreo, but our camaraderie is what's going to fill that void," and in doing so we become healthier. So to speak. Totally. I love that point. That's a great point.

In "The Mighty Ducks," as you said, every character has their role, and of those roles Goldberg is the big goalie who farts a lot, and people kind of think he's gross. As you said Karp to an extent is kind of comic relief, not really a main driver of the plot or an active guy on the ice. How would you compare the treatment of overweight characters in "The Mighty Ducks" and "Heavyweights"? Or to put it differently, how would the "Heavyweights" characters feel about those "Ducks" characters?

Hmm. Huh. That's a good question. Josh and Goldberg are the same person. Karp and Gerry are the same person. Let's take those people since they would be most like themselves. I think Goldberg would think Josh was the coolest thing alive. It's basically Goldberg in "Heavyweights." The thing about the way Josh is written, he's kind of a rebel, and he kind of goes against the grain and he's like, "All these rules, all these regulations, a bunch of BS." Oh my god, there's a crazy guy. That poor dog. Oh my god, man. I'm sorry, but this guy's carrying his dog and screaming "F you!" to the world. And this poor dog is just sitting there being carried. I think of the dog's position in that, thinking, "What's wrong?" Oh, man, that's sad. Anyway, sorry. Where was I? What was I talking about?

Goldberg and Josh, Gerry and Karp.

I think Goldberg, they would love these characters. I think Karp and Gerry are two completely different characters. I think Karp would think it's a bunch of BS. He'd think that "Heavyweights" was like, "Oh, please." He'd think be like almost fat shaming as a fat person himself. He'd still be fat shaming. [Laughs] And I think Goldberg would be like,

"Rock on." I think Goldberg would love Josh, or vice-versa. I think Gerry would look at Karp like he has some therapy to go to. [Laughs]

That's a big contrast between the two characters you played. That Shaun's characters would hang out, and your characters would be repulsed by each other.

We would not like each other. Gerry was kind of shy, good kid, good heart. Was kind of being bullied, not being the one who started the bullying. Even though I think Karp was still a good kid, he was kind of a bully, kind of a roughneck. And Gerry was this quiet, down-to-earth, scared-of-the-world kid, until he ended up taking over the camp and keeping Tony Perkis from doing anything. Yeah, they're two completely different characters.

Did you say Karp would see Gerry as fat shaming? I thought you would say it was the other way around.

Oh, no, wait. I think Karp would look at the character—did I say Karp would look at it as fat shaming? Yeah, I guess I did. Yeah, maybe he would. I do think he would look at it as fat shaming. I don't think he would be protective. I think he would just be like, "This is ridiculous. Who cares about these fat kids?" [Laughs] I don't know. You have to ask Brill about that. Brill wrote that character. He didn't give a lot of intricacies into Karp's backstory, so I couldn't really tell you.

You had mentioned in another interview that like many who have had success, you weren't sure who your real friends were, and after "Heavyweights" you didn't know who was just your friend because you were now a lead in movies. Is there a specific story that comes to mind about that?

Yeah, let me think. There have been a few. I think one time maybe going out with a girl, I think she was a huge fan, and I think that was one of the main reasons she went out with me, not because of who I was. And it got to a point where I fell for her a little bit, and I realized maybe she didn't feel the same, or she wouldn't have felt the same if I wasn't in the movie. That was a situation that kind of upset me, I remember. There was a friend of mine, it was after "Heavyweights" came out and I was in high school. I ended up switching schools to a place called Beacon High School, which was like two blocks away from PCS. I wanted a real school; I also didn't want to spend $20,000 a year on my school. [Laughs] I was like, "Let me not spend all my money on this." And so I went to a real high school, so to speak. And I became really good friends with this kid who almost pretended sometimes he didn't know who I was, but he knew 100% who I was. In Beacon people would call me, "Oh, it's the 'Mighty Ducks'" or be like, "What's up, Mighty Duck?" I was treated normal at times, but there were times that I realized that maybe some people were friends of mine because they wanted to say they were friends of mine. And I ended up having a girl I was going out with, one of my first girlfriends, who ended up cheating on me with him. It was a very big moment in my life. The rejection of that really got to me. And I went, "Oh, wow." I looked at my fame at that point in a negative way for the first time, when I hadn't before.

This might be a dumb question, but I think when people hear a story like that, they ask themselves how you can tell when someone isn't in it for the right reasons? Are they always bringing posters for you to sign?

[Laughs] It's very subtle. I think you learn over time. Some people are super obvious with it, and those are people either I'll have them in my life as acquaintances and they won't really be good friends of mine, and what ends up happening is those people get disappointed in your humanness. In you just being a normal person and having faults and not being this idea of a famous person. All famous people—I wouldn't consider myself a famous person now. At the time, I would say I had a little more of that, and I would say that anybody who has any type of fame, a lot of people will look at them like they're not real, like they're not a person. They won't subconsciously think of them as a person that has the same feelings. "They're gifted or they're better off because they have more money or more popularity," but it's complete BS because it isolates a person. It makes them even more of that human aspect. It makes them even more vulnerable and lonely. I think you can kind of see through when somebody's like that, especially when you're younger. And as you get older, and years and years of experiencing that, you can kind of wean it out. You get fooled sometimes, but most of the time you can wean it out when somebody's like that and they're ultimately there for the wrong reasons.

As you mentioned, at 14 or 15 you got in shape to get more attention from girls and chose that over acting opportunities that were happening because of being overweight. Do you ever think about how those impulses would have been different if you had felt differently about acting at the time? Or if "Heavyweights" had been such a smash that you had to do sequels and stay heavy? The way that those two things played off each other seems like such a major fork in the road in your life.

That's interesting. I do sometimes think about that. In the beginning I would think about that in a nostalgic, "What if?" kind of, "Goddammit, why couldn't I have become more successful through that?" And later on, I think about it in the way you're asking. Almost like, "What if?" I'm so happy with the way things turned out. I'm happy with who I am as a person right now. I think I could have easily fallen into a narcissistic type of personality with the way I was as a child, and with a bunch of fame. Would I have stayed heavy? I probably even more so would have become skinnier earlier with all that fame just because I think it would have put me into a narcissistic mindset. I think I would have been a workhorse; I think I would have been a workaholic, and I don't think I would have stopped to smell the roses so to speak. I wouldn't enjoy the small things in life, the important things in life that I do now because I was able to take a step back and have the freedom of not being famous as I got older. I'm grateful for the fact that I had that break, and I didn't become an A-lister. Of course I want to continue acting and make movies and do what I love, but I'm also grateful for the anonymity that I was able to have, from a late teenager to an adult, there were moments I didn't have it, but for the most part the anonymity and the ability to live somewhat of a normal life allowed me to become an empathetic person and to become a real, grounded human being.

So I take it you were not recognized very often during your time in Israel?

[Laughs] No. Not at all. It's so funny, these movies became cult classics. "Mighty Ducks" was huge. People found out I was in "Mighty Ducks," some people recognized me, it happened once in a while. But in Israel, it was a great way to get away. I look at that now and I think that was what I was trying to do, just get away from it all for a little bit. I feel like I subconsciously knew things could get bad if I became famous and I stayed in the business.

On that note, I want to ask you about the documentary you're making about child actors, "Raised in Hollywood." What is the biggest thing you learned about yourself through working on that? Is there something you didn't know when you started that changed through the process?

Yeah. I feel like there's a sense of trauma in my life that caused me to act. I feel like a lot of child actors either had before they got into it, or it ended up happening. There was some sort of trauma happening. I was starting filming it and was a champion for child actors, and as I've been filming it, I'm starting to defend the idea that maybe children shouldn't be allowed to become famous. I have my foot in both puddles, so to speak. I want to be a champion for child actors, and that was the basic idea of "Raised in Hollywood." There's a stigma attached to being a child actor, and I don't think it's fair. I think that the stigma is not accurate. And so I want to pinpoint where the stigma comes from. I'm sure there are many facets to where it comes from, but ultimately pinpoint the major aspects of the stigma attached to child actors, why it's there. Is the narrative something that is perpetuated because it's created by the outside world and we just play out what the outside world is stating we are? Or is there something to this trauma and this idea that what we have in us that makes us unique. That we all have somewhat of a connection to each other because we all understand the way our world works is a little different than the way everybody else's world works. I think that was the idea behind it. It was the reason I wanted to make it, is because I think a lot of people are misunderstanding these "Where Are They Now?" posts and these clickbait posts. People want to see a disaster, and they want to see the disaster cleaned up. But you can't see that disaster cleaned up without witnessing the disaster, and ultimately people want news. When you see a child actor going through all this trauma and BS, like Macaulay Culkin with his father, taking his father to court. You got Lindsay Lohan, you got Britney Spears shaving her head. You have all these child stars going through all this shit, and that's one of the main reasons I ask everybody I talk to, "What's the first thing that comes to mind when you hear the phrase 'child actor'?" And that's to prove the point that ultimately everybody has that stigma in the back of their head, that it's a bad thing. And I think that's a horrible thing for young actors who are starting out to know right off the bat. You're getting into this, and right off the bat you know you're going to be traumatized. I think that's a crappy situation for a young adult or a child to be put in. So my goal was to expose some of that to the world. At least have a conversation and have the conversation be out in the public so people will think twice before demonizing or thinking that, "God, you're a child actor. You must be screwed up." For the most part, I don't think that's the case, and my goal is to provide a narrative from the inside and from the reality of what Hollywood is and the reality of Hollywood as a child. An aspect of it is I'm going to have therapy sessions that are going to be on the documentary, and it's going to get a little deeper into the idea of what is the trauma of a child actor? Why is it so traumatic? Or is it? Or is it just we're all human, and the only difference is child actors are in the public eye and regular kids are not?

Are you saying that kids who succeed as actors are subconsciously being identified because of trauma they've experienced, or that some child actors are not coming from trauma and then become traumatized? Or both?

Both. I think that's the idea of the whole thing is that when you have a child actor getting into this business, is the narrative of being a child actor pushing them toward allowing that narrative to come to a fruition? Was that narrative not going to exist unless there was an outside source feeding it? I think that's the aspect for some people. I think that happens to some people. I think some people come from great families. They saw something and wanted to become an actor and they become an actor, and somehow they become famous. Next thing you know they're going through all this stuff and looking at media or being told, "So and so is smoking weed," and it becomes this big—like Miley Cyrus doing tons of drugs and becoming this drug addict. Were they going to become like that before it was already becoming this idea? That's the touchy part of the documentary. I don't know. I don't know the answer to it. I still don't know the answer to it as I'm doing it. There are aspects of child actors that go through this business unscathed until TMZ catches them doing something and all of a sudden now they're that person who did that thing. Now they're this person who had a keg party. That was one thing Macaulay Culkin did. When I was growing up, I went to a keg party. Should a 14-year-old be going to a keg party? No. Do they do it? Hell yes. It happens all the time. But we don't see it in the public eye. So now a normal kid who went to a keg party and nobody saw it and didn't get caught is still that normal kid. Grows up, had that keg party, didn't do anything and is no worse for wear. Maybe shouldn't have done it, it was a mistake. But the kid who was a child actor and it was all over TMZ or whatever National Enquirer at the time, now they have been identified as that person, and now they ultimately consciously or maybe subconsciously identify as that person, that messed-up child actor. And I think that's a big aspect of why a lot of child actors fall off the wagon or go into those insane moments because we're all expecting them too, and it's creating the story for them that they haven't even lived out yet. That got very passionate; I'm sorry. I'm literally doing this as a passion project. I don't know if it's going to make any money. I don't really care. I want to create it and put it out there so people can see this side and understand that idea behind it.

Of course I don't expect a painful story when I ask this, but when you talk about trauma as it pertains to you, are you able to identify what you mean by that?

Sure. I've never hit that status of Miley Cyrus or Britney Spears or Macaulay Culkin, so I couldn't feasibly tell you what it's like to walk down the street and have to hide or be hesitant to go into a supermarket because then you get bombarded or have security guards around you. I couldn't begin to tell you what kind of trauma that brings to a person because I'm sure it has to do something, especially in your formative years. For me I think the trauma happened before I was acting. My mother and father split up when I was young, it was a bad breakup, big custody battle. And I think that created some sort of sense of abandonment in me, which ultimately led to me looking for some relief from that abandonment, which was acting. So I think my choice in acting most probably stemmed from that. But a lot of kids don't choose acting. Or a lot of kids choose acting when they're a little older just because they saw something on TV and they came from a family that didn't have a lot of trauma, there was nothing wrong. It's an individual story each time you tell it, but I think there's a running theme along all of it. Me as an actor, let's say I did become an A-lister, even with my childhood trauma and then all of a sudden I became an actor because of it and I became an A-lister. Would that trauma rear its head? Probably. Would it be exacerbated by the idea that there's paparazzi everywhere and people saying I'm somebody that I'm not? And then I become that person? I think I've had that trauma. I think I'm a pretty well-rounded individual. Long-winded, as you can tell, [Laughs] but I'm pretty grounded, and I think I'm a pretty good person, and I don't think there's a lot of traumatic things going on in my life. And I came from that childhood trauma. I think everybody has some sort of trauma when they're kids. That's what turns us into who we are. I think the difference is when you're a child actor and you're in the public eye, there's a compounding of trauma added to whatever you already had as a kid, and it creates this narrative which would normally not be there unless you were in the public eye. And I think mostly at the fault of the outside narrative, not the inside narrative.

And it's not like art is going to stop casting kids. So it's just a question of how do you protect the kids who are in that world, and how do you undo the label of, "Who cares if you were the lead when you were 10? Show me what you can do as an adult."

That's a major aspect of the documentary that I've been hesitant to put in there about abuse and about those kind of things that are happening in the world. I think a major point—I talked to Corey Feldman, and everybody knows he's been trying to get out that there's a lot of abuse happening for kids in the business. It's fortunate I never experienced any of that, thank god. But it's there, and I believe everything he said. He did say that if you're a mother or a father and you're allowing your child to possibly become famous, you are abusing your child. And I had a problem with it because I know my mother is one of the sweetest persons in the world. She is wonderful, and she would never want to abuse her child, and I don't think she did. But there is some truth to that. This business does have a lot of that abuse happening, and they're not checking it. Which they haven't been for a while. And to be honest, and I hate talking crap about a union that I'm a part of, but there is an aspect of Screen Actors Guild that still allows—I don't even like talking to this level of it because it's not a fun topic to talk about—but they're allowing pedophiles to still work in the business with kids. There's restrictions, but they're still allowing that. I think these people should get their SAG cards taken away and never work again. And the fact that that's not happening is a huge issue. So those different parts of this, I don't know how much I'll be able to put in the documentary with not even being able to get it out in public. There are some documentaries that are made talking about that, and you can only watch them on Vimeo because no streaming service would allow it because the financing behind a lot of these streaming services is coming from the same place that the financing is coming for Screen Actors Guild and for other things. So it's a messy thing, and it's a hard thing to talk about without ruffling a lot of feathers, but it's something that I'm planning on talking about.

I can't wait to see that. I also wanted to mention that when this book comes out I'm hoping people will want to learn more about everyone included and what they've done and have coming up. Your IMDb page says you're in a forthcoming movie called "Trailblazers." Is that accurate?

Yes, that is happening. It's been taking a long time to be made. One of the writers is playing my wife. It's Antonio Sabato, Jr., right? Is that the one who's part of it?

Yes.

Yeah, it's happening. I think it's going to be filming in July in Texas. RJ Mitte, who was in my documentary, he's going to be a part of it. Yeah, it's something that I'm going to be in. Not a huge role, but I play a fun drunk father whose daughters went missing, and he's looking for his daughters. I guess people like me to play these interesting characters, drunk or ... I was in a short film called "Ponyboi" where I played a bisexual pimp. So it's [Laughs] been an interesting career I've had, but I'm excited to play interesting characters. To cross out of my wheelhouse a little bit.

Sure. I hope you understand why I mention this: While I am allergic to anything salacious, I have to ask the questions that anyone might be wondering about. With that said, you're Jewish, as am I. On social media you shared video of you celebrating the Biden/Harris victory, so there's that. It strikes me that the cast of "Trailblazers" is kind of a who's who of pro-Trump celebrities—

I didn't notice that. I didn't see that.

Yeah. Kevin Sorbo, Kristy Swanson, Scott Baio, all people that, speaking for myself, I used to have fond feelings for and now I don't for reasons that are widely available on the internet. So I was surprised to see that and felt like I had to ask what decision goes into that sort of thing for you.

Well, if I find out that any of these people are aiding something that's not good for other people or saying something that's—here's my position on anti-Trump, anti-Biden, all of that. I celebrated Biden because I think that Trump's a moron. I didn't celebrate Biden because I am an extreme leftist who agrees with anything that's not Trump. I will say one thing here real quick: I think right now this world, and I hope this doesn't sound bad, but I think this world right now the way we are with politics is we are kind of in a cultish mentality. If something is left, then everything that's left you have to agree with. If something is right, everything that's right you have to agree with. I wouldn't call myself a Democrat anymore because I'm not in full agreement with the blanket of what Democrats believe in. But I'm not a Republican at all. I'm a human who believes in being a good person. I think Trump is a moron. For the people who were voting for him, he would state that he believed in everything that they believed in, which was completely BS. I think he was a complete opportunist, and I think that's the main driving force for Trump. So I think he was a complete idiot because he wasn't doing anything other than what would suit him or be good for him. That being said I also disagree with some things that extreme left people are believing. I think there's something to be said for having your own choice and the freedom of choice, and I think we're kind of losing that in this cult-like mentality from left to right. So that being said, if the whole crew are Trump supporters but they're good people and the script is not in any way trying to dictate some pro-Trump or pro-hate message, then I don't care. I don't care if all these people are believing in a bigot, as long as they are not being bigoted toward me or the rest of the cast or anybody in the world, then I'm not going to take offense to any of it.

As you said, because you are someone who believes in the importance of being a good person, I was curious about your take on it. It's a difficult point that the world has come to. To me, the degree to which some of these actors involved have been very outspoken about being in favor of the persecution of a number of groups, Jews included, in the last few years.

Oh, is that within Israel, like anti-Zionist, pro-Zionist, that kind of thing?

I just mean the embrace of white supremacy of the last few years.

Has there been an embrace of white supremacy? Or has there been an embrace of a person who's condoning some sort—like I said before, Trump is an opportunist. A complete opportunist. So the stuff that he's spewing and him condoning certain actions by not saying something, I wouldn't consider white supremacy. I would consider that a dangerous opportunist. And I think some of these people that supported Trump supported certain ideas and retroactively supported white supremacy when that wasn't their intention. Until you know the person and you've talked to them—that's the whole thing. I don't want to be considered somebody who is in support of something. I will distance myself if I see anything or hear anything, whether it's through the script or though anybody that's involved, if I hear some horrible, horrible anti-Semitic remarks. I would do a movie with Mel Gibson right now. Because I think there's another thing to be said about people who have made mistakes and who have said certain things. We're not the same person we were a year ago. I probably said something a year ago and if it was put into the news, I would be canceled immediately. I think there needs to be a little leniency, and within that leniency I think we'll find leniency on the other side as well.

It's thought-provoking. You're touching on forgiveness and empathy, and I appreciate you understanding where I'm coming from and why we're talking about this.

And I don't disagree! Man, I'm a born-and-raised New Yorker. I might be white as white can be, but I'm also a Jew, and my father was a Hasidic Jew. I'm completely against any type of hate toward anybody. That breaks my heart, but at the same time that goes along with also being empathetic toward people making mistakes.

I like the people saying that "consequence culture" is more accurate. To that end, without diving into that rabbit hole, if you were to work with Mel Gibson, would there be any litmus test you would need in order to feel comfortable in knowing that he had changed?

Yeah, I would have a straight-up conversation with him. I'd be like, "My father was a Hasidic Jew." I'd straight-up make the most uncomfortable situation for him to say—I would make it comfortable for him, but I would bring up the most uncomfortable thing off the bat. And I am not just saying this because I'm being interviewed. I am somebody, and people who know me know this, I have a filter, but I also filter very carefully. It's very New York of me. I will say something if it's bothering me. I won't beat around the bush. I come straight for it, and I tell it like it is. I've always been that way. And I would do the same thing no matter if it was the Queen of England, the Pope, Mel Gibson, whoever. If I'm going to be working with them and I have an issue with anything they've said or said in the past, I would bring it up, straight up. Would I lose a job? Maybe. Then that would be the answer, and I wouldn't work on the project. I think to put a point on what you said about cancel culture or consequence culture, what's happening is not consequence culture. I think there are aspects that are, but there's a lot of cancel culture happening, and there used to be a lot of forgiveness. We're all human. We're all doing stupid things. James Gunn wrote something that was a dumb, idiotic joke years ago. And somebody saw it, and immediately he was taken off of—everybody's afraid. If it was consequence culture, Marvel would not have been so afraid. They would have been like, "OK, let's have a conversation about this." Instead, there are thousands and thousands of trolls, which are immediately canceling a person because that's what they do. I think there's a group of people that are consequence culture, and there's a larger group of people that are cancel culture, and I think it's getting caught up between the two, and I think ultimately it's bleeding out, the consequence culture, and turning into cancel culture. I think we have to go back to the time where we forgave everybody. That time is the most important time because we're all making mistakes. Yes, we have to pay for these mistakes, but we also are human, and we all make mistakes. If we put people in a box and this is what they said and they're forever this person, then we're not doing what we're preaching, so to speak. So that's one part of the whole equation which I find to be disconcerting. And I understand if you disagree with that, but I personally feel like people need a little room. I think there's a lot of bad things happening. There are a lot of bad people doing bad things, and I don't think they need room. They need to pay for what they've done. But I also think there are a lot of people that did things years ago that might not be the way they are now. And I think we need to look at that and decide whether we want to just immediately write that person off or welcome them back in.

I appreciate where you're coming from, and we could talk about this all day. To me so much of it is about opportunity. At this point there are so few opportunities in the world, and so many people are just trying to fight for equality and being on the same level, that when someone identifies themself as having been hateful—I don't think everyone has a horrible skeleton in their closet at all. It's a spectrum. The dumb thing I said when I was seven that was mean was not hateful.

Not you, right. But then again you get somebody like a Hitler or somebody who's hurt a lot of people or done something treacherous and horrible. Then that's another story. But a lot of the things we're talking about are people like Mel Gibson. I hate even putting Trump in this category because Trump has hurt a lot of people. So I'm not going to put him in that category. I think he's an idiot, and I think he's harmful for America and for fellow human beings. But that being said, there are people out there who are Trump-esque that didn't have the platform that he had, and thank god. But these people are harmless, and they are opportunists who try and do anything, and maybe they've learned their lesson. I think that some people have learned their lesson and paid the cost of what they've done. And I think to not allow any forgiveness is a bigger crime. That's world war or civil war. We take this pain out of anger and sadness and we don't even realize we're doing it, and once we realize it it's a little too late because nobody's giving you the time of day. I think that's the saddest thing. I understand the anger on the other side as well, so it's not me justifying any type of wrongdoing or hate speech or hate actions. But I think there needs to be, just like you said, with everything there needs to be not moderation but not just, "[Incident], stamped, and you're out." There needs to be more room for discussion I feel like.

It's a forgiving way to look at things. To apply it to the reason I asked the question, it's interesting that you said you didn't know about the rest of the cast of "Trailblazers." I'll be curious if anything changes with that.

Yeah. I'm going to look into it for sure.

I think the hard thing everyone has felt in this moment is, for example, I had a close friend who is not a close friend anymore. And if I had to summarize that in short, it would be because he is on the side that to me is harming people and advocating for that, and that makes a lot of people less safe, including my son, and even if you realize that was wrong, that harm is—

That's totally understandable. I totally get that. I would ask myself a question if it was my friend, personally. Is the reason this person is taking that side, what is it based on? What are their beliefs? Are all their beliefs in line with that, or only some of them? And maybe they're making the mistake of taking the side, but is what they're doing in their beliefs harming? I think there's a cultish mentality that just because you believe in certain facets of somebody's belief system and then you find out that are harming people or doing things to be harmful, it's an issue if they decide that they don't—ultimately I think that we will never get to the place where we're not fighting with another person that doesn't believe we what we believe in if we don't take that mentality of forgiveness. Not saying that we have to forgive all but saying that we have to open up a dialogue. More often than shutting a person down or pushing a person away, even if we believe that maybe this person is in line with something that's extremely dangerous. I still think there needs to be this dialogue because if not, we're going to become this perpetual argument that will never cease to exist because anything that the other person says is already wrong. There needs to be a gray area. It can't just be black or white. There needs to be an understanding of why a person does something, and then make the decision. I really think that just throwing out a person's—I don't even know how to phrase this. I'm being very careful with saying this, and I understand it's something personally that happened with you, and I don't know the situation, which is also why I'm being careful. But I do think that if we don't open that dialogue up and we don't look at it with more of an empathetic eye as opposed to a fearful or danger, eminent danger eye, that we will ultimately stay in this vicious cycle of just hating each other.

I guess for me it boils down to if it's a back-and-forth learning about something, that's one thing. But if it's you in a situation with another actor and you say, "I think everyone should be treated equally," and the other actor says, "I think whites are the best," to me that's not a two-way learning. That's either you sitting and educating them, or—

If they state that and it's a solid statement, as opposed to the person who said that is friends with somebody who's friends with that person, it's a different thing. If somebody says straight up, "White people are the best, and nobody else deserves what white people deserve," then that person will not be a part of my life. Straight up. But if they are in connection with somebody who said that and because of that connection that person is not part of my life, I would look into it a little more. Because what if their belief is different than that person's belief on that aspect? You could say that the person's supporting that line of belief just by supporting the person, but I don't believe that. I think I would definitely keep a greater distance from that person because of the idea that it could possibly be that, but until I had a conversation with the person and understood exactly why they supported a person who believed these things, I wouldn't write them off 100%. I wouldn't have them part of my life until I had that conversation, but I wouldn't write them off because I would want to understand the other person's side. I think that's the major key here is a lot of people are not understanding another side. They're just understanding the major alert from that side, and they're not looking at the intricacies of what's under it. And this is not in any way supporting any horrible—I'm a Jew, I don't support any of that [hate]. But my opinion is people should look at the human side of even somebody supporting a hateful person.

I think the way you broke that down was useful.

I'm a New Yorker, a Democrat. Man, Alexandria Ocasio[-Cortez] is my friend. I worked with her at a restaurant. She's Xandy, she's my friend. I support everything that you're talking about, but I don't want to throw the baby out with the bathwater. I think that's a detriment to what an ultimate Democrat should be.

I'll be curious to hear if there are any updates about "Trailblazers."

Oh, yeah. I'll keep you posted. Thank you for that information. I'll definitely look into it. And also I don't want to be looked at as somebody who is supporting something like that. But I also don't want to leave a job because I could look like somebody who is supporting something like that. Because that would be completely the opposite of what I'm even stating right now.

Update: In May 2022, a little more than a year later, I spoke with Schwartz again after seeing that he is no longer listed on the film's IMDb page. Indeed, he isn't part of the project anymore but not for any political reasons. (The script contains no political ideas, he said, and he hasn't spoken with any cast members about Antonio Sabato Jr.'s film. For what it's worth, Scott Baio, Kristy Swanson and Kevin Sorbo are not listed on the film's IMDb page anymore either.) Rather, Schwartz left "Trailblazers" because the production—which had been slow to gather funding and set a solid start date—couldn't find union affiliation, and the size of the role and compensation weren't enough to justify being involved anyway. He remains open to working with anybody—as long as that person isn't treating someone poorly or prejudiced against anyone. "The only thing that will stop me from working with somebody is if I truly believe that they're hurting people or they're doing something that in my opinion is a detriment to another human being," he said. "And I don't think any of them have."

Ariana Richards of 'Jurassic Park,' 'Tremors,' 'Spaced Invaders,' 'Angus,' 'Boy Meets World'

If you weren't paying attention, or maybe if you were just 10 years old, you would have thought that Ariana Richards was plucked from obscurity for the role of Lex Murphy, the computer whiz with the incomparable scream who survives near consumption by a T. rex and numerous raptors in 1993's "Jurassic Park."

In fact, the actress, who as an adult has dedicated herself to painting, was in some ways the established and clear choice for the role, having already proven her ability to convey intelligence and/or fear on screen in "Prancer," "Spaced Invaders," "Tremors" and "Grand Tour: Disaster in Time." Whether shouting or trembling in terror or mastering the Unix system in the tensest situation imaginable, Richards is excellent in Steven Spielberg's undisputed classic and did a lot of other smart, thoughtful work in movies like "Angus" and "Broken Silence" (a TV movie about a high school track star sexually assaulted by her coach), and in a memorable episode of "Boy Meets World."

When you think back to the '90s, what's something you're nostalgic for? It can be anything that you miss.

Gosh, one of the things that I love is—for example, part of "Jurassic" was the way that they used actual animatronic dinosaurs. There was so much put into making these films, and that's something absolutely from that era that is not something that you see anymore these days.

Obviously you have a unique perspective, having been involved in that. For the general moviegoer, do you feel like something is lost because that isn't done anymore? Why is that what comes to mind?

It just comes to mind for me because I feel like that particular era was kind of a golden age of special effects in a way because the guys like Stan Winston and his crew were so hands-on that it gave a particular sense of richness to the set, to the filming. I'm not saying it's better or worse; I'm just saying it's different.

It was almost like a happy in-between point where things had progressed to a certain point that was utilized really well, but also it hadn't gotten past the place

where things shot into space and were less hands-on. Maybe it's an odd connection, but it reminds me of how people my age talk about how we had the benefit of having a little bit of technology growing up, but it hadn't blown up too much. So it was the happy medium that you're talking about. A sweet spot in a way.

Yeah, actually that's true. Interesting, that thought about a happy medium. I was remembering back to the late '80s, and I did a movie like "Tremors" for example, and that was where the special effects were at more of a beginning stage. They had models. It was funny [Laughs]; they were just kind of starting out, "Let's see how we can make these creatures look kind of real." They hadn't gotten to the point of what they got to at all with "Jurassic," for example. Yeah, you have an interesting point there.

I don't know if there's anyone in film history who has spanned the special effects spectrum in the course of three years the way that you did between "Spaced Invaders," "Tremors" and "Jurassic Park."

[Laughs] I know! "Spaced Invaders," oh my gosh. That was so funny. I still remember my alien costume. I don't know how I remember these things that far back. But it was funny. Basically the wardrobe people handmade my alien costume by gluing pieces of foam onto this thing they had fit to my body. It was so funny. And my helmet. It was just hysterical!

Slightly different from the "Jurassic Park" approach, but only a little.

Yeah, slightly different. And while we're on the "Spaced Invaders" topic, I have to talk, since we're talking about technology and special effects, that little robot in "Spaced Invaders," it was so fun. It was named Spiff. It was real; they made this little robot; it was in quite a few scenes with me. I was eight years old or so, and I was just thrilled to have this little robotic co-star. I thought he was the coolest thing ever. I was always telling the director [Laughs], "He's so great. Can I keep him?" [Laughs]

If you had to think of a movie or show that you were not in but enjoyed as a fan, what comes to mind?

"Batman Returns" was great, with Michael Keaton and Michelle Pfeiffer. That was pretty fun. And that was close to the '90s. I guess it was '92. That kind of thing was really fun. I like seeing the superhero coming into more of a serious role, not the kind of goofy, comic-book thing that was done before.

Are you more of a DC person than Marvel?

Which one are you?

I won't win any fans by saying neither. Do you tend to go more for Batman and the darker characters?

Out of Marvel and DC, I think I'm more of a Marvel girl.

I know Steven Spielberg told you he didn't want to know where your scream of terror came from, but I couldn't find anywhere that you explained it. So he may not want to know, but I'd like to.

That was a funny moment with Steven. I think it's really about the acting. That's what it is; acting is putting yourself in that zone, where you actually are feeling those real emotions. That's the type of acting that I do. I wouldn't call myself a method actor, but I would say that when I'm in character I am absolutely in character. Even as a child actor, I was very serious about my craft. I would get in character as Lex, and I'd be feeling all these real feelings of imagining, "OK, put myself in a situation. How would I really feel?" And let that come alive. So that's really it. I was feeling those emotions.

To what extent did you feel a different challenge when working with the live dinosaurs versus reacting to nothing? Maybe it's an obvious, simple question to think it was easier when the live dinosaurs were there, but maybe not.

Yeah, of course. Of course it would be easier. I mean, can you imagine trying to act with a co-star that is a piece of tape on a long stick? It's a lot harder than to actually have a co-star with you there in the scene.

Assuming you're not someone with an illogical fear of tape, I suppose that makes sense. It's the difference between your imagination and reality. I guess the reason I asked was if, in theory, even though the dinosaurs were so extraordinary, I'd wonder if having them be physical and in person and you knowing it's not real and there are people working on it would then be less scary than totally going from your imagination.

Yeah, working with the imagination is something that you do as an actor, and once you really set up the reality for yourself of what the dinosaurs are like, what they are, you have to block out the fact that … I wasn't stupid. I knew that there were guys working on the dinosaurs, moving its toes and mouth and eyes and all that, so you block that out and you experience the moment and let your imagination take flight. So whether it's a dinosaur or a piece of tape, you're still working with that imagination and making sure it feels real for you in the moment. It's like the interview initially when I first interviewed for the project. It was just so mysterious. Of course, you don't have anything to look at in the initial interview and the initial taping. They just said, "Pretend there's a terrible dinosaur that's going to attack you." And you just imagine it, and that's it.

I definitely remember that summer when the movie came out and I was 10, I was interested in the movie but nervous at first to see it. It's interesting to think about movies playing a role in making young viewers scared as a way of confronting emotions and experiencing life and going back to the safety of reality. Do you think there's value in that?

Hmm. That's an interesting question about that. Because movies and stories in general are absolutely geared to be able to take people out of their current reality and experience a new reality for a time, and then go back to their current life feeling different. Feeling happier; they got to experience some awesome movie. But to your question about feeling scared, like a young person watching a show and feeling scared and going back to their life and [Laughs] maybe their life doesn't feel as scary anymore or they're not as anxious about stuff as they were previously. I don't know. Is that your opinion? Is that really how you see it?

I guess so much about growing up is figuring out how to understand the world and overcome various fears and uncertainties. To overcome your fear of seeing a movie and love it and see it a few more times is much different than a social situation.

Absolutely. It's totally different. But the thing is that a movie is an escape. It absolutely is an escape from whatever your current life experience is. And I love that about movies, and I'm sure you do too. So absolutely. There's something really, really extraordinary about people at a young age. There's a lot of plasticity. There's a lot of change, and young people's personalities are just forming. So absolutely, for them to be able to get inspired by something or, like you said, be really scared to see a movie and then think, "Whoa, this is an amazing experience! I feel so great. I want to see it again." That kind of makes them look at the world in a different way. I think that's absolutely possible. In fact, I loved inspiring young people. That's one of the things I'm crazy about. I was really honored. In 2018, I received a Reel WiT award from the National Center for Women & Information Technology. NCWIT. They were great because they validated something that I experienced for years; whenever people did send fan letters in [Laughs], I would get a lot of fan letters from girls and young women saying, "Hey, your role as Lex inspired me to jump into technology and the world of information and computers, engineering, that had previously been male-dominated. I just love it. I'm passionate about it. Thank you so much for inspiring me." So I love my award; I have it in my studio, and it's fun to look at. So that's been pretty special.

Definitely. The movie does a good job of flipping the perception of "computer nerd" and showing what she can do. And in terms of flipping perception, I was also thinking that I can't think of a side mirror without thinking of a dinosaur charging. I'd like to think I'm not afraid of it now, but it's that sense of conquering something that you were afraid of or shifting the fear of the unknown to not being afraid of it anymore. Can you think of a movie you were ever afraid to see?

[Laughs] Oh, gosh. A movie I was afraid to see. That's an interesting question. I guess I was kind of afraid to see "Arachnophobia," but then I actually did get arachnophobia about spiders. [Laughs] I was actually OK about spiders before that movie. That was so funny because I was invited to the screening for "Arachnophobia" by the leading actor who I'd worked with before, Jeff Daniels. I had to go, right. I wasn't really excited about seeing this movie, but I thought, "OK, I better go." But, yeah, it totally freaked me out! [Laughs] I was nervous, and it was worse than I imagined. Totally looking for spiders everywhere after that.

It's a good thing to mention that sometimes a movie can have the opposite effect.

[Laughs] It totally can! Yes, I know.

I still remember going to see "Problem Child," and there was a trailer for "Darkman" and I was having a sleepover at a friend's house and had to come home because I was so scared from the trailer. The things that scare us as kids.

Just the trailer alone! Exactly. Yes. Yes. It's crazy, isn't it. Isn't that weird? You look back on it, and doesn't it seem like such a long time ago?

It does. Maybe I'm late to this, but I only just discovered, after seeing the movie for the 100th time, that there's a 20-year age difference between Sam Neill and Laura Dern. You being 12 or so during filming, was that evident to you, engaging with colleagues mid-20s versus mid-40s?

Oh, no. Gosh, I was 12. I mean, think back to when you were 12, right, Matt. Were you that focused on whether an adult was a little bit older or a lot older? Honestly, I don't think so. At 12 you're either a kid or you're an adult, and you don't really make a lot of distinctions between—I thought at 12 when I was 17, I was going to be an adult. You'd have all these thoughts at 12.

You're right. For a 12-year-old, a 15-year-old is a veteran of world experience.

Right! [Laughs] Yeah.

On that topic, I wanted to ask: Whether it's being a computer expert in "Jurassic Park" or an intellectual who knows trivia in "Grand Tour" or even a Santa skeptic in "Prancer"—

Oh, you did your research! Yeah!

Thank you! This might be hard to answer, but every actor is chosen for a particular reason. Do you have a sense of what about you tracks as an intellectual or

someone with a degree of authority? For that to be said for someone so young, it's worth asking if you have a sense of where that comes from.

Hmm. That's an interesting perspective. It really is. It's something that I haven't been asked before, but I absolutely can see the parallel in the characters I've played. I would like to think that it's something that I brought to the table, my personality. But honestly these characters were already written before I came to the role. But I guess the people, the producers and directors, thought that I would be a good fit for it to be able to express that character. I definitely have a side of me that loves the intellectual side of life. Very much interested in exploring that. For example, even during the filming of "Jurassic," I was extremely interested in spending time with the late Stan Winston and his crew and learning about how they were manipulating these models and learning how they worked together in concert six guys at a time. I found all that fascinating. And when I wasn't hanging out with Stan, I was usually hanging out with Jack Horner [Laughs] and hearing all about dinosaur information and actual paleontology and what the discoveries were currently at the time and started to get really interested in learning about that. So I've always had an incredible hunger for learning. I just kind of follow that.

About spending time with Stan Winston and his crew, you've said they were really patient with you because you were so curious. Why did you put it that way? What did they need to be patient with?

Well, anybody on a movie set—as you know, a movie set is extremely fast-paced, extremely structured. Everybody has to keep playing their role to keep things moving, to keep the shots being filmed on time. So just to have a 12- or 13-year-old sitting there with you and all your guys, and Stan taking time to actually explain things to me, talk to me. Those were seconds he may not have had. So he always made that time for me.

Do you remember what you were most curious about? Or was it just everything?

I don't know that I can remember just one. It was just lots of conversations about the workings of these creatures and how they built them from the ground up and how this particular dial moved this particular part of the dinosaur. And sometimes he would let me actually manipulate parts of the dinosaur! That was so fun. I was at it again with the computer people, though, too. I was incorrigible, wasn't I, on that set? [Laughs] I was doing the hacking part when I'm into the Unix system, and it was really old school. They've got the back room with all the computer tech guys manipulating the screen, and then I'm there with the mouse and the controls and everything, looking like I'm pretending to move around the screen. I was so bold. [Laughs] I just started talking to the computer guys and saying, "You know, I would really like to be the one to start moving this cursor around the screen myself in the scene during the shot. Can I do that?" [Laughs] So they actually said OK and let me play the Unix system, which was really fun for me. And it just felt really real. I've always been interested, even as a child, in making the scene feel as real as possible. [Laughs]

Curiosity and that sense of authenticity and wonder goes a long way. Whether you're making a movie or playing a game with your child. It's committing to the moment.

Sure. That's a good word. Authenticity, wonder, those are really, really good. That's right; what do you have except for the moment you are in? If you can make that the richest experience, you're doing pretty well, right?

On that subject, as you said, the early-to-mid-'90s were a special time for special effects, and "Jurassic Park" will be a classic forever for good reason. Much has changed about the world and what movies get made since then. Is there a sense of wonder that gets lost because of what movies get made now and how, or is it just that we're older? To put it another way, is it possible for people to have their minds blown in movies anymore the way that it was in 1993?

That's a good thought. To have people's minds blown like it was then, because it was—it was a huge leap in what someone could achieve in the theater at the time, that's true. So can people have their minds blown now? That's a good question. With what's out there, all the technology that's been available for a long time, gosh, it really depends, doesn't it, on the person. I'm kind of looking at this in terms of a young person. I feel like when young people hit the theatres with "Jurassic," it was so mind-blowing to them to step into that new reality and have it just kind of take you, just grab you and take you on a roller-coaster ride. Such a good question. I think it's a case-by-case basis, but I do believe that young people, just by nature, are always open to a new experience. They're not saddled with all the preconceived notions that adults can attain being jaded and what have you. So they are an incredible audience because they will take on that raw experience of that movie and just run with it.

I'm trying to think of the last thing that really shook me awake. My mind goes to being lucky enough to be at the Sundance premiere of "Me and Earl and the Dying Girl." Every single person was crying, and it was so beautiful, and I loved the movie. It sold for a ton of money, then came out and made no money, and now just feels like this quiet, unknown thing. Which is extremely different from a big-budget sci-fi movie, but maybe it speaks to us being at the point now where what blows your mind has to be something that just blows your mind as opposed to everyone's mind.

Hmm. That's an interesting thought. Do you think we're at that point that it's a different genre that we're in, that we passed that genre of the '90s, and the type of thing that can have the possibility of being mind-blowing is actually going to be a little different? A different angle, a different take on a story?

What do you think about that?

Gosh, I don't know. You were the one who came up with the idea, the concept. I think it's interesting. I've never thought about that before. It's an interesting concept that you brought up.

It's hard. As time goes on, you don't know, like, am I jaded? I loved the Oscars when I was 12; I don't particularly love them now. Did they change, or did I just change?

[Laughs] That's right! Yeah! Or is there a third thing: Did what's popular now change? Trends change all the time. Yeah, it's funny, we kind of watch ourselves and what do we like over the years. Yeah, that can be an interesting question. [Laughs]

Of course any experience someone has leads them to where they go. But in terms of work like "Spaced Invaders," "Tremors" or anything else that preceded "Jurassic Park," was there anything in any specific way that you learned from the earlier works that you changed later on for "Jurassic Park"? Or any way you can identify how your previous work prepared you for that?

Hmm. Yeah. Let me think. I started acting when I was 6, so I kind of grew up in the world of performing. I love it. It's part of who I am, and I had a great time. It was so much fun. I didn't feel like I was going to work, which was great. And that's what you hope, right, for a child actor, is it's just fun. It's a game. Yeah, preparing for it, I'm just imagining what if I hadn't had any of those previous experiences filming all those years before "Jurassic," what if I just entered it cold, right? Is that what you're thinking, like how did it actually change me to be ready to play that character?

Yeah, that's a great way to frame it.

Hanging out on different locations, I think, was a big deal. Just being part of a family on a movie set for so many years growing up, I became really comfortable in that life. I loved it; I was comfortable meeting people. It's a whole other reality. You're not in a structure like you would normally be, going to school every day and seeing the same people every day but for months at a time you were part of a family on a film set. You might be on location; I was filming in places like Hawaii or out in Lone Pine. You become aware of the different terrains when you're out there looking for things [Laughs] like rattlesnakes or whatever. You just have so much variety. So I think that absolutely prepared me for it. If I had just jumped into "Jurassic" without having any of that before, it would've been a learning curve for me. A huge learning curve. Sides, script, you've gotta memorize this, you've gotta get in character. There's a lot that was already normal to me. And actually our first day of filming, it was a pretty cold-water dip for me to just jump into the most emotional scene when it comes to crying, just absolutely in tears about my brother, it looked like he was going to be dead falling off the fence and all of this right out of the shoot. Not even having time to get to know my co-stars before just jumping in, just being on the island.

So I think I was prepared by the earlier work to do that, to do my job, to be a professional and just go for it.

If you think you asked a lot of questions in reality, think of how many more you would've had in this scenario.

Oh! [Laughs] It would've been crazy. It takes time to learn this kind of thing, just to get accustomed to it. So that was great. I felt right at home on set right away. I loved that. I liked just going for it, and I liked that Steven knew what he wanted and would help me contribute to the scene. Because I always like to put my take on the scene, and he wanted me to be natural. He wanted me to be me. And we didn't have a lot of takes, which was great. He was really, really decisive. So we would get it, and I'd be super excited if I actually hit it right the way he was hoping for the first, second or third time. It never gets old to hear "one-take Ariana." You're a kid, and you're so excited. "You're one-take Ariana!" "Yay!" [Laughs]

That's incredible. You mentioned how you felt so happy acting as a kid. Why do you think you were so interested in the first place at such a young age? Some actors talk about not knowing a sense of self and feeling comfortable as anyone but themselves, but I'd be a little surprised if that was your answer too.

Yeah. That's an interesting perspective that some people have. But I could see why they would have that because a lot of young people really don't have a sense of themselves at all and maybe they find it as they're trying out different roles and acting. That could be an experience for them. I feel like I kind of came at it from the opposite direction. I just always felt really grounded as a little girl. Really confident, and I was just excited about learning and experiencing the different roles from that perspective. Meeting people, going to different locations. I was kind of outgoing to a fault sometimes. It's pretty funny to look back on my interview for "Spaced Invaders." It worked out, I guess. I was sitting in the waiting room and looking at the poster. The producer had a company called Smart Egg Productions, and I just thought that was so funny. I was 8 years old, this little, tiny girl, and I meet him in the room, and no prompting from my mom at all on this, believe me. I just thought, "I'm going to talk to him about his production company." "By the way, I really like the name of your production company. It's called Smart Egg Productions. That's a great name!" Apparently that won him over. [Laughs]

That seems to make sense.

[Laughs] It's so funny!

That's awesome. It's funny; so much of being a kid is so instinctual, what seems right to you and what you're drawn to. So the idea that that is what a producer or director would see in you, and then it leads to you getting cast in a number of roles

that show what an intellectual and curious person you are, to the point that decades later someone is asking you about that.

That's weird to look at the span of that. But I didn't actually notice that so much. I just thought, "That's who I am. I have that perspective on the world like that." But it's interesting that it actually was reflected in the roles that you pointed out. That's an interesting thread that carried through.

The one question I wanted to ask you about "Tremors" was that I have long been curious, fascinated and amused by the pogo stick. You talked about getting really good at it. I want to hear about that. What type of demands, practice, evaluation was involved? Or am I blowing that way out of proportion?

No, you're not blowing that way out of proportion. It was one of those things where, yes, I was ultra-confident, and I also wasn't dumb. By the time, what was I, 9 or so in that audition for "Tremors," and I'm getting to the final callback and I know that they're really interested in me for the role, and I'm excited about that. And they ask me toward the end of the reading, "By the way, Ariana, do you know how to pogo stick?" I probably paused for a second. [Laughs] And I said, "Yeah! I can do that." And they thanked me, and I left, and my mom had to buy one for me so I could practice. [Laughs] I guess as an actor I've always wanted to go a little further in preparation than even was necessary, especially with physical preparation. So even at that age, I just didn't need any prompting. I got a pogo stick in my hand, and I just practiced every day until I could get up to jumping about 500 times without stopping. So I was ready for the scene, and that was great.

Is that like riding a bike? Could you do that tomorrow if someone asked you to?

[Laughs] That would probably be a really funny thing to put on Instagram! I could completely crash [Laughs] on a pogo stick, I bet, if I tried one tomorrow.

I admit I was also imagining the idea of someone pogo sticking away from a dinosaur.

Oh. Oh, yeah. See, now you need to start writing for "Jurassic." That's it! It's settled. You've gotta write the next scene.

The movie may be acclaimed and made all this money, but without a pogo stick I don't see how it can even be worth seeing.

Well, there you go. You've got to talk to Steven and Frank Marshall. They've got to listen to you, right?

In researching for this conversation, I remembered your "Boy Meets World" episode well. I also watched "Broken Silence" and the Ben Folds Five "Brick" video.

All of those involve serious, heavy, emotional issues. Those are all very different, but I'm wondering if you have memory of the prep for that material or if anything in particular required special preparation because of the subject matter?

Yeah. The Ben Folds video, and all of the projects you mentioned, as well as "Angus"—my character was bulimic in "Angus"—so I did a bit of prep into whatever character I was playing as these teens going through some challenging life experiences and some pretty devastating experiences, like when it comes to "Broken Silence." So I do some research. I always did, when it comes to what some of these people might be going through. Even when it comes to something like bulimia, trying to learn more about what it was. I feel like people in that era, if you didn't have an issue you weren't really very aware of what the issue might've entailed for other people, so I tried to learn a little more about that and was pretty surprised at how horrible it could be to be trapped in that experience and learn a little bit more about that. I even lost a few pounds for that project just on purpose to feel like that person who is so thin, just painfully thin, just to get into that zone.

I realize these aren't issues that people might be eager to talk about, understandably. Have you heard from anyone about any of those projects because of difficulties they were going through and how they responded to what they saw?

Yeah. I received a lot of great letters from people of all different types. Yes, people have gone through every one of those experiences, sure, but I feel like a lot of people wrote to me about "Angus" in particular. It wasn't just about my character; it was just about the message in the movie itself, that they were struggling as a teen and trying to find themselves and get through that. Whatever issues they happened to be going through, and that movie actually did give them a little bit of a push to getting through some of those things and coming out on the other side and feeling a lot more like they wanted to feel. So that was interesting for me. It had a great cast. "Angus" had a really incredible cast. It got very, very little attention. Even so, people still found the story and experienced it, and it meant something.

Definitely. That movie is hiding for people to find and connects in a unique, vulnerable way. I really like teen movies when they go well, and that's one that has its own distinct personality. So that's great that you heard from people who recognize that.

Yeah! Exactly. It's interesting because you heard from people in that old way, when people actually wrote fan letters. And nobody does that anymore! But that was how it was then. You get the hand letters, and they would draw art for you and all sorts of things.

Speaking of which, your art is beautiful, and you've talked about how much you enjoy getting to know the people you're working with when you're painting them. What's your process to get to know them? Are there unique questions you like to

ask to get a sense of who they are? What makes you feel like you know them enough to be ready to paint?

Yeah, I do. I love getting to know people. I don't go searching for people; they come to me when they're interested in having me paint them. A lot of times it is about painting a person because people love their families. They want to create a moment or capture them doing something they love to do, a feeling that they want to remember. Being outdoors, for example, natural light and that spontaneous feeling of impressionist brush work. That's what I do a lot of times. I do enjoy the process of getting to know someone, but you asked what's the benchmark of me—when do I feel like I know a person well enough to say, "OK, I'm going to paint you, and I'm going to put my impression of your essence down on that canvas?" The main thing, I feel like as an art form, really, it's kind of how I would approach and how I do approach looking at an acting role to play. I look at it in terms of how does it make me feel, what am I resonating with here, what is the story of this character. So I see a person the same way, as a character, who they are. What are their motivations? How do they see the world? Are they super shy? Are they super outgoing? Just kind of get to know the basic type of person they are, the things they like to do. Then I'll often have a conversation with them, a video conversation or on the phone, just get to know them that way. Then once I feel like I've got a little bit of a sense of, "OK, I think I've got a little sense of what you're about," then I go for it.

That's a cool and intimate process. I imagine you saw the movie "Portrait of a Lady on Fire" and were like, "Damn right."

Yeah. Actually, no. I did not see that. Was it good?

It's incredible, and I would be shocked if you didn't love its presentation of how knowing a person allows you to capture them differently.

I will put that on my list. [Laughs]

This question is not to get you to say anything bad about anything. That's not the point at all. Because "Jurassic Park" was so incredible and impactful, it's easy to imagine that anyone who goes through any sort of insane life peak has a certain degree of comedown for other things. Was there any sense for you of having to emotionally re-regulate or change expectations? Especially for a kid, it would be easy to be like, "Well, everything from now on is going to blow my mind." Did you have to adjust that or learn from experience that that was the exception and not the rule, despite doing a lot of other cool stuff too? Does that make sense?

Yeah, it totally takes sense. I get that. Absolutely. I guess your perspective on it definitely could have been the case about me taking that as, "Whoa, this mind-blowing reality where I'm known all over the globe and insanely famous and can't sit down anymore at a cafe to even have a bit without a humongous line of people coming up to me to talk to me and tell me how much they loved my character." All that stuff being the norm and then dissipating and having to be like, "Whoa, what's going on here?" It really wasn't like that for me because I grew up in the acting world, just being a working child actor and living a fun childhood. Having an awesome time doing competitive horseback riding and dance and music and schooling and hanging out with friends along with my acting. So it was like that was the exception. That was the shock for me. I guess being naive and young, just going into "Jurassic" feeling like, "OK, this is just going to be another fun project like I've done before." Not really thinking through, "Wait a second; this is a Steven Spielberg project. This is probably going to be a gigantic blockbuster." Just kind of living in the moment, one day at a time. And when it literally exploded, it seems like overnight, that was the anomaly for me. That was the anomaly that, "Whoa, wait a second, my friends are starting to get jealous of me? This is new." [Laughs] So you kind of hit all that. So I think it was kind of the opposite perspective for me, like, "Wow, this is really different."

For sure. That's well said. I guess I meant more so that some of the work would be fulfilling in different ways, but it would be hard to match the high afterwards.

Oh, yeah. You can never match a particular high of that type of experience. It is and always will be, what we achieved with that film. And what we achieved with how it affected people. You feel like, OK, you bond, you're working on this project, you made it happen, it affected people to this level, that is a high that absolutely it was incredible. You can't match it. That would be like machines. It's an art and a piece of art and anyone involved in it created it and put it out there and the impact was really, really something, how it reverberated over time is just really something we're seeing now. That absolutely can't be matched again. I'm really, really happy I got to be part of that at that time. It's a good thing I didn't go to Disneyland that day instead of meeting Steven [Spielberg]. [Laughs]

If you don't mind me asking, how did you deal with that recognition of your friends being jealous and that hard, real-life emotional stuff? Was that hard to navigate at the time?

You know, teenage years are hard for everybody. You're kind of forming who you are as an adult. You're kind of in the in-between place. It's always awkward for everybody. So I think that it probably made it more challenging for me to get through those years because of things like that, that level of unusual nature of, "Whoa, so much excitement and fun opportunities," the same time as weird stuff around your peers and jealousy and so forth. That kind of I guess shows you, "This is my real friends, and these people I guess weren't really ever my real friends." It was a weird way to navigate. I definitely haven't lived a normal experience growing up from the get-go. It's been a completely out-of-the-box experience from the beginning. But you know what? I love that. [Laughs]

Let's go out on a couple lighter ones: If you had to fight against real dinosaurs or real underground worm monsters like in "Tremors," who would you choose to battle?

OK, so quick question: Are you talking about raptors right now? [Laughs] Or not? There are different types of dinosaurs you have to deal with here.

That's true. You can answer any version you want. Does that change your answer, with or without raptors?

Oh, yeah. Raptors, hands down, not interested in battling. No. Hands down, that is not happening. So if they're going to be involved, I'm going for the underground monster battle. I'd definitely go for that.

Once you survive a T. rex attack, you become arrogant that you can do it again.

Yeah. I need to call Chris Pratt to get involved if we're going to go for the other ones. [Laughs]

If you could ride in an alien spacecraft or meet a real dinosaur and not be attacked, which would you choose?

Ooh, I would totally choose to meet a real dinosaur. Alien spacecraft, no. I think that a real dinosaur would be way more exciting for me.

And which dinosaur would you pick?

OK, so I wouldn't have to be interacting with it, right? I'd be in my own bubble or something? [Laughs]

Yes, it would be safe.

Oh, wow. I guess let's say the T. rex. I've gotta see the T. rex again. That would be something else.

Red Williams of 'American Gladiators,' 'Mortal Kombat: Annihilation'

Considering the remarkable ubiquity of "American Gladiators," both as a phenomenon in the U.S. and as a property that was adapted for many other countries worldwide, it now feels at least a little surprising that none of the Gladiators went on to become a household name as a performer after leaving the show.

The closest to movie stardom was Red Williams, who, after four years as Sabre on "American Gladiators" following an injury-plagued professional football career, starred as Jax in 1997's box-office-dominating, critically less-commanding "Mortal Kombat: Annihilation." While the movie is, let's say, a product of its time and choice of effects, it's easy to see the type of presence Williams brought to the role translating to exposure beyond the handful of TV appearances he made on shows including "In the House," "Babylon 5," and "NightMan."

While Williams, who now runs a ministry and focuses more on the spiritual than the physical, couldn't talk about "American Gladiators" due to contractual obligations with ESPN's "30 for 30" documentary about the show, I'm confident you'll still be glad I included our conversation about why he turned down a chance at stardom, his difficult upbringing, and much more.

What are you nostalgic for from the '90s? It can be anything you miss.

The music. The hip-hop music was at its peak. You still had messages in your music. It wasn't cursing every other sentence. It wasn't about sex every other sentence. You actually had music that would empower you, and I really enjoyed the hip-hop aspect of the music back then. And Arnold Schwarzenegger was still pretty big at the box office, and I was an Arnold Schwarzenegger fan.

That's quite a combo of things to put together. Are there any particular artists you think of when you talk about the music?

Oh, man. Outkast. Tupac. Biggie. Public Enemy. My whole playlist is pretty much '90s music these days. Souls of Mischief. Nas. Enigma. "[MCMXC] A.D." It wasn't hip-hop, but that was a great album.

It's so cliche for generations to look at new music and say it was better in the old days, but I feel like the era of rap you're talking about is so objectively better than what's happening now that it's not even a comparison.

It's not even a comparison. It's almost like there's a systematic attempt to dumb the population down. And I can't [mention favorites] without saying Ice Cube and Snoop too.

So Snoop gets a pass in terms of profanity and sex, then? You're OK with it in his voice?

It was just his first album. His first album was probably the greatest debut album for a rap artist in history, to me. He was such a different dude. *[in Snoop Dogg voice]* He was smooth like this, you know. [Laughs] Snoop D-O-Double-G. He talked a different way, and it was a change of pace.

What's a movie or a show from the '90s that you loved as a fan?

Can I just be generic and say movies? My daughter calls me the "Eddie Murphy and Denzel groupie" because whatever they're in I go see. And generally I give them thumbs up. No matter what it is. I think Eddie Murphy should've got nominated for "Nutty Professor" too. He should've won an Academy Award for that. I like movies in general. I was a movie guy. I had two young sons and a daughter that was born in '91, so we had to go to the movies every weekend to entertain the brood. I liked movies, and so every weekend we would go to a movie. If Denzel had a movie out, we went to see it. If Eddie had a movie out, we would go see it. If Arnold had a movie out, we would go see it. If Will Smith had a movie, once he got started in '96, we would go see it. I even gave permission to my wife to be able to say, "Will Smith is my boyfriend."

Some of those actors made a lot of movies people wouldn't call family films. Did that make a difference in what you see on those outings?

It did. Because some of those Denzel movies, "Out of Time," and the more adult versions, it would be date movie for my wife and I. But I saw some movies in the '90s that were hysterical kid movies. One of my favorite kids' movies of all time, and we saw them all from "Home Alone" to "Dennis the Menace" through whatever, I really enjoy "Baby's Day Out." I have a granddaughter now, and I make her watch it right now on TV at night when we're together sometimes, and she likes it also. She calls it "Baby Gorilla," and you have to watch the movie to understand why she calls it that. Because the baby was protected at one point by a gorilla in the zoo. I watched every movie that came out. There were some kid movies that I couldn't stand; oh my goodness, some were horrible. But for the most part I had fun at the movie theater. Then once I became kinda famous as Sabre or Jax in "Mortal Kombat" and some of the other stuff, I didn't have to wait in line. I could get my ticket ahead of time, and they would escort me in so I wouldn't get pestered by the fans.

Did that impact what you went to see? Like if someone said, "I can't believe Sabre is going to see that," did that change what you saw?

No. No. Once I became grown and learned how to fight, peer pressure disappeared.

And if you want to see a Julia Roberts movie, you should feel comfortable doing that.

I saw Julia Roberts movies too. I told you, I saw 'em all. I'm a moviephile. I tell you this: I met Quentin Tarantino probably in '91, '90. I should say re-met him because we watched movies as kids at the Carson Twin Cinema, but when I met him and was introduced to him, we were able to talk about obscure movies that you have to be a real movie buff to even know. Like "Phantom of the Paradise." I told him I had just seen "Phantom of the Paradise" again in the middle of the night, and I said the soundtrack was off the hook. And Quentin said, [in Quentin Tarantino voice], "Hey, wait a minute!" He ran to his room and came back and gave me a cassette tape for the soundtrack for "Phantom of the Paradise." I said, "I can't take your cassette!" He said, "That's OK! I have another!" I'm a moviephile like that. I'm that kind of nut. One of my favorite movies is "Cyrano de Bergerac," the 1930s version with the subtitles. And Quentin Tarantino's "Pulp Fiction" is the greatest movie ever made. And I say that from an analytic standpoint. You know how a movie can be great, but at the end it will do something that breaks the rules that it already set in order to tie the movie together nicely? Like the movie "Heat": All through the movie he says, "Always be able to leave within 30 minutes notice." And then at the end of the movie he goes back to kill somebody and then Al Pacino kills him, so the movie was tied together nicely but only because he broke a rule. "Pulp Fiction," every character stays true to themselves, and the movie turned out perfectly.

Is it true that you had to wear 40-pound metal arms to shoot "Mortal Kombat"?

Yes. Yes. Yes. I had to do that. They weren't metal though. You have some metal pieces. They were like fiberglass and some other type of substance. They were sprayed up and painted to look like metal, but they weren't metal.

What do you remember of the added difficulty of maneuvering on set with that? Or once you did it for a day or two it became standard?

I had to be careful because we only had one or two sets of arms, and I believe one. Because I really wanted to take a set with me, but they wouldn't let me have a set. I guess because I was a new star. I bet you if Denzel would've wanted a pair of arms, they would've given him a set. But I had to be really careful because if we damaged the one set or the two sets then there would be a lot of downtime. So I had to be careful. There were some things that kind of constricted movement because it was bulky. You saw it in the movie. But like you just said, after rehearsals and filming, because it was a five-month shoot, it was new at first but you got used to it and you were able to move pretty good with it. But you couldn't bend your arm all the way, so there were certain things that you couldn't do.

It's such a physical role for a physical movie, but do you notice the way the physical limitation impacts your thinking and speaking?

The character was kinda close to me. I was able to put my own personality into the lines that they gave me, so I was just acting like a bad, macho-man dude with cybernetic strength enhancers. The one thing at the beginning of the movie, I had to play with the arms like I had to get used to them. So at the very first fight scene it was like I was out of control and didn't have control over the arms because they were new to me, so it took a little acting, even if you didn't notice it.

People don't always appreciate the behind-the-scenes technical aspects of that, especially when it's something real on set, not CGI.

So you know I was very disappointed when I didn't get nominated for Golden Globes and Academy Awards.

The whole movie was shockingly shut out.

Yeah. But I saw the new one, and I'll take mine against the new one. The only thing we had, at the end of the movie we had CGI with the dragon fighting, and that was kind of crazy. But for the most part I'll take our movie over the new one any day. Hallelujah.

How did you feel when Jax was killed early and violently in the new one then?

No, Jax didn't get killed early! No. I don't think Jax got killed early in this one. Did he?

Yeah!

[Laughs] I don't care about the character. Like I just told you, I'm a moviephile. I understand. Listen to this: I bet if you did a study, 60-70% of the black actors are going to get killed in the first part of the movie anyway, right? So I guess that was par for the course.

I listened to an interview where you talked about having to convince the government in Thailand that you weren't desecrating sacred spots for the movie. What specifically did you say? Did they just take it at face value?

I said that the story we're telling is a story about faith, and in order to tell a story about faith on a high level you have to go to the holiest places on earth in order to tell that story. And we look at these temples here in Thailand as symbols of the holiest places on earth. And they liked it. I remember one of the producers saying, "Man, I was really impressed by what you said." And that was the story. Because we filmed in the temples of Tetra also. We went to Wales, a couple of holy sites. It was a story about faith in yourself, remember. That's what he told me. "Faith in yourself is all you need; you don't need those arms."

If those people who you sold the movie to that way, when they saw the film do you think it would've matched up with what they imagined when you described it?

I think so. All the way up until when the two dragons fought at the end. I think when the two dragons fought at the end, all bets went out.

I think part of the reason some movies like this are beloved now is because they feel handmade. Of course some of these weren't well-reviewed at the time. Based on the way people perceive different "Mortal Kombat" movies, did it feel like everything was working on set? Did you feel surprised at all when it came out and wasn't met with the same reception as the first movie?

At the very beginning, it was well-received. We opened up No. 1 at the box office. After that, it wasn't received well after the initial crowd came in. And I'm going to say this again, and I'm going to keep saying it: The CGI just hurt so bad! It just hurt bad. It took away from the actors. Listen to this: Brian Thompson is a quality actor, and his Shao Kahn role that he played was excellent! Excellent. James Remar is a quality actor that has been in several quality projects. He's one of my most beloved actors, and he did a wonderful job. We had a nice little idea for a script. I think they fell short in the visual effects, and that hurt us. That's what I believe.

At that time you were in this big movie, as well as episodes of "In the House," "Renegade" and "Babylon 5." If you could've had the trajectory of Dwayne Johnson, did you want that? I guess most people would say yes, but in terms of acting, was that the direction you hoped to go in your career?

Yes. Yes. And I went from a boutique agency to a big agency. And the big agency, did you ever watch the TV show "Entourage"?

I did.

And in "Entourage," they wooed Vince to this agency. Remember, they had him at the long table, and they had all the agents telling him how, "We're going to have writers, and we're going to have this, and we're going to have that, and we're going to make sure that you take off, and you're going to be the man." Remember that? I sat at that table. My movie opened up No. 1 at the box office, and then I signed to do "Hulk" for Universal Pictures. Got upfront monies and everything. So I was on this trajectory to be that star. I got a script, and in this script I'm a drug dealer, of course. I'm already going, "Oh man." The drug deal that's happening on Imperial and Crenshaw goes wrong, and I bust out of the McDonald's to get away, and I carjack a car at the light. It's a white man on his way to the Laker game with his Laker gear on, and he has a baby in the car seat. We struggle over the gun, the gun goes off, kills the baby in the car seat. Later they find the car stripped of its tires and its radio, and the baby is still in the car seat, dead with the shoes stolen off its feet. And I said, "No, man! This is not what I want to do!" And they said, "OK. You're free to find different representation." I could've said, "OK, OK. I'll take the meeting." But something in me was wounded. I got to see the real monster. The real one. The one who portrays certain people a certain way, and the one who makes stars out of people. And I could've done it. I had opportunities back in the day to do beer commercials. I had opportunities to do certain things. But since I didn't drink beer, I wasn't going to sell beer. And since I didn't want to be just another black dope dealer in the movie, I didn't take the role. And from that moment on, I kind of slowed down with the acting and the spirit in me just kept raising, and before you know it, I was given the title rabbiyah by my instructor, by my rabbiyah, so I teach scripture full-time now. I teach about Israel. I am Israel. We are Israel. So that's what I teach. Forgive me; that's what he teaches through me. I don't teach anything.

Was that 1997 when that movie was being pitched to you?

Yeah, I would say '97.

And obviously it didn't get made in that version.

Not in that version. It could've been a litmus test just to see if I would do it. And I look at some of the big stars, and I'm not going to call out any names. I look at some of the big stars that did projects that were beneath them, hallelujah, and maybe they were tested. Maybe we were tested with those. But I always wanted to be something positive. I came from an era where gangbanging was really real in my day. And I always wanted to unite the world. When the spirit of the creator woke up inside of me, I became a TV star in 50 countries. And I wanted to just keep feeding that energy and didn't want to go backwards and start cursing and slinging dope. And I wasn't corny; it wasn't like I was a nerd or anything. It's just that you had a whole bunch of actors that would take those roles. I was foolish to believe I could be Denzel and play only positive roles. I was foolish.

Was there any regret or any temptation of maybe, "If I do this, then I can do something else?" Or it didn't matter what would come after it?

I used to have those thoughts. Like if I would have just played the game a little better, I could've have had at least four or five … you know how they give a star like myself, who starred in a No. 1 box-office movie, had a nice body, that's what they would tell me: You have a nice personality, you have a nice look, blah blah blah. You're personable. Maybe I would've got at least four or five movies to see if I would pan out at least. You know what I mean? "We gave him four or five movies, and he's not a leading guy. We'll just make him a supporting actor." Maybe. But now that I teach scripture full time and I teach about the Father full time, I think that maybe if I would have gone all-in, then I may not have the spiritual connection with the most high, so I can live with the choice that I made.

When you think of the other work you did, the handful of TV opportunities you had, is there one that sticks out the most? And if so, why?

I did a guest star on a show called "NightMan." I played a black superhero called The Black Knight. And that's Marvel. That was before the big Marvel things that are going on now, and there was talk for a minute of a spinoff, to do "The Black Knight." Now that would've been very nice because it was syndicated, and syndicated television means that you film all 26 episodes. And it was 26 back then. So that would've been nice to get a spinoff to see what would've happened with my own syndicated superhero show. But the talks faded because "NightMan" ended up getting canceled that year.

It's amazing how many close calls there are in the history of the entertainment industry. I'm sure the '90s are no different than any other time, but this book has certainly illuminated a lot of them.

I almost did projects with Steven Seagal. I almost fought in the UFC. I can probably find the letter still that my management wrote to the UFC back then. Because I had retired from the Gladiators. They retired my uniform. And the UFC was at show 1, 2 or 3, and I thought that was it. I said, "That's my calling right there. I'm going to fight in this thing, and I'm going to whoop everybody in the world over and over again." And they said they had been getting inquiries from other athletes, so they were thinking of putting together an athletic UFC competition, so I didn't get a chance to fight in that. That's one thing I really wish I had been able to do at my peak, fight in the UFC. Back when the UFC used to throw elbows downward and stomp and do everything except for eye poke and bite? That was me. I could do that. From the age of 29 to 40, I was the baddest dude on earth, bar none. There was nobody on earth that could whoop me in hand-to-hand combat from the age of 29 to 40. I don't care who you are: boxer, wrassler [sic], karate man. Nobody in the world on planet earth could get any of me from the age of 29 to 40. And the only reason I stop at 40 is because when I woke up the morning I turned 40 years old, this is what I said to myself. I said, "OK, you 40 now. I wonder if you're still the baddest dude on earth." And that's when I said OK. That little doubt of me saying, "Are you still?" Because before that, I knew I was. Does that make sense to you? That one little second of doubt made me be realistic to myself and say, "OK, you might be slipping a little bit because you just questioned yourself."

You referred to hard times in your upbringing. I'm not intending to open old wounds or make you tell hard stories, unless you want to. But so many performers talk about using their real-life experiences to drive their performances, and I'm wondering if some of the things you experienced when you were younger, that you alluded to here and in other conversations, were utilized for some onscreen moments.

Yeah. I think that type of energy that I came from is the reason why I didn't want to do that role that made me stop being serious about acting. I didn't want to perpetuate that drug deal going bad and the kid getting killed in the car seat because I've seen it happen for real, and it wasn't fun. "New Jack City" and those other movies that we watched, they're cool to see, but what if you lived it? Is it fun? Do you really want to perpetuate it? I was outnumbered when I was growing up. We were in a little neighborhood called CenterView. We were a Blood neighborhood, but we were surrounded by Crips. We wore red, and we were surrounded by Crips and other gang members. So me not taking the beer commercials and the liquor commercials, that's because I see the beer and liquor every day in the 'hood. And September 1991, my nephew, my sister's stepson, was shot 29 times in the back by the West Covina S.W.A.T. team while he was asleep in his bed. And I was with him six days before he got murdered, and I had some weed, I had some Seagram's 7, and I had some beer. And we were sitting in the backyard, and he was sitting in the jacuzzi. I asked him, "Do you want a brew?" He said, "Nah, I'm cool." I said, "Do you want a seven-and-seven?" He said, "Nah, I'm cool." I said, "Do you want to hit the joint?" He said, "Nah, man, I'm cool. I just want to kick back and listen to the Dodger game." And in my mind, I said, "Whoa. He has changed." That was a conscious thought in my mind. And then six days later, he was dead. The police murdered him while he was asleep in his bed. I started drinking at three o'clock that morning when I got the phone call. I drank that whole day, and I never got a buzz. The Creator never let me get a buzz. I woke up the next morning and I was completely hungover. I said, "That's it. I'm done. I'm not drinking no more. From now on, I'm going to live completely Black." That means acknowledging my blackness at all times. So that when people see me, I want them to say, "Look at that strong Black dude right there." And I want it to be something positive so that they wouldn't have an excuse to kill me. So I didn't want to perpetuate liquor. I didn't want to perpetuate the stuff. Because I grew up in that hard life for real, and I don't want to make it seem like it was the hardest in the world. It wasn't. We had nice houses, but when I leave this neighborhood and I go somewhere else, if they weren't from this neighborhood, whatever I'm wearing they might want it. Whatever I'm driving, they might want it. Whoever I'm with female-wise, they might want her. Whatever I'm doing and they don't want me to do it, they might try to stop me. So I became an expert at hand-to-hand combat. I was able to locate weaponry when you couldn't. If you watch those "Rambo" movies and I say, "OK, I'm sitting in this house. There's a trophy; the top of it is metal. I can hit him with that. And there's a little statue of the Eiffel Tower. I can use that as a knife." I was able to formulate weapons in my mind where other people look at it as a trophy. So I was battle-ready. Not to mention, my father was a macho man. I mean, my dad was a macho man. My big brother was a macho man. So I'm from a long run of macho people. Self-preservation was high on the list, and me perpetuating the stereotypes that they had us on, I just couldn't do it. So it keeps going back to that again when you have those questions because I had a physique. I had a personality. I could read the lines. So, yeah, I probably could've been a nice little action hero. But they gave me the wrong role at the beginning. Maybe if they would've given me the superhero stuff first and then came back to it, it would've been good.

Certainly. I so appreciate you sharing that, and I would never pretend to be able to understand it first-hand. As we know, there's a long history in Hollywood of there being far fewer roles for Black actors, and limitations in the types of stories that are

told. The '90s in particular, though this wasn't everything, had a lot of movies focused on crime in the Black community. Would it have been possible for something to come along about that world that would've humanized the character in a way that you would've been interested in playing? This is not the same, but something like the Morris Chestnut role in "Boyz n the Hood" where he's the innocent victim. I'm not saying anyone necessarily wants to play that role of course, but do you see what I mean? Or was it anything having to do with that world at all you didn't want?

This may sound corny. But Piru is a street in Compton, and CenterView was the name of our neighborhood. So CenterView-Piru, we wore red. Now listen to this: In the movie "Boyz n the Hood," Morris Chestnut was a football star. I was a football star in high school. I only played four games of high school football in my whole career, but I had 26 scholarship offers after that. Twenty-six scholarship offers. I didn't have any grades, but I had scholarships. I had letters from Oklahoma, Nebraska, you name it, I had letters from 'em. Because I played against Banning, which the 1980 team was ranked as one of the top teams in the history of California football. So the similarities in that movie was almost like, "Oh my goodness, it's like they are following me." In the movie "Menace II Society," which is the bookend for "Boyz n the Hood," there was a character who was a low-rider, and I was a low-rider, who was going to Kansas to play football, and I went to Kansas to play football. So I'm saying, "Maybe my reputation was such that it was about me in a pseudo-form." So the movie you brought up, "Boyz n the Hood," that was real life. It was exciting to watch, but it's nerve-wracking to live. And I lived it. If you can put it in a poetic, cultural [context] where people can feel the pain and the cats that are doing the killing can go watch the movie and they feel the pain, then, yeah, it's worth it. If we can get the feeling out there. But just to have gratuitous violence just for the sake of violence because it looks cool, nah, I didn't want to partake in that.

Absolutely. And you said that you felt like coming from where you did informed the toughness you were able to bring on screen to a degree, and it of course shaped you so much. Are you able to share a specific moment you experienced that you can connect, between the real event and the performance?

When I was in high school, I told you we were outnumbered. I was involved in the biggest gang fight in L.A. city school history. It was a bunch of Crip neighborhoods against one little neighborhood, which was ours. It happened because earlier that year they had disrespected our neighborhood by burning our flag and throwing it where they shouldn't have thrown it. And we were kids, of course, but we were playing that game, and now that you get older, you realize it is just a game. But later, some of my people put hands on some people that maybe they shouldn't have put hands on because it wasn't their affair. So just like I had to organize our [people] to [have them] answer for what they did, they had to organize and try to make us answer for what happened. And we were vastly outnumbered. Of course I'm putting hyperbole on it, but like the movie "300": vastly outnumbered. Vastly outnumbered. But we prevailed. And that was kind of like that scene close to the end [of

"Mortal Kombat: Annihilation"], the climax, where I said, "Are we really ready to die here?" In other words, let's fight as hard as we can. If we're going to die, they'll have to kill us because I'm not ready to go yet. So that was kind of a parallel to that old gang fight that I was in back in the days where we were vastly outnumbered, but we still had to handle our business because they're going to try to take you whether you give in or not. So why give in? Go for it! You might be surprised! Hallelujah. And that's what happened. They were surprised. [Laughs]

So when shooting that movie, did you find yourself thinking about that real-life event? Or you just see the parallel now?

No. It's just something that I thought of when you brought it up. I'm like, "Wow, I could've used that for motivation." But being outnumbered all the time kept me in the frame of mind of always being ready. My wife will tell you. I've been married to my beautiful wife for 38 years. When we go places, she knows what she's going to take, and she knows what I'm going to take. I'm going to have my back to the wall, and I'm going to look out, and I'm going to make sure that I get her away first. So I'm battle-tested. I used to tell my wife, "Duck!" when we were girlfriend and boyfriend just to make her duck when I say "duck." I don't want you to look to see what you're ducking for; I just want you to respond to the word "duck." Because it was the wild west.

In a heated moment, even if it's when you're supposed to get a free meal at Sizzler and you don't, is there even 1% of you that's tempted to reference "American Gladiators" or anything from your past, like "Don't you know who this is?"

When I told you I quit drinking, September 1991, when my nephew got killed, I haven't had a drink [since]. In the old days, if I had a drink back in the early '90s, '90, '91, then yeah. One time, an old buddy told me, "Man, remember what you did last night?" I said, "No, what'd I do?" He said, "You grabbed that guy and put him in a headlock and started holding him up, talking about, 'We twins' because he was red like you." The guy was mad and trying to get away from you, but he couldn't. He wanted to fight you, but he knew that if he couldn't even get away from you there's no way he could fight you. So once I became sober I was able to use my vocabulary, and instead of just being a fly-off-the-handle kind of guy, no, I have a mouthpiece. The Creator gave me a mouthpiece with a vocabulary, so I can cut you up with my words. Hallelujah. And if you decide to get [aggressive], I can protect myself. But I was never a swing-first, push-first guy. I used to get bullied when I was in elementary school. I fought the bully back in the sixth grade, and he never bullied me again. And it was like an "A-ha!" moment because my big brother kept telling me that I could whoop this guy, but he was just so mean, and he was just so confident. But once I fought him back and he knew it was going to take some to get some, he left me alone. And I was able to start blossoming to be who I was going to be. So I was not a bully. If anything, I would bully bullies. So if you were over there with your girl and the bully came over there and wanted to bully you, I would bully the bully. "Hey, man, instead of messing with him, come mess with me! Oh oh, it's a different thing now, huh? OK, well, I'll tell you what: anything you say to him, say it to me. I'm going to take it like you talking to me now." "Hey, man, you ain't in this." "I am; every time you say something to him, you saying it to me. So you walk up on him, you walkin' up on me." That's the kind of guy I was. And now I'm 58. I think I can still do it, but I ain't got time to be doing that right now. [Laughs]

That's admirable that you were a defender.

Absolutely I was. I'll show you text messages where a guy says, "Man, I appreciate you protecting me when we were young." I said, "Don't worry about it, man. I used to bully a lot of people." He's like, "Nah, man, you helped me. Thank you." All right. I was just being me. My mom was a wonderful lady. The most wonderful lady in the world. And she used to help me so many ways. One time when I went from elementary to junior high, that same bully that I had to beat up, now in I'm in junior high school level, and I had new friends now. I'm a social butterfly. And he starts calling me a f**. "You a f**, you a f**. You and," well, I'm not going to say the other guy's name, "Y'all busting booties." He was talking bag and talking mean. I could take it because I knew how to bag back, but the other guy was new to this kind of bullying. He told his mother. So the mother goes to the school officials, and the school officials call people in the office, and to me, it's like, "Oh, man, I can't believe you went and told your mother." So now that makes the teasing go up. And my mother told me, "He talks about you like that because he's unsure about your own sexuality. You can be friends with whoever you want to be friends with, and you don't have to apologize to anybody." And from that moment on, it didn't matter to me. As long as my moms had my back, I was OK. And so I had all types of friends. White friends, Black friends, gay friends, straight friends. My granddaughter says right onw, "Grandpappy, do you have to talk to everybody?" We are the world ... this was pretty fun. This was an interview that I liked, so I enjoyed this. I need to get back to some of my music so I can get some of those memories for you from the '90s.

And you didn't even say A Tribe Called Quest. I thought that was guaranteed.

You know, A Tribe Called Quest wasn't one of my favorites. They were nice, but I was more gangster. I think Ice Cube "Death Certificate" is the highest-rated hip-hop album ever made. If you had an alien that said, "What is hip-hop music about?" It was about that. It was about "Death Certificate." That was it. But you had other classics in there. Nas' "Stillmatic," top five. Biggie "Life After Death," that's right there. Maybe Tupac's "All Eyez on Me." Outkast's "ATLiens." You had some songs on certain CDs that stood out to me because of the soul and because of what I was going through when they came out.

Common too. I'm trying to remember when "Like Water for Chocolate" came out, but "Resurrection" and some of the earlier stuff is good too.

There's only one Common rap song that I liked, and it came out in the movie "Smokin' Aces," and it was called "Aces High." You're naming those different types. The raps are cool, but they weren't the songs that you would hear when you would go hang out in the 'hood. You wasn't bumpin' Common. [Laughs] No disrespect to Common, but you didn't bump Common.

William Daniels and Bonnie Bartlett of 'Boy Meets World'

Yes, we know that actors are not their characters. But sometimes it's hard not to wish that they were just like them. How thrilled I was years ago when I interviewed Taylor Kitsch and he said things that made it seem like he and Tim Riggins are alike. That doesn't mean they are the same, but the parallels to his "Friday Night Lights" character are there, and when you admire someone, sometimes you want to see things a certain way.

Also, Kitsch at the time was building a house in Texas and said Riggins-like things like, "We're the type of guys, if we're going to fuckin' fall doing something, we're going to do it falling into a fucking vat of crocodiles with chainsaws."

Anyway, I bring that up because as much as we would like to think otherwise, especially in a tumultuous period in need of any moral stability it can find, William Daniels is not his legendary, "Boy Meets World" lesson-dispenser Mr. Feeny. Trust me: After reading/listening to many interchangeable interviews with Daniels, I was excited to try to get some new thoughts on the educator that still means so much to "BMW" fans. The character is an important icon for work ethic and integrity, even in a decade when so many shows for kids were trying to create that type of role model. Through Daniels' presence and George Feeny's blend of patience and BS-free motivation, the teacher, neighbor and friend became a source of reassurance to all of us.

But for Daniels, who does all of his interviews with his wife of 70 years Bonnie Bartlett, the role was just a role—one that followed work in "The Graduate," "1776," "Knight Rider" and an Emmy Award-winning turn on "St. Elsewhere" while preceding a few years as president of the Screen Actors Guild. Daniels says he didn't bring home any of Feeny's wisdom to use on his kids or in his daily life, and he doesn't feel any softening he's done over the years is because of Feeny.

The character is obviously meaningful to him, and he still gets tons of fan mail. Though when I ask for anything specific that people cite as inspirational to them about Mr. Feeny, or any advice that they seek from him, Daniels, 95, and Bartlett (a two-time Emmy winner for "St. Elsewhere," including winning on the same night as her husband), 92, tell me that most fan mail just cites Mr. Feeny's iconic advice to "Believe in yourself. Dream. Try. Do good," and the final episode in which he told an empty classroom, "I love you all. Class dismissed."

Seeking something different, something specific, I ask if he's someone who is typically as friendly to and close with neighbors, as Feeny was with Cory's family.

"Bill is not particularly a good neighbor," Bartlett says. "He's the kind of guy like his dad, 'You're on my property!' That's all in the play; that's not Bill at all. He's not a bad neighbor, but he's not a good neighbor. He's not somebody who would chat over the fence."

"I'm a kind of private person, to tell you the truth," Daniels adds. "But I'm not disagreeable with neighbors. I've never had any problem being the neighbor of people. But I'm a private person, and being an actor I kind of try to protect that privacy."

Which doesn't mean that he doesn't engage with people in many ways, including Cameo. When it comes to requests, he says people ask for messages offering answers to their problems or expressing sympathy for losses they have had. Daniels' son Mike helps him film those messages, Bartlett says, and then continues about the nostalgia that powers these inquiries.

"It's kind of weird that this whole fan thing is, that people have this nostalgia for the '90s and people watch this—it's OK, it's fine. And I think it's healthy. But it isn't reality," she says. "What's going on in the world is the reality. And I think this is a distraction from that. And a welcome distraction."

Neither knows why this is happening. I suggest that the '90s seemed simpler, and Mr. Feeny was such a strong, kind, moral presence. They recommend that I talk to series creator Michael Jacobs when I ask if Feeny would have been motivated, despairing or both to teach during the Trump era. I ask if Mr. Feeny would make a good president. Daniels laughs, then tells me that's kind of a weird question. Bartlett reminds me that Mr. Feeny is a fictional character that doesn't exist, then notes that Joe Biden is much closer to Mr. Feeny, not explicitly identifying that other president who was not at all like him.

"[Biden] has a great deal of empathy," she says. "He cares about people. He wants to help. He's not interested in money. Teachers don't make any money. They're not out for themselves, they're out to help people. And Biden seems to be the same. It's such a relief after what we've been through."

As far as what he misses about the '90s, Daniels, who is finishing a late breakfast when I call at 11 a.m. his time, is nostalgic for playing tennis. I offer a sampling of '90s movies ("The Fugitive," "Braveheart," "Forrest Gump," "Titanic," "Saving Private Ryan," "American Beauty," "Magnolia," "Fight Club") to see if anything struck a chord, and Bartlett, who appeared briefly on "Boy Meets World" as (eventual Feeny spouse) Dean Bolander, says none of them did, at least not compared to "Gandhi."

Daniels declines to comment on if young people worry too much or not enough about their future, saying that's a personal question for the individual in terms of optimism or anxiety, but that he knows there's a lot of the latter out there.

"A lot of suicides," his wife says.

What sparks more discussion is when, after reading Daniels' comments about being forced into performing as a child, if he ever thought about or discussed that when coming into a show that was going to be full of child actors like "Boy Meets World."

"I didn't lecture these children. I treated them as adults. And I did not interfere with their performance," Daniels says. "I did not give them advice. I let them do what they are prone to do, and I stayed apart from that. And I think that's the best way to handle that situation."

"When we're watching television and they put on a commercial with kids, he'll turn it off," Bartlett notes. "He cannot stand to watch a commercial with kids. He cannot stand it. He just turns it off."

Daniels: "They're being taken advantage of. And it harps back to what I went through when I was a child and made to perform under sometimes very difficult situations where me and my sister were really taken advantage of. We were very, very nervous about performing in certain situations, but nevertheless there it was. So I'm very aware of that. And naturally I'm against it."

Bartlett: "[Michael Jacobs] was wonderful with the children, with the kids. I won't call them children. He was wonderful with the kids as they were growing up. He was very good. And they all had wonderful parents, the ones we met anyway. Very lucky. That's very unusual on a show with a lot of kids. That their parents were good parents. That's unusual. That's one of the things that made the show very pleasant to do."

When I ask if Daniels ever struggled with or questioned anything Mr. Feeny was doing, Bartlett shares when the script called for her husband to get stung by a bee and she told Jacobs, "This is the worst script I've been in since high school," while also recognizing that writing weekly scripts is going to lead to some that aren't brilliant. We talk a little about Daniels playing many doctors ("St. Elsewhere," "Scrubs," "Grey's Anatomy," many more) and authority figures in general; if he liked silly, physical things like Mr. Feeny riding a roller coaster ("Not as much"); the importance of adapting to change in a marriage; and bringing their own life experience into their roles if they're cast as spouses. ("They're buying a whole lifetime of togetherness," says Bartlett.) Bartlett says that she thinks "The Graduate" is funny, whereas young people like her granddaughter, and girls in general, disagree.

"When I watched it, coming from a different era when sexuality was very different, I thought it was very funny," she says. "But not the young people. They think it's sad."

No matter what, there's no denying the presence in Daniels' voice, the wisdom in his performance. More than anything, talking with them left me reflecting on why "Boy Meets World" and Mr. Feeny remain so comforting, and reckoning with how much people continually seek a persona like his. After so many years, it feels like the questions have changed, but the answers remain the same.

Leanna Creel of 'Saved by the Bell'

The question all along has been whether or not Tori Scott made sense. Her existence, her role at Bayside, her disappearance. For many, the narrative was always that the short answer was no: Because where were Kelly and Jessie, and why did no one talk about them, and where did Tori disappear to after her 10 episodes.

If you are a "Saved by the Bell" fan, you know all this, and can surely see where this is going: That Chuck Klosterman's essay about "The Tori Paradox," included in his 2003 "Sex, Drugs and Cocoa Puffs" collection, over time has threatened to redefine the understanding of Tori. That, Klosterman argues, the bizarre appearance of Tori as a de facto replacement of two-thirds of the gang's core female characters is in hindsight an accurate portrayal of high school and shifting friendships and cloudy memories. It's a poetic way of justifying what, in reality, was merely producers wanting to film another batch of episodes after the series had already filmed its high-school graduation episode and Tiffani-Amber Thiessen and Elizabeth Berkley were no longer available.

That's the elaborate and necessary lead-in to this conversation with Leanna Creel, a legend of sorts even though Tori Scott, a leather-jacket-wearing, motorcycle-riding badass who also didn't drink and for a short time served as the group's moral compass, was by far her most significant onscreen credit (aside from, being a triplet, numerous appearances with her sisters in TV movie lead roles [two "Parent Trap" movies!] and smaller parts on "Growing Pains," "Beverly Hills, 90210," "Parker Lewis Can't Lose," and in 1996's Reese Witherspoon/Kiefer Sutherland vehicle and the disturbing 2000 movie "The Cell"). This was by design: Creel never intended to become an actress, really, and in the years since has been a successful film producer ("But I'm a Cheerleader," "Six-String Samurai"), philanthropist, photographer and content creator through her company Creel Studios.

Wait, though: This is probably an appropriate time to remind you that I wrote a book about "Saved by the Bell" called "Zack Morris Lied 329 Times!" I'd talked with Creel about interviewing her for that project but the timing never worked out, so I was thrilled at her enthusiasm to try again for this book. Before our call I sent her "Zack Morris Lied 329 Times!" but she didn't have a chance to read it, so for the first 10 minutes or so we talk as she reads portions out loud, leading to exclamations like "It's so hard to read this stuff!" and "It's so sexist in a lot of ways" and "[Zack] is such a dick!" She is surprised to learn that "Drinking and Driving" is Zack's most dishonest episode (13 lies) and that there were no lies in "Slater's Sister," and has no recollection of "The Will." ("Earthquake," in which Mrs. Belding delivers her baby in a Bayside elevator during an earthquake," is Creel's favorite.)

It may not be a paradox, but listening to the real Tori read your thoughts about Tori in preparation to talk about Tori and the question of the Tori paradox is certainly some kind of meta example of the world collapsing on itself.

What's something you're nostalgic for from the '90s?

For me, it was my college years. Where I got to just go to school and go to class—I was working, obviously, to pay for college—but life sure was a lot simpler back then. And so I miss those days, that age, where I was going out mountain biking, going on auditions, and going to school and having deep discussions with people on campus. I'm just kind of nostalgic for that age, I guess. I was raised in a pretty sheltered environment, so any pop culture references prior to 1988 are pretty lost on me anyways. It was all brand-new culture for me, really. The '90s were kind of when I joined the culture world. Ironically, I find myself on "Saved by the Bell" [Laughs], a touchstone of the '90s, apparently. The irony is I wasn't that tuned into the broader culture. I just joined society, I guess, after I graduated high school.

When you think of those deep conversations on campus and being in that college environment, is there anything specific you remember?

A lot was going on. It was right around the time I did the show. I had just come back from a summer working in a housing project in downtown Philadelphia. Like I said, I came from a very sheltered upbringing in Orange County, in Fullerton. I didn't even know what a housing project was. I remember having to raise my hand and ask. I was very, very sheltered about a lot of things. So that summer rocked my world. Then I rolled into UCLA, and I had I think a semester at UCLA before I came and did "Saved by the Bell." And it was either just before or just after I did the show, the L.A. riots happened. So that was deeply moving for me. It was just like every time I turned around, some new, major revelation about the world and life was happening. It was just a time when my eyes were wide open, and I was learning and experiencing so much and meeting people from around the world, very different from myself and my background. It was just a wide-eyed time. That's what I remember. And also the great luxury of college is just the time you have to develop friendships and get to know people and study things and read books. It's a great privilege that I had of having that time. It was a really crazy time.

What's a movie or show from that era that you weren't in that meant or means a lot to you?

Oh, easy. I remember right after I graduated high school, right around the time just before I did the show, I watched "Mystic Pizza" [1988] and "The Karate Kid" [1984] and "A League of Their Own," I think, was that same era. Let's just focus on "Mystic Pizza"; that is a classic. I remember just really relating to it and I was like, "Who is Julia Roberts? Who is she? She's amazing!" I remember seeing those movies in the movie theaters and being very inspired by them. [Laughs] I'm trying to think what was on TV at the time. I think right around then, it was probably a little bit earlier, it was a mystery show and they just redid it and it was really long and slow.

"Twin Peaks."

Thank you! The original "Twin Peaks" really blew my mind. I remember seeing that and I was like, "TV can be like this? What?!" It was one of those times. I remember also seeing the English version of "The Office" and the same thing; my mind just was like, "What? TV can be like this? What? Mockumentary?" I gotta tell you, "Nomadland," the film I saw recently, was kind of like that as well. Where you just feel a fresh new combination of elements in a fresh way that feels like it's going to change things. I was a history undergrad, but I wanted to go to film school. I loved watching films and stuff, but I didn't get into filmmaking really, behind the camera, until I got into grad school. Which was after "Saved by the Bell."

Speaking of which: We talked about Tori taking the place of both Kelly and Jessie. What do you remember about the way the character was described initially? Was there a sense that they knew what they were looking for or not really? What did you feel like you were auditioning for?

It was weird. I remember reading for a role like maybe a year or so before. So I knew the show. I didn't watch it regularly, but I knew about the show, and I had done acting class with Elizabeth Berkley. And I think I met some of the [actors] on the show through some other things. And I remember they told my agent, "Oh, we really liked her. She just wasn't right for this, but we'll remember her in the future." I was like, "Yeah, right. [Laughs] Heard that before." And then, it was. I just remember, and again this was all when I was going to college so I was busy with school, but I remember I got a call and they worked out the deal, and I don't remember auditioning for the role. I remember we went in and there were like five of us who went straight to the producers. So we just walked in, one and done. Because they had remembered me, allegedly [Laughs], from some time before. So it was really fast. I think they were just hiring me. I don't think I really, totally comprehended or understood the weird role that my character was playing as this asynchronous character [Laughs] that comes out of nowhere and is unexplained. I definitely didn't have an understanding of that at the time at all. I just showed up and went to work, and only much later did I hear that people were [perceiving] my character in some nefarious plot to undermine or get rid of these other characters. I just was unaware of it until a few years ago when the "Saved by the Bell" nostalgia resurfaced, particularly with the Saved by the Max [pop-ups]. I wasn't aware that my character was so random. It was a random kids' show, obviously. I remember asking, "Is every single episode a thinly veiled morality tale or commercial for something?" It was like "Teen Line," drunk driving, earthquake safety. I was like, "They practically turn to the camera and give the social message right to the screen." So I was kind of learning as I went along. I don't know how much thought went into it, other than, "Oh, that's cool. I'm a tomboy." I remember they even put in my first episode or in the masquerade ball, they were going to have me wear a dress, and I remember marching into the producer's office and saying, "My character would not wear a dress. Tori definitely would not wear a dress." [Laughs] I must've had some understanding, deep internal monologue about my character being a tomboy and should not wear, would not wear a dress to do the limbo dance or whatever it was. [Laughs] So I think they were figuring it out as well. When we did the show, I brought in—my sister had this, it sounds so ugly now, but it was a motorcycle jacket but it was green leather, and I remember asking if I could wear that. And they were like, "Definitely no. We want you to wear this." It was just a regular, black leather jacket. I remember being bummed. I'm like, "Can it at least be a biker jacket?" If it had been me, my choice, it would've been more of a biker jacket instead of that regular, black leather jacket that was five sizes too big.

What did you think then when the ultimate decision was to put Tori in a dress and have her put a leather jacket over it?

Well, no, no, the dress thing was from the first episode, and that fit my character, I thought, because my character was trying to be something she wasn't. But in the masquerade ball, they had me back in a dress, and I was like, "No, that's the whole point. We learned in 'The New Girl' to be yourself and not try to change for anybody." [Laughs] It obviously wasn't a real deep show. It sounds so arrogant now, but I remember thinking, "Oh my gosh, if adults would leave this show, we kids could do this show in three days a week." I was already thinking like a producer. [Laughs] Like, "We do not need five days for each of these episodes." [Laughs] I remember even at that time I must've been thinking about becoming a producer because I remember telling Peter Engel that I wanted to be a producer, and I remember he laughed. I look back now, and I think I was probably so precocious. I did look 16 or 17 even though I was older, so I'm sure I came across very precocious and surprising that I would say that. But it was true; I was looking around going, "I want to be Peter Engel. He's the one that has the power in this situation." I never was super comfortable in front of the camera, if we're honest. I'm very comfortable behind the camera. I think I was aware of that even then, even when I was doing the show. Which was one of my first big things. One of my only big things [Laughs], however you want to put it. In front of the camera. I think I've been more successful behind the camera for a reason.

So why do you think that Zack Morris has been such an enduring character? When you opened the book, one of your first reactions was to laugh and say, "So sexist." Why has there been longevity despite his behavior?

It's interesting. He definitely was filling a stereotype that was very common in the '80s and '90s, that good-looking jock. But you love to hate him. It's kind of "boys will be boys." It was a little bit of that old-school [mentality] … his smile was so cute, he just got away with it. I don't know. There's obviously an arrogance to him, but maybe Mark-Paul's just a super-charming guy. It's amazing because sometimes it doesn't feel like we've made as much social change, but then when you look back at shows and things because I think it was right around then that MTV was fairly new, and they had that character Pedro came on, and he had HIV, and he was the first gay kid that everybody knew on TV, and it was so radical. We've come a long way.

You say Zack is someone people love to hate, but somehow despite Zack's behavior, Zack and Kelly I think people lump in with Ross and Rachel and these iconic couples no matter the details. I could post something from my book about Zack's bad behavior, and Mark-Paul in the most recent episode he says Zack and Kelly have no chemistry, he's terrible to her, there's nothing between them and he'd rather watch any other couple, and meanwhile someone will still be really protective of him. People hold their childhood loves close to them, which is fine, but the people who love him love to love him, not hate him, which I think is weird.

It's sort of like I think how a lot of boys feel about baseball. It's like, do they really love baseball, or do they really just love that time they got to spend with their dad at baseball games? Do you really love the show, or does it just remind you of those carefree Saturday mornings that you got to watch TV? So maybe it's just a reminder of that time in our lives when we had less pressures on our lives and it was a simpler time, and everything was so simple and came together at the end with a bow and Zack always learned his lesson. That's why we tell stories, to remind ourselves that life's going to be OK, we're going to get through this, the good guys win in the end. Usually. I don't know if it's more of that. And he had a really cute smile! [Laughs] It's an era. It's weird to me, honestly. I've said this so many times, but I don't think people really believe me. But if you had told me back then that people would care about this show in 2021, I would've laughed. I'm like, "No no no. This is just a dumb Saturday morning show. There's nothing to it." So there's also that je ne sais quoi. That magic quality. I don't know if it was just because there was no other live-action programming on Saturday morning, and is that why everybody got so emotionally attached? I don't know. It's a phenomenon, and you can't really explain why. Why this show and why not some other show. Yes, it was on in every timeframe and every time schedule around the world, and it's G-rated and doesn't have any conflicts, so maybe just numerically it just beat us down. I don't know. [Laughs] But people are very, very, very attached. I don't think it even appealed to high-school students at the time. I think it always appealed to junior-high students. So never the reality. It was always an aspirational thing. It was never meant to be real. So it was always this weird fairy tale, I guess.

You alluded to this a little while ago, but the idea of the Tori episodes being controversial. What's your first memory of becoming aware of that and the way those have existed for fans over time?

Truthfully, it wasn't that long ago. Maybe five or six years ago I was invited to participate in this parody called "Bayside! The Musical" in New York, and it was watching that parody that I realized it. How people were reacting. They'd just make fun of all the different tropes of the show, and it was that experience, and watching that. People still love my character. Everybody's like, "Oh, Tori!" And there were other times I read a couple of online things and people would be like going off on Tori. Oh, I know! There was another really specific time. Right around that time, maybe five years ago, it was on Funny or Die, and there was a parody written as if I had written it. But I obviously didn't write it! Because there was some other name on it, but it was a parody and as if Leanna Creel, who played Tori, was upset that I wasn't part of the reunion episode on Jimmy Fallon or whatever it was. It was actually really funny, I thought, but I had people, even my brother-in-law, that thought that I wrote it. He texted me, he was like, "That's so funny, Leanna! That was hilarious." And in the notes, people like, "Leanna, you're just jealous! Because you were a loser, and no one ever liked you." [Laughs] And it was like, oh my god! A. Whoa whoa whoa. I didn't write this. And B. You're missing the humor. And C. Now I know what you're really thinking. So it was probably those two events. Watching the parody, which actually was really funny. I actually went back another time and brought all my friends in New York. And this piece. I can't remember who wrote it, but it was actually really funny. But misunderstood. So many people read it and really thought I wrote it sincerely with my feelings hurt that I wasn't invited to be part of [Fallon]. And people took it as an opportunity to—it's just this weird thing that people think that my life ended after I did "Saved by the Bell" or that I just could never get another job so I left Hollywood. But it was then that I was really aware of these deep-seated questions, these existential questions. [Laughs] The timeline. What happened? What did Tori do to Jessie and Kelly? Why wasn't she in the graduation episode? I completely was not aware until about five years ago-ish. When all this was coming on, which was funny.

And it's interesting to think where that negativity would come from. On the subject of trying to make Tori both Jessie and Kelly at the same time at least for a little while, one of the things I think is great about Tori is that she is the voice of reason in a way they never let Jessie be. Every time Jessie pointed something out from a moral standpoint, Slater would say something sexist, there would be a laugh track, and the point was lost. But Tori, whether in the "Drinking and Driving" episode or identifying that Lisa is being mean to Screech in "Class Rings," she's being the moral voice. Yet the show also eventually transitions away from her as a romantic possibility without any explanation, so I wonder if that sort of left the character hung out to dry from the perspective of the people who would be inclined to feel so negatively.

It's really strange, and definitely an interesting window into the men that wrote the show and their ideas. And their ideal. I think it says a lot more about when they grew up in high school, which was in the '50s and '60s. It's hard because when you're young everybody seems old. Franco [Bario] was young. He was probably still in his 20s or 30s, but the guy that was directing it, Don [Barnhart], I think he was in his 50s. And so was Peter Engel, I think. When you're still barely out of your teen years, everybody seems like they're 50. They probably grew up in the '50s and '60s, so this was sort of a lot of how they remembered high school and the dynamics that were going on for them. And they were working out their issues. [Laughs] Very interesting when you compare it to a show—have you seen HBO Max's "Generation"?

I haven't.

So good. And it is so of the moment. And one of the writers is 18 or 19 years old, and you can tell. It feels so of the moment. And there are obviously adults who work on the show and producers and stuff like that, but it does not feel like—it's the anti-"Saved by the Bell." [Laughs] It's like brutally honest and very now. It's a totally different show, obviously. It's single-camera and handheld and a little bit "Rashomon"-style. There's kind of three points of view each episode and the timelines get mixed up. It's very different. The reason sitcoms have gone away is they're just so inauthentic. There's nothing real about that. There's nothing real about a soundtrack and people basically winking at the audience and saying a dumb joke. I feel like audiences today and youths especially are not going to put up with that. So they demand an authenticity today that [make older shows] just seem so quaint now. Even "Growing Pains" and ["Family Ties"], all those shows, they all seem almost so quaint because they're all three-to-five cameras and everything's from the same angle, and it wasn't really until I was out of grad school and I did some shadowing on "ER" and "The West Wing" and stuff like that, and those shows, it was quite a bit later, but that's really the first time they were shooting with single-camera and steadicam and even shooting the ceiling, which was so radical. [Laughs] Up until then, people didn't really do that. I'm having a flashback right now. When I was on "Saved by the Bell," because remember I said I was a history major, and I went to my advisor and I said, "Can I design a class or an independent study around doing a history of children's programming in television?" So I went and I got eight units for writing this research paper. And I went and interviewed all these executives at NBC, and it's interesting because I'm basically doing the same analysis right now for where we are today. There's a reason for "Saved by the Bell," where it was, and it was like the first—it's like they never thought kids would be interested in seeing live-action on Saturday morning. It seems so obvious today. Now it's 24/7. But back then it was just cartoons. You probably know all this because you're written the book, literally. And I can't remember how I was tying that to today other than there's a 24-hour news cycle that was just beginning back then. And it's like kids are just used to fact-checking, and they demand authenticity. It's just such a different era.

I definitely think you're right, but it also makes me think about that 1. "Fuller House" came back on Netflix and lasted five seasons and 2. Peacock's "Saved by the Bell" reboot, which I thought was done really well and was effective in making all of its updates, there were still a lot of people who said, "I liked it the way it used to be. Hard pass." So it's notable how many people reject the authenticity you're talking about.

I know, it's so weird. It's true; "don't screw with our notions of our idolized youth." "Make high school great again." It's like, really? Was it really that great? Do we really want to go back to that? "But don't screw with it; don't tell me I can't have it that way." And then they brought back "Karate Kid" too. And that apparently has been doing really well. People loving that. So that sort of reboot, which I watched one episode of. I want to watch more. I've heard it's great; everybody I talk to loves it. But the "Karate Kid" movies, even all put together it's only like six or eight hours. But there's I don't know how many hours of television; maybe there's just too many episodes of "Saved by the Bell" to really reinvent it. Did [the reboot] get canceled? I'm bummed! Because I did hear that they had reinvented it. I never saw it; I've gotta see it.

It's coming back for a second season, actually.

Oh, it is? OK, good good good.

So I have to ask you: Have you read the Chuck Klosterman piece about the Tori Paradox?

I have! It has been a while, but I remember—I guess when I read that I must've been aware of how crazy the storyline was. And I was very, very, the Brits say "chuffed"; I loved that my character was part of naming—it's so meta—a phenomenon, or I don't know if phenomenon is probably too generous of a word, but when a show does this. Because we all have seen this happen before, but I love that he put it into words. I thought that was pretty great, and then to call it the Tori Paradox, it's funny. I was proud to be affiliated with that. [Laughs]

And do you think that there's merit to that idea that high school allegiances are so fluid that it's reasonable to think that Kelly and Jessie were there at the same time?

Oh, that part. Oh, that's interesting. It's weird. What did you think? Were you watching the show in real time and then wonder where they went? Did it matter?

What did I think back then?

Yeah, were you like, "What happened?" Or did it not matter?

So many episodes were aired out of any sensible sequence anyway that I think if anyone paid attention to it that way, smoke would've come out of their ears. It was alternating in a way that was trying not to be chronological.

Yeah, because you have many more options for how you can syndicate the show if it's linear. [Laughs] So the producers had their eyes firmly on the bottom line. So I'm sure they just wanted to not ever address it, and they just wanted to make 10 more episodes. That's how it seemed to me. And as a producer, I understand that. They had a really good thing going. They're like, "Let's make 10 more." So they did. They found a way to make 10 more, for the price of probably 9 more or 8 more. [Laughs]

So when you think about your own high school experience and that theory that the Tori episodes are actually a profound way of identifying that high school is fluid

210

and sometimes people are there for things and not there for things and that's just the way it happens, does that track? Or does that not seem authentic to you?

No, it does. It does. I very much have gaps in my memory all the time. And I remember certain things. It's sort of like with me and my sisters—I'm one of triplets. I think you probably know that. But we, maybe more so than other siblings, but we put our stories together, and we're like, "Wait, do you remember that?" And one of us remembers one thing, and another remembers another thing, and we kind of piece it together, and it's really interesting how Joy will hold onto one part of the story that I've completely forgotten, and I've held onto something that she's completely forgotten. So I think that's how memory works in general. We remember the things that strike close to home. Like that one episode that I've completely forgotten, "The Will." Or "Class Rings." Both of those episodes, no memory of those whatsoever. But some of the other episodes I really remember strongly. There was one where we had to sing, and I hated that. It was so horrible. So geeky. And I hate to sing, and I remember it was so embarrassing. And I had to dance a little bit, and I was horrible. But I remember it because of those reasons. I think that's how life is. We just remember things out of order. Something takes center stage or are a bigger deal in my timeline, and even though you were in my timeline it wasn't as big of a deal in your timeline. So I readily admit to a very, very biased and skewed memory. I'm not one of those people— some people can recall conversations word-for-word. I'm not like that. I could never do that. I just remember the emotional things or the things that made an impact. But maybe I've forgotten a lot more things than the average person. [Laughs] It is interesting, what I remember and what makes an impact years later. It's not always what you think.

And I know you said at the time your perspective of what they were doing with the character was just sort of letting it happen in the moment. Was there a statement about feminism that they did make or tried to make with Tori? At first Lisa's telling "You've gotta turn on the femininity," and they did allow her to recognize that she wasn't the dress-wearing type and embrace that, and that's great, but she also eventually stopped being a romantic possibility, and Screech has a line like, "Just like Tori; not feminine at all." At the time, was there any alarm bell going off for anyone about what was actually being said about any of that? Or did it just happen quickly and only decades later anyone talked about that?

Yeah, I think, as with the grand tradition of women in Hollywood, we, as characters, are fillers. We fill the stories where we're needed. We're girlfriends, we're best friends, we're sometimes love interests, sometimes not. That's how I think—it's an ongoing, somewhat subconscious thing that the male storytellers have done with our characters. They just use us to fill in the gaps, I guess. [Laughs] As needed. But the focus was definitely on the boy characters, for sure. That's who Peter related to. He didn't relate to my character. If there had been women writers and girl writers on the show, maybe they would've called out Zack a lot more. [Laughs] Maybe the women would've been allowed to be more nuanced. I'd like to believe so. It's so weird; it's so hard to even imagine back in that day having a woman director or a woman writer. Isn't that sad? But I can't even hardly imagine it from that era.

Someone who creates graphs to do stats about TV, yesterday created a graph about "Saved by the Bell," charting the number of episodes that were named after each of the main characters. The most frequent times it happened were Zack, Screech, and Slater, with Lisa, Kelly and Jessie falling far behind. It shows where the emphasis was of which characters were thought of as the focal point.

Oh, absolutely! It was all a fantasy. It was all a male fantasy. Absolutely a male fantasy. I had been on a few sitcoms, and often the producer or somebody introduces the cast ahead of time because it's sort of like a little play. You have a live audience, and you're about to run through the whole show. I remember the very first night, and Peter Engel, he either ended with Mark-Paul or he started with Mark-Paul, I couldn't remember, but I definitely saw that he saw himself in Mark-Paul. [Laughs] It was really clear. He was the darling. He was who he saw himself. And maybe that's how he either wanted to be or saw himself as in high school. I'm sure of it. I guess glee clubs have become cool again because of the show "Glee," but at the time there were no such thing as glee clubs anywhere! And so to have an episode about that, I feel like we laughed and were like, "Yeah, it's because these old-timers had glee clubs back in their day." So we were somewhat aware. I'm pretty sure the other cast would be somewhat aware that there were these weird holdovers from the '60s or '70s or something that were not consistent with the early '90s.

Are you saying I'm lying when I say that my high school had a weekly sock hop, like Bayside's sock hop?

Yeah, exactly. [Laughs] True. I guess I'm not the first one to notice this. I have to admit; I even got Peter Engel's book and I was going to read it, and I never read it. I don't know why; I just have a block against reading about "Saved by the Bell." Although I'm enjoying your book. So some of the stuff I'm saying right now might be completely boring and regurgitated from things that people have already noted and said about the show. I'm probably very, very late to the game. I usually am.

On that topic, I wanted to ask you about that. You'd talked about previously wanting to set that part of your life aside but over time you weren't as worried about being defined by it. Is there more of an answer than just time passing that explains why you feel differently now about "Saved by the Bell" and more open to acknowledging it? Did anything happen to change your perspective? Or it's just that enough time passed that you stopped caring about what was holding you back before?

Yeah, I don't know what was holding me back before. I guess I was just like, "On to the next, on to the next, on to the next." Honestly, it was going out and doing that show ["Bayside! The Musical"], it really helped me laugh about it all and see how absurd it was. I honestly did not wear a black leather jacket for years. I don't know why; I didn't want to be defined by something in my past. I wanted to look forward. It's weird; I produced a movie called "Six-String Samurai" that's about to have a Blu-ray, remastered re-release, and I'm so excited to show it to my son because he thinks I'm so uncool. He has no idea that I had this other life and that I made this movie years ago. But he loves Godzilla movies right now, and he loves kung fu movies, and I'm like, "Oh my gosh! I'm going to be cool in his eyes." I'm not the kind of person that has pictures from my past around my house or anything. I don't know why; I've just never been that sort of, "Look, I met this person that one time." I just have never been that kind of person, I guess. I try to be in the moment. But it was wild. I had a conversation with the director of that movie for the behind-the-scenes DVD or whatever, and it felt really good to talk to him about those memories and chat about it. So being at this stage of my life and looking back and taking some enjoyment from it—I'm still barreling ahead at 500 million miles an hour on all my other projects, but I feel more comfortable looking back and laughing at it and not taking it so seriously. I think also I feel less defined by it. Less people know about it. I do feel like it's not in my face anymore. Growing up, getting older, perspective. Also people forgetting about it. [Laughs] No one under 35 even knows what it is. So it feels like a new era. But I am fine with being part of it, and I'm proud of it, actually. I'm glad to have been a part of it. I'm kind of paying my penance. Because I never responded to any fan mail. I was such a jerk. Mostly because I don't have headshots. But I do Cameos, and I'm late on the Cameos because you have to do them within three days. And I'm like, "Oh, man." So I end up doing like half of them for free. I feel like if people remember me and [care] enough to track me down, I can at least leave them a one-minute message on Cameo. I definitely enjoy doing those and hearing from people. I guess just getting older. Long, long, long answer just saying, yeah, I'm getting old.

Did you say before that someone wrote you a letter addressed to Jessie/Tori?

Yes! I remember I got a number of them, which was funny because Elizabeth is like three feet taller than me, but we both have big, curly hair, and I'm sure there was confusion. We both have these strong characters, I guess. Strong-mouthed characters. I remember getting a number of 'em. I don't know if Elizabeth got them as well, but I remember getting a number that were like, "Dear Tori/Jessie." But none that I know of ever got me confused with anybody else. Just Jessie.

My brain scrambles trying to understand the logic of addressing something to two different people.

Yeah. Because I feel like we're very different looking. But I grew up as a triplet looking like both of my sisters, so I kind of have this weird thing that I look like everybody else. [Laughs]

When I saw that you were actually the student body president and the homecoming queen, my belief about you being used as both Jessie and Kelly at the same time exploded. The show couldn't conceive of one person doing those two things, even though you did it for real!

That's funny. That's funny. Yeah, it's wild. It was such a weird time, the '80s and '90s. I guess people may be looking back on this time in our lives saying, "That was such a weird time."

Do you remember what the part was that you auditioned for originally?

I don't. I really don't. It's weird what I remember. I remember, one of the last auditions that I remember auditioning for was for the show "Friends." I remember for not the Monica part; I read for the Rachel part. I remember thinking, "This is so good! This is so funny." Some roles you just read and you never forget. Oh my gosh, it was so good. But I don't remember what part it was [on "Saved by the Bell"]. Robin Lippin was the casting director; I remember her.

How far along did you get in the process for Rachel?

Not very far. [Laughs] I'll tell you another weird piece of trivia that is even hard for me to believe. It's kind of crazy. I got down to the "Tool Time" girl on, oh god, what's the name of that show?

"Home Improvement."

"Home Improvement"! I got down to—it was me and, oh my gosh, I'm totally having a senior moment. Can you tell I haven't slept in three days? Anna Nicole Smith? Is that right? No, Pamela Anderson! It's so weird! Because you would think that we have nothing in common. But she and I; it was the two of us. They were obviously looking to go in two very different directions. But isn't that funny?

There's something profound in there, I think.

Me or Pamela Anderson. That is just nuts. I can barely believe it. But I remember I played it really comedic, and obviously they went a sexy direction for sure. But it's kind of funny. Weird.

Which is more ridiculous: A clean delivery in an elevator or getting extremely hammered off of one light beer?

[Laughs] The earthquake in the elevator. To me that is the zenith of absurdity. An earthquake in an elevator is something you only see one time. And my character is the one that delivers the baby. Which is even more absurd. Like how would I know anything about that? How would Tori know?

On that note, in "The Will," which I know you don't remember, it becomes a battle of the sexes and Tori is a specialist in putting a carburetor together. Do you know anything about carburetors?

I know zero about carburetors. But I am now remembering an episode—were we wearing all red, and the boys were wearing all blue?

That's right.

Oh my gosh. That to me, honestly, bless the writers on the show, but that's just lazy writing. [Laughs] "Let's have a competition." That's just bad writing. That's, "We've run out of ideas, so let's have a competition." That's not good.

Do you remember any conversation on set involving the writers, cast, anyone, about continuity or talking about things making sense? Or was that not talked about?

I don't think it was talked about. Or I just wasn't aware of it. I wasn't like in the writers' room or anything, so I have no idea. I would just be handed the script and go on set. I was blissfully unaware of if there was any discussion. I wasn't aware enough to even ask. I was super green, and I didn't know even what was going on. I was definitely in the dark.

When you think about the movies you produced, is there one really vivid thing that comes to mind?

I'm very proud of "But I'm a Cheerleader." And "Six-String Samurai." Those two felt like they were passion projects through and through. "But I'm a Cheerleader" we developed from a two-page treatment, and it came from the idea that there wasn't any John Hughes-style, any fun, lighthearted films for gay kids. And it was the time when teen suicide we were just becoming aware was a third of teen suicide was gay kids. We were just like, "We gotta do something." It was the very beginning of some of these cultural wars. Maybe not the very beginning. But I didn't know that convergence therapy would still be controversial this many years later. So it feels like it was about something, so that's why it resonates with me. It was about something, it was about something important, and everybody that was involved was really passionate about it. I am really proud of that movie, and I think that's why it has staying power. Some of the other movies—it's why I say I don't need to just produce or direct a movie just to produce or direct a movie. The ones that stick and last are the ones that mean something. And so those are the kind of projects I get involved with now and the kind of things I want to get involved with in the future. Stuff that is meaningful because that's what lasts.

That's awesome. And my last question: There was an L.A. Times story in 1988 about you and your sisters that was basically like, "Triplets, wow! Who knew?!" Recently I watched "The Cell" for the first time because you and your sisters are in

it, albeit very quickly. I felt like I had to ask what you remember about that period and that movie, and that decision. That movie is so weird.

So weird. [Laughs] Here's the thing: We did that very late in our triplet acting days. And it was when I was already interested in directing and producing, and Tarsem was the director. It was as simple as that. I had already produced a bunch of movies. I was like, "I want to see what it was like on a $60 million set." I knew it was going to be weird and visual, but I was a huge fan of Tarsem's, and I just wanted to see what the spectacle was all about. [Laughs] Just to see what that was like. Because I've only produced little, tiny indie movies. But, yeah, it was weird. It was one day, I'm sure. Tarsem was sweet, and it was a spectacle. [Laughs] It was just for the experience. But it was one of the last things—it may be the last thing my sisters and I ever did together. So it was actually later, after film school, after I had been producing for a while. I think I wasn't even acting anymore. That's the way I remember it. Again, I probably remember things out of order. But the way I remember it was that I had already left acting and then was like, "No, no, let's just do this one thing. We have this opportunity. Let's just do it." And Monica [Lacy] stayed on and continued to act, and she's been acting all these years. My sister, Monica. But I remember when I graduated with my MFA, I called my agents, I'm like, "I'm done! I'm going to be a producer, and I can't be going off on auditions. I'm out." I feel like this was after that. I remember being able to really look around and take in what a $60 million set looks like. [Laughs] Which I wouldn't have totally appreciated before.

Do you remember the first thing you thought when you then saw the movie?

I remember it's so vivid, and the script was so out there. I don't think it was as successful in its execution as I wanted it to be, but it was a pretty crazy idea. You know, going into the killer's head to catch the killer. [Laughs] It's definitely not my genre, but it was a really fun experience. It's one of those that I did for the experience and the story of it all. I was a huge fan of Tarsem's; I still am, as a visual storyteller. He's a unique voice. It was a really fun experience.

And the idea that there's something that can blow your mind that you were in, there's some universe where the Tori paradox exists in the world of "The Cell."

Oh my god. That would be one big paradox. [Laughs] They broke a lot of rules, and Tarsem paints with a big paintbrush on a big canvas. He was very absurdist in a lot of ways. I haven't seen it in all these years. I should probably go back and re-see it. I don't even remember what I thought when I saw it. I just remember them saying, "You're going to sit here and put your head back, your mouth is going to be open." We were going to be painted white, and "We'll bring you these black shawls with these black things in our eyes." And going, "All right. [Laughs] OK." As you can tell, I'm too aggressive to be an actor. I'm too proactive. It's hard for me to sit around and be told what to do. So I was never going to make it as an actor. [Laughs] I do not miss it. That was definitely not my calling. But it was fun; because I was a triplet, it opened these doors. It was absurd. My whole life has had some absurd moments. [Laughs]

Ernie Reyes Jr. of 'Teenage Mutant Ninja Turtles II: The Secret of the Ooze'

Among the many strange things about the 1990 movie version of "Teenage Mutant Ninja Turtles" is that there isn't really a non-adult human on screen to root for. So it's not surprising that for the (even weirder but more kid-friendly) sequel, 1991's "Teenage Mutant Ninja Turtles II: The Secret of the Ooze," a non-turtle teenage character was added for young viewers to identify with more than they did for Danny (Michael Turney), the son of April O'Neil's boss, in the original.

That was 16-year-old Keno, a pizza delivery boy-turned-ninja-turtles-ally played by Ernie Reyes Jr., who was not only a child karate champion, co-star of Arnold Schwarzenegger's 1985 film "Red Sonja" and star of the "Sidekicks" TV series but also the actor who wore the Donatello costume in the first movie. For many kids watching "Secret of the Ooze," Keno felt like a chance to vicariously hang out with the turtles as they continued their battle with Shredder, took on the mutant snapping turtle/wolf combo of Tokka and Rahzar, and, um, crashed a Vanilla Ice concert.

As an adult, Reyes—son of legendary martial artist and trainer Ernie Reyes Sr. (who appeared with Jr. in "Surf Ninjas")—has been a successful kickboxer, the vice president of a nonprofit organization that empowers kids through STEM education, martial arts and bullying prevention campaigns, continued acting ("Rush Hour 2," "The Rundown," "NCIS: Los Angeles," "Brooklyn Nine-Nine," "Superstore"), performed motion capture stunts ("Avatar," "Alice in Wonderland"), founded a virtual training program called Kick Punch Club, and, well, spent 12 hours a week undergoing dialysis for years due to kidney failure.

What's something you're nostalgic for from the '90s? It could be anything you miss.

For me, the '90s was kind of like hanging out in Hollywood. Getting into Muay Thai. Hip-hop. Just being young, really, and not really knowing that you're young. And just riding that wave of the '90s. It was a good time, but I don't necessarily miss it. I'm kind of grooving on what's happening now.

I like that, being young but not knowing it. Is there a moment you look back on now that you realize you thought you were old at the time but laugh in hindsight about how young you were?

Yeah. Just like when I hit around 30, it's like now you're feeling like, "OK, I'm not necessarily young the way that I used to be." But you didn't realize how young you still actually were. [Laughs] And I'm sure that I'll look back at this time and go, "Man, I was so young then." [Laughs]

No matter how many times that happens to us, we keep doing it.

Exactly. Today's the youngest that you'll ever be.

What's a movie or show from that era that you weren't in that made an impact on you?

Man, that's a good question. '90s for me was also the birth of like modern indie cinema. With Quentin Tarantino and Robert Rodriguez and all of those. All of that stuff was super cool to me at that time, which was also the beginning of a whole thing and careers you'd see go into the future. Like "Reservoir Dogs" and all of that early stuff that was going on in the '90s as far as indie cinema, that would've been cool to be a part of. Even the "Kill Bill" [movies] and stuff like that, but that was a little bit later on.

Why are those movies and those filmmakers the ones that come to mind as the ones that made a connection?

Because it was probably where I was in my life. Being a part of things, even the "Ninja Turtles" in a way, it was something that was coming kind of from left field and it wasn't something we had seen before. So those filmmakers like Quentin Tarantino at that time— what a lot of times people don't know about the ninja turtles movies in particular is those movies were made and produced by Golden Harvest, which is a martial arts film company that built the movies that Bruce Lee and Jackie Chan, Jet Li, they were making a martial arts movies and it happened to be in the world of the ninja turtles. So those early-'90s filmmakers were carving a new voice, like, A. Anybody could do it. It was Sundance, and all that kind of stuff was like young filmmakers who were just like, "Hey, man, anybody can do it." So that was super cool, and of course they had a unique voice as well.

There are a lot of places we could start about "Ninja Turtles." While there are many acting challenges on a set, not many actors get to sit and listen to a long story about the history of the characters from a giant talking rat. What do you remember about the process of keeping a straight face and listen in a serious moment like that?

[Laughs] Oh, no, it was amazing. It was kind of one of the most memorable parts of making that movie for me. Because I came in there [in the original] as a replacement guy on the stunt team, which the "Ninja Turtles" was the first time they were bringing Hong Kong stuntmen over to work on American productions. So I was a replacement for one of the guys who broke his back in rehearsals, so I was on there, and then to get bumped up from stunt guy to co-star of the sequel, that was an amazing moment in my life. So for me to be there, it wasn't even more like "Look at how silly this was" and "Now I need to keep a straight face." I was just truly in awe of the moment. And kind of just soaking it all in. It was a really great moment.

Do you remember what it was like to execute a scene like that though, with the characters and costumes?

It's a huge set, and we were on a stage. The apartment was built on a stage, so we were on stage, and there's like three or four people per ninja turtle that have some sort of role in making it come alive. From being the person in the costume to the person that's controlling the facial expressions and on and on. It's almost like being in front of a live audience; there's so many people around trying to make it all happen. But it was the second movie. We had just filmed the original movie the summer before, so we were just with each other 12 months prior, so everybody was doing their thing. It was all just good memories, man. [Laughs] The ninja turtles is just good memories. Great memories, actually.

Even though Keno isn't there for most of the giant monster battle during the Vanilla Ice concert, did you watch that unfold on set?

Yeah, I didn't see all of it, but I was definitely there while they were doing it.

What do you remember of how that was set up and done?

The one thing is it's just in terms of rehearsals and that kind of thing, Golden Harvest in terms of action, they'd been doing that for decades. And a big part of that is the rehearsal process, so everything was always well-rehearsed, and then it just comes down to execution on the day. But everybody was pro that was there. That movie was as fun as it was, but it was always a lot of work involved. Everybody was having a good time.

Part of what has made that so enduring is that it's a wild movie in a lot of ways. If you had to identify one of the craziest aspects, could you pinpoint what seems like the craziest?

I think it's really just the concept in and of itself. Teenage Mutant Ninja Turtles.

I was thinking about specific events, like that someone could knock over a dangerous villain by playing a keytar at peak volume.

There was some cool moments and stuff that we shot that never made it. Which was just training sequences and stuff. That was interesting because it was like basically we were out there training for real, and we were shooting b-roll really, and it was quite crazy to think that we were out there for hours training in these suits. But that's always the way that I took it when I was actually in the costume was this was all training. We had these huge suits on in the first movie, and we worked for 12-, 14-hour days every day, five days a week, and it was just crazy training. So by the time we got to the second movie, it was all just awesomeness. It was just one of those moments that you'll look back and go, "Man, that was pretty much my childhood growing up like that." Super cool.

And the movie holds up because of its silliness, actually. Some people have had fun writing articles questioning things like why a huge rap artist is playing in this weird warehouse space. Do you remember any conversations that anyone had at any point questioning the logic of anything, or is that antithetical to a kids' movie about human-sized ninja turtles?

Yeah, again, what's the concept? Teenage Mutant Ninja Turtles. Now what are you discussing to me about the logic of what?

That's fair. Anything can happen at that point.

It's world-building. And anybody who wants to spend their time nitpicking on things like that is doing exactly that: nitpicking on something that doesn't mean anything.

Of course the tone was changed between the first and second movie, and the sequel definitely feels lighter and hits a different spot for kids. The martial arts movies of the early '90s often were rated PG and had an innocence or comedy to them whereas nowadays, a movie like the new "Mortal Kombat" is very violent and very R-rated. I'm curious about your thoughts about the PG-rated versus the R-rated martial arts movies because I'd argue the people seeing them are probably pretty similar groups.

I think there's a place for both of them. I think there's a place for "Kill Bill," and I think there's a place for something like "Teenage Mutant Ninja Turtles." And each comes with a different tone in terms of the choreography. But great choreography is great choreography. I'm into both of them. I like the idea of being able to take the violence to a hyper-real place, and I like also doing comedic things in fight choreography, which tends to be more family friendly.

Is there any consideration people give to that in terms of the way young viewers react to the different paths those presentations take? I know you're a dad yourself; the conversation one would have with a 10-year-old is very different between those two movies.

I don't know because we're a martial arts family. So martial arts is part of our world. The understanding of violence is part of being a martial artist. So we'd probably have a different perspective on all of it. Not only that, even my kids work on fight choreography for films and television and that kind of stuff. We'd look at movies and TV a little differently, knowing the process of it and being part of it. I think it's just up to each individual, and each individual family is probably different in their ways of doing things.

We're a martial arts filmmaking family, so my kids will watch "Kill Bill." [Laughs] It's a different time and place.

And you could argue "Kill Bill" is an example of being in between on the spectrum because it's hyper-violent, but it's also comedic.

And I think what it comes down to for me really is not so much those fight scenes but the storytelling. If the storytelling didn't work on the movies, it wouldn't matter. They kind of toned down the violence from the first [movie] to the second—it wasn't so much the violence; it was more the tone of it all. To balance out the violence. A kick to the face is still a kick to the face, but when you tell a joke around it everybody seems to be more OK with it. So it really comes down to great storytelling. Tell a great story, and have great action be part of the structure of that great story, and to me that's great. Just action for action with no story, I don't care.

I know you've talked about how hot it was in the Donatello costume. Is there an untold story from that experience, or something that gets lost over the years that you go back to as a memory from that?

It was a couple things. Ninja turtles and all that, it became meaningful to me in my life after working on the movie. I had a younger brother that was into ninja turtles at the time so I was aware of it, but it became meaningful because of what it became to me. Golden Harvest, on the other hand, was already cemented into my mind as a beacon of greatness when it comes to what my dream was since I was a kid, just to make martial arts movies. So to be working on a Golden Harvest production, even though it was ninja turtles and Jim Henson and all these cool things, kind of the overriding thing for me was Bruce Lee and Golden Harvest and Raymond Chow, who was the producer who made the Bruce Lee movies. That to me was the thing that stood out. So Keno was a character that Golden Harvest created. It wasn't part of the ninja turtles universe. So at the end of [the original], Tom Gray, the exec at Golden Harvest, said to me, "We're going to take you out of the costume and give you a role in the next movie." Then I get the script for "The Secret of the Ooze" and I'm looking at it and I'm like, "Oh, this is cool." There's a little handwritten, personal note: "This is your character, Keno." And I open it up and read this script and I was like, "Holy shit. I'm starring in this movie." I was a stunt guy in the movie before. Which was awesome, but it was a totally different experience. That was the thing that really stuck out to me in my mind. Things were happening for me, like, "Wow, I'm doing a Golden Harvest thing. This is so cool." And it's with all the people that I just made this big hit with the summer before. It was a big marking for me just in life in terms of dreams of making martial arts movies. With Golden Harvest, there was no other place to go. It was Golden Harvest and the Shaw brothers. I grew up on those, when I was eight years old watching those movies, seeing that Golden Harvest logo come up and watching Bruce Lee kick ass. It was an amazing moment.

It's one of the coolest promotions of the '90s when it comes to onscreen leveling up. And Keno is such an important character as an access point for young kids.

Yeah, it was cool to be part of it in that way and have a connection with people basically all around the world because of that movie. So it was cool like that.

Do you remember the first or biggest thing that struck you when it came to the animatronic characters or Jim Henson or the way the creature shop operated?

When you go into those things, you never know what the hell costumes—it can go real bad real fast. But when you see to the level that it was done, you instantly knew, "Whoa, we're doing something amazing here." Just by looking at the way that they were able to bring those characters to life, you knew instantly, "Wow, this is awesome. I've never seen anything like this."

Do you remember a moment when you became aware of that? Or something you saw that made it real, to be specific about it?

It was mostly just when I went over to London and I was at the shop, and you see the work that goes into the making of these things. There's a process there. It's not something that's just being thrown together. And Jim Henson is just a super OG when it comes to great work.

Speaking of a lot of work going into something, your fight sequence with the Rock in "The Rundown" is a classic for good reason. I know it took three weeks to do all that. When you think of the choreography or something you learned, do you remember any conversations or where does your mind go about that experience?

I worked with Andy Cheng on that, and he's part of the Jackie Chan stunt team. Again, Hong Kong, for the world that I live in, action and martial arts fight scenes and that kind of thing, they've always been a leader in the space. So Andy came from Jackie Chan, all-time-great stunt guy, martial arts action guy. So it was always about pushing the envelope. And that's what I remember about that. "We're really doing something special here." I really did know that when we were rehearsing and putting it together. I'm like, "Wow, this is going to be amazing." Mostly when we were actually shooting it. Because you never know; sometimes you rehearse and then when you get there on the day it ends up just, "Oh, it's going to be boom-boom-bap!" [Laughs] And you're like, "Hang on one second! We just did six weeks rehearsing this fight scene. It's all laid out." "Yeah, well, we gotta cut it. We don't have time." [Laughs] So when we were filming it, like, "Shit, they're really [doing it], and it's awesome." I remember Peter Berg, the director, and Andy Cheng, the way that Peter was covering the fight scene and the choreography with Andy and all the stunt guys because it really was a tribal thing. In "The Rundown," a lot of that is Hong Kong action because of the way that Andy was putting together those fight sequences and second unit directing.

"Red Sonja" and "The Rundown" are different movies, but how would you compare how Arnold Schwarzenegger and Dwayne Johnson work?

I don't know. I was a kid when we were doing "Red Sonja." It was early childhood memory, and it was just the time of my life. "The Rundown" was basically the first real movie I'd done since "Surf Ninjas." It was a good 15 years in between. So totally different mindset going on. The one thing about those guys is both Arnold and the Rock is you know people that are driven to be great at whatever they do. None of those guys got there because anything was handed to them. They worked hard to get to the places that they were. They were both at similar places when I worked with them in their career. Because Arnold had done "Conan," but he one night gave a VHS to my dad and me after work and was like, "I just filmed this movie; it's coming out this summer." And we went and put it in the VHS at the hotel, and it was "The Terminator." He went on to become the biggest star ever at the time. And similar to that with "The Rundown" when I worked with the Rock he had done I think one other movie, and he has gone on to be the biggest movie star on the planet. So that's always something that you can kind of look toward for inspiration. And I have. It's cool to be able to work with those kind of people all along the way. People that have gone on to become great in their careers and what they've accomplished. The main thing is they all have great work ethic. Even after work: "OK, now I've gotta go work out." Work never ends.

And certainly the choreography in a lot of these movies is so remarkable. I'm not saying these are the same, but do you see a parallel between martial arts acting and dance movies?

I think in some ways. I think you have the classics, like Kurosawa, where we really mark the beginning of seeing martial arts movies. Those are also classical films that major filmmakers draw inspiration from that have also been major movies. But I think "Kill Bill" is a good example of how—it answers that question, ultimately. And the filmmaker in and of himself answers that question. As easy as it is to break into a dance number in "Pulp Fiction" is as easy as it is to break into a sword fight in "Kill Bill."

That's a great comparison. And now I see why Tarantino connects with you.

Yeah. And it's because you come to the genre that I grew up in and do something great. That's a cool thing because then I see you have the inspiration too. You can see the Bruce Lee inspiration. I was graduating high school in the '90s. So those filmmakers were making their debuts pretty much right around that time. And so you're coming off of movies like the ninja turtles and being part of 'em, and you're also growing up and developing a taste for filmmaking and you have on the other side of the coin [Laughs], you have "Ninja Turtles" and then you have "Reservoir Dogs."

I wonder if any kids who didn't know the turtles' names referred to them as Mr. Purple, Mr. Orange, Mr. Red, and Mr. Blue.

[Laughs] Exactly.

Did anyone on any other sets talk to you about their "Teenage Mutant Ninja Turtles" fandom? On "Brooklyn Nine-Nine," "Superstore" or "Indiana Jones and the Kingdom of the Crystal Skull"?

I know that Shia LaBeouf hit me with the "Go Ninja Go Ninja Go" when we were on the set. [Laughs]

I definitely would've been more surprised if you said Harrison Ford did that.

No, Harrison Ford was cool. Super cool. We were sitting there while they were lighting, and I told him I was Filipino, and he was like, "Yeah, I went to the Philippines to film once." I was like, "'Apocalypse Now'! One of my favorite movies!" So that was kinda cool. Just the fact that we had a conversation about "Apocalypse Now" and him being in the Philippines, that was legendary to me. I was like, "This is great." Honestly, working on ["Crystal Skull"] was super cool to me because I grew up on all those movies in the '80s. And seeing 'em, a lot of times in 70mm in an old-school theater, packed up in the Bay Area. So to be on a set with Steven Spielberg on "Indiana Jones" having a little fight scene and smash him over the face with a shovel [Laughs], it was cool. I remember when I got the phone call for that, I walked through the door and they were like, "Hey, Indiana Jones just called for you. Indiana Jones is looking for you." [Laughs] "Let me see what Indy has got to say."

I have to ask when it comes to the roles that are available for Asian actors and the type of characters we're seeing, and of course "Minari" was recognized by the Oscars in an unprecedented way. I don't intend to make you the mouthpiece for the community, but I feel like I should ask if you have a sense of how far representation on screen has come and how far it has to go? Or where we're at in the stories that are told about this community?

Yeah, for sure. When I started there was nobody. In 1986, I was on a show, network television, ABC, called "Sidekicks," and there was nobody. Nobody in sight. [Laughs] So to see somebody like Chloe Zhao winning the Academy Award and everything else that's going on in between all of that, yeah, there's a tremendous growth that's happened over the last 35 years. It's remarkable, actually. Forget the actors and all that; it's also behind the scenes because in order to have representation in front of the camera and all that, you need behind-the-scenes structure as well to help champion and support those stories because they're familiar with that material. So we're seeing that more and more. It's awesome to see it. At the same time, there's always more room to grow. But things are changing; the way that movies are made and distributed has completely changed. So I see the future [having] a lot more opportunities.

Representation is obviously so important, and people want a variety of stories to be told. I read an interview where you talked about just being seen as a karate kid. The martial arts stuff is great and important, but you don't want the community to be seen as only that. So when something like "The Farewell" comes out that's the opposite of that, in a lot of ways maybe it feels like finally filling in more of that space.

Yeah. And I think that's super important. For me, that's my lane, so of course I'm going to champion my lane, but at the same time we need all of those stories. My thing has always just been martial arts and action and that kind of thing, but with the quality of acting that not just a martial artist can pull off. Those are the kind of movies that I always like. Starting with Kurosawa and Toshiro Mifune, who's like the super OG of it all. He was a legit actor, like one of the greats. Like the Asian Marlon Brando, but he did samurai movies with Kurosawa, who's considered one of the greatest filmmakers of all time. So we like to see that. But I understand that there's a lot of people who are Asian that they don't live in the world of martial arts. We need those stories as well. It just happens to be that we do live in the world of martial arts. [Laughs] So it's not a stereotype; it's just our reality. [Laughs]

That's a good way to put it. It's cool that you've trained people like Wiz Khalifa and Snoop Dogg, and of course people's personas may not be what they're really like, but many wouldn't think laidback stoners would be hardcore trainers. What's a memorable story from working with those guys?

I always try to keep the training on a real authentic level. Before movies and TV and all of that, I grew up as a martial artist. So anybody that I get to spend time with training, I always keep it 100 when it comes to the martial arts. Everyone who trains with me trains hard. We're all at different places as martial artists, but we all go hard when we train. So it's all good. [Laughs] You'd be surprised; with Wiz, if you think laid-back stoner, he'll definitely put in the work. That's why he's gotten good so quickly.

Is there any more gratification for you as a trainer if there's some reluctance at first?

No, not really. For me, I want to get people to a good place as fast as I can. That's always the thing. Not faster than they can get there because then it's just not there. But as fast as I can get you to being at a place of being legit, I'm going to try to do that. So spending time with people that you have to convince, I don't do that. They can go disagree with somebody else. [Laughs] But I don't have any problems like that. I don't even get into situations like that really. But I have, having met people and trained people along the way. But I don't want to spend my time convincing people of anything. [Laughs]

I can't talk to you about "Secret of the Ooze" and not ask this: What do you remember about the shooting of the Vanilla Ice performance?

It was Vanilla Ice! At the height of Vanilla Ice! He was a young dude; he had his crew. They came in there, doing their thing. I was on my own trip too, so I wasn't really checking for him too hard. I'm like, "I'm good doing my thing over here. I'm cool." So it was all good. I grew up listening to hip-hop, raised on hip-hop, so I wasn't too fazed by Vanilla Ice. But I knew that he was huge at the moment. So I was like, "Damn, this movie's going to be big." The little dance routine, I remember. [Laughs] I was there; I actually watched them film that too, some of those dance scenes because I was waiting for fight scenes at the end. It was all love, man.

It certainly puts a perfect time stamp on the movie.

It definitely time-stamped it. The movie would've been cool, I think, either way.

And lastly I want to circle back to one thing. You've talked about the prejudice you experienced growing up, and the challenges you experienced personally and professionally. I don't want you to have to go into anything difficult from a long time ago, but I'm wondering as the world goes through an ugly period of intolerance, are there any conversations you wish people were having, or any way we can get out of what's going on now?

I don't have any kind of messaging I'm trying to push out when it comes to that other than from my own personal [perspective], I'm on the pathway of trying to make better every aspect of my life. So it's a constant focus to try to make that happen. I have children; my daughter's an actress. She was one of the leads in Robert Rodriguez's film "We Can Be Heroes." Her name is Lotus Blossom. So for me it's being that thing that you want to see in other people. So my focus of concentration is working on that. All the energy that people spend criticizing other people's points of view, I choose to spend that on trying to improve myself. [Laughs] So that I can live my best life.

Shannon Elizabeth of 'American Pie'

Shannon Elizabeth and I begin our conversation discussing how a rhino orphanage is only a Band-Aid because it doesn't stop poaching, and that legislation can make big change but only if the political will is there, and that harming the Amazon is a destruction of the Earth's lungs. Anyone who cares about animals and the planet (this should be everybody) would be impressed and inspired, and it's great to hear Elizabeth—an actress with a gift for upbeat comedy and inherent sweetness, arguably best utilized in 2001's "Jay and Silent Bob Strike Back"—so clearly using her passions and influence in the way she always intended.

"I've always had a love for animals, and I knew that was what I wanted to do once I was in a position to give back," she said via Zoom from her current home of South Africa, where her charity the Shannon Elizabeth Foundation—launched in 2001 as Animal Avengers—is currently looking to purchase a piece of land to use to protect all species and habitats within the area. "So as soon as I felt I could start to give back, I'm just that type-A personality that wants to do everything myself."

It's also hard not to notice how the idea of a webcam interaction with Elizabeth, one of many breakout stars in the massively successful, franchise-spawning "American Pie," has changed enormously since the film's release in 1999. That was when, in one of the most enduring, heightened comic set pieces of the '90s and one of Jim's (Jason Biggs) most humiliating sex-related disasters in a movie full of them, premature ejaculation ruins the moment not once but twice after Jim walks in on Czech exchange student Nadia (Elizabeth) touching herself in his room, and she humors his attention—all while being secretly broadcast via webcam to his friends and (accidentally) everyone else in the area.

Surprisingly, Elizabeth says, Nadia was never discussed for one of the series' many spinoffs.

I really appreciate you taking the time to talk for this project about the '90s. What's something you feel nostalgic for from that era?

Gosh. It's funny. For me I feel like so much of the '90s were a blur. I wish I could go back and relive them all because that time of my life went very fast. It's like everything was fast-moving. I was always busy working on something and being whisked one place or another, being told what to say and not to, how to act. Looking back on it now, it's such a blur. I feel like I slept through it almost. I don't feel like I got to live and enjoy those moments because it's almost like you know how people say youth is wasted on the young? It's like I was so young then, and now I have so much more wisdom now; I wish I could go back and live all of that knowing everything I know now and being the person I am now but [do it] again. It was such a fun period of time, but I don't know if I enjoyed it as much as I would if I was doing it now. And I loved every moment of it. So much that I just wish I could do it all again. It's hard to say just one thing that I miss because it was an amazing experience for me. It was really an honor to be allowed to participate in a lot of those things that I was invited to do because of the work I was doing. And whether that was a talk show or an awards show or getting to work with actors that I admired, all of that, I look back on it now and feel really blessed that I got to do all that and am very, very grateful.

The nature of that time in anyone's life, and also being in a competitive field where you always have to focus on what's next and how you get to here and here and here, I would think it would be hard for people in that world to take a deep breath and say, "Wow, I can't believe I'm doing an episode of 'Step by Step'" or whatever they're doing.

Even in the moment, when you're younger, for me anyway, you don't know to take a breath and do that. You don't really know that you're not grounded. You just keep going and keep fighting and you keep doing. And you don't realize how fast it is all going to go by. For me it doesn't feel like it was that long ago. It doesn't feel like that much time has passed. But then people like you tell me that the time has passed, and I'm like "Jeez, I can't believe it." It doesn't feel like it to me at all.

Seriously! And 1999 was an unbelievable year for movies. Besides for "American Pie," is there another movie that came out that year that struck a chord out of "Magnolia," "The Matrix," "Fight Club," "Being John Malkovich," "The Sixth Sense," "The Talented Mr. Ripley," "The Insider," "Eyes Wide Shut," "Notting Hill," "Election," "Varsity Blues"?

Without you telling me what came out in a year, I wouldn't even know what year a movie came out. All of those were massive movies that I remember watching all of them, and they're amazing. It's such a different thought when you think back to 2020 and what came out and what happened. Not much came out because they couldn't. Not much happened. That was a whole different time.

Do you feel like any of those connected with you in particular?

What stands out is "Being John Malkovich" because I'm a huge fan and I just remember it being an amazing movie and I love him. And it's funny you say "The Sixth Sense" because we were just talking about "The Sixth Sense" earlier because my partner's mom was telling me how a friend of hers is very psychic and has had some experiences lately in her home and that movie came up because my partner's dad and his sister were talking about how they went and saw that movie together and how scared they were, and I was saying that I think more and more right now you see a lot of these movies and TV shows that are very supernatural because people are having experiences. They're having some sort of experience that they can't explain, and they're putting it into the work. So whether that's hearing something, seeing something, experiencing things that they can't explain that seem like they're from a parallel universe but is spiritual in some way. The reason you're seeing more and more of that—this is going into my spirituality—the vibration of the earth is rising, and as that vibration rises we all have to rise to that occasion, and as we start to wake up and become more grounded and more aware, we will have these experiences and of course it's going to go into the work of the writers and directors and producers of these films. I think we're going to see a lot of that happening. For me it's cool because I love that kind of stuff.

Sure. When it comes to "American Pie," a lot has changed in terms of how the movie is viewed now and the character of Nadia is viewed in terms of the webcam—

[Laughs] I can't imagine how it's viewed now. I'm not up to date on this.

Well, obviously the conversation, for the better of course, has changed about what people recognize as a violation and the—

The "Me Too" movement.

Certainly. And the necessary rejection of the predatory bro-ness, for lack of a better term. Is there something else about the character that you've been hoping people recognize but haven't yet? A lot struck me as I returned to the series and revisited what Nadia does and doesn't do.

No. [Laughs] It really wasn't that deep. There's a time for being politically correct, and there was a time in the past where it was just don't think, and just escape into something else that isn't always so heavy and always a specific way. I really haven't thought anything about it. [Laughs] I could see why it wouldn't hold up today because we're in a different time, and people and everything is evolving in a direction, and film and TV is going to have to evolve with it. Imagine "American Pie" and everyone's wearing a face mask! [Laughs] It wouldn't have worked! I don't analyze it like that or think about it like that. It was supposed to be a fun movie that made people laugh. The whole job of the movie was to have fun and make people relate to a character because "I was that guy" or "I was that girl." I was a fantasy character! I wasn't really real. I wasn't representing much of anything; I was just a fantasy character. I don't really think too much more into it than that.

One of the things you talked about previously with Howard Stern was fantasy vs. reality in terms of people and roles. And I watched the "Skin" documentary about nudity in film that you participated in, and it's interesting to think about these fantasy characters and how they evolve. The concept of "Does the nudity make sense for the character?" is the question people like to ask, but when the character is a male fantasy, how does that color that question?

Well, if it's a male fantasy, then of course there's going to be nudity. That's the fantasy of it. I don't think we were making a movie completely set in a grounded reality. I mean, look at some of the stuff Jim does in the movie. Not saying it couldn't happen, but again it was to make people laugh and be a little bit out there. It wasn't a story about me. It wasn't about me and me being a certain way, me being a feminist. That wasn't it. I think the main thing to remember too is this was my first studio film. I was just very excited to have a job. [Laughs] It wasn't about being a politically correct character. For me especially looking back, it was all about—I didn't know this at the time—but it was all about building a presence so that I could have a platform today to do work that matters. Was I performing a female movement back then? No. Because I was just trying to get a job. But now that I have that platform, I can do what I can to help women, people, animals, kids, whatever it is. So for that I'm very grateful. We weren't trying to make any big political statement with "American Pie." [Laughs] It was escapism for people to laugh and have fun, and I think it should only be viewed as that.

Do you have a sense of why Nadia connected the way she did? In "Skin" you talk about seeing Phoebe Cates in "Fast Times at Ridgemont High" as a kid. Was there ever a moment where you allowed yourself to think you could be the Phoebe Cates of the '90s?

People said it to me, but I never said it. But people would say that. For me it was just about working. I loved working, I loved being on set, and I love acting. So if I was able to do a job that allowed me to get another job and then another job, that was my goal. Just to be able to keep working. So that was all it was. Now I can look back and see that I feel like the universe was helping to build a platform for me so that I could [do this work now]—my mission on the planet is the work that I do for charity. So I think the universe was supporting me in my job so that I could then complete my mission before I leave this planet. That's kind of how I look at it.

I totally appreciate what you're saying about "American Pie." It's easy for people to look at something from the outside or in hindsight that's incredibly different from the way it was at the time for people involved. I find myself struck by teen comedies almost being a window into how young people, particularly young men, are being raised. Eight years after "American Pie," "Superbad" came out with a more feminist viewpoint. Twelve years later was "Booksmart," and now you're co-directing "Losing It," in which young women have a pact not to lose their virginity until college. Do you track an evolution there through that lens of teen comedies as a window into how American kids are being raised?

Um, I never really thought about it that way. For me it's just about making people laugh. And to make people laugh you have to ground it in their reality. It's fine for you to have your reality, but without the parallels of them having a similar experience or being like, "Oh my god, I've done that; I've been there," where they can relate to something. So you want to make people laugh, but it still has to be grounded in reality, unless you're doing a supernatural thing, but for this kind of work you want people to—obviously you need to know something about people's reality. I don't know anything about boys' reality per se unless they tell me. [Laughs] But even now I don't think I understand guys all that well. You try, but you're never going to see it the same because you never lived it in their shoes, their body. So you just don't know.

I find myself wondering if a guy is doing something obnoxious or sexist in a movie, does that result in people thinking about the consequences of that? In "American Reunion," Stifler, who is past 30, is doing "vagina shark" at the beach and violating women's boundaries, and while they scream and turn him away, I'm curious how much people learn from moronic behavior. In my book about "Saved by the Bell," I explored how so often when Jessie, the feminist voice of the show, would say something, Slater would say something sexist and there was a laugh track and male viewers would just think, "Ha ha, they made fun of her." Now, in the reboot 30 years later, there's a much different perspective where they're not mocking her viewpoint and there's no laugh track. So in terms of "Losing It," then, do you find that you are wanting to create that recognition behind when people do stupid things? In "American Pie" or '90s movies in general, we laughed with the obnoxiousness, but I'm not sure if we learned from it.

I don't know that we were supposed to learn from a movie like "American Pie," per se. I think it was entertainment. But I do think for a movie or a TV series to work, you have to either be a period piece or you have to be up with what's happening in that current day and age. So what happened back then [is different] from what's happening now. In the same way, if you go further back you've got stuff like "All in the Family," which was extremely controversial for the time. And some things like that that came out today would be like the way they did "The Conners." That's a thing that comes to mind that might be kind of similar in a way. Now it is about learning something, whereas I don't know if it was as much about learning something then. Maybe, but people were more accepting of it. I'm living in a country where apartheid happened. Things were acceptable in the past that aren't acceptable now. And they should've never been. So many things that should've never happened in our history and they did, and we can't change that in the past, but we can change it going forward. And I think now we are in a day and age where you want to be able to make a statement with film and TV, but you also need escapism too. And I think there is a fine line now, and I think it's going to be an ongoing process for me to find that line. Especially as a director, especially working with people, directors, and actors, and what is acceptable now and what is not. And what is the right way to portray somebody. I think it's a collaboration. It's not up to one person to say that it should be a certain way. That's where you've really gotta trust your team and work together to make sure what you're putting out will be entertaining and make people laugh but also that it's putting out the right message. And I never thought about that with "American Pie." That's not where I was at in my life, and I don't think society was at that point either. But now it's a different day and age.

Did you ever hear from anyone from the Czech Republic about Nadia?

No, but I was hoping to! [Laughs] But we messed with the accents so much in post, that I'm sure the Czechs were like, "That's not our accent. I don't know what she's trying to do." I started with a very thick accent, and in post they had me bring it down, down, down. I'm like, "You know there's no accent left on here, right?" "No, no no, we want her to have been here for a while." "OK. I give up."

As you think about "Losing It," do you have any sense of how being 18 is different now than it was in 1999?

I have no idea, but I can't imagine what it would have been like growing up with the kind of access to technology and internet and social media and YouTube. I always said that if I was a kid now I would probably do anything I could to be creative and create my own YouTube channel. Why not? It's such a creative outlet, and even though people criticize some of them for what they're doing, I think it's a great way of being creative and learning and teaching yourself skills that can really help you. Kids now, with technology and all this stuff, I'm still trying to understand. There's too many things. I don't even want to learn another thing. By the time I realize it's even available to learn, the kids already know [about the next thing]. If I had that kind of time, like when you're a kid, I think it would be awesome.

Where does filmmaker or actress land on your list of roles you're playing in your life now?

I want to do more directing. I really want to do more directing, but I also want to marry my two worlds where if I am on camera I'm going out and introducing the world to animals in different places around the world and the people that are protecting those animals and that habitat. So I can be on camera as the actress, but I can also be doing the conservation work at the same time.

Charlie Talbert of 'Angus'

Remember the movie that ended with so many high school students recognizing that they'd been victimized by the most popular and feared kid in class?

No, not "Mean Girls." First there was 1995's "Angus," which starred the girl from "Jurassic Park," (Ariana Richards), two screen legends (Kathy Bates, George C. Scott) and in just a few years, the star of one of the generation's seminal shows (James Van Der Beek). Add in a soundtrack featuring Green Day, Weezer and Goo Goo Dolls, and the movie made ... no money.

Whatever. "Angus" is (to an extent) a little like the sweeter, smarter younger brother of that year's far more successful "Tommy Boy," with Charlie Talbert, in his first onscreen role, starring as the titular, awkward high school freshman. He's forced in from the fringes after his nemesis, Rick Sanford (Van Der Beek), pulls a prank that names Angus the winter ball king and his crush, Melissa Lefevre (Richards), as the queen.

The character is an endearing, vulnerable representative for how it feels to be young and insecure, and how scary it is to suddenly have a chance to get what you want. Talbert may not have starred in any other big movies, but he's still grinding it out in small roles in major movies and shows like "Watchmen," "The Big Short," and Barry Jenkins' "The Underground Railroad." And remains the heart of an empowering, overlooked piece of the '90s.

What's something you're nostalgic for from the '90s? It could be absolutely anything.

I gotta tell ya. First and foremost, the first thing that comes to my brain is just having a pager with no cell phone. Having my sweet little green-and-black Motorola pager, with the blue LCD screen, and I don't have to call you back right that second. I don't have to [get] the bad news, whatever the bad news is for the day. Or the good news. It's all coming to me when I get home, or I decide I want to go to a phone. So that's the biggest thing I miss about it. And being an actor at that age, at that time, that was the first thing you had to get. It was non-negotiable when it came to communicating with your agent.

Did you have a pager before everything happened with the movie, or you just had to get one after?

As soon as they were a thing, after I booked the movie, [my agents said], "Well, we can't rep you if you don't have a pager." I was like, "Really? Alright."

Now I feel like some people who don't have certain social media accounts are pressured to create one to promote certain projects. I never thought of pagers as the original Instagram.

Pagers were the original Instagram for me. [Laughs] I have a couple social media accounts. I don't really use my Twitter that much because, let's face it, I'm just not that fuckin' witty. As far as my Instagram I kinda like it because I can judge how famous I am as well as [Laughs] put out new content, fuckin' around with people and having fun, whatever comes to my brain. I remember one of coolest things I ever did was I was one of the first few independent people to have their own phone show, and it was "The Charlie Talbert Show" for CBS. And they had it on the Verizon phones. I remember we beat out Letterman, and we beat out "Big Brother" that week. It was pretty awesome. So I did two seasons of that. It was like 2008. It was at CBS … I used to steal all my guests from Ferguson. That was my one agreement with him. I was telling a joke in line—which is funny because I'm always telling a joke in line when I book something—and these guys were like, "Hey, do you want your own show?" And I had to come in and pitch it and I paid a little person to come in and dress up like me and do jazz hands whenever I said a keyword. And it turned into me doing 24-hour access to both Redford and Television City and I could run back and forth and shoot wherever I wanted to. My office was right next to Ferguson's, so I would just steal his guests left and right. It was awesome. I think one of my first guests was Coolio.

One of your first guests was who?

Coolio.

That's what I thought you said, but I wanted to make sure I wasn't imagining that.

It's funny. He was with the producer of his cooking show at the time, and I remember Henry Winkler was there, and we got along great. I don't talk about this story very much. And the producer, funny enough, a few years later, ended up being my neighbor, and now he's one of my best friends. He was the best man at my wedding. I have a tattoo of my buddy on my leg right now, actually. His name's Dan Smith. He runs a division of Rockstar Games overseas in India.

What do you remember of your interview with Coolio?

We had worked together years before. I wanted to learn everything there was about filmmaking. I think it was my third film—which I actually live with one of my co-stars of that now down in New Orleans, Christopher Berry. You might remember him from "Django Unchained," "12 Years a Slave," "The Purge." A bunch of stuff. We're both in [Barry Jenkins'] "The Underground Railroad" comin' up too. I think he had a full day of shooting and I had off, so I showed up to meet him. The sound guy hadn't shown up, so I picked up the boom and ran it for two days until they found a replacement. I did such a good job they brought me back for another movie, and it was a Coolio movie. And I had to sit under Coolio in his white Humvee for eight hours, so I just shot the shit with Coolio. So we basically just improv'd a whole bunch and just had fun. It wasn't an interview; it was just us going back and forth playing improv games.

That sounds like a fun day at the office.

It was awesome.

I've also been asking everyone about movies from the '90s. To focus on 1995, when "Angus" came out, some others were "Apollo 13," "Braveheart," "Usual Suspects," "Heat," "Devil in a Blue Dress," "Clueless," "Desperado," "Before Sunrise." Did any of those make a particular impact with you?

Well, man, I gotta tell you, the thing that I love about film and television—I sound like I'm really doing an interview, which is good, like I'm sitting on a couch; "let me tell you what it is …"—the thing about movies, man, is, and I'm going to say this when I refer to the movies we're talking about, like "Apollo 13." The thing about movies is they affect your life, and that's why I continue to do it. I don't know if you've noticed my resume, but I used to be the lead in a bunch of projects. Now I'm a co-star and a couple big guest stars because they're bigger projects and different characters, and I'm no longer the funny fat guy. When I was younger, it was always, "Oh, he's the funny fat guy." So I got to work with William Atherton on "Who's Your Daddy?" and Dave Thomas. And they were sitting with me and they were like, "God you remind us so much"—Eugene Levy was there and Martin Short, and we're all shooting the shit—and they were just like, "You remind us so much of John Candy." I gotta tell you, man, that fueled me for at least another ten years. From now. So when I go to sleep at night, I'll throw on "Apollo 13" because I know that Tom Hanks and Bill Paxton and Bacon and those guys, they're comforting voices. They've let me cry when I need to cry, and laugh when I need to laugh. That's kind of my catchphrase when it comes to doing film. I hope you cry when you can cry, laugh when you can laugh. And those movies do that. I worked with Justin Walker; I think it was on my second film. Justin Walker, I don't know if you remember, was Alicia Silverstone's love interest who turns out to be gay in "Clueless." And it was so neat just being there and knowing that there's that fourth wall. I'm on both sides of that fourth wall. I'm enjoying it as a fan and I'm indulging in it as an actor. So those kind of movies, no matter what your taste is—and for me, my taste is all over the place, especially with movies—so yeah, those movies really impacted me. I don't compare "Angus" to those movies. It was kind of strange. "Angus," the original script wasn't what everybody saw. And that was truly one of the most disappointing things for me was when I walked in on an ADR session that Chris Owen was doing. They didn't know that I was in town, and they had reedited the movie, and it had changed a whole bunch. That's OK; that's their prerogative. But it changed what that movie was to me. But it's nice to know that it found an audience that says, "Hey, I was an outcast," and they see the bigger picture of that story and they inserted their own life experience, and that kind of did the trick for me and made me feel really good about "Angus" in the long run. That was a long-winded answer, I'm sorry about that.

Not at all. I like the way you discuss responding to "Apollo 13" specifically for a comfort factor. It's an empathetic portrait of what art makes people feel. We know the world has changed so much since the mid-'90s, but so much of the material is darker and isn't necessarily comforting.

Same with "Apollo 13"! The ship blows apart. They still make it, but you know, you're still finding comfort in that. It's weird.

Well, as long as you make it to the end when they're OK it shows you're rooting for things to be alright. It's only weird if you turn it off after the ship has problems, as if that's what gives you comfort.

[Laughs] Well, that's why I also like to watch "Red Dwarf" when I fall asleep. Because nothing ever goes right for those guys. When I'm feeling sadistic, I'll watch Rob Llewellyn and those guys and [Danny John-Jules] in "Red Dwarf." And Chris Barrie, which is funny because one of my best friends is Chris Berry. The one I live with.

I guess that's a good segue then because the first thing I wanted to ask you about "Angus" was that at the top of the movie, Angus points out that Angus is a cow's name. To what extent do you think names impact personalities?

I can't remember if that line was one of the originals. Because that whole opening monologue was changed when they cut out Larry Drake and Robert Curtis Brown, the gay fathers. Because originally they both walk in the frame with [Kathy Bates]. Because she and my dad divorce and they both turn out to be gay. So it's one of those things where I think that was a fill-in. But as far as names, sticks and stones, but, yeah, they can mess you up a bit. It's very much like that Johnny Cash song "A Boy Named Sue." And I kind of respect that. Because though my mother is dead now—she died last Valentine's—I was thinking, even now she knew I was OK because she didn't give me a bad name or anything like that. But genetically she gave me man boobs and a flabby stomach and not a fat neck. So I've got a lot I'm fighting against. It's like if you give a man a fish he eats for a day, you teach a person to fish they eat for a lifetime. And I think that kind of is parallel to what we're talking about here.

How different, if at all, would Angus' life or teen years have been if his name was Clive or Antonio or something?

[Laughs] I often think about that for myself. Charlie never had enough anything for me. If I was skinnier, I think Charlie would have taken me farther. A lot of my best friends growing up through life, including Chris Owen, Chris Berry, Chris Shelton, Chris Heiliger, have all been named Chris. It's a weird fact and phenomenon. I've got five really close

Matt Pais

friends named Chris, and I've always had close friends named Chris. It's kind of strange. I always find that when I meet someone named Chris, I'm always at ease with them and think they're cool. Until they do something to put the switch on me. So I think a name really does have a large impact on who you are, and shame on so many of these parents for some of these names they've given their children.

I definitely do find it hard to not groan at some names I hear.

Absolutely. I hear a name and I go, "How?! How do you spell that? Honestly, dude, what is your name?" And I'm like, "You have a relative named that? It's a combination of favorite furniture and food? What is your name?" And it's OK. Some people can wear their exotic names. Some people get a thrill out of people saying their name wrong. Right now I'm on that app Clubhouse, and I don't know if you're familiar with it, but it's like another way to be social and chat with people you don't know. We spent the other night hanging out with all these different celebrities. But I've been working for free, pro bono, for the Laugh Factory comedy club because I used to do standup for a few years, and that's actually what helped me transition in my move back to film and television. So every day I'm listening to these guys and I'm helping them with their jokes and they make me a moderator and I come in and work on people's jokes and sometimes take people aside and try to help them find their voice. And I hear it from these comedians, "No, that's not how you say it." And they won't tell you. They won't tell you [Laughs] how to say their names until someone gets it right. And I'm like, "Oh, you're sick. I love it. You're the kind of person who watches 'Red Dwarf' before they go to bed, and I like it." So there's definitely something to that. But for those that it doesn't work for, I always feel bad for 'em. Because they didn't really have a choice and they kind of went with it, and even now when they can change their name, they still don't have a choice and they kind of went with it. And even now when they can change their name, they still don't have a choice because it was still a gift from their parents and god knows what it means, but maybe it meant something to them and maybe that's the piece of them they hold onto. Now if you adopt a child and give them a messed-up name, well, shame on you! You had time to prepare. You had months of paperwork; you should have thought it out. But my dad's name was Bradley, and I was like, "God, I wish I was a Bradley." I look like a Bradley. "Yeah, Bradley, come on over." I don't look like a Bradley Whitford, but I look like a Bradley. Just a lovable dude that you can tell stuff to, that'll crack jokes with you but in the end you know will pick you up in the desert even if he doesn't have gas.

Then do you think Angus' experience would have been different with another name? Say, Brian Johnson or a different member of AC/DC?

Well, Angus is a cow's name—no, just kidding. I think based on the story scenario it could've been a little different. It could've been a little more under the radar. Because in this particular [case] he pays so much attention to his name. I think if you believe, or you say you are, you are. Until you say you aren't. So I think focusing on it made him a glutton for punishment. If he had had a different name—if he had the name Bradley or Johnson or

238

what have you and he focused on his name and said, "Johnson is the name of a male member." It's just about the circumstance. And I think that's true for a lot of people. I don't meet a lot of Charlies, which is kind of nice when I go into social groups. I meet tons of Chrises and Jeffs, but it's one of those things that I kind of lucked out in the gamut, but Angus did not.

I saw an interview that James Van Der Beek did recently where he said he based Rick on guys who used to bully him when he was in school. You've talked about the relationship that developed between you two over time and him being a really good guy. Did the two of you ever talk about your experiences being bullied?

No, not really. When we did "Angus," it was kind of separated. Chris and I would hang out, and we wouldn't really hang out with so much the other cast because we wanted to keep our relationship genuine and stronger than the relationships we would have with the other performers around us, if that makes sense. So a bit method. So, no, never really got into it. And after "Angus," I know people tried to hire us together again. I went out for Pacey 12 times, and ended up getting paid a bunch for that, on "Dawson's Creek," and then finally it was down to a couple of us. I didn't have the right appeal, but obviously they liked something about me. And I went out for Billy Bob in "Varsity Blues" and I picked up Billy Bob in the TV series, but in the TV series Billy Bob was the lead telling the story. So we never really got into that. And when we just saw each other, it was usually not the scenario where after that you would sit down and talk about that kind of stuff. I did, however, call him once when I was doing that show on CBS. I was like, "Hey, I want to do this whole 'Crank Yankers' skit, it's going to be awesome." And he was totally down to do it, and then they pulled the plug because the show got canceled. Actually all the shows got canceled because CNET bought 'em out, and somebody had put porn up on the website so they were nervous and afraid that they [would offend the advertisers]. I think after that I saw him in Vegas, we had both worked for the same producers, and spent a nice dinner together, but never really talked about our previous bullying [experiences].

So many stories about bullying find the person being victimized being passive the whole time, but Angus at least isn't afraid to get physical in his own defense from the start. How if at all do you feel like your perception about the right way to stand up to a bully has changed since then?

God, man. I don't think there's a solid answer for that because I do what I've always done, and I just rely on humor. Heck, that's how I got "Angus." Telling a joke. So it's one of those things where I'm usually good at coming into a room and defusing it before people have to blow up and show who the alpha is. So I'm a bit of a beta's alpha with pretty much every group I'm in. Which means I get along with the alphas and I get along with the betas, and it kind of works. If I were getting bullied like I did when I was younger—I got bullied a lot when I was younger—humor. Because most of the people that bullied me when I was younger—not most of them. Some of them are my friends. I even had a dude reach out on my Facebook the other day, and they'd heard the interview I did on "The Coogan

Chronicles," and he basically apologized for bullying me when we were younger in junior high. On a public forum. And I hadn't talked to this guy since 19 diggity doo. So it was kind of like, "Wow, I'm not going to like that comment, but I appreciate you."

Is that how you responded? "Thanks. I appreciate the apology."

No, I didn't respond. I just thought it would be funnier not to respond. Hence the humor factor. "You sit and think about what you've done now that you're thinking about what you've done!" [Laughs]

It's hard to know what to do with that. It's easy to have the inclination to write, "It's OK," but you're like, "It's not OK. I don't think about it, I'm glad you realize you feel badly about it …" Do you think that person is looking for you to absolve them of the guilt?

I can't answer that. I can answer to the fact that I think everybody that's been in my life, whether they bullied me, whether they hurt me, whether they made me laugh, whether they made me feel great, whether we had sex or not, whether anything. Any kind of interaction. Because without all of that I wouldn't be on the phone with you now.

That's a good way of looking at it.

And I wouldn't have cannon fodder for the jokes either.

Obviously you and Chris Owen connected so much on set and in your friendship and working together and living together in the years after. One of my favorite parts of "Angus" is the relationship between Angus and Troy, and when they say "Buds!" In the moment when they say "Screw you" but still walk into the dance together, is that a sign that friends like this are connected, codependent or both?

It's both! I lived with Chris for years upon years. In fact, I just finished my first pilot script that I adapted from a book last night. Seventy pages. And the first person I sent it to was Chris. I said, "Tear it apart, man. Just rip it apart." And he was like, "Absolutely." And we hadn't talked since he got married last March, I think it was. It's hard to remember. Sometime during the pandemic. Sometime during lockdown. And I was so bummed because I couldn't go to his wedding. Heck, I'm ordained; I would have married him and his wife. There is that codependency when you're together. And even now, now that I'm 1,200 miles, 1,300 miles away from him, I feel like he's right in the next building. And when I fall asleep at night, I take comfort in that. So because "Angus," our two characters, the ones that we portrayed in the film, were based off of our relationship—you've heard the interview; they left us in a room and we just started finishing each other's jokes and they were watching us from another room, and they came in and were like, "Do you want to go to Disneyland and see if you get along?" And we both looked at each other and were like, "Hmm, you're giving us 200 bucks to go have fun at Disneyland and see if we get along?"

We both had this, "OK, buddy, yeah, we'll take your $200." The fact that we shared moments like that only having met each other 30 minutes before. It was meant to be. So when we did "Angus," that was really just Chris and Charlie. So there's no real difference between what you saw on screen, except Chris is a hell of a lot cooler than I am.

And it becomes a great time capsule to an offscreen friendship.

Oh, 100%. And I don't know if you remember, but the young kid who goes "That was your underwear, Angus?" That was Tony Denman, and we met him when we shot that scene in Minnesota, and he ended up signing on with our manager in Los Angeles, and we became super friends too. It's just one of those things where I consider all of those guys my family. I don't consider all of the cast my family because some of them I haven't seen in years and years and years, but the ones that I bonded with and spent the most time with absolutely. And like I said, we were a bit method on set, so I really just focused on mine and Chris' relationship and mine and George C. Scott's and mine and Kathy's.

And I think part of what makes the movie resonant is the way it taps into a particular feeling at a particular time in a unique way. My son is 3 now, so hopefully he'll go a long time before having to deal with any real social challenges. But I find myself wondering if there's a way to out-think the teenage experience. Is there a way to avoid some of the hardships that Angus goes through? To program a kid with confidence and balance?

If you're going to help him out, just listen to what he's saying or what he's joking about or what he's reading or what he's watching or how he's playing. Is he playing by himself? And if he's playing by himself, throw him a few extra dollars and tell him to go play somewhere. Tell him to go find a friend. Keep him away from the house. If you shelter your kid—and this isn't advice to you, it's just advice in general—it's going to be tougher for the teenage experience. If you make 'em go out and play in the park every day from whatever time to whatever time, I think it'll be a little easier for him. Me personally, I was sheltered a bunch because I got picked on and my mom babied me a little too much when I was younger younger. Like elementary school younger. Then in junior high she realized she needed to loosen the reins, so what she did was she kind of made me leave the house and I found out people that were picking on me from time to time actually became my friends because I was forced to not run away from the problem. And it's kind of reversed because of how everything is with keeping an eye on your kids, and I know it's a dangerous world out there, but also it's always been a dangerous world; it's just more people are talking about it now and you can see your phone better. That's kind of a long-winded, convoluted answer to that. So I hope that helps.

I like that. Do you remember a moment when those relationships flipped for you? Or was it more gradual than that?

It took a week or two when mom started letting me hang out with a family that lived around the corner and the kids would kind of bully me but then mom would be like, "You go hang out with them!" And she wouldn't let me come home and stay in the house. And because I was around them so often and I started getting quicker and wittier and listening to what they had to say, I learned my own personality. I didn't have to be defiant of my mom's personality. I got to use a bit of my mom's craziness and a bit of my friends', who were my enemies for a second, their craziness, and turn it into this wish-wash. "What would my mom say to this?" And then I would use that on them, but then I would make fun of it because it wouldn't be something a kid would say. And it just kind of flipped a switch for me. Because even if there's a little bit of bullying going on at the beginning, eventually if you stand up to it long enough, if you prove that the element is brave—[Laughs] I don't think that I've ever said that in an interview—that was one of the things I loved about "Angus." He just stood there, and you couldn't knock him down, so you kind of had to make him part of your thing. That was kind of what I did with these [people]. If I were to go in the other room right now and ask Chris Berry, "How did you feel about me when we first met?" He'd go, "I hated you. I thought that you were an obnoxious know-it-all, wannabe center-of-attention dude." And by the end of the movie, we were like besties. It's one of those things where you've gotta go out there and you've just gotta say, "Dammit, this is me." And one of the things I used to do when I was younger—a lot of traumatic stuff had happened to me, and you've heard the interviews with my mom, and my dad dying, and all that stuff, and I would meet people and I would tell them right away, I was like, "Hey, what's up, I'm Charlie. Things you should know: My mom accidentally shot my dad in front of me when I was 8, he kind of died in my arms." And I would go on these tangents about my entire life story and my family's history in like two minutes flat. I'd be like, "That's all of me. There ain't nothing left." It was like when Eminem went out there and was just like, "Yeah, so what, I'm a white rapper? So what, I live in the 212?" You disarm them before they have any fodder against you. So I think it makes kids stronger if you push 'em out and make 'em do that too. So I think that coincides with your last question as well.

I don't even know what someone would say in response to a monologue about someone's background like that.

That's the beauty; they couldn't say much. They would just kind of shut down and be like, "This guy's got a lot going on." [Laughs] And it would just be a moment of silence. "This guy's got a lot going on; let's see what he does." And then when I come out and I'm jovial and I'm funny and I'm happy and I'm goofy, it's like, "Oh, he does the thing you do, you just jam it down there and you make it funny and hide your real feelings." It works. But to see the look on their faces sometimes … and I kind of slowly went off of that. I was like, "Maybe it's better if I time-release it."

Obviously to be coming from that place, there's no easy way to deal with that or communicate that.

I gotta tell you just to add on to that, it's kind of hard to time-release that information. You'll be hanging out with somebody and you're friends for a couple months, and they're like, "My dad blah blah blah, what about your dad?" It's hard to slip that in. So if I get it all out we can avoid that awkward moment when you find out later on.

I don't know if this is a good idea for society or a "Black Mirror" episode if everyone is walking around with a name tag that includes their biggest trauma written on it.

Well, actually, that was an episode of "Sliders," so … I knew that would be confusing people when I would do that to people. I knew that would be overwhelming. And I did that so I could play the room, control the room, dish it out and assess how everybody takes me in, know who I gotta shut up around, know who I get to play around with, etc.

Speaking of playing the room, admittedly I only saw "Angus" for the first time recently as I was preparing to talk to you—

Well, you have a beautiful night. Thank you so much for calling. No, I'm just kidding.

It was one of those I'd always meant to see, and for whatever reason just hadn't. The reason I mention it is that one of the things that struck me was that the speech at the end about people being victimized by Rick is almost the same as the one in "Mean Girls," which was a huge hit. Did you have a visceral reaction to that the first time you saw that movie? Or thoughts on the trajectories of the two movies?

It's kind of strange. I would tell you that I worked with Jonathan Bennett, who played the boy that she's in love with when she gets to school. I worked with Lizzy Caplan, but her friend, do you remember what he wore to the prom dance?

A very familiar tux to Angus'.

Exactly. So I knew right away when I watched that that it was truly inspired by that film. But they did it at the right time with the right writers and the right footage, and it's a better movie. "Angus" itself was ahead of its time. Because in 1994 there was no script with two gay fathers and a mother who was potentially gay floating around, mixed with bullying. We were tackling everything in that project. And I remember sometimes working 17-hour days, which was ridiculous. But I was doing it because I was like, "We have to get this done." And when I found out they had taken out the fathers and watered it down a bit, it took it away, but I don't have the same memory of "Angus" as you guys do because I remember what it originally looked like and originally felt like. So it's one of those things where I'm like, I'm glad they did that. I'm glad they approached that, I'm glad they took another stab at working that out. And I remember when the distributors were putting us out, I think they only advertised it for a week before the film came out. And we were in New York doing a press junket and all that stuff, and I remember just thinking, "They didn't do it right." And

I'm watching this movie and I'm like, "This isn't it. This is not going to do well." I told my mom. "It's not going to do well, Mom, it's not going to do well. But at least I've got my foot in the door and I'm not going to be working at Wendy's." She got it. And she was with me through a lot of that stuff. I didn't even bring her actually [sometimes] because she and I had such a rough, rocky relationship physically, that I was like, "I have to bring my [family member] with," which ended up being another weird thing that went on. [Laughs] Let's just say it was only three years ago that it was discovered that the backs of the chairs for "Angus," mine, George C. Scott's, Kathy Bates', Chris Owen's, were all snatched up by a family member. And I ended up mailing them to everybody that was supposed to get 'em, and I sent George C. Scott's to Chuck Logan, who does all the DC stuff. I sent it off to him with a letter going, "I'm so sorry that this happened, I just realized it." I sent Chris' for his birthday, I was like, "I got mine. I was so happy to see it again after 25 years." I lost the question. What was the question? Forgive me.

It started about "Mean Girls."

Oh, yeah. So looking at that movie now, and that somebody went in there and took another shot at it but decided it was going to be a heartfelt comedy, that was it. When "Angus" was edited down, they were shooting for a heartfelt comedy, but the problem was you were missing all the heavy moments that really balanced that movie out. I remember there was a podcast that I hopped onto, I think it's called "High School Slumber Party," and they were talking about "Angus," and one of the gals on there was like, "It just felt like he was [the same] all the way through without many levels." And they were also saying, "Yeah, but he was also just being a 15-year-old kid." That's the thing. Everybody only got half of the movie that we shot. And Chris and Patrick and I have talked about it a bunch—I just left a message for him yesterday, the director, Patrick Read Johnson—it just was missing half of its heart. But you could tell. And I think that's why this movie works so well with overweight kids and kids with disabilities and things like that because they can insert their own painful memories and balance it, and it kind of works for them.

Speaking of Wendy's, I wanted to ask you: While I imagine everyone recognizes the importance of timing in life, you have had a life particularly reflective of that, from being discovered making a joke at a suburban Chicago Wendy's to a family member's theft of chair backs impacting your promotion of "Angus" to running into Blake Soper on a night that you say saved your life. To what extent do you feel like you're an example of life swinging at random? Does that ever make you think, or do you not think about it like that? You have so many incredible stories.

For me, my life has been a series of "What the __ just happened?" In fact, with the script that I just wrote, I ended it with the line, "What the fuck was that?" [Laughs] It was just about the entire day that this guy had had. I told a joke in a Wendy's, I ended up doing "Angus." I told a joke while I was shooting "Angus" in another restaurant and got tickets to the Billboard Music Awards. I made somebody laugh and got another job blah blah blah. But if I hadn't been there, if I hadn't stood … I did a show with Kevin Farley that his brother was going to do because I was supposed to potentially in the long run I was going to play Chris Farley's kid. This was about a month or so before he died in a show called "Head Over Heels." With Peter Dobson and Kevin Farley. I remember standing in front of the audience with Chris, doing an impersonation of Chris, and then doing it for Chris, and he goes, *[Chris Farley impression]*, "Man, do you want an autograph or something? You're flippin' awesome, man. I hope we get to work together." I saw him and I knew something was going to happen. He was wearing sweatpants, his regular pants, and he was wearing a button-down shirt that was kind of ripped in the back but he had a jacket over it to kind of cover that, so he was kind of heavy at the time. And as a guy who has always been into people's clothes, I kind of watch people's mannerisms and stuff. I'm like, "I know how he feels right now." Just physicality, not the drug stuff. I just knew that physically he wasn't doing well. And I told him, "Chris, no, man, I want to cherish this moment forever." Somebody took a Polaroid and I had it and it disappeared somewhere down the line. I have Chris Farley's jacket from "Beverly Hills Ninja," which I wore in "Who's Your Daddy" and a couple other films. It's one of those things where those moments, every one of those is like getting discovered. Sitting there with Dave Thomas and those guys and having Dave Thomas go, "You remind us of John Candy." It's one of the proudest moments of my life. Farley was very gifted, very talented, but he was a big guy who used that in his performance. And John Candy was an actor who just happened to be big. And he rode that out. And that's kind of what I've been doing in New Orleans. I got on the phone with my buddy Chris, and I've spent like every holiday with his family for the last 20 years since we did that second movie—the guy that didn't like me—and he's like, "Yeah, man, there's plenty of work down here, you should try it." And the company I was working for got bought out, and I blind moved. I just got in the car one day and sold my stuff off ... and next thing you know I'm in New Orleans, and four days later I'm working on "The Big Short." And when I got here the first thing I did was I kept these big mutton chops because I was like, "I wonder if this takes place in the past or the present, and if it takes place in the past with the Louis Ranieri stuff maybe I can do that." I read for Louis Ranieri, and I wasn't right—I wasn't old enough—but hanging out in the room, Adam McKay goes, "What's with the chops, Charlie? I gotta ask you." Of course I'm nervous as well, it's Adam McKay. And I just went, "I have been growing these chops because I knew you were going to be shooting this film down here. And he goes, "What?!" So I get a phone call later that day and they're like, "Hey, you didn't get the part, but he wrote in another part for you." He basically split up one of the parts and gave me a chance to be in his movie. That was another one of the happiest days in my life, going, "Hey, I made the right choice to get back into acting." I made the right choice to tell a joke in Wendy's that night and be myself. And flirt with a gal who I knew from school who was working behind the counter. I made the choice to tell the guy my info even though he was a stranger at 12 at night asking me to be in a movie near Chicago. So you kind of push and force and make your own luck to an extent. I've been fortunate since I've been here to be in a bunch of award-winning projects, and there's more coming. Working with Barry Jenkins last March—in fact, when I was done filming that, I got in the car and I drove back here and I went out for Martin Scorsese for a film, and I didn't even know the casting director. I just got the call, "Hey, can you audition?" I didn't get the part, but that moment that that casting director somehow stumbled across my name, that's the same moment as Patrick Read Johnson stepping up to me and saying, "Hey, do you want to be in a movie?" So me pushing myself in these situations, it's kind of like my own personal life—I'm a thrill-seeker for these kind of moments, and to fulfill your life I think you've gotta be. I'm also a lazy dude. So I just kind of push myself. I do the work when I gotta do it, I get it done on deadline, but I do like to enjoy my surroundings and make fun of it and have fun with it and run into those moments again. It's kind of funny that I've been saying moments so much because the theme of "Angus" is a brief moment in the life of Angus Bethune. That was the original title for that project, and it's all about having your moment. Those moments where I met all these people, they lead to all these different things, so I don't even know they're coming. I like to look for it, and the fact that I'm looking for it, I get to acknowledge it when I see it and go, "Oh, this was that moment I was looking for, dude!" [Laughs] And I'll tell everybody in the room. If something dope happens to me, I'll just be like, "You're not going to believe this!" I don't care if I know you or not.

Which is more true: That actors are only as mature as they were at the age when they got famous, or that people still carry wounds from high school around with them?

I know a few actors like that, sure. But I think you're talking about two different people. My thought is, yeah, I know some people that stunted their mental growth because they want to continue to live in that time and play that, and some people it really works for them. Performers particularly. There are some people that are just absolutely different than when they were in high school. So even the people that their mental growth might be stunted a bit because of that particular bookmark in their life, those two are also scarred, and this is a way for them to massage or change those scars and let that moment fade from life.

It is sort of strange to put those two things against each other because they both mark a stopping point, but for one it's because something great happened, and the other is something bad probably happened.

Right, right. Like I said I used to tell everybody my life story when I met 'em, but now I don't. I learned to gently leak that information, if tell them at all. And when I'm doing comedy, I'm telling that information. And when I'm just being me, I'm not really laying that on 'em anymore. So there was a time when my growth was stunted after "Angus," for sure. Absolutely. But there's also a time that I am nothing like I was in high school. Not a thing. Except for maybe being a smartass and enjoying life. But being a smartass is just taking the pink elephant in the room and saying, "This thing's crazy, right?" So that's kind of my humor is whatever the thing is we're not supposed to talk about, that's my thing is let's talk about it. And I think that's what helped me move on from it. Those that don't talk about it, that probably sticks with them for a while and can easily stunt them or drastically change them as an adult, but we'll never know the opposite.

Which has changed more since the '90s: the type of teen movies being made, or what it's like to be a teenager now vs. then?

I think there was an innocence. And I think this relates to my very first answer. I think there was an innocence to the non-pager pager era in the fact that because everything is so readily available at your fingertips [now], it's hard to pin the two against each other. I think it's much more intense for anyone that's young and growing up now because like I said before, you can wait until you got home to find out if it was a bad day or a good day in the rest of your life. You booked this movie, or you did something. So I think that kind of reflects in film nowadays is the pressure that's put on kids. And I can remember a time during quarantine, which I'm so happy the "Me Too" movement came out, I'm so happy that Black Lives Matters is being reexamined and pushed, and we have tons of other things that are being dumped and it's been such heavy information, and I know that if I was 15, 16 hearing all this information, my fat little head would just explode. I wouldn't know how to put it in its pocket and try to work with it and try to be the better version of myself in any of these scenarios or be helpful to anybody else in any of these scenarios. It was kind of heartwarming when I saw the big writing in Washington on the streets, just like "Watchmen." I was like, "Wow, I got to be a part of something in some obtuse way, and it's how I feel." And that's great. It's a lot of information, and I think films really reflect that. I miss the innocence that was in film up until the time that "Angus" came out. That was the last film that I did that I think came out on VHS. That time, that switch, when everything starts to become readily available, that's what changes. The difference between my era of movies vs. the 2000s.

I was rewatching "The Mighty Ducks," and there's a moment when Emilio Estevez is going to pull out a checkbook from his jacket, and the kids think it's going to be a gun. Maybe that's just a misjudged moment in a beloved movie, but it's weird to think about how much the world has changed, and what we see on screen has changed as a result. To say nothing of how the entertainment industry itself has changed.

The moment that happens on film, it's immortalized. It becomes part of the staple if that film does something. I remember when it came out, "D2," I couldn't skate. Because I have thick ankles. I was thinking, "Oh, that would be great." But there's moments in films that change the way you look at films. Like when swearing became heavy. George Carlin's seven dirty words, I think maybe one or two of them are left that you [can't] say or be classy enough to get away with, but by the time that record came out, "Ohhh, don't you say that! Don't you dare!" So I think that goes to my previous answer. The change of innocence. That moment when he reaches in and they think it's a gun, that's a moment of innocence. But it's also a commentary on society which might have needed to be said at the time. That's hard for me to judge because that was a weird time for me in my life.

And my last question, to go back to our discussion of names: There's a documentary on Netflix called "The Strange Name Movie," featuring people with

unusual names. Which would you rather have as your name: Tim Burr, Harold Schmuck, or Ronald McDonald?

Tim Burr. 'Cause if you're going to fall, you gotta fall hard.

Jason James Richter of 'Free Willy'

It would be hard to overstate what a phenomenon "Free Willy" was in 1993, despite its biggest star being Michael Madsen ("Reservoir Dogs"), who wasn't exactly known for his work in family films. Yet the movie, about a kid who bonds with a whale and helps lead him to safety and freedom in the wild rather than confined in a park with owners who don't protect him, spawned two sequels and made a household name out of both the starring whale (Keiko) and Jason James Richter, who played Jesse, a kid without a family seeking not just something to care about but someone to care about him.

Richter went on to appear in movies like "Cops and Robbersons" and "The Neverending Story III" as well, took a break from acting to play music and then returned to the film world about a decade and a half after "Free Willy" was released. Lately he has appeared in movies like "The Little Things" (with Denzel Washington, Jared Leto and Rami Malek) and has been doing character work more in line with a journeyman actor, not a former child star. And it's great to hear how happy he is with that.

For so many of us, it feels like the '90s just happened, not that it was more than 20 years ago. What's something from the '90s that you feel nostalgic for?

That's a tough one for me. Only because any time I hear music from the '90s, I just change the channel. I know there's this nostalgia right now for the '90s, and it just hasn't struck me yet. Like you said, it still feels very recent in my mind even though I know that it's not. I'm definitely not 21 anymore. [Laughs] I guess some of the music, some of the styles; I see some people pick up some of those old things. There are just some weird things about that era that I do miss, and then just things that I absolutely don't. I'm sure if you grew up listening to Led Zeppelin your whole life, you'd be kind of sick of it by the time you're 40. Maybe? I really used to love what they had on MTV, the old lineup. If I miss anything, it's that. The late-night music videos, the "Yo! MTV Raps." Those shows that I grew up watching as a kid were a lot of fun. I miss that kind of stuff.

Do you remember any particular video that you loved at the time?

A lot of the grunge music, and I liked the Wu-Tang Clan and the East Coast rappers a lot more than—some of the West Coast rappers were cool, but I liked the East Coast rappers because it's a more stripped-down style. I thought there was a lot of good music from that era from a lot of different genres. So probably the music. And MTV that actually showed music videos.

I agree. A Notorious B.I.G. documentary just came out on Netflix, which reminded me again that I do prefer the East Coast stuff from that time too.

I think they had a little more substance. The West Coast was a little flashier, it was a little more fun, party music. Which is cool; there's a place for that. And the East Coast stuff, they had some of those elements, but some of those guys were thinking a little deeper about things.

And you reminded me that one downside you can argue about the perpetual recycling of things is that song you hated when it came on in 1997, it's still being played.

It's insane! There are so many bands that I thought, "You'll never hear them again." And you'll go through different stations and pods and music—no offense to Lit, but their one hit is still somewhere playing in Iowa! [Laughs] Kinda funny.

I think I saw earlier that that song was released 22 years ago today, actually.

Oh, really! That's so funny. What a coinkidink. That's random.

Well, "Free Willy" of course came out in 1993, which also had "Jurassic Park," "Dazed and Confused," "Rookie of the Year," "The Sandlot," "The Firm," "The Pelican Brief," "Cool Runnings," "Homeward Bound." Which one of those, or something else from that time, had the most impact on you?

Oh my gosh, from the early '90s? "Reservoir Dogs." Some of the bigger films. Definitely "The Pelican Brief." Some of the bigger stars. Julia Roberts. Tom Cruise is of course very much still a movie star. There was a great synergy between studio films and independent films. All the Kevin Smith stuff, "Clerks" and all that stuff. It was a unique time for a lot of different filmmakers to get heard and seen in different ways. "Free Willy" is a result of Warner Brothers trying to compete, from the way I understand it, with a few other studios for the family market. It was their first big family feature film that they pushed. It was written by a guy named Keith Walker, who had played the father in "The Goonies." He had a really great relationship with Dick Donner and Lauren Donner, and he had this project called "Free Willy." And I guess the origin story is there was a film called "Orca" in 1975 that was very negative to killer whales, orca whales. So there was this internal push between Dick and Lauren and Jennie Lew and Mark Marshall, Penelope Foster, our producers, Simon Wincer, our director, to make a film that had a more positive message about this particular issue. So things like "Free Willy" got made. I don't know if it would get made now. If it would be made now, I don't think it would be quite the same in many ways. But there's a lot of great films from that era. There are great films like "Doberman." "Black Cat White Cat" from Bulgaria. There's a lot of stuff I can point to back then that I was really absorbing. "Pulp Fiction." There's a lot of stuff.

The degree to which the industry has changed is undeniable. And 1993 in particular felt like a good year for kids' movies and movies about animals. How would you characterize the type of kids' movies being made at that time? We're similar ages, I'm in my late-30s; at the time it felt like there was so much for us, and kids now don't get that.

The early '90s, there was just a lot of creative expression going on. On all levels. The studio level, the independent level, musically, artistically. There was a lot of awareness happening. Our generation—we're similar in ages; I'm 41, you said you're in your late-30s— we were invited into these conversations. I know back then that's when a lot of the Rock the Vote stuff started to happen with getting youth involved in politics and getting to think differently. There was a transition from the '70s, '80s, and our parents. Suddenly we were all in our early teens, and there was this—these creative things happen in spurts. There are periods in the '70s that are prolific. There's people like Martin Scorsese out shooting movies in New York, and there's a hive mentality, and there's a lull in the '80s of a lot of bad stuff and just garbage, but there's gems floating here and there. But the '90s I think was this resurgence of a new way of thinking toward a younger generation that had different opinions and feelings than their parents, and they were being heard a little bit. It's a good thing.

And it's been notable as I've returned to this era to realize how many movies there were about kids needing homes. Between "Free Willy," "Newsies," "Angels in the Outfield," "Dick Tracy," and more. And as a parent now, it affects me more than I'd think.

Yeah, I think some of the issues they were allowed to go a little deeper. I would put "Free Willy" in the more kid-ish category, but it still had a pretty serious message about captivity and animals in the wild and stuff. I was just thinking about what you just said. Leonardo DiCaprio, "This Boy's Life." I don't know if you'd be able to get that made [now]. With the abusive father. It's based on a book by I believe Tobias Wolff. "Stand By Me." I know that's the late '80s, but four kids smoking cigarettes, lying to their parents to go look at a dead body? There's no studio that's going to sign up for that now. [Laughs] It was a very different time. It was different. Subsequently the late '90s, 2000s, you have this very different attitude about youth and young people, and like the book you wrote about "Saved by the Bell," it's a little more, "These are kids! What's the message we're sending here?" There were debates about whether or not video games create violence in youth, and that started parental warnings on CDs and albums and things like that. There was this rumbling of no more "Bad News Bears"-type movies about coaches doing blow and drinking. Which [Laughs] Walter Matthau in a kids' movie doing blow and drinking before he goes to coach the kids, I don't think you could get that even made in the '90s! So things kept changing as eras go on.

That's a great point.

The kids' movies are a little soft now. And ironically they're being exposed to so much garbage online with no filter whatsoever. It's really weird, the schism that we're in at the moment.

As things were starting up with "Free Willy," how nervous were you or what do you remember about feeling the scale of that, having had pretty limited acting experience in just a local commercial previously? Was there a "Holy crap, I'm the star of a movie" moment?

Yeah, it was a big shock. There's a story that I was a model when I was a baby for Japanese commercials or something. I don't know what that story is. I don't remember that; I never did that. I had no relationship to the acting world prior to—what I had was my mother was a struggling actress. She'd do background and stuff for "Magnum P.I." when we lived in Hawaii. My father was in the Navy. And so we were stationed back to the mainland, which was California. So things got financially tight, and my dad was like, "Maybe getting something else other than trying to act is maybe a better situation for the family." So she agreed. It was very hard for her to put down the acting thing because she had been passionate about it. And I don't know what possessed me, but I was just like, I loved movies, I was obsessed with them. I could recite dialogue I just heard. I told her I wanted to do it, and she was just like, "Absolutely not." So I begged her for a little while, so we got a six-month calendar out, and she said in six months if you still want to do this … I think she knew a local agent in San Diego. So six months to the day I came back to her and said, "I still want to do this." So she called up the agency that she knew of in San Diego, which was this legitimate little child-actor, mom-and-pop kind of thing. And when I started going in to read for stuff, I was terrified, super nervous. I was shaking in front of the camera, and people were like, "Oh, he doesn't look like he's having a good time. He doesn't want to be here. Maybe he shouldn't be doing this." I don't know; just going into those rooms, getting comfortable, and not really having any experience, just kind of winging it. I don't have anybody connected to the movie business. I'm not a child of celebrity or wealth or status. I have no connection whatsoever to it. So the first few months were tough. And then I got a call, it was a cattle call for "Free Willy," and it was a trailer in a dirt lot in Culver City. There was probably 100 kids waiting to go inside the trailer, and my mom and I had worked on the part together, and I had gotten dressed in what we thought Jesse looked like. I did something because they said we want you to come back, and the next time I came back it was a nice big building [Laughs] in a fancy part of L.A. And I was like, "Wow!" And I came back again and read for more people and more executives and more so-and-so from Warner Brothers, and the last audition I remember doing there was like 7-10 people in the room. You could cut the tension with a knife. It was a lot for them to risk; I was literally a kid off the street, so they were riding $15 million film and a lot of workers' paychecks on whether or not I was going to be a pain in the butt or freeze up and all that stuff. It just all kind of worked out. I don't know. I got the part. I'd done one commercial in San Diego for a board game that never got produced. It was a Milton Bradley game, and it was some take on, I believe, "Wall Street." And they had me dress up like a little Donald Trump with my blonde hair slicked back with a jacket and a little red tie. I was supposed to be this money mogul.

It was shot down at KTTV11, which was the local affiliate in San Diego at the time. We shot on this television stage, and that's what got rid of my stage fright. Because I got onto a real, working television stage for the first time, and I saw how big the cameras were. And so I was like, "Either I'm going to be totally terrified of these things, or I'm just going to forget that they're there." And that was kind of how I got comfortable was just to ignore the fact that they had this giant camera. But it worked! They never produced the board game, but that was it. And then "Free Willy."

So on the movie, were there any nerves? Anyone leveling up that way at that age would probably have some fear of, "What have I gotten myself into?" Or was it just, "They cast me for a reason; I can do this."

I was too young to know what I had truly stepped into. I know my parents were in a huff and buzzing around and there was something big going on and I was like, "Hmm, things are seriously changing." But I was a tad naive. And my parents tried to protect me from a lot of the chaos that something like that creates. So I have mostly fond memories. I remember the agent calling and saying, "You got the part, kid." And literally dropping the phone and running down the street to tell my friends, "I'm going to be in a Warner Brothers movie!" They were like, "Get outta here! You're lyin', man!" [Laughs] I was like, "No, I'm going to be in a movie!" And they were like "Holy crap." They had a big party for me when I left three or four weeks later. I cried because I had to tell my baseball team that I wasn't going to be able to be their catcher for the season because I was going to go make a movie. I was so upset to walk away from this obligation; I took baseball very seriously at that time. So I remember the coaches giggling, "It's OK, Jason; go make a movie, and baseball will be here when you come back." There was a lot of chaos, absolutely. There was a lot of good, a lot of joy, a lot of incredible first-time experiences. The first time you walk onto a set. And you realize the magnitude of what it is. I don't know if it was because I was too young to know better. Maybe if I had been a 21-, 22-year-old kid it would have scared me in a way that that kind of pressure can scare an adult. But first off, there's a killer whale in my face, and you got a camera, and I'm like, "I'm allowed to touch this animal and work and play with this giant whale? Are you serious?" They're like, "Yeah." I was just enamored of all of that. I don't think I had time to really process it. Especially at 11, 12 years old, I didn't have a lot of world experience to compare this to. Sitting on a private jet with Dodi Fayed [Laughs] and these really, really important, famous people, and a day before you're a kid from a middle-class military family. It's earth-shattering. It's earth-shattering.

For a second, I was imagining you and Keiko flying together but then realized that wouldn't make sense.

[Laughs] You know, they couldn't fit him onto the private planes. It was kind of wild. I lived in a house with a TV in the living room. I didn't know that people had money to the point where they had a whole room that was just for sitting and talking. There wasn't a television, and there wasn't a video game console. It was a big deal. It was a huge life shift. [Laughs]

On that note, while no one thinks actors have lived the experience of their characters, you have a real authenticity and vulnerability for what Jesse has been through. Did you ever get in trouble as a kid, even a minor infraction you were able to draw from?

I think a lot of that stuff came instinctually. I had worked with a coach; I think they were concerned, so they had me work with a coach for the first two weeks just to [teach] me how to hit a mark and yadda yadda, work the camera, turn this way and that kind of thing. And after that I was kind of left to my own devices. The best acting advice I ever got was from my mother, which is just, "Listen and react." Which is an old, common tool. You just listened and you would react how someone would in that moment. I think it was later on that I began to investigate acting on a more serious level and started to understand the tools of the trade and how people draw on emotional experiences. Some people use method, some people use sense memory and that kind of stuff, but early on a lot of that was just the instinct of a young person. It was very easy for me to make-believe. It was very easy for me to fall into an alternative reality. I had an overactive imagination as a child. Like I said I was obsessed with movies and television and could recite anything I'd seen. I have kind of a photographic ability to look at something, absorb it and interpret it. It's just natural. And it's a complete blessing. But also something that you have to work on. No artist wants to stagnate. You can always learn something new about whatever it is that you do, whatever craft you're a part of. Whether you're intuitively good at it or you've put the 10,000 hours in. You can always learn something. So as a young person it kinda just came natural.

That's a testament to your ability. Yet there's also the cliche about working with kids and animals. Who more often needed additional takes to get it right: you or your animal costar?

Oh, me of course. Keiko was perfect.

There must have been times the humans got it right and the whale didn't.

Oh, yeah. Oh, yeah. We would do takes, and he would get irritated. They have personalities. They're wild, but they're highly intelligent creatures and they have mood swings and they get irritated, and after four or five hours he didn't want to play anymore and he was like, "I'm going to go away." And we'd just have to find something else to do. Because the last thing we ever wanted to do was to upset Keiko. And I know everybody working on that film, from the director to the producers, everybody on down, everybody at Warner Brothers, once they had [an issue] they had some way to help him. That was always in the cards. So they were always very careful with him, and I think with me as well. I did my own jumping into the tanks and doing a lot of wild stuff because I was young and fearless and it was like an adventure every day you get up and like, "What are we going to be doing?" "We're going to be hanging a two-ton truck off the side of a cliff." It was an adventure every single day for me. I do recall Augie Schellenberg, he played Randolph in the film, making a joke about never working with kids and animals and what the F was he doing in Mexico. [Laughs] We had a lot of fun on that set. I have a lot of fond memories of little moments like that, things before takes, little jokes and then we'd go into a really serious scene. [Laughs]

So when a whale actor gets mad they just swim away, it's not an Alec Baldwin stereotype of onset rage?

No, you deal with the agent, that's it. Once the whale/animal talent has left, that's the end of conversation. You have no recourse. Talk to his guy at CAA.

I know you've gotten a lot of the same questions over the years, if you rode him, stuff like that. I want to know if he really blew your hat off with his blowhole on command.

I would imagine that it was done on command or that they enhanced whatever the effect was, under the camera they did something. But I do recall something like that. I never rode him. Any time I'm in the tank with him I'm partitioned between a net and I because he's a 14-ton killer whale, and if he decides he's going to drag you to the bottom, he's going to drag you to the bottom and you're not going to come back up. [Laughs] So I never physically rode him. They usually had me on a board or something. I did feed him. I did help train him. I did help clean up the tanks. I did pet his tongue and rub his belly and get him to come up onto the platform and interact with him and stuff. He was a very special creature. No doubt about it.

One of the strangest parts of the "Free Willy" pandemonium was you being nominated for an MTV Movie Award with Keiko for Best Kiss. Demi Moore and Woody Harrelson won for "Indecent Proposal." Do you remember thinking anything of that at the time, or afterwards?

It was just silly. It was just funny. It was a popular film, and they were trying to find a way to work it into the ceremony, and that's what they came up with. I change the channel here and there and you'd see mid-'90s sitcoms, and there'd be a "Free Willy" joke. It permeated the culture in a way that I don't think honestly anybody expected. The story that I have, that I understand, is when Warner Brothers first screened it for executives, they thought it was going to be a wash. They don't get it. I think they had reached out to Michael Jackson to get involved with the music, and they ended up screening it for an audience and as far as I know to this day is the highest audience score they had ever gotten for a film. So they suddenly had all this interest in promoting it and it was weeks and weeks and weeks later after the first viewing. The first three weeks it was in the theaters it was number five. Nobody had any interest in it. I don't know what happened. This was a different time; films didn't come and go like they do now where if they don't produce in the first weekend, they're gone by the second. It had time to find an audience. It had time to build. And then that third week all of a sudden it shot up to number one, and then for the next five, six, seven weeks, it was number one in the theaters. And like you said it was a cultural phenomenon. And that was probably more shocking and had more of an effect on me than getting to make a movie was the subsequent hoopla that [comes] into your life where you can't go to the store without creating a ruckus. You can't go to a movie with your friends. Your life changes. And that was probably an unwanted side effect of that period of my life. It just comes with being famous. I'm older now, it makes more sense to me. I can handle it a different way. But when I was younger it was very overwhelming to me, having people staring over my backyard. I ended up on a "Star Map" tour, and there was like 12 people suddenly peeking over my fence one day. I'm in my backyard playing with my dog, throwing the ball around, and I go in the house and I'm like, "Uh, something's going on outside." My mom is like, "What?" She goes and she looks and there's like 20 people milling around this bus and talking, and everyone piles into the bus, and they keep going. [Laughs] It was so surreal, dude. I'm telling you: I was born in Medford, Oregon. Dad was in the Navy. My mother was a homemaker, occasionally had a part-time gig. We're not famous, wealthy movie people. So it was definitely shocking. I struggled with that a little bit as the years went on, and of course you get typecast and that makes it hard to keep going forward as an actor.

If you don't mind me asking, what was it that you struggled with? Just the whole celebrity world forming around you?

Yeah, you're constantly in the teen magazines, and I was trying to go to school and people would tease me. It just disrupted my life in a lot of weird ways. There was a lot of great stuff, but there was also just these other things that just come along with, that's just part of your life.

How much do you feel like that part of it developed, changed, became a problem, became OK as one "Free Willy" movie became three?

Yeah, once you crack a certain strata of fame it does change your life and the circle around you. I made some other films, and then it was time to go make "Free Willy 2." I had a three-picture deal with Warner Brothers at the time. So coming to "Willy 2," the production was suddenly a lot bigger because the first one had been successful. So now there was a lot more involved. The director, Dwight Little, he had an action background and he was used to big, logistical films, so it became this huge thing. So there were boats and barges and animatronic whales and helicopters and fires. It just becomes this insane, carnival circus. But I think my family, my mom, my dad, everybody around me, they did really well to insulate me from a lot of the pitfalls that a lot of young actors go through. Drugs and alcohol and getting caught up in scandals. We just didn't do that. Went to school during the week, and in the summer I was making films. They just tried to create as normal an environment as they possibly could. So I don't know if that much changed around me a lot. Like I said, going from being a face in the crowd to suddenly there's a traffic jam because you went into a Ralphs [Supermarket] and there's people gathering, that stuff was happening. [Laughs] And it was wild, and it was a little bit scary. I remember one time I was in Germany, I was doing an autograph signing, and there was over 5, 6, 7,000 kids that crammed into this very small area that they had put together, thinking that maybe a few hundred, if that, would show up. I remember having to stand up on top of this table and telling the crowd, "Please stop pushing on the front row. I will stay here all night and sign every single autograph. Nobody has to push." And I stayed there for hours. So every single person that was there got something. So that kind of stuff I was like, "Whoa." [Laughs]

Did anyone ever ask you to recreate the iconic moment of Willy jumping over you? I'm reminded of the "Simpsons" episode when Bart becomes a breakout star and is exhausted quickly because everywhere he goes people say, "Do the line, Bart." I wouldn't be surprised if someone asked you to pretend there was a whale jumping over you, to replicate the movie in real life.

That kind of stuff usually only came from hacks on VH1 doing interviews, or people that are hacky. They're like, "Can you give us a little bit of that for the camera?" I'm like, "No." [Laughs] "I don't mean to be rude, but I'm trying to get some attention so I can get something else so I can keep working. I'm an actor. I'm not an actual homeless kid that freed a whale. I know it's hard for people to understand this …" I get it; movies feel real. I understand. The first time they showed a Charlie Chaplin movie in a theater, people went looking behind the screen to see where he went when he went off-camera. I get it. The illusion [of film.] [Laughs] With most people, it's a happy memory. Now, if I do get approached or anything, which is pretty rare, it's usually somebody our age that tells me, "I have kids and I showed them 'Free Willy' and they totally loved it." And that's the best and coolest thing. That they loved it, they enjoyed it, it gave them a happy memory, some good feeling, and they were able to share that with their kids. You can't beat that. That's pretty awesome.

And you of course took a break to get into music for a while, and then came back into acting. What do you remember going through your head when you returned to that environment? Did it feel like starting over? Was it exciting, scary, both?

Yeah, a little bit of all that. I think it was around 2008, 2009, I sort of got burned out on the band thing and touring around on tour buses and living in hotel rooms and being stinky and playing in random towns and stuff. I had fun playing music. It was a lot of fun touring with cool bands, nothing major, but it was really fun. And then I decided that I wanted to come back and pursue acting and pursue the craft of film. So I started behind the camera. So I got a [production assistant] job. People were laughing, "'Free Willy' is bringing me my coffee." "That's right; can I get you anything else?" [Laughs] I took my fair share of abuse is what I mean to say. But I learned a lot. I learned from being a PA all the things you go through in the AD department, then I would drift over into this part and learn about gaffing and all these different things, and I'd start to get a different picture from when I was a kid. I would show up and things would kind of happen. And as an adult I began to want to take the reins of my own projects, so to understand, to know how the mechanics of these things work I think was really valuable. I came back with a humble heart.

I don't expect people to roll out a red carpet for me because I was in a movie 30 years ago. If they do care about it, if they have some memory of it, that's fine, but I'm happy to come work and do whatever. I've been really lucky the last couple years, I've been working a lot in New York for a producer. I've done a lot of his projects, and he's been very generous. I just got to shoot a thing called "The Little Things," which was really cool to be on a set and watch three Oscar-winning actors work their craft. You bet your butt I took notes, man. Every time they were on set, I was real quiet. Real quiet. [Laughs] And listening and learning. It's been a journey back. A detour, a continuation. I love film. I love making them, I like acting in them. It's an adventure. It's a challenge, and it's a privilege to be able to do it.

Could you pinpoint something you learned on "The Little Things" from any of those guys?

Oh, for sure. I think one of the most fascinating things was to watch Denzel Washington go through his process with John Lee Hancock. How thorough he was, how many questions he had, the kinds of questions he was asking the director. A lot of that good, meaty actor stuff I think sometimes you don't have an opportunity to get into because A. you're not Denzel Washington and B. you're making something that maybe you just don't have that kind of time. So getting to work on that film, and that was such a huge film, that you had all the time in the world to sit there and work these scenes and go through it to some degree. It was just fascinating to watch the process between the director and his actors. And John Lee Hancock, even for me, was very generous with his time. Very generous. And I am eternally grateful for that. And I got to have scenes with Rami, who is absolutely astonishing. He's a great actor. I'm in the scenes with him, I'm watching him, and sometimes I'm forgetting. Because I'm just watching Rami. He's that good. My experience with him was brief, but I learned a lot from him too. It was really awesome.

So when you show up to "The Little Things" or anything as part of your adult career as an actor, is there anything in your mind about, "I really hope no one comes up and makes a lame 'Free Willy' joke today"?

Honestly, no. [Laughs] First off, [Laughs] if anybody recognized me, which nobody did, I would have been in complete shock. There's Jared Leto and Rami Malek and Denzel Washington and Chris Bauer and Natalie Morales and all these incredible actors. Terry Kinney. There's so many other people to be interested in, and it's not one of those things that's in the forefront of my mind anymore because it has been a long time and I have regained a certain amount of autonomy from that to some degree. It will always be with me, and I'm extremely proud of it. I'm glad that I was part of a film that had that kind of a cultural impact and had a really positive message. I think it's even more relevant and impactful today than it was when the film was released just because I think it spawned a generation of kids to be curious and concerned about things that maybe they weren't before. Marine life, etc. Maybe it wasn't on their radar, and it was a new thing for them to explore and discover. I'm grateful for that legacy. But I don't walk around thinking, "Oh, god, I hope they don't call me out." [Laughs] When people do that, I'm like, "Cool! Yeah, I know.

I'm old." "Oh my god, you're the kid? Holy shit!" I'm like, "Yeah." I did one signing a couple years ago, it was called the Hollywood Show. I've only ever done one, and that was a little interesting. [Laughs] The people that come up to you at those things, god bless them, they're very sweet, take pictures, sign pictures, whatever. But they are kind of people that are a little stuck in the past I would say.

And everyone is so different 30 years after they do anything. I think of things I did at that time, and it almost feels like it happened to somebody else.

And same with me. It is a weird thing to talk about something you did when you were 12. I'm 41 now. "Oh my god!" "I know, I know." I kind of have the same reaction to certain people, I guess. Go, "Oh, yeah. I remember when they were much younger." Like "Dick Tracy," Charlie Korsmo. He's like off-the-charts genius. Crazy IQ. He became a lawyer or something, got a degree at Harvard. [Editor's note: It was Yale.] I don't have anything to show for it. I stuck around and kept trying to do it. I don't know what was wrong with me. [Laughs] He took the money and ran. It was a smart move, that kid. We had the same studio teacher.

Is this something you've ever talked about with other kid actors or people that went through what you did?

Um, yeah. I keep in touch with Jeff Cohen. He played Chunk in "The Goonies." I saw him a few years ago; I think we went to the Palm for lunch. It's nice to communicate with him because he went through, like you said, something similar. It's sort of like walking on the moon. You recognize each other across the room, like, "Oh, yeah; you did something too." He's an entertainment lawyer, he's very successful. I believe he went to Berkeley School of Law. When I did that signing, I ran into a few other child actors, and it was interesting to listen to their stories. You did have a different childhood. You did have a different experience than other people, so it is a unique thing to sit and compare notes.

Do you think if the opportunities had been there you would've wanted to continue through the teens? Or no matter what would have happened you would've needed a break?

I think it was a little of both. I'm grateful for the amount of time I took and stepped back and went and had life experiences. I started when I was 12, and like I said it came to me instinctually. It was just a natural thing. As you go, you get older, you need life experiences to be able to have a truthful moment, if you will, in front of the camera. You gotta go out and live your life. I'm grateful that I was able to take that time eventually and step away and discover myself a little bit more. I think it was just really hard for me to get out from under my own shadow at that point. Because I was just so distinct looking and so synonymous with "Free Willy," and it was just very hard. I got some very nice notes from Ang Lee and other people I read for, Gary Ross. And he just passed away—Joel Schumacher. So I had some opportunities to go and read and meet with people. I just think it was difficult for them from a financial, business standpoint, for somebody who's branded one way. And it was a different mentality too. But I'm grateful for the time. I had fun playing music and just not being the kid from "Free Willy." It was nice.

So that was "The Ice Storm," "Pleasantville," those are the kind of movies you went out for?

Sure, yeah, I went out for that stuff. Baz Luhrmann when he did "Romeo and Juliet." There's always one guy that always seemed to get the part. [Laughs] You're always up against him for the one role, and they keep hiring him. [Laughs]

That's what Charlie Korsmo was saying—that he got really close on "The Ice Storm" and "Wonder Boys," and Tobey Maguire got both of those.

Yeah. Yeah. I have my own similar story about "Pleasantville." I got very close on that, but for circumstances it ended up going to Tobey. It is one of those things. You live to fight another day. You keep doing it. I've had opportunities to do stage plays now. Expand my craft as an actor. Last four years I've been playing cops a lot. I guess the mustache and my general look people just think I look like a cop. [Laughs] So it's been fun.

This is an odd place to take it, but when I think of an edgy movie about animals I think of "The Lobster" or Kevin Smith's "Tusk," which no one but me seemed to like.

I really enjoyed that movie. With Justin Long? I thought it was a great film. It was f'd-up, man. [Laughs]

So being so many years removed from when you were understandably intent on being separated from being seen as the kid from "Free Willy," how would you feel now doing something offbeat with animals like that?

I think I'm open to anything. I'm open to have an opportunity to have an opportunity to work. I just shot a pilot I'm tentatively calling "Dolphin Boy." It's loosely based on my experience as a child actor with the "Free Willy" franchise. There's some cajoling going on where instead of a movie it's a television show and instead of Willy it's a Flipper-esque jokey thing, and I got some people to be a part of it. I got David Boreanaz and his wife to do a cameo for me, and this great little cast of local actors to do it. We're almost through the complete first edit. And it's pretty funny. I didn't realize how absurdly strange my life actually has been to some degree, so to put it on paper and go and do it, it's really entertaining. I don't know what it will turn into, but maybe it will turn into something. This is very tentative, preliminary. I just finished shooting it and am just now through a month of first assembly and all that kind of stuff.

That will be cool to see. I also wanted to ask if you remembered what you did, if anything, when you found out Keiko passed away in 2003?

I do remember that happening. I was up in Berkeley; I was visiting my cousin who is a Doctor of Literature. He used to teach at Berkeley and stuff, and we were going over to Rasputin's music. It was a music store in Berkeley in the early 2000s. I know I sound like such an old man. I had a cell phone, and I got this weird number, and I wouldn't normally pick that kind of thing up, and I just did. I was on the street, and I picked up the phone and it was somebody from CNN or People Magazine. I was like, "Hello?" They were like, "Is this Jason James Richter?" "May I ask who's calling?" "Oh, this is so-and-so from such-and-such publication, and we just wanted to get a quote on what you think, feelings about the death of Keiko?" I was like, "He died?" I didn't even know! [Laughs] So I just said, "No comment," and I hung up the phone. And then I called one of the producers or something and said, "Oh my god, is this true?" They said, "Yeah." And it was sad. Of course it was one of those things where you sit there and redigest everything. I feel like ultimately the film getting made was the best thing that could've happened to Keiko because it got him moved from that tank in Mexico that was too small for him to a much nicer facility in Oregon and subsequently got him moved to an open ocean pen where he was from up in Norway. So he's I think one of the only whales in captivity to ever attempt to be reacclimated to being in the wild. So because of the film and my happenstance of being a part of it, I was able to contribute to something that was great that ended up changing not only his life but got people to think differently about how we treat these animals. I think that's a really great thing. The last thing I remember filming in "Free Willy," we'd been shooting, we were over a few hours, it was late, it was a 14-hour day or something, a really long day. Totally illegal probably to be doing that with a child actor and a whale and everything else. But it was like the last day we were there and we had to leave to go back to the United States the next day, we were going to be out of Mexico. So they're trying to get every last thing they could. At some point he got really frustrated. I remember he was swimming really fast around the tank. I think he could tell we were going to leave. He was going so fast, and this entire shoot, three months we were down in Mexico we were making this movie, he could never seem to go fast enough to breach his entire body out of the water. And that night he did it in one fell jump right out of the pool and slammed down into the tank and water went everywhere, all over everybody, all over the crew. And it was one of those wild moments and we all collectively experienced it all together. Everybody on set was like, "Holy cow." Because we had been working for him for months, and it was very hard for him to get nearly his entire body out of the water because his tank was too small. So we always kind of felt like that was his way of letting us know that he was disappointed that we were leaving him.

Absolutely. Animals are so powerful and so emotional too. Then my last question, and feel free to say nothing about this, but in writing a book about the '90s and how perceptions may have changed, I feel like I wouldn't be fulfilling my duty if I didn't ask. Michael Jackson was such a big part of the "Free Willy" moment at the time, and of course the conversation about him has changed a lot over the years. Is it strange at all to have been involved on the inside of that narrative for a little while and see how that has played out over time?

Oh, absolutely. It may have been six months after the film was released that all the accusations of child molestation started to percolate about him. I think that's what you're referring to. It was just really terrible luck that he had lent his name and his energies to a children's film with that sort of thing going on. I never met him. I didn't know him personally; I didn't know anybody who knew him personally. I know that it was litigated in court, and there were agreements and conclusions made. But I don't have any insight about any of that. I never even got to meet him. I made a music video for him for "Free Willy 2." And I didn't even meet him then. We just shot it on a stage somewhere, and it was completely assembled after the fact. I've heard a lot of jokes about me meeting him. I've heard a lot of weird innuendoes. I can assure you I do not have a Swiss bank account somewhere with $20 million in it. [Laughs] I never met him. I don't know if what he did is true or not. I would have a really hard time believing somebody would make that up. And at the same time, he's a famous guy with a lot of money. So I don't know. I know the courts apparently worked it all out though.

Those jokes aren't happening still, right? That was a long time ago?

Yeah. Sometimes you'll get some knucklehead that'll be like, "Did you get to meet Michael Jackson by any chance?" And they're inferring that child rape is funny, I guess. I'm like, "No, I didn't!" I don't know why that's so funny to people. Because it's not. I never met the man. I don't know what his demons were.

I appreciate you understanding why I'd need to ask about that.

Of course. It makes total sense, Matt. He was part of the film; you have to ask, of course. "Will You Be There?" the music video, the iconic thing. It's an elephant in the room. It's a big elephant.

Marguerite Moreau of 'The Mighty Ducks,' 'Blossom,' 'Boy Meets World'

In an episode of the Disney+ reboot of "The Mighty Ducks," Guy Germaine (Garette Ratliff Henson) gazes at an old picture of himself and his then-girlfriend from their early days on the Ducks. "You look amazing in that hockey gear," he tells Connie Moreau (Marguerite Moreau).

Now married to Guy while working as a Minnesota State Senator and being mother to their three children, Connie replies, "I looked even better kicking butt in hockey gear." Later Connie shows girls on the team how to deliver a hit on the ice, and one tells Connie she's her hero.

It's a great continuation of the way that the 1992 original film put boy and girl hockey players on equal footing—something that wasn't exactly common in the male-dominated products of the time. It was also, you know, the only kids' movie to spawn not just a trilogy of movies, not just an animated series, but a real-life franchise as well.

It also, importantly, gave us Moreau, an actress who is more prolific than you realize and almost certainly way better than you appreciate. In addition to being arguably the most under-appreciated part of 2001's extraordinary "Wet Hot American Summer" and its eventual Netflix prequel and sequel series, in addition to having more multi-episode arcs on TV shows ("Blossom," "Grey's Anatomy," "Shameless," "The O.C.," "Parenthood") than almost anyone, in addition to doing a short film about addiction ["Viral"] and a lot of Lifetime movies and a horror series on Facebook Watch, she simply elevates everything she does, from the sci-fi "The Tank" to the romantic comedy "You Can't Say No."

Hell, even her Cameo videos are so endearing they might get you choked up, and talking with her reinforces where that charm and appeal come from.

What's something you're nostalgic for from the '90s?

I think it's being a teenager and driving around in your car and listening to music and that first taste of freedom. Especially in California, where things are so spread out. You really just can't wait to get your license so you can feel that taste of autonomy.

When you picture yourself in that moment, do you have a sense of what you're listening to or where you're going?

263

Oh, yeah. I'm definitely in my first car that I bought with the money from "Mighty Ducks," [Laughs] which was this cool Jeep Wrangler. My parents didn't tell me that they were letting me buy it, but it had the smallest get-up-and-go. It was a tiny engine. [Laughs] It looked great but was very big. I'm on PCH, and I'm flying down the street. What am I listening to back at that time? Uh, the '90s? What was I listening to in high school? Oh, man. It's like college is definitely stuck in my brain, but what was it in high school? We'll have to come back to that one. It's like there was Madonna, and then there was a big jump and then there was all the college stuff. I can't remember. Not Sugar Ray. [Laughs]

You remember specifically it wasn't that.

Yes. Yes. Yes. [Laughs]

I'm trying to remember when Hootie and the Blowfish hit their peak.

That was after me, I feel. I missed that. But it was sort of, who's the other great band— Counting Crows. That one album that everybody knows the lyrics to. It was my senior year, with the Jeep, and I was shooting in Couer d'Alene, Idaho, and I remember driving all around there with it.

Windows down, cranking "Rain King" has a sense of freedom for sure.

Totally. Or going to coffee shops. Independent coffee shops was a really big thing then. And "Reality Bites" and Lisa Loeb and going to thrift stores. I remember shooting "Mighty Ducks," and they had the most amazing thrift stores in Minneapolis. We'd take the bus across town and walk over to find the perfect flannel. I remember there were tickets that all the boys had to go see—well, I had tickets too, but I didn't know who Pearl Jam was— and they were in the most tiny theater in Minneapolis called First Ave. It was this tiny club that was all ages. And that night, for some reason I was like, "You know, I don't know. I'm tired tonight." And I didn't go. And it was Pearl Jam! And I kick myself all the time for not going!

Wow.

I know. I know. I can't believe I just said that out loud! Say that instead of the Sugar Ray quote. [Laughs]

When you think back to the period and the movies and shows you were not in, is there something you watched at the time or still watch these days that really connects with you?

Oh, yeah. I definitely watched "Party of Five." And I loved "Troop Beverly Hills." [1989] I was always like, "Why didn't I audition for that?" It's like one of my favorites from that time. And also another movie, it's getting pretty specific, but god, it's so good: "Shag." [1989] Which for the people who know about "Shag" from this time, they love "Shag."

I'm not sure I know what that is.

It's Bridget Fonda, Phoebe Cates, Annabeth Gish. And they all go down to Myrtle Beach for the summer, and it's sort of a coming-of-age film, but it's also about friendship. It's sort of when the kids were getting older rather than the kid-based films. Because it's like romance and all that. And also "Goonies," [1985] obviously. [Laughs] Who doesn't want to be in "Goonies"? Has to be in "Goonies."

Where I wanted to start with "Mighty Ducks" is that I was thinking about the kids' sports movies of the early '90s and how it felt like such an explosion. It was such an important part of my life, but I also recognize how such a high percentage of those movies were about boys playing sports. How much did you at the time get a sense of the stories that were being told and how "Mighty Ducks" fit into that? To even look at 1992 alone, there was also "Ladybugs," which we could talk about for a while, and "The Cutting Edge," which is figure skating, something people arguably see as a sport more traditionally associated with women.

I remember watching "Ladybugs" and going, "What? I was just in 'The Mighty Ducks.' How did I not audition for that? I actually play soccer!" So that was one that I was so confused because I didn't really understand how the business works. I just thought you just get a call one day and have an audition. So "Ladybugs" was cool, but I was all of a sudden after being in my first movie seeing it through the lens of work instead of just more innocently. So "The Cutting Edge" came out before, and so that was something that I could still get lost in. Or "Goonies" was made before I even thought of starting to act, so the magic is still there, where you imagine yourself going on the journey. In terms of sports movies, I just remember "Rudy." I remember "The Bad News Bears," which was the generation before. And that's what they compared "The Mighty Ducks" to. I just remember loving "The Bad News Bears" but also being kind of scared of it because I was so young and I was like, "Well, there's beer drinking and the guy on the motorcycle, which was a little too dangerous, but I knew he was supposed to be the guy that I was supposed to be attracted to. But I was confused because he was doing all this dangerous stuff and I was [aware] of that being too scary." So this new comparison to "Mighty Ducks," I was like, "Yeah, I know the reviews are it's just that, but somehow it seemed fresh and sweet from a kids' point of view because it was fun." Even the serious stuff was still relatable for us. There was nothing really in our age group. And in terms of the gender, because I grew up being used to it being more the boys' movie with a girl in it, if there wasn't a girl in it then it was just a film for everyone. And then if there was a girl in it, then you're like, "Oh, OK, this is supposed to be for me too." And you never thought, "Why is there never a team of girls where the guy is lucky to be on that team?" So that's how the conversation feels different now.

So you're saying that because the expectation was to see stories about boys, that didn't push anyone away because there was no thought that it could be anything else?

Yeah. The universal understanding was the movie is for everyone, even if it has a male lead. But a movie with a girl in it is for girls, if the lead is a girl. So now we're having the conversation or expanding kids' opportunities to see different people as the lead but being a universal story for everyone to enjoy. I think parents are really trying to encourage that for their kids, but back then you didn't think, "Oh, 'Empire of the Sun' is Christian Bale; that's a boy movie." You just were like, "That's the movie we're going to see." Or "Free Willy."

Obviously being a teenager is such an emotional time of life, and a lot changes over the course of a few years. Making three "Mighty Ducks" movies, I imagine the dynamics among the cast changed to a certain degree as you all grew up. Do you remember at all about the awareness of being one of a couple girls among a lot of guys on the team, and how much that dynamic did or didn't change as you guys grew up a few years at a time between each movie?

Oh, yeah. I was the tallest in the first movie and the shortest in the last movie. So I stayed at the same height, and they all got better at hockey and taller. So I had to really check myself. Because anything I got away with in the first movie came back to haunt me in the last movie. [Laughs] In terms of scrimmages and stuff. I remember being like, "Ugh, why did I think tripping was OK? Nobody could skate." But I was 12 or 13 and a little bit of a bossy know-it-all. And also, I liked all the attention. I was just a girl at that time, just coming into the self-consciousness of being a teenager. So I was like, "Look at all these boys. I could probably kiss any of them that I wanted to. How many do I want to kiss?" I was definitely boy-crazy, and it was so fun. And by the third one, they were like, "Ugh, Marguerite." And I was like, "Ugh, those guys." We had all been turned outwards. But they are all my brothers for sure. So that was sort of my trajectory with them. I definitely was going out with Elden Henson for a while, and that was like so fun. And by the third one I don't even know what he was doing. [Laughs] I think I was hanging out with someone who was a double from the first movie that I had met in Minnesota or something.

In the second movie, we see the guys being idiots and pulling pranks and being a bit ridiculous, but we don't get to see what Connie and Julie are doing at that time. What do you think they were doing in the dorms when the guys were up to those shenanigans?

Well, I feel like we were probably chatting and doing our nails, or we were playing in the hallway, actual stick-hockey, goalie stuff while chatting. It could've been either of those. I was always asking about that. Always wondering.

Wondering yourself or asking that of other people?

Asking the writers and stuff: "What about us?" But there's only so much time in the movie. [Laughs]

That was going to be my next question, actually. With playing this character for so long, how much did you ever imagine her interior life, whether her hobbies, the music she likes, and what else she has going on?

No. I'm trying to think—I feel like that kind of work that I started to do on characters and really enjoy happened probably after that. Because I had to make a decision whether I was going to keep acting as an adult or do something else when I went to college. So that's when I really started to study and go, "I shouldn't just be crossing my fingers and hoping it works." Because as a kid I wasn't around anybody who acted before and sort of just felt into it by accident. And even though of course I wanted to be an actress, it was more of like how I also wanted to be an astronaut and the president of the United States. It wasn't something I really knew how to go about doing. In my family we know how to become nurses and teachers.

I think you could get some people on board with you as an astronaut or the president.

Thank you! I was very convinced. It's a little easier to figure out how to go about doing those two jobs than it is about becoming an actress.

I've never thought about that. That's an interesting question.

Yeah. When I went to college, I majored in political science. Then I quickly realized that the compromises that needed to happen when it comes to creating policy and working with others—I wanted my thesis to be about pop culture and its influence in political elections, and they were like, "I don't think that's a thing!" And now I look at Trump winning the election before last and go, "Uh, I think so!" So I actually thought that maybe the acting world was a little healthier for me than the political realities of Washington and where it was headed. [Laughs] So that was in college that I decided to jump into theater and finish my degree in poli sci. I just really felt I learned a lot about myself and humanity within acting, and that was really healthy for me.

Just think how different the events of the last few years could have been if you had written that paper. It would've been like "The Pelican Brief," and you would've changed history.

I know. But you know what, at Vassar they don't require you to write a thesis. So I was busy running around with flowers in my hair and growing my armpit hair in order to play different characters while skipping into my policy classes to finish up my major. And I didn't have to write a thesis, so I was like, "Great! I'm going to be in another play instead!" I had never acted for no money before. But with all my friends, just for fun. It was like, "Ohhh! OK, this is what it can be." I had done it with "Mighty Ducks," but there were so many adults around, and it was such a huge production that it was a bit intimidating.

I think that's fair then: We won't put the fate of the world on your shoulders in a "Back to the Future" sense.

Well, if we're in "Back to the Future" you can because that's another movie that I was obsessed with. Whereas I always wanted to be Michael J. Fox, but I never thought of it as a movie for boys or girls. I was like, "'Back to the Future' is everything." But, yeah, don't put the fate of the future on me. I already do it for me; it's unhealthy. So I don't need the pressure from others. [Laughs]

Which do you think is more unethical: Dating a player's mom or dating a rival's trainer?

A rival. Because we're playing against them, and if it's someone on the team—I can't get in the way of love, but have your ethics. If you have to pick, I would say, "Don't be doing it with our competition. Do it within the fold."

Do you think the Iceland trainer was really interested in Gordon, or was she just trying to distract him?

See, I always thought she was really interested and that the boys took it the wrong way, but that's because I'm always looking for love. Connie was always like, "I really love playing hockey and don't get in my way, but also, Guy, you are so sweet. Let's hold hands." I think that Connie would feel that way, and I guess I did too when I saw the movie recently. I was like, "Wow, maybe she was doing that. I never thought that."

There's a line on a recent Taylor Swift album about the greatest love stories being over now. I think she's talking about Gordon and Iceland's trainer there.

I mean, you can see the longing in her eyes. Because her coach is so tough. She longs for a team that she can work for that brings more hope. We all want to love what we do. We don't want to hate to go to work.

Do you have a sense of the public opinion when it comes to the trilogy in terms of favorites or a ranking?

Hmm, no. I think that's one of the fun things too that fans reveal is that everyone has specific relationships to the whole thing. But just the overwhelming meaning that it seems to have for people who reach out, and how it has been part of their childhood in a way that has been impactful. Otherwise, it's very specific to each individual. Especially when it comes to three. I'm always excited to hear about three. I think I need to see it again.

Because your perception is that one is loved less?

Because I don't think I know it as well. I went off to college. I didn't have a VCR or a DVD player or whatever was happening then. And I had to leave college to go into New York to do the press for it, so it seemed like I was juggling these two big worlds, so it was slightly different than the other two where it was like I was just in high school with my normal house with my brother and sister. I just feel like my concentration on it was less. Whereas with the first one, I could tell you every line in it. As a young kid being like, "Can you believe this? This is the craziest thing that ever happened?!" I went to the video store, and they had that three-dimensional triangle of movie posters. I forget what was on the other two sides, but at Blockbuster there was like a pop-out Emilio. It was the cover of the movie. And I had it in my room for the entire year faced out the window onto the street! It was just so exciting. I was just the dorkiest, most excited kid ever.

That's awesome that you were excited and proud.

Yeah, but then my parents let me get a license plate that said "Mighty Ducks" on it. Like an official Californian one to drive to high school. And I wanted to kill them when I realized later, like, "You let me do what?" They were like, "It was so sweet; you were so proud." I was like, "It was high school! You could've protected me!" I'm sure everybody was like, "Good god, let it rest." I mean, I don't know. That mortifies me to this day. But kids are kids.

Yeah. If John Cusack were driving around Chicago that had just the consonants of "High Fidelity," would people think that was strange for an adult to do? Or does it just matter how beloved the movie is?

Well, I think if you're a kid it goes a lot further than if you're an adult. You don't want John Cusack riding around with that. Because he's trading on that. If you're an adult, you may be trading on that, so it's kind of sad. My parents thought it was sweet, but now I'm like, "Oh, god." I just have to cover my eyes. [Laughs]

I know "Wet Hot American Summer" didn't come out in the '90s, but with all of the other unique, memorable movies that came out that year between "Fight Club," "Magnolia," "The Matrix" and more, I feel like "Wet Hot" should've been a '99 movie.

[Laughs] They were certainly trying to make it in '99.

Perfect! I think most people would probably agree that Coop is good for Katie. Do you think Katie is good for Coop?

I think when she drops her popular-girl thing and just chats with him, she's got a really good heart. But aside from that, she gives him confidence to believe in himself that he has worth as a person. She sees him, and she can give him some things that he thinks down on himself about, she's good at saying, "That doesn't matter. That's not what I had a problem with." Except at the end when she does say that. So she's a teenager; she's very complicated. She's a very conflicted person. [Laughs]

So when they're connecting, is there pity there or is she feeling deeply in those moments?

Oh, I think that she starts with pity because she doesn't know any better, and she all of a sudden—when you have a real connection with someone at that age, it can seem a little magical to just really connect. Especially for her. She seems like that cool girl thing; you're not really sitting and hanging out too much. You never see her with lots of other girls or anything. So I think that he takes her by surprise, and she loves that.

With the Netflix series and the ways in which Coop always wants her and when she's finally ready for him he's taken, I was thinking if they're more like Ross and Rachel from "Friends" or Jesse and Celine from the "Before Sunrise" movies.

Well, I feel like Jesse and Celine are like a great love story, but am I not remembering it right?

By the time they get to "Before Midnight" they're a married couple with challenges.

But I thought they were together, but Chris Rock was in it, and they were a couple, right? Or is that a different movie?

That's a different movie ["2 Days in New York"].

It is?! Oh, I thought that that was how it ended. That she had married him. What happens at the end? I don't remember. It doesn't turn out well; it's not as beautiful as the falling-in-love romance.

They don't see each other between the first and second movie, and then they stay together between the second and third.

And does their relationship turn out good?

I think the trilogy ends at a point where we feel good about them.

God, I have to watch those again. Because I definitely have the first one. I even have the screenplay. I feel like that's depressing. Oh, god, I don't know. Were Ross and Rachel good together? They were, weren't they? I don't know; I think Katie ends up probably a divorcee. Even though she's well-meaning with Coop, I don't think she ever develops the relationship competence to treat him the way he deserves ultimately. OK, I answered your first question! No, no, she's not that good for him. [Laughs] Not in the long run. [Laughs] It's hard for me; I have to defend my character, so you're testing me! That's your only job as an actor: Fight for your point of view. So of course Katie's going to think that. But it's hard to think outside of that. Like, "Oh, yes, she's going to fuck that up."

I feel like I tend to have unpopular opinions about onscreen relationships. I liked Rachel and Joey together. I saw the Mashterpiece Theater that you did about "Saved by the Bell," and you and your husband played Kelly and Screech. I liked when Kelly and Screech were together, at least for her to be with a person who wasn't terrible in one episode. So I'm the wrong person to ask about Ross and Rachel. It's interesting to wonder later if the stories we grow up with and think of as the perfect love story are actually good.

I agree. I totally agree with you. I love that you did such a deep dive and that you care about those heroes too. Because it's good to think beyond that, right? Like what the hell does happily ever after mean? What does it really look like? Oh, man. What do you think about Katie and Coop?

Part of the tension of that relationship is, like you said, what impulse and what side of her is she going to give space for. We get the sense that Coop is there when she's ready, but we don't know what her priority will be.

Yeah. Especially when it gets into the shows later, she's still kind of looking to the left. Isn't she? God, is that how it ends? I don't remember. I think that we get interrupted by a big bomb. She's kind of like a Barbie in that sense. A Barbie back in the day for girls was not a mom. She had the great clothes, but she had her job. That was the independence, and she didn't have both. So at the end of the shows, Katie has the job again. She doesn't really have any dudes or anything. So I don't think they've really developed her world beyond that, which is why I think she'd probably end up being a divorcee and not good for Coop.

When you think of "Wet Hot," what's a memory that you look back and say, "I can't believe that that happened"?

Oh. I think that I got the part to begin with because it was a few days before shooting, and they didn't have a Katie. Elizabeth Banks was going to play Katie, and they were going to maybe push some of the shooting for the barbecue girl. That's what her name was in the script that I read, 'cause I read for her first. And then they said, "Oh, no, I think we know what role is better for you." I feel like if Bradley hadn't mentioned it to me, then I wouldn't have known about the audition and called my agent, and I just happened to be in New York, and I just happened to get the materials the night before I flew out, and then I changed my ticket. It happened that they could make an appointment. It all was by luck. I think that's the real thing I can't believe. Once I was at camp I just sort of was like, "Where the hell am I? What the heck is going on?" I kind of held on while all these older kids—I was used to being the oldest of all of the group with "Mighty Ducks," and then I was in a group where I was definitely the youngest by like 10 years. So I just tried to not say too many stupid things [Laughs] and just keep my mouth shut and learn ... while not falling in love with any of the dudes. Because they would have been open to smooching, but then they don't understand that I'm like a real fall-in-love type. And I won't be able to have any casual [relationships]. So I tried to stay away from the boys and not say anything stupid and have as much fun as possible. Without getting fired. I think it went great!

That's something you had to actively implement?

Oh, yeah. I think I knew in my 20s, "If we were to really take this to the next level with these guys, you couldn't break up with me during the shoot. I would just leech on." So I knew that would be problematic for work. So I was like, "Oh, no, no, no, no. Let's not do that. Let's keep it all—you cannot read me at all." I already knew that about myself. Not a casual dater. I will make your life hell. Now I'm healthy and married and it's all fine, but definitely back then.

Based on what I know of what it's like to be on set and go from project to project, that seems like that mentality might present some challenges.

Uh, yeah. Your job is to fall in love. So of course in every job you do, if that's required in the role, a little of you is going to love the other person. I just had to be really careful with that because I knew myself.

Sort of on that note, a pattern that I noticed in your work is this: You initially read for Lindsay but became Katie. You're in a "Boy Meets World" episode that starts out focused on sex but then has a discussion of love superseding that. In "Blossom" you're Joey's first, but you get engaged to him. And on "Parenthood" you have a physical relationship with Crosby that almost gets really serious. Have you noticed that pattern of playing characters that might be established as the object of lust but then turn into marriage material?

Ohhhh! That's so nice that you pointed that out. Because there was a while in my career where I feel like I started as the girl who seemed like she would be great to have but then was a total nightmare. They would turn the character, like in "What About Brian." But that's really lovely. Because I think that the one character that's most like Ross and Rachel is Connie and Guy. They're the most healthy probably of all these characters that you mentioned. But, yes, definitely, I was a teenager who liked falling in love, so these were all the parts I kept getting. [Laughs] But I also personally love anything that has to do with relationships and family connection and how we speak to each other and how we grow together. Those are my favorite kinds of material, although I would also like to run around

Kazakhstan solving mysteries. Definitely want to be in "Mission: Impossible." I don't know why I keep getting this one, this kind of storyline.

Does that say anything about you or the characters, or it's just a coincidence? The representation of marriage material?

I don't know. Of course I wanted to think of myself as marriage material. [Laughs] Personally. [Laughs] I was very into that idea. Thankfully I didn't date any guy that would marry me. They were smarter. They were like, "You're not ready yet." Who knows? You connect with what you connect with, and then you get lucky if you get it. I think it's a combination of me having an interest in that experience and also everything colliding at the right time to actually get those roles. I loved those roles growing up. I remember "Mighty Ducks," there's the big kiss at the end. I was so excited to do that, and I imagined how it would go over and over. And I remember somebody saying, "Maybe we should rehearse it," and me being so nervous but like, "Yeah, definitely, let's rehearse it." Then when we actually shot it and everything else was going on and we like crash into each other and almost fall over, and when I saw it I was horrified and so disappointed. Because I had imagined it to be like on the quality of like "An Affair to Remember." Like it's not going to be lit and quiet, and they come in for this big—I definitely want to think about that other question that you said about did I have the thoughts and feelings of Connie and hang out in her mindset back then? Only probably around when I got to hold hands or give a smooch. Planning for that big moment is very much like Connie looking forward to smooching Guy. And now it's just like amazing because it's two little kids, and it's hilarious.

Now I'm imagining if the kiss between them turned into a big, 15-minute, romantic musical sequence, like in "Singing in the Rain."

Right? Totally. Oh my god. I think they probably put us together in the show that's coming out because both Garette and I are very happily well-adjusted and married and have great kids, and they were like, "That probably works."

I also wanted to note that I've never seen anyone with as many multi-episode arcs as you've had in your career on shows, including "Blossom," "Grey's Anatomy," "Shameless," "The O.C.," "Parenthood." You are not a one-and-done person. Do you have a sense of that being a rarity or why that happened?

No. I just feel very lucky to be a little bit more a part of these awesome stories. So many of those shows you just mentioned I'm a huge fan of. Yeah, I don't know why. I'm stuck between a guest star and a series regular! [Laughs] Come on!

Earlier you mentioned putting the weight of the world on your shoulders, and in another interview you mentioned a moment that Leonardo DiCaprio has in "Once Upon a Time in Hollywood" and how hard it is to talk yourself out of pressure. Can you elaborate on that? What is the pressure you put on yourself?

Probably wanting to tell the best story I possibly can. Knowing how much movies mean to me and stories, the ones that I love, is just wanting to do a service to the story in the same way. The best thing is to just think about what you're trying to do, but it can sometimes—what's that word? I'm not good with euphemisms. I want to say spinball, but that's wrong. It's tailspin; you go into a tailspin or something.

Is there a specific time that was especially difficult for you?

I think sometimes the first day is really hard, and then it takes off. And I really enjoy being the lead of something because then I'm too busy, so if I can't overthink—the same thing that makes me good for my job and is my superpower, which is being sensitive, is also something that can get in my way. So it's just trying to negotiate with those parts of yourself to do the best job that you can.

On Cameo you sent a message where you said, "Your family sounds great and that they really love you," and I thought that was such a beautiful sentiment. Do you think the way a person does Cameos says something about them?

Probably. [Laughs] I haven't really watched any. I just watched one or two when I first started, and I was like, "Oh, I don't ever want to be wearing the same shirt in every single one so someone thinks I'm just ripping off a bunch in a row." People take time to reach out. I don't really know what anyone else is doing. I feel like it's sort of replaced the fan letter, and I've kind of tried to keep my price low as long as it doesn't get too crazy so I'm able to do them. Because I really like connecting. It's so sweet; I've gotten to be part of people announcing that they're getting married or they'd like so-and-so to be in their wedding party or birthdays and helping people cope or who have a hard time with COVID and needing some company. It just feels like a nice way to connect with fans.

Let's wrap up with some lightning-round questions. If someone says they want to do a Guy and Connie spinoff show, what are the first questions you ask about that?

Are they going to hit a bump in the road where it looks like they might have to separate? Is this a comedy or a drama? [Laughs] I always had this fantasy—I know this isn't lightning round—that when everyone would talk about the Ducks getting back together that it was like that old movie—I think it was in the '90s; you tell me. Maybe it was in the 2000—remember that movie "Beautiful Girls" with Natalie Portman? I always thought that that would be a great way to do a dramatic sequel of "Mighty Ducks" because they're all small-town, and they all still live in district five, and it's hard to get out when you're from a working-class family, and I think that while Connie maybe got out, I think she still lives there. So that would be my other question: Can you keep it true to the movie? Can I keep it true to the movie? [Laughs]

Do you get free Disney+ for life?

No.

How many dekes is enough? Would there be any benefit in trying the quadruple or quintuple deke?

I think you should deke 'til you score.

Is there a point at which it becomes too much?

No. It's all about getting what you want. It's all about the actions you take to get your objective.

As I mentioned, you're so great in those Mashterpiece Theater segments, which I know were a few years back now. Did you ever have any interest in being on "SNL"?

I never miss an episode of "SNL," yes. I never auditioned. I mainly watched people in my high school improv. It never occurred to me that I could audition in college when I saw all the other improv groups, and then I was in a movie with all these other improv-ers and was like, "Oh, well, now it's too late. Now I'm so busy in my 20s, and it just kind of got away from me." But I never have given up hope. "SNL": Call me.

"Wall to Wall Records," your pilot with Bradley Cooper, was about running a record label. If you had your own, what would you want to focus on?

Oh my god. If you can take Ani DiFranco and singer-songwriter and mix it with pop but also dancing and Motown, so you're always dancing at our record label. You never sit down.

And lastly, who is a better person from "Wet Hot": Katie or Andy?

Oh, Katie, all the way. She's the only one rooted in any sort of reality. [Laughs] And in that sense, I think you can have something to hang on. Otherwise, everyone, you don't know what they're thinking. They're all nuts.

That's fair. If I were to play devil's advocate, I would say that Andy doesn't motivate anyone to trust him and then let him down. People get what they think they're going to get from Andy, but with Katie you're not as sure. That would be the only way I'd debate those two maybe.

Right, like he is who he says he is. Well, you make a fair point. [Laughs]

Doug E. Doug of 'Cool Runnings,' 'Operation Dumbo Drop,' 'That Darn Cat,' 'Hangin' with the Homeboys,' 'Class Act,' 'Where I Live,' 'Cosby'

We are overdue to properly praise the career of Doug E. Doug.

It is likely that you remember him primarily as Sanka, the goofy, pushcart-driving joke machine of 1993's "Cool Runnings." And you should—he's a delight in it, a breakout part in a breakout movie. But you should also remember that he was nominated for an Independent Spirit Award, alongside names like Robert Duvall, Gary Oldman, and River Phoenix, for his leading role in 1991's "Hangin' with the Homeboys." In 1993 he had his own short-lived, funny ABC sitcom called "Where I Live," based on his life, and was celebrated for his supporting work as Griffin in the mid- to late-'90s "Cosby" series.

Even in largely dismissed Disney movies like "Operation Dumbo Drop" and "That Darn Cat," Doug—who in recent years has published a novel ("The Fall of '87") and directed multiple features—demonstrates unexpected skill for character work and can take a silly line and get a laugh. "I need to bag this, label this and catalog this," he says at one point in "That Darn Cat." "Do you have a bag and a label?"

What's something you're nostalgic for from the '90s?

I feel nostalgic for fashion of the '90s. I recall that it was a time where there was sort of an opening of the floodgates in terms of expression. I may be a little biased since I entered into my 20s in the '90s, and I just recall the rules had changed. The '80s, there were specific types that you had to fit into fashion-wise and culturally. And I think people started to experiment with it, individual expression in all kinds of dramatic ways, in the '90s. I miss that.

When you talk about the floodgates opening, what images come to your mind for that expression?

From my vantage point, there was an explosion of hip-hop culture and quote-unquote urban fashion. It was brewing from the '80s, but it matured in terms of its relationship with the commercial world in the '90s. So my career, my life, it all came together in terms of feeling mainstream in the '90s. There was just a broader acceptance and also a value associated with urban culture in the '90s that was exhilarating.

When you think of a movie or show from that era that you weren't involved in but meant a lot to you as a fan then or recently, what comes to mind?

There's a show that I wasn't involved in and didn't watch, but I occasionally look at "Martin." [Laughs] I go, "Oh, wow, this is a product of its time!" I don't look at it a lot, but I refer to it because it's just sort of something that happened that probably wouldn't happen again that's a product of the '90s.

Can you elaborate on that?

Yes. It was a time when there was a lot of trust in people who came from the culture. The corporate world didn't monitor its urban product in the same way it eventually learned how to do. So artists from the '90s, particularly Black artists from the '90s, had a lot more autonomy and more meaningful influence over what they produced. So there's a sort of, I guess you could call it a cultural authenticity that that show has, that you can tell that a lot of the humor—like the whole fashion thing of FUBU, how that emerged. For Us, By Us. It's sort of a concept that manifested itself in television shows. There was a lot of meaningful contributions from Black artists, and there wasn't the kind of interference that eventually ended up happening. So you got expressions that I think were very, very, for lack of a better way of saying it endemic to the community. And that show was an example of it. It rang very true.

Is there a contemporary example that you point to that shows the lack of authenticity now?

It's a different kind of authenticity. The contrast that I would make is not the lack of authenticity because that existed in the '90s too. It's just that that particular show was very, very bawdy and unfiltered. When I say true, I don't necessarily mean positive. It's sort of like it unfiltered. Almost everything today seems to have a filter in my view. There's a kind of aspiration to be recognized as like everybody else. So most shows today, to me, are like that. It's like, "Let's expose the humanity that we have like everybody else!" I'm not saying that's a good or bad thing; I'm saying that that's a facet of modern television that obviously existed in the Civil Rights era, the '60s and so forth, but now it's less bawdy and raw. That show "Martin" was raw! [Laughs] Now people are very meticulous in terms of how you present people, Black people, for example. It's more of a craft than then. Then I think it was a question of a fascination with the culture. The people who were producing those shows didn't know what people were fascinated with or not. They were just being themselves. I think now people are much more sophisticated about showing what they think people want to see or need to see.

For your work, I want to start with "Hangin' with the Homeboys," a really good movie that you're really good in. This is the early '90s, and a leading role for you that explores male friendship and discussions of the value of college and relationships informed by racial dynamics. When you think back to the period of that film, where does your mind go regarding the subject matter or your experience?

It goes to what we're talking about; it goes to this place of resonance. In terms of thematically and in terms of the situation, it was so resonant. Because it had that dynamic that I'm talking about. It was unintentionally universal but very, very culturally specific. So specific that it was like THE BRONX! [Laughs] And "What are the kind of people in the Bronx that you would find really? Well, these are the guys that you would find in the Bronx." It's interesting, that film was compared to films like "Diner" by Barry Levinson or "American Graffiti." It had all the elements of coming-of-age, it just happens to be in the Bronx. So it was very resonant. That's the first thing I thought about it, that it was very specific but also very universal at the same time. As a young actor and being my first film, I thought all films were like that when I first started. "Wow!" I thought everybody could be that skilled in terms of representing such a thing. It was a fantastic entree into the film business.

And speaking of comparisons, a few years later another movie about guys out on the town came out, "Swingers." That was lightning in a bottle. Did you feel like "Hangin' with the Homeboys" got its due as part of the discussion when the "Swingers" moment was happening?

I think it was getting its due in certain quarters, in certain circles, definitely. But as far as the general market was concerned it wasn't as big of a financial success. Relative to what it cost, it was financially successful, but it wasn't a cultural flashpoint like "Swingers" was. But I didn't feel like it didn't get its due. It was a Sundance film. It was nominated for awards. I was nominated for Best Actor! In the Independent Spirit Awards. So the industry at large embraced it. And certain fans of a certain kind of movie embraced it. But as far as its due in the general market, no.

Was that just because the independent film community didn't really have its moment until later in the decade?

Exactly. Exactly. Exactly. It was very early in the Sundance experience. It's a combination of the independent thing didn't yet have its moment, but also it was competing with the so-called commercial urban films. I think the audience didn't, and I think this is still true to this day—there isn't a real acceptance of films with urban characters. There's a presumption that they have to be wildly commercial, and that was true then. So there isn't this idea that you can tell simple stories and small stories with Black and Latino characters or Asian characters. Especially Black and Latino characters. At that time, it was like, "Look, we're looking for low-investment, high-return here. We ain't looking for *art*." It's not like the motive as far as the company was concerned, New Line Cinema in this case, was, "We really want to tell an important story about coming of age in the Bronx!" [Laughs] I think that they thought they had like "House Party"—they wanted to capitalize off of a particular phenomenon, and they were willing to invest $1 million in it. It wasn't like the art house films where they just were like, "We don't have high expectations on a return, but we think this is an important film."

So you're nominated for an Independent Spirit Award alongside some major names. What are your feelings about your career and your plans at that time?

My mind was spinning. I was a fish completely out of water because I didn't understand why I was there in the company of these people. I had no idea that I would be plucked and put into a category with anybody who was of note. [Laughs] So I had no concept of what to feel about it. I just felt, "Wow! OK." And going to the awards and seeing the other actors, like, "Whoa!" I just thought, "OK, this is what people I've seen on TV [do], and I had no concept of how people got invited to [something like this] or included in [something like this]."

Then you wind up starring in "Cool Runnings" not long after. I know you didn't really bobsled in the movie, but Sanka is very scared of several things like the ice and the bobsledding itself. Either because it was your first big-studio starring role or any other facet of the character or the movie, was there anything about "Cool Runnings" that scared you?

What scared me was the studio politics. [Laughs] Because I had done a television show for ABC called "Where I Live," and I had been embroiled in all kinds of politics in terms of the studio, Disney Television, who produced the show, and ABC, who broadcast the show. I had gotten in all this controversy trying to make the show what it could be, should be, and it was never resolved. They tried to recast me. It was crazy. And in the meantime, during hiatus, I do "Cool Runnings." So I was very skittish because I had been very bruised by the experience of working with these major companies and trying to produce shows. So when I had reservations about some of the portrayals or things of that nature, it was terrifying because it was like, "I would like to raise my voice, but I know how these people feel about that." [Laughs] So that was the most scary part of that experience. I felt like I had to point out things that I thought could be improved or focused on that I thought needed to be focused on. Because there was a very narrow idea of what we should do. For example, they wanted the characters not to speak in an accent. [Laughs] Out of fear that the audience wouldn't understand them. So that seemed to be ridiculous to me. I was like, "Well, they're Jamaican!" [Laughs] So we had to find a way to come up with a compromise where they sounded Jamaican but not so Jamaican that people couldn't understand them. The studio's suggestion was that we all sound like Sebastian the crab from "The Little Mermaid." [Laughs] Which I thought was ridiculous. Leon as well, for that movie, they also suggested that he sound like Aladdin, which is obviously a Middle Eastern character, so that didn't make any sense as far as being Jamaican. So it was notes and suggestions that we had to navigate through … that all of us, and me in particular, found particularly objectionable, and they had to be sorted out somehow.

How did you feel about the resolution of those issues?

I think the proof is in the movie, in the pudding. We were able to get through it; it's just there's always a toll. Even if you succeed, there's always a toll because people don't like to be embarrassed about their bias. And sometimes they misbehave when you bring to their attention, or they get defensive, that something they believe in and they think is funny is objectionable. [Laughs]

I'm now wondering what type of story would be concocted for a spinoff movie featuring Aladdin and Sebastian the crab.

[Laughs] Exactly.

Is it fair to say that the Winter Olympics sports are harder than Summer Olympics sports?

I think that they are because of all the gear involved. [Laughs] Like a bobsled is an extra thing you gotta deal with. Or a toboggan or luge. If you're a track runner, you just gotta get your shoes. But if you're a hockey player, you gotta get the skates and the pads and the … And of course there's the added challenge of weathering the elements. So, yeah, I think that the winter sports are probably more challenging.

Every so often there will be an unfortunate incident in the sports world, and the video will go viral. Are you the type of person that has to see that or tries to avoid it?

I try to avoid that. I think that at my age I've seen a lot of those things, and I get the general idea that someone is hurt. When I hear, "Oh, someone was hurt," I assume it's not good. So I just leave it alone.

I agree. Of course "Cool Runnings" has been so inspiring for so many people. Are you more inspired by stories of defeat or victory? Is there a sense that part of the movie's power comes from how it wraps up?

Yes, definitely. Definitely. Because I think it was unexpected gain in defeat that the movie depicts. They gained the respect of others. They gained a lot. And I think that's part of the power of the movie. I think it's probably something that most people wrestle with. What happens when you don't get what you want? John Candy, when we first met each other, he played music that he thought consolidated the themes of the movie, and that's what he played: The Rolling Stones' "You Can't Always Get What You Want." [Laughs]

"You try sometimes; you get what you need." So he was very in touch with that message. It is a very powerful message.

I know your dad is Jamaican. What did he think of the movie and the issues with the accents, and your character being named Sanka Coffie?

I didn't have a problem with my character being Sanka Coffie. I thought that was a very clever thing. Nicknames are obviously a big part of most cultures, and certainly [in] Jamaica, it's not outside of the realm of possibilities. You look at dancehall music, reggae, people are very big on inventing yourself. So it's within the realm of possibility that someone would be like, "I'm Sanka Coffie." [Laughs] So that I can wrap my head around in terms of believability and come up with a rationale for why that might be what someone would call themselves. Accents were a lot more tricky as I mentioned because it was a fight pretty much for the first month of the film. [Laughs] Even to the point of the director Jon Turteltaub being threatened by the studio that he was going to lose his job if he didn't get it under control. [Laughs]

Did you have a sense of what your dad thought about all of that then?

I think that my father, being Jamaican, is aware of the range of ways that people talk and express themselves. Particularly around issues of class, which is true of America too. So there is a range in terms of the way that people talk, but obviously there's these popular ideas about what a Jamaican accent is. So all of his having insight into Jamaican culture or to Caribbean culture broadly knew that. So obviously some characters' voices are more British inflected because that's obviously a facet of speech in Jamaica for people who are of upper classes. So the rest of us tried to concoct something that was authentic enough, but we knew that were up against it in terms of having characters that spoke in full patois. Because that would put us out of the realm of being comprehended, being understood. So it remained a struggle. From my father's point of view it wasn't an issue, but there's a lot of people that take exception over the accents in the movie.

The movie was certainly a phenomenon and a breakout for you. People tend to judge actors based on the success of a movie, and what you do in "Cool Runnings" is much different than what you did in "Hangin' with the Homeboys." What do you remember about the impact on your career of "Cool Runnings" and the type of parts that were coming your way as opposed to what it was feeling like a few years prior to that?

After "Cool Runnings," I was in a different category in terms of the industry's perception of my value. And so the things that were coming were very vast. In terms of film, they came mostly from Disney itself because they look at me as a homegrown talent. If I was pigeonholed in any way, it had to do with the fact that the things that were coming were family films. And I had already been working in that area anyway in terms of my television work and so forth, so it wasn't in terms of the individual portrayals that I got the same kind of roles. It was in terms of just the genre. There was no interest in me playing anything edgy after that. As a matter of fact, when I have played things that were edgy after that, people really, really missed Sanka. [Laughs] They were like, "Sanka wouldn't stab anybody!" [Laughs]

People love the dark origin stories now.

Yeah, but they weren't as narratively sophisticated in the '90s. [Laughs] They weren't challenging audiences in the same way. It's even a challenge to say, "This is a prequel." I don't know if there was such a thing even thought about until "Phantom Menace" or whatever.

Talking about the homegrown talent of Disney reminds me of old Hollywood.

Yes! I was under contract. I was. Three pictures.

Let's turn to "Operation Dumbo Drop" then, which I hadn't seen in a long time. I remember not liking it as a kid, probably because I just didn't know what to think of it when I was 11 or something. When you think of being pulled by an elephant's tail or interactions with countless extras, what do you think of? It seems like that movie was a lot.

Oh my god. [Laughs] Yeah, it was probably double or triple the budget of "Cool Runnings."

Denis Leary said, "The movie was so painstakingly terrible because it took a long time to shoot that all of us had pictures of the things we were going to buy with our money to keep us going."

That's true! That's exactly right. I mean, I made so much money on that movie, and I still wonder whether or not I should have done it. [Laughs] Just the per diem alone because the exchange rate in terms of Thai baht—we were in Thailand—was so ridiculously outlandish that I actually just had to give money away. It was like, "This is ridiculous." "There's too much poverty in this country; would you like to have some money please?"

What was the hardest part of that experience?

Oh, man, everything was hard about it. We shot in the jungle. We had so many company moves. The company moves all had to be taking a very small, rickety plane. There was exposure to all kinds of unusual bacteria. I was hospitalized. It was just a very, very difficult movie. We were in Thailand, so we were many, many, many miles away from anybody, different time zones, so we can't really get the kind of support we need if you have family or friends you want to talk to because it's three in the morning or two in the morning and you're up. Everything was rough about that movie. We actually had to leave the country because there was a travel advisory that American citizens would have to leave the country because there was a hunt for them at the Burmese border. So we finished the movie in Florida and Los Angeles. There was an untold number of company moves, and we shot it in so many different places.

Did you feel like you guys were prepped for that at all?

No! Absolutely not. [Laughs] As a matter of fact, I didn't really understand the script at all. But when I met with the director, Simon Wincer, he described it almost like it was "Apocalypse Now" with an elephant. [Laughs] I was like, "This is either going to be the best movie ever or a shitshow." So, no, I was not prepared for what it was. No.

There are Disney movies I love, and ones I don't. I'm not bringing this up for you to have any particular feelings about the company that did so much for you. But these concepts of Disney versions of history, whether the things that were changed for "Cool Runnings" or hearing about moving an elephant in Vietnam and thinking, "Oh, we can make a PG-rated movie out of that. Doesn't matter how much gunfire there is." What do you make of these Disney takes on history? Was it ridiculous then? Was it reasonable then and ridiculous now?

[Laughs] I think that it was definitely ridiculous then. I think now let's just call it historically inaccurate. But then it's just ridiculous. And what's more ridiculous was the rationale behind it. That in order to get people to participate in it, you had to make it make as much sense as possible. So the way that they marketed and justified these stories was probably the most egregious thing. If they had just said, "OK, this has nothing to do with history. We just want to do a movie with an elephant." And then it happened to be during a war, you could stomach it. Because there's no disingenuousness in that, in my view. And I don't think that everything that is Disneyified is bad. "Cool Runnings" is based on a true story with enormous latitude and creative license. But it works because the spirit of that story is true. I don't know if the spirit of the story in, for example, "Dumbo Drop" is true. I'm not as familiar with what happened there. When they told me the story, they were like [Laughs], "This happened. They dropped an elephant out of a plane. And the only reason why it didn't get international news is because it was the day that Martin Luther King got shot." And I'm like, "Well, that's a good reason." [Laughs] But they were talking about it like it was a slight. Like, "They should've made some room for this elephant in the headlines!" [Laughs] So that's the absurdity of it. But because they think it's an important story, it should trump all, which is profoundly self-centered and ridiculous.

Like the newspapers should have done a split cover on that day: Two big stories today!

[Laughs] "Soldiers drop elephant! Oh, yeah, and Martin Luther King died." Come on, y'all. [Laughs]

It is funny. Most movies that have truth to them will say "Based on a true story" or "Inspired by a true story." With "Dumbo Drop," it's not until the movie is over that it says, "Inspired by a true story," and you're just like, "What?!"

[Laughs] I know, I know. [Laughs] Look, they paid Danny Glover $3 million, and he said, "I did it for the money. That's it." That says it all.

When you talked about the challenges about making the movie, you didn't say anything about the elephant.

That was the beautiful part of the movie. That was the blessing of the movie because I ended up being so comfortable with the elephant that I would sleep under its feet. That almost makes it all worth it because the movie gave me an opportunity to be exposed to an actual wonder of the universe. This is a powerful, serene and wise and beautiful thing that people are afraid of. But like anything else, you develop a familiarity, a relationship, and it ends up being commonplace for you to be like, "Oh, good morning, Tai," which was the name of the elephant. [Laughs] So that was something that was unexpected. Because you had to adjust. This thing that you initially think will kill you, you have to learn how to be around it. And we did. I know I did. I have pictures of me sitting at the feet of the elephant. It's astounding. Once you achieve something like that, it does change you.

In what way?

You don't have the same perception of danger based on reputation. Or based on previous exposure to the idea of something. You realize that dangers a lot of times have to do with familiarity and understanding the rules of what it takes to be around someone or be somewhere. There's rules. So once you learn the rules, you can coexist with anything and anyone.

I may not be right about this, but I'm curious if you know: Did you see Spike Lee's "Da 5 Bloods"?

Yes, I did.

There's a scene toward the end of "Dumbo Drop" where there's talk about the elephant being father of God, and I could have sworn it was the same place used in "Da 5 Bloods."

I doubt it because that set was built for "Dumbo Drop," and I'm sure they built a set [for "Da 5 Bloods."] Maybe they didn't. And I know they shot in Thailand too. But when I saw that, I was like, "Yeah, that looks just like it!" I mean, it might be. Maybe they left the set. But I doubt it.

I'm glad to hear that stuck out to you too. The thought of those two very different movies using the same set is interesting, possibly. And now to "That Darn Cat," which I had never seen and really enjoyed its ridiculousness.

[Laughs] Thank you. Me too.

I was expecting one thing and really enjoyed how zany it turned out to be. But the one thing I wanted to ask you about was that in "Cool Runnings," Derice looks at a framed picture of his father on the wall and wants to live up to that if he can, and that's the same thing your character does in "That Darn Cat." What's the motivation behind this through line, and is that good?

Well, in the case of "That Darn Cat," when I went to meet the director, Bob Spiers, in England, I took my father along with me, who is Jamaican. So we went and had dinner with the director, and my father and the director hit it off. So that picture is a picture of my actual father. They painted a portrait of him.

That's awesome. Then the idea that there were multiple movies starring the same person within a couple of years that were both touching on this element of parental success and becoming your own, is that just a kids' movie trope?

Yeah, I think it's a particular trope in movies in general. For example, the [1986] Tom Hanks and Jackie Gleason movie "Nothing in Common." It's just a facet of life, and people given the opportunity to tell those stories take advantage of the concern about that. Less and less you see that these days because the current industry, I don't know if they really explore actual, real dynamics between people in the same way. In particular when you have to focus an inordinate amount of attention on older people because the emphasis now is on a younger demographic. So you don't see that explored as much, the perspective of someone and their relationship with their parents. Not in that way. There are adolescent concerns like "Freaky Friday" or "Parent Trap." But not like a grown person is reflecting on their parents' expectations and things like that.

I want to go back to "Where I Live." It sounds like there were a lot of difficulties behind the scenes with that. The '90s was huge for comedians getting their own sitcoms. Watching some of the show on YouTube for the first time, I think it's good. It's a winning and funny show. What do you think of the way it was received and turned out? When it seemed like every comedian imaginable was getting a sitcom in the '90s, was that good?

[Laughs] Well, it was good for me. I loved the show. I loved the show. There are some episodes where I say, "That's as good as it gets," as far as what I can make meaningful contributions to and create, or at least be part of a creative team. The show was based on my actual upbringing and my life, so it's very, very special to me. So I loved the show. There were things about it that I didn't like, and that's probably where the fights were. It was among the first of that era for Black comedians. Because "Martin" aired first, but it was shot afterwards. Because we were a midseason replacement, so actually Carl [Anthony] Payne [II], who played Martin's friend on the show, auditioned for my show first. So it was very, very early in terms of young Black comedians getting shows. But obviously Cosby opened up the door for Roseanne and for Tim Allen and for basically everybody else. And a lot of the writers and the people that he had that worked on his show worked on my show. Ehrich Van Lowe, who was the ["Cosby Show"] producer, [was] one of the ["Where I Live"] executive producers; Sullivan Walker was on "The Cosby Show" as one of his friends. We just basically poached talent from that show. [Laughs] It was great for me. I think it was great for the industry, and based on what we said earlier, there was a sense that comedians had a built-in audience and also that they had a particular point of view and an understanding. They knew what was funny. It was really a golden age in a sense in terms of someone basically from obscurity, relative obscurity, being put in a position like that where you're one of the few people in American history to have a show of your own on network television. That's some very rare air to be breathing. So, yeah, I thought it was fabulous. Was I ready for it and all that it entailed with ratings and network notes and the stakes of all these salaries that depend on you behaving and not upsetting people? The whole politics of it was difficult to mine and master. Remember, I was 21, 22 years old. I was just a baby. I'm a co-producer on the show. So it was really a lot.

And did you say at one point they tried to recast you on the show about your life?

Yes, they tried to recast me on "Where I Live," yes. I think it was more of an empty threat. They were concerned about silly things. Like I was playing a teenager even though I was in my 20s. But my character was going to college, and he had a couple of schools he wanted to go to. One of them was St. John's, which is where I went. So I was like, "Oh, cool, let's put that in there." And I was like, "What about a Black college?" They were just like, "Oh, no!" Little things that I didn't think would be controversial or would upset anybody they were really upset about, and I just didn't understand at the time where the fears, in this case racial fears, that they have about alienating white people when you suggest something that they think they can't handle or don't understand. So that was a big part of the challenge between myself and the producer of that show, the main executive producer, which was Michael Jacobs, who had this whole empire of shows like "Dinosaurs" and "Boy Meets World." He was sort of a big cheese at Disney as far as a producer, so he felt I couldn't tell him anything. I shouldn't tell him anything. And he also resented the power dynamic of when the show gets on the air, the talent gets exponentially more powerful and so he was always worried about having the show taken from up under him. So any suggestions were threatening as opposed to, "Oh, that's an interesting idea." I went on Arsenio Hall's show as a matter of fact when promoting "Cool Runnings," but there was also ancillary attention paid to "Where I Live." So Arsenio asked me about "Where I Live" and pointed out, "Hey, you're also a co-producer." My comment was, "Well, all that means is that occasionally I have a say." Michael Jacobs was livid: "How dare you say you have a say! I only gave you a producer credit as a courtesy!" It was really just mean-spirited, ugly. It came out of nowhere. I was very young, I didn't understand the fragile egos that some people have around being perceived as the main creator. So I was completely blindsided, so they tried to recast me. [Laughs]

That's a lot that goes on behind the scenes. Was "Where I Live" always the title of the show? Were there any others discussed?

Uh, no. The working title I think was "The Untitled Doug E. Doug Project." So they didn't have a name.

It's challenging to encapsulate in a title sometimes.

[Laughs] Yes. I think that was part of the issue. He was trying to do Thornton Wilder's "Our Town." With this literary concept of the show. As opposed to what I thought the show was, [which] was a family show like "Roseanne." But he was like "Our Town"! Because he had aspirations, I would say pretenses, for being Gary David Goldberg or Norman Lear or people with real talent. [Laughs]

And you were also in "Class Act," of course. The early-'90s world of Kid 'n Play is so fascinating.

Yeah! Oh my god. I was hoping you would ask me about that. The most fun I ever had in my life! Let's just face it.

Why?

Because they taught me about what it meant to be a celebrity and the perks of it and the fun of it and girls and parties. It was the kind of fun that any young man would love to have when you're 19 or something. [Laughs]

What did they teach you?

Mostly Chris Reid, who was Kid, he was the main person, but I met Play—because I was working as a comic at the Apollo Theater, and when I got off stage and started leaving, I bumped into Play. And Play was like, "We gotta work together!" And I Just didn't know how that would happen. So I was like, "OK, cool, man!" [Laughs] But mostly Chris Reid, Kid, would teach me about clubs and VIP section and how to utilize your success or perceived success to try to get access to people, places and things. They were very skilled at that. He still is. [Laughs]

That's cool to have someone who's been there to help you out when you're getting started.

Yeah, big time. Because I was totally mystified, like most people are, by celebrity and the so-called celebrity lifestyle. And really these are things that people have to do in order to compensate for the fact that you can't do the things that other people can do anymore. Instead of trying to put a round peg in a square hole and trying to get people to treat you like you're normal, you've gotta develop strategies in terms of how to live given the nature of your profile, given the nature of whatever, maybe your new tax bracket, whatever the hell it is. You have to find a way to create a life for yourself without denial for what you have become and how people perceive you.

Was there a moment that you could tell that knowledge was benefiting you?

Oh, yes. There were many situations in which I felt stymied, and then I realized, "Oh! This has to do with celebrity." I've been utilizing that knowledge ever since. Because you can't be sane and walk around saying, "I'm a celebrity!" all the time. But it does occur to you when certain things happen, when certain people talk to you in a certain way. I remember John Travolta saying this very eloquently by saying, "Sometimes you just have to allow people to experience the joy of seeing you." Sometimes there's a lot of exuberance about you, but you're not thinking about, "Oh, yeah, they must've seen me in a movie or something." You're not thinking about it. You're just getting tomatoes. [Laughs]

I wouldn't be doing my job if I didn't ask this next question. It's an inevitability, I know.

Cosby.

Well, you're in a unique position where Russell Simmons was very helpful for you at the beginning of your career.

Yes. He was!

And of course you were very involved with Bill Cosby as well. No one is happy to hear about the terrible things that anyone does. You are in the position where you are learning things about people who were very helpful to you. I hate questions that say, "What was that like?" But that puts you in a strange and terrible place to learn things about people who were so helpful for you, so I wanted to throw that your way.

Yeah. I'll start with Russell. I love Russell, but I have always had issues with Russell [Laughs] in terms of things I saw. And not in terms of sexually or anything, but in terms of just business dealings. But on the other hand, he opened up a vortex for a lot of, at that time, really, really young, Black, urban kids who really had a lot of creative energy and didn't have a vehicle and means by which to get to audiences. They didn't understand the marketplace, etc. So I'm on the side of being skeptical about believing everything, but I do accept that there are things in his case and in the case of Mr. Cosby, that there was something untoward that must have occurred. I kind of keep it in that space. But the details I couldn't possibly know. I don't have a problem or conflict with maintaining affection with people when they do wrong. So that's not really something I wrestle with. Or when they are reported to do something wrong, or when somebody says they did something wrong. I have no conflict with that. I've had family members that have gone to jail. I don't have the same trip I think a lot of people have when someone close to you—in this case, probably Mr. Cosby is closer to me than Russell—but when someone who's close to you is in trouble. I no longer feel the burden of having to as I would say rep him, as I have over the years. This is not the first controversy he's been involved in. When we worked together, there were controversies. So it's like any intimate relationship or close relationship. People have their own side, their own explanation for their conduct. So you just have to maintain your affection if you happen to love them and acknowledge that there's definitely something not right with the way that this person operated. Certainly morally, if not criminally, repulsive, So, yeah, that's how I look at it.

I guess that speaks to a complex and difficult thing, what to do when someone you love turns out to—I mean, I'm not here to debate the truth of anything. I'm on the side of believing accusers in these cases; false reports are extremely rare. But to the point of maintaining affection, is that something you have talked about with Bill Cosby? How do you reconcile that in your mind about someone beloved hurting a lot of people?

As I said, this is not the first time that someone I've loved has hurt people. I've watched people have their feelings hurt, and I've [Laughs] had my feelings hurt in relationship to him. As far as hurt is concerned, I think that that's something I've acclimated myself to. The whole psychological term "hurt people hurt" is I think a very realistic and grounded way to look at human beings. It's not something that people want to accept when it comes to someone that has accusations because they presume that they're sympathetic. You don't have to be sympathetic to acknowledge that a hurt person hurts people. But if you were to acknowledge that someone's hurt, that people who do bad things are hurting, is against what a lot of people want to do because they want to demonize. And that I will never do and cannot do with someone who I have so much information about so many experiences with. It's actually cruel to even expect someone like his children or his wife—I don't care that people do it to me—but it's really cruel to expect someone that really loves somebody to have the same perspective on things as the general public who hears something about somebody. It's just not fair.

As you said, life is not binary, and I think people want to know what to do when they hear about something terrible happening. And they might think that the thing to do is lock that person away. Sometimes that is what should happen to keep people safe. It sounds like you're sort of talking about rehabilitation vs. incarceration to a degree.

Well, rehabilitation has to do with the presumption of guilt. I don't even assume. I just recognize that something untoward has occurred, something wrong has occurred. The nature of it I will never really know, so I try not to make presumptions when it comes to anything.

289

Shane McDermott of 'Airborne,' 'Swans Crossing'

The reviews were lousy, and the movie didn't make any money. But several decades later, the fish-out-of-water-romantic-sports-drama "Airborne" remains less derivative and more rewarding than its 1993 performance would suggest. And not because it's one of the very few movies you will find that makes rollerblading a major plot point but because its main character, Mitchell Goosen (Shane McDermott), had such a uniquely upbeat, deceptively complex view on life (a mentality that immediately makes him the target of bullies after moving from Los Angeles to Cincinnati, where apparently there is no greater insult than "pretty boy" or "surfer boy"). Which is notable at any age and especially in high school, when laid-back optimism is not exactly the standard.

Anyone who responded to the movie (which costarred Seth Green and Jack Black) at the time or more recently must credit the likewise underrated performance of McDermott, who previously starred with Sarah Michelle Gellar and Brittany Daniel on the teen soap opera "Swans Crossing" and later appeared on the adult soap opera "All My Children." Though that—plus a "Baby-Sitters Club" here and a "Law & Order" there—was the extent of McDermott's onscreen career, the actor made a huge impact in the limited amount of time he had in the spotlight. He's now in Galveston, Texas, selling real estate and original artwork—check out his paintings at sfmcdermottart.com; they're fantastic.

What's something you feel nostalgic for from the '90s?

During the '90s I was living in New York City, so the experience was kind of unique. I was living on Roosevelt Island, and I was rollerblading a lot. I used to rollerblade through the streets of New York. Used to go to auditions that way. So rollerblading was a major, major part of my life in the '90s. … Of course we'd get around on the subways, but once you got off the subways you'd still have long walks. And we were just young enough and maybe a little bit crazy enough to get very excited about skating the streets in New York. Especially during the summers.

I know you've mentioned you don't do too much rollerblading these days, and I can't say I do either. I wonder if my old ones are still in my parents' garage.

[Laughs] Recently I just got a new pair. I have young kids, and they're just getting to the age where they're either starting to skate or rollerblade. And I said I'm going to get a new pair of rollerblades, and it felt great. It felt good to get back on the blades for sure.

Did that make you feel old, young, or both?

290

Made me feel young, very much so. Brought back some great memories. Galveston, Texas, which is where I live now, it's a fairly small town but it's a walkable city. So if you know how to rollerblade you can get around it pretty easily. During this pandemic I think people have really started to embrace skating again, so there are large groups of people that got on their roller skates and rollerblades, and I was lucky enough to get involved in that group. So it's been wonderful. It definitely makes me feel younger, thank god. [Laughs]

There were a lot of major movies that came out in 1993. Of these, which most struck a chord and why: "Jurassic Park," "Dazed and Confused," "Rookie of the Year," "The Sandlot," "The Firm," "The Pelican Brief," "Cool Runnings," "Homeward Bound," "Mrs. Doubtfire"?

I would say "Dazed and Confused" was a great film. Definitely something I saw in the theaters when it came out and left a great impression. And actually moving back to Texas— I was originally from New York, but at a young age I moved to Texas and lived in Texas for a number of years and I have a lot of family down here. We moved back to New York when I was maybe 10 or 11, when I started in the acting business. "Dazed and Confused" has a great feel of Texas. Not only that, that '70s era was just—it seemed like it was a simpler time. So that movie definitely was a big deal.

If you had been a couple years older at the time, would you have auditioned for the laid-back Matthew McConaughey role?

Very possibly. Very possibly. That's the one thing is when you're auditioning, you audition for a lot. These films that it didn't really register when you're doing the audition, and then a year later or so it would come out and you would realize how great a film [it was and] what was going on there. So for example I auditioned for "Clueless," which is still one of my favorite films. So just going into the audition you read through the script, which was amazing, but when it actually comes out and you see it on screen, even though it was just an audition it was really wonderful to be a part of even that.

Was that for the Breckin Meyer part?

It was, it was.

Something that really struck me about "Airborne" when I originally saw it and when I returned to it a couple days ago was the peacefulness of the movie and the vibe of Mitchell knowing who he is and how to get what he wants. How much did that match up with who you were at the time? I think part of why I, and probably many people, responded to it is because that part of most people's lives is defined by not feeling that way at all.

I don't know. First of all, very, very good question. I would say first of all I was young. Being 16—I don't think I had just turned 16, but I was pretty young. And at that point I had lived in New York City for a number of years, which is absolutely opposite from the character. [Laughs] Somebody who's from California … and I did surf at the time, but I would go out to Long Island and surf and the weather was nice and cold. But it's very possible that in the casting, the director, Rob Bowman, and the other individuals, the other folks that had choice in choosing who was there, maybe they saw that in me. Because it's definitely a part of my personality. I tend to be a little bit laid-back. I don't know if doing the movie made me more like Mitchell or if I was Mitchell originally [Laughs], and through the years it started to come out. Especially now with kids, I'm Mitchell Goosen all the time. [Laughs]

Mitchell's not afraid of bullies and is so easygoing whether with girls that come into his orbit or any situation. Can you think of any time in your life before the movie that you either drew from, or a situation in the movie that replicated even slightly? Whether someone was messing with you, coming onto you or otherwise?

When I first moved to New York, New York was—I think this was maybe '88—it was a little bit of a rough city. I look back fondly on those years in New York because there's a grittiness to it. I love New York City; it's an amazing city to have been lucky enough to grow up on and also where I lived on Roosevelt Island. But I remember the first couple years I was there was a little bit rough because it was a little bit dangerous. There were a lot of muggings and stuff like that, and as a young kid who spent a large amount of time walking through the streets of New York, whether it was to get to auditions, to get to school or so forth, you always had to sort of watch yourself because there were times that the city could be pretty dangerous. So multiple times you're confronted with a situation which is a little bit scary. And my response to that was always to relax and try to be as smart as possible and try to figure out how to get yourself into a better place. [Laughs] So I never really dealt with bullies in school, but there were definitely some bullies walking through the streets of New York, and I definitely was confronted by 'em a couple times. But I'm still here and I have some good stories to tell.

I certainly don't intend to make you relive something terrible, but in terms of stories to tell, if you feel comfortable, is there something that stands out most vividly in your mind?

[Laughs] Well, there was an interesting story. It didn't happen in New York; of all places it happened in Los Angeles. It was during the filming of "Airborne." I became very good friends with Seth Green, and Seth and I decided to meet up with some friends and go to a park and have Chinese food. So we had ordered the Chinese food and found this nice park, and I remember we were in the park, and it was kind of surreal because there were kids playing in the park and parents and everything like that, and I just remember these two kids sitting on the fence, kinda staring at us. I didn't think much about it. And after five or so minutes of them staring at us, one of them walks over and lifts up his shirt and under his shirt he had a gun. [Laughs] And I'd been mugged before, but I had never been mugged by a gun. Which being mugged by a gun is a whole different thing. What stands out the most is how cool Seth was in this situation. Of course the guy says "Hey, give me your money," and I just remember Seth being so cool about it. He had one of those wallets that had the chain that was attached to his belt, and—I don't know if this is the way to describe it—but he was a total gentleman. He gave him the money, and of course I just followed his lead, gave them the money. The guy took the money and ran off through this field of kids. It's one of the memories that sticks out the most because of the terror of the gun, but in the end it was a beautiful day in a park, and watching Seth and how he dealt with it was quite impressive.

It seems like it would still be hard to get back to work after that. Not that this is the most important part of that experience, but did you get a few days off of shooting after that happened, to recover?

Actually that was at the end. The first part of filming was all done in Cincinnati, Ohio, and that's where the bulk of the work was done. This was the first movie I had ever done—actually the only movie I had ever done at this level, at this budget. But after you finish the filming—the California aspect of the film, where in the beginning [there was] surfing, rollerblading—then you have reshoots, voiceovers, you have a good amount of time you spend in Los Angeles finishing up the film, they're editing and so forth. That was what we were doing in L.A. at the time. So it wasn't full-on production; you'd just go in and [fix] something that wasn't recorded right. I think if I remember right, [the robbery] didn't affect us all that much. Because first of all nobody was hurt, which is the most important, and also it turned out to be an interesting story to tell. But I remember there was a—whenever they have a first draft or a second draft of a movie, they bring it to a movie theater and have an audience come in and kind of critique it. I think it was the day or maybe two days after that, and I remember Seth came up with the idea—first of all, it was a very surreal situation because I guess when they're looking for audience occupants to go to these movies they go to very busy areas like malls and say "Hey, would you like to preview a movie?" And sign you up. So Seth and I were walking around, maybe it was Universal Studios, someplace where there are lots of people, and this young lady walked up and said, "Hey, there's this new movie coming out and we'd like you to preview it, it's called 'Airborne.'" Of course Seth and I both look at each other [Laughs] and we're like, "Really?" She said, "Yeah, all you have to do is write down your names and we'll give you a call and you show up at this time and you preview the film and tell us what you think." We said, "Oh, OK." So we wrote down our names. And it was like two days from then. And we were a little bit nervous that we would be recognized if we went into the movie, so we actually dressed up like the two guys that mugged us. We had tats and we had sunglasses on and we kind of got into character a little bit, and we stood in line, and that was the first time ever that I saw myself on screen. So Seth and I got great seats in the middle of the theater, he was to my right, and I just remember the movie starting. It starts out so great. The opening is great. And also there's a close-up of my face, and I just remember going, "Oh, man." Just blown away. And the audience reaction was great. Watching the film in that environment was great. So I don't know if that answers your question [about] how we recuperated from the experience [Laughs], but anyway that's what we did.

Where did you get the costumes to dress up as your attackers?

It wasn't so much costumes—if I remember right they had ski caps on or something like that. I can't remember—first of all, this is many, many years ago. It wasn't anything unusual. Maybe it was a hoodie or something like that; something real simple we could've gotten dressed up in. Anyway, it was a really fun experience, and I look back so fondly at that time with Seth. Because Seth is so creative and so funny, and anytime you spend with him, it's always an adventure and there's always a good deal of humor. So it was a good time.

On the topic of adapting to that world and the zen mentality of Mitchell, was anything done on set to create that easygoing vibe?

At the time I was very into acting, really working on the skill. What I think you're asking, as far as Mitchell Goosen, for me I got into character once I actually got to Cincinnati. I did my best—I was there a week or two before everyone else showed up, the rest of the cast, and that gave me a good week of reading through the script, really trying to get to know Mitchell and spending a good deal of time trying to figure out who this character was. A large amount of it was there, but thank goodness Bill Apablasa, who is the writer of the film, was also there. He was in Cincinnati the moment I was there, and we would work on the character of Mitchell Goosen pretty much all the way until we started filming. But I never knew if I had captured it until the first scene. I remember a big moment is when Mitchell meets Nikki [Brittney Powell] at the hockey game, and they're in the stadium and they start talking, and it shows Mitchell Goosen for who he is. It talks about his beliefs and why he acts the way that he does. That was the first scene we ever shot. [Laughs] I just remember walking onto set that morning, and Steve McEveety, who was the executive producer of the film and one of my greatest inspirations, he was really positive and really wanted this film to be a success. Of course you're always nervous for the first shot. And there are so many people on set that it's electric. The energy on set was just great. I had been in my room or trailer or whatever they had me in, just tried to get into character, and I remember walking out onto set and to see in Steve McEveety's eyes just saying, "You can do this." And we shot the scene, and I think maybe we spent 2-3 hours going over the different parts, and you never know how you're doing because there's so much stuff and they cut and start over again, and I just remember getting up when they said, "Hey, we got it" and starting to walk over to Steve, and I knew the moment I had captured Mitchell Goosen because he didn't even say anything. He just gave me the biggest hug and patted me on the back and then said, "Bravo. Well done. Let's keep it up." That was the moment that the character had been born, and we were able to keep that throughout the whole film. And I am so happy that I've been lucky enough to be involved in a project like this because it's been such an inspiration to so many people in my generation and a little bit younger. And the message is so positive and so good. I feel honored to have played a part. It's a real big deal that I got Mitchell right, and I think that's what Bill the writer wanted and what Rob the director wanted and what Steve wanted, so I was happy to be a part of it for sure.

And the scene you mentioned when he meets Nikki—one of the things that's underrated about the movie is that Mitchell is someone who makes a complete 180 in his life at 16 in response to near-tragedy, and spends the rest of the movie reconciling what that new outlook is going to be. I feel like the degree to which it's psychologically interesting from that angle hasn't really been discussed a lot over the years.

Yeah, that's what I love about cult classics or about film actually. Not only "Airborne" but a lot of these great films, what I love about it is you can watch a film again and again and again and the greatest part is you know it's a great film and can take new things away from it every time. See something new. And I'm happy that you say that about "Airborne," that it has a depth, and it must be why it's 25 years afterwards and still I get people who come up to me and it's so important, they say, "That movie was such an influence in my life at a young age." I'm blown away that 25 years afterwards people are saying that about that film. It just makes me so proud. [Laughs] And I'm excited for my boys to grow up— they're still a little too young right now, but let me get them into rollerblading now and then I'll start showing them the movie. [Laughs] I hope they will take some good things from [it] just like I have and I guess others have too.

Is it wrong that Nikki doesn't tell Mitchell that Jack [Chris Conrad] is her brother?

No. [Laughs] It adds a dimension to the film.

If that situation were playing out in real life, though, should she have told him? Because she sees that the two are clashing.

Well, think about it on her level or bring it back where you see somebody that you like. Obviously there's some tension between the brother or sister and this other person. You don't want them to not like you because of your association, so maybe when she started the discussion, she figured let's just see who this kid is, and at that point the chemistry starts mixing and she doesn't want to mess it up. Actually I think that happens quite a bit [Laughs] in relationships. I think there are a lot of people who don't tell the other person about something important just because they don't want to mess it up.

Well, the movie obviously hinges on Mitchell moving to Cincinnati. How do you think he would have spent the time if his parents let him stay in L.A. when they were in Australia for six months?

Surfing and rollerblading, and I think he would have been totally fine. He's one of those people that he knows who he is, and he's going to go about his life. He knows what he wants. That's what made the movie interesting is he was taken out of his element. When he was in California, life was good. He's surfing everyday and rollerblading, and it's a good life. And all of a sudden, he's put into a challenging situation, and I think that that's great. For him to really test his resolve, I think you have to be put into situations that are a challenge. That's how you grow. That's another nice part—I feel Mitchell came out better in the end than when he started. He learned in that film. He learned that he could love a place like Cincinnati because you can find the good in any situation. And that's what you do need to look for. And sometimes not only do you find the good, but you find the great. You find something that you wouldn't be able to find in a non-challenging situation. Just another cool element in the film.

To what extent on set did you feel like the new kid in school, similar to Mitchell?

Oh my goodness. It felt so much that way. The most difficult scene of the film by far, by far, was when I had to get up in front of the class and do that monologue. When you're in an acting environment when everybody's in character, you feel out of place. I never liked getting up in front of class anyway. [Laughs] That wasn't uncomfortable enough. But to get up [there], I felt absolutely exactly how Mitchell should have felt in that environment. It was not his comfort zone. When you are confronted by individuals who don't understand you and you don't understand them and you're trying to work it out, which is another element of the film, which is great they accept each other and start to understand each other, that was definitely pretty uncomfortable. I did not enjoy getting up in front of that class. [Laughs]

When selling a house and explaining what's great about it, have you ever used Mitchell's phrase, "liquid Drano, wannabe Bullwinkle"?

[Laughs] No. I probably should with this current generation of homebuyers. I really like real estate, and real estate's been wonderful to me. And I like selling the houses I do; I sell a lot of old, historic homes. Which I absolutely love old homes. I rehab them, I live in them, it's just a wonderful way to live. But it's interesting because when I started out most of the homebuyers were older than me, and I was pretty young. But I'm starting to get up there, so now my generation is buying a lot of property and maybe I should brush up on my Mitchell Goosen [Laughs] dialogue so I can bring it into my home sales. Maybe I should do a little video and post it.

Just challenge yourself and say, "Today I'm not going to say anything Mitchell Goosen didn't say."

[Laughs] There you go. I should do that! That is a great idea. And I'll take a little video of it and we'll post it, and we'll make sure that I send it your way. [Laughs]

I appreciate that. Who is more of a fish out of water: an actor getting into real estate or an L.A. surfer going to Cincinnati?

It's a little bit unfair for me to answer that because as much as I was an actor and I got into real estate, my family was very involved. My grandfather was a realtor and broker. My mother was and still is a realtor and broker in New York City. So I grew up with her selling real estate. And just knowing about it. Of course New York City is very different than Galveston. But my father was a realtor. My sister was a realtor for a number of years. So it's kind of in the family. So whenever I was trying to figure out whenever I moved back from L.A. and I moved to New York, I actually got my realtor license in New York. At that point I was kind of searching, and I knew that I wanted to make a living but do something I was passionate about. And real estate is what I kind of fell into. And it wasn't until I got to Galveston that I really got into it. I think the best thing in real estate is as long as you believe in the area you live in, it's not so much a sale as it's you tell 'em how you truly feel. And that goes a long way, and Galveston real estate has been wonderful for me. So I'm very happy.

I appreciate your honesty about that. In terms of either becoming Mitchell after the movie or embracing the Mitchell within you that already existed, how do you define or articulate how doing the movie changed you as far as the character and what he believed in? Could you point to anything specific you feel like you did differently or reacted to differently as a result?

Hmm. I think I was a different person after the film. First of all, I'm just thinking here. It's a very good question. It's making me think, which I love. So thank you for that. I think that I was young enough when I was doing the film that the Mitchell Goosen character was a major part of my development. Does that make sense? When I actually went out to Cincinnati and for a very brief moment really became Mitchell, I think there was a big part of Mitchell that never went away. [Laughs] I think that even though afterwards I was in L.A. for a while, but I was still young. I didn't move elsewhere out of New York City until I was maybe about 21. But I think the movie helped define my character maybe just because I was young enough, and a big part of that has always stayed. I really got into surfing whenever I went out to California. I was surfing every day. In New York City you can't do that. [Laughs] I just loved the way that the character looks at life. I think it's a great way to go about living a life.

Absolutely. And I think that translates so much, and it's part of what makes it resonate over time. It leads to my next question, which is maybe a surprising place to take it because there's nothing political about "Airborne." However, in returning to the movie this week, it was hard not to see that one of many aspects of why some of the students reject Mitchell at first, from a 2021 perspective, is the narrative of a person who is happy and comfortable and at ease with the world being rejected by people who seem to prefer a more aggressive, argumentative viewpoint and division. Has that ever crossed your mind about the enduring nature of the way that that conflict is initiated and then resolved? That doesn't mean Americans can look to "Airborne" for an answer right now, but do you see where I'm going with that?

Wouldn't that be great? [Laughs] "'Airborne' has the answer. For all things." No, that's great. I don't know. I hope I'm saying this right that tolerance is important. Understanding that people are different than you, and there are also different circles. The difference between someone who grew up in New York City or New York/East Coast and somebody who grew up West Coast and somebody who grew up in Spain. It's really interesting; the humor is different. There are so many things about who they are that's different. And I think that there is a certain element that the movie does teach a little bit about that there are people who are not like us, but that's not a bad thing. If anything, that's good because you can learn from people who don't think like you. It's good to see how other people think, and you never truly know if some of their ideas are good unless you hear them out. It is an element of the film. If somebody comes in and he's foreign, he's not one of us, we have our circles, and he's coming and messing things up, because he's now here and he's blonde and talks weird and he's confident and laid-back, and that's not good for us. It's almost like a testing; they're trying to test who he is, and they're challenged by him. That makes them insecure. But in the end you look for the things that—rollerblading in the end was the thing that bonded them together. And you search for those things in everyone and try to learn what you can from them. You can learn from everyone. So maybe that's another dimension of the film.

And the direction of the narrative is not Mitchell becoming a bully. It's the bullies learning to be nice.

Yeah. That's a great story! Let's keep it up! Let's keep it going. [Laughs] We want bullies to be nice. And that's maybe how you win. I think it is how you win; you lead by example. You be nice. Be as nice as you possibly can, and there you go.

I admit that until recently I was not familiar with "Swans Crossing," so I enjoyed watching a little bit on YouTube. For someone who didn't see that series or know much about it, how would you summarize that show in a sentence or two?

Uh, in just one sentence: "Saved by the Bell" on acid. [Laughs] It was a wonderfully written show. The production schedule was very heavy. We shot 65 episodes in 65 days. It was the first big show that I ever did. How many episodes have you seen?

I just jumped around to find some memorable moments of yours so I felt familiar with the character.

There was so much going on, and it was written as a kids' soap opera. The writers had no boundaries. They could do whatever they wanted, and it produced something that was really interesting where they had characters living on submarines and people build rocket ships and all kinds of interesting stuff. And I thoroughly enjoyed shooting it.

Because of the similarities in title and location and soapiness and age of the characters, what went through your head when you first heard about "Dawson's Creek"? Were you like, "What the hell? We already did this."

[Laughs] Funny enough, I auditioned for "Dawson's Creek." [Laughs] I kind of look at "Swans Crossing" as a little bit younger. If you see the episodes, some of the stuff is outrageous, which I love. There was like a spy element, Eastern European spies that came on and were trying to abduct different characters. It was just really interesting. I go back now, I've watched it with friends, and it's kind of hard to make heads or tails, just seeing a couple episodes. You almost have to really get into it and watch a number of them. It was fun; it was absolutely a blast to shoot "Swans Crossing."

Which character did you audition for on "Dawson's Creek"?

Honestly I do not remember. I'm sorry, it's been so long ago. But I do remember getting a callback for "Dawson's Creek." For some reason I thought I was in L.A. It's hard to go back. [Laughs] Especially these days, I can't remember yesterday. With two kids. [Laughs] But it's also fun to go back, so I really want to say thank you for all the questions because it gets that part of my brain working, and so many of those memories are so good, so I'm smiling this whole time. I want to let you know.

I appreciate that. What do you think your "Swans Crossing" character Garrett would think of "Airborne"?

[Laughs] He probably wouldn't think of it too fondly. He'd probably be the bully in the film. [Laughs] Maybe he would learn some good things from "Airborne." [Laughs] How to treat others nicely. If I remember right, Garrett was kind of a spoiled kid. He was a great soap opera character. He's the character you want to be if you're in a soap opera.

He did seem more like Blane than Mitchell, but I also saw him say "Normal kids make mistakes." So maybe he would relate to what Mitchell was going through.

Oh, absolutely. We all make mistakes; that's life. And I'm going to absolutely brush up on all my lines from "Airborne" and now I'll do some lines from "Swans Crossing." I'll start going through those 65 episodes.

Because of the way things played out over time, is there a part of you that feels like the cliched expression of "the part you were born to play" applies to "Airborne"? I'm so happy you've made the transition to a more stable environment, as you've said, with real estate and your art, which is beautiful. And to pull the curtain back: I quit a full-time movie critic job for a different, less-glamorous writing job for the same reason of stability and lifestyle. So my question is when you think back to that transition, was it sort of like it happened gradually, or was there a moment where you felt like "I did what was right at the time, I did what I could, and I'm good with that"?

Another great question. If I look back on my life, it changes quite a bit. [Laughs] And I don't know if that's my personality. I am very Irish, so maybe it's an Irish characteristic. At a young age I was very heavily into gymnastics living in Texas. Then at a young age moved to New York City to do modeling, then moved back to Texas, then moved back to New York and got into acting, and I jumped around a lot. I lived in Europe for a while. I went to L.A. and lived in California for a while. I did a huge amount of traveling. But my life changes, and it's never kind of stopped changing. And I like that. I like trying new things. The stability is absolutely important, especially when you have kids. You want to provide that kind of stability. But even when I moved into the art, the art was a challenge. So as far as the transition, I remember whenever I decided that I was no longer going to do acting, and so many of my friends looked at me, like, shocked. They would all say, "Well, what are you going to do?" I just remember thinking, "What am I going to do?" But I think you figure it out. There are certain basic things which are very important, which is working hard. You work hard and you want to love what you do, which I hope with your writing, I hope that that move is something that you're passionate about. It seems that you are. Your questions are great. I say never stop changing. Always search. Always look for something new, and I kind of do that still to this day. I got into real estate, but then I got into rehabbing houses. The art has probably been a consistent theme through my life, and I really appreciate you saying that you like the work that I do. Thank you; that means a lot. But now it's raising kids a little bit [Laughs], which is a true adventure.

For sure. I appreciate all of that, and thank you for your kind words as well. So my last question is if you were to stumble across an ad about auditions for a movie called "Rollerblade Dads," would you audition?

[Laughs] You know, it's funny, I guess the quick answer is yes. Absolutely. Especially at this point because somehow, maybe it's because I've found a certain amount of stability, but with my kids, last night my boys and I were watching "The Greatest Showman," which I'm sure you've seen. When I was in New York, my mother used to love Broadway, so we used to get the discount tickets to any shows we could. So we saw lots and lots of shows. And it brought back some great memories of being lucky enough to be in the film, and I still remember the experience of walking on set at night and they're doing a day shot and the cameras are all set up and you walk into that bubble of daylight, and I think so fondly back on those experiences of shooting and how much I enjoyed being on set. I think if anything it would just be another adventure and it would be fun, so, yeah. I don't know if I would get the part, but I'd definitely audition for it. [Laughs]

I'm going to have to add "Write script for 'Rollerblade Dads'" to my list of things to do tomorrow, and then send it your way.

There you go. [Laughs] Absolutely, count me in. I would love to audition for it. So you go for it. That would be a blast. It's just really nice that "Airborne" is something that has stood the test of time. So many years afterwards you have people still watching it and loving it, and that's a great thing.

Trivia Challenge

1. What "Avengers" star is, according to Luke Edwards, a diehard "Newsies" fan?
2. What Oscar-winning film did Gabrielle Anwar turn down?
3. What TV theme song does Tom Everett Scott want to hear at a faster tempo?
4. What is Karyn Parsons' favorite Will Smith performance?
5. Charlie Korsmo lost two movies to the same actor. What were the movies, and who got the parts?
6. What "Dawson's Creek" star used to have sleepovers at Amy Jo Johnson's house?
7. What '90s movie especially motivated Hill Harper with its storytelling and message?
8. What "Futurama" creation does Billy West wish was real?
9. To what real-life sports star does "The Mighty Ducks" star Aaron Schwartz compare his character, expert agitator Dave Karp?
10. What movie gave "Jurassic Park" star Ariana Richards the same fear it depicted?
11. What major TV role was Leanna Creel extremely close to landing?
12. True or false: Shannon Elizabeth received considerable feedback from people in the Czech Republic about Nadia's accent in "American Pie."
13. What song did John Candy play for the "Cool Runnings" cast to capture the movie's themes?

Trivia Challenge Answers

1. Chris Evans
2. "Shakespeare in Love"
3. "The Love Boat"
4. "Seven Pounds"
5. "The Ice Storm" and "Wonder Boys"; Tobey Maguire
6. Michelle Williams
7. "Jerry Maguire"
8. The holophoner
9. John McEnroe
10. "Arachnophobia"
11. Lisa the "Tool Time" girl on "Home Improvement," a part that went to Pamela Anderson
12. False
13. The Rolling Stones' "You Can't Always Get What You Want"

Acknowledgements

First, I have to thank my wife, Dana Pais, for her support of this project, including adjusting her schedule to accommodate the interview schedule and listening to my assessments of the material. I'm so grateful to have a supportive, generous partner in long-term writing efforts like this.

To my son, Theo, who is too young to read this book but never ceased to ask me "How was your interview?" after one took place or tell me that he was proud of me for my interviews. I can't wait to watch some of these movies and shows with you, my man, talk about the conversations that resulted, and have more of our own.

To my son, Bodie, who was born not long after these interviews were completed and whose enormous smiles and upbeat personality are as irresistible and inspiring as anything. Already you show us how engaged and curious you are.

To my mom, Faye, who read the entire manuscript twice and helped to identify what worked best, what could be trimmed and where the book's heart came through strongest, along with spotting typos. Thank you for always supporting my writing and providing a chance to discuss.

To my dad, Shel, a fellow author who has always made me feel supported. Thank you for being there no matter what I'm working on or passionate about.

To my sister, Lauren, who read many of these interviews and talked about many aspects of the book to help refine the approach and content. Thank you for being such an advocate for pop culture reflection and for supporting my efforts in that regard.

To everyone who spoke with me for the book—Gabrielle Anwar, Megan Cavanagh, Leanna Creel, William Daniels and Bonnie Bartlett, Doug E. Doug, Luke Edwards, Shannon Elizabeth, Hill Harper, Dave Holmes, Amy Jo Johnson, Charlie Korsmo, Shane McDermott, Marguerite Moreau, Karyn Parsons, Devin Ratray, Ernie Reyes Jr., Ariana Richards, Jason James Richter, Aaron Schwartz, Tom Everett Scott, Charlie Talbert, Billy West, Red Williams—thank you so much for being so generous with your time and your words.

And to the many people who responded positively to the concept and provided feedback on the writing and other ideas (or helped in other kind, impactful ways)—particularly Brett Schacher, Mike DePilla, Marc Peckler, Drew Fortune, Keith Phipps and Alex Dowd—thank you for your time, insight and support.

About the Author

Matt Pais spent 11 years as the movie critic and music editor for the Chicago Tribune's RedEye, reviewing more than 2,000 movies and interviewing Will Ferrell, Brie Larson, LeBron James, Margot Robbie, Harrison Ford and hundreds more celebrities. In 2020 he published "Zack Morris Lied 329 Times! Reassessing every ridiculous episode of 'Saved by the Bell' … with stats," promoting the book on Mark-Paul Gosselaar's podcast "Zack to the Future" and much more. He released his debut collection of fiction, "This Won't Take Long: 100 Very Short Stories of Dangerous Relationships, Impaired Presidents, Frustrating Jobs and More," in 2019. In his current work at MDRT, he has won numerous Excel Awards (in the podcast and blog categories) and covered topics including cybersecurity, elder financial abuse, and what to say and not say to people who are grieving. He has been a member of the Chicago Film Critics Association since 2006. He majored in journalism at the University of Illinois at Urbana-Champaign and won a William Randolph Hearst Foundation Feature Writing Award in 2005. He now lives in Chicago with his wife and sons and, no matter how many times he sees it, still worries that Bryant's throw to end Game 7 will sail over Rizzo's head. Follow him @mattpais and mattpais.com.